LIFE WITH BILLY

ALSO BY BRIAN VALLÉE

The War on Women
Torso: The Untold Story of Evelyn Dick
Edwin Alonzo Boyd: The Story of the Notorious Boyd Gang
Life and Death With Billy
Life After Billy
Pariah
Life With Billy (1986)

www.brianvallee.ca

BRIAN VALLÉE

LIFE WITH BILLY

SPECIAL COMMEMORATIVE EDITION

KEY PORTER BOOKS

Library and Archives Canada Cataloguing in Publication

Vallée, Brian
Life with Billy / Brian Vallée.

ISBN 978-1-55470-002-8

1. Stafford, Jane, 1949–1992. 2. Wife abuse—Nova Scotia. 3. Marital violence—Nova Scotia. 4. Homicide—Nova Scotia. 5. Abused wives—Nova Scotia—Biography. I. Title.

HV6626.23.C3ff34 2008 364.152′5092 C2007-906975-4

The publisher gratefully acknowledges the support of the Canada Council for the Arts and the Ontario Arts Council for its publishing program. We acknowledge the support of the Government of Ontario through the Ontario Media Development Corporation's Ontario Book Initiative.

We acknowledge the financial support of the Government of Canada through the Book Publishing Industry Development Program (BPIDP) for our publishing activities.

Key Porter Books Limited
Six Adelaide Street East, Tenth Floor
Toronto, Ontario
Canada M5C 1H6

www.keyporter.com

Text design: Martin Gould
Electronic formatting: Jean Lightfoot Peters

Printed and bound in Canada

08 09 10 11 12 5 4 3 2 1

For Maggie, my mother, who taught me from an early age about the worth and equality of all human beings.

and

To the memory of Jane Hurshman, a woman who made a difference.

As time went on, I lost everything: my confidence, my self-esteem, my pride—with time, I even lost the ability to care or to feel. Bill took everything from me, a bit at a time, until there was nothing left but a shell.

—Jane Hurshman

CONTENTS

ACKNOWLEDGMENTS

I wish to thank Jane Hurshman's family, friends, and associates; her caring and tenacious lawyer, Alan Ferrier; and the many others who provided insight and information necessary to write what I hope is a thorough and accurate account of her life and death; and a tribute to her bravery and enduring compassion for other battered women and abused children.

AUTHOR'S NOTE

November 20, 2007, was the twenty-fifth anniversary of the landmark "not guilty" verdict in Jane Hurshman's first-degree murder trial in Liverpool, Nova Scotia. To mark that event, Key Porter Books agreed to publish this special, updated commemorative edition. This book will replace all previous editions of Jane's story including the original *Life With Billy*, published in 1986; *Life After Billy*, published in 1993 following Jane's death; and *Life and Death With Billy*, which combined the earlier books into a single volume. This new edition reverts to the original title: *Life With Billy* but includes the complete story of Jane's life and death.

In her introduction to the original *Life With Billy*, Jane Hurshman wrote: "I hate to think how many other women are out there this minute, living that same fear, and how many kids are being abused, all behind closed doors. I don't think a day goes by when I don't get up with that thought going through my head."

It was that concern which motivated Jane to agree to have me tell her story. "I want this book to be written, not for myself, but for all of those others out there who are living the same hell as I did. If even one person picks up the book, and is helped by it, that will be reward enough. I hope it also helps professionals understand the dynamics of abusive relationships.

"My life has been filled with many different emotions—heartache, disappointment, pain, tears, anguish, sadness, loneliness, suffering, and evil. But most of all—guilt. Guilt over what the emotional and physical abuse did to me and guilt for what it drove me to do. To think that one so-called man could instill so much hate and resentment into another human being...I felt like a wild animal that had been cornered or caged, and I fought back the only way I knew how."

PROLOGUE

In the last years of her life, as Jane Hurshman struggled with her own demons—the legacy of the physical, sexual, and emotional abuse she endured in her common-law marriage to Billy Stafford—she fought fiercely to put an end to the criminal domestic violence suffered by other women and children. Her contribution was huge but, twenty years later, the alarming rate of criminal violence against women by their male intimate partners persists at an unacceptable level.

How unacceptable? Research for my recent book *The War on Women* revealed that in the seven-year period from 2000 to 2006 more than five hundred women were stabbed, shot, smothered, strangled, or beaten to death by the male intimates in their lives. That number was five times higher than the combined total of all Canadian military and law enforcement deaths in the same period.

Continuing the war analogy, about eighty Canadian soldiers were wounded in that period, while back home the annual medical bill for women injured by their male intimates was estimated at $1.1 billion in direct medical costs, rising to more than $4 billion when social services, lost earnings, and police, court, and prison expenses were factored in.

Wars spawn refugee camps. Canada's refugee camps are the more than 550 overcrowded shelters and transition houses where between 90,000 and 100,000 women and children flee each year to escape the violent domestic terrorists living in their homes.

The number of shelters has more than doubled since Jane's story was first told in 1986. Have the shelters helped? They've certainly helped men. The number of male intimates killed by their spouses has dropped by about 70 per cent as the number of shelters increased. But the number of women killed has dropped by less than 25 per cent. So the irony is, shelters save men's lives.

It was these startling facts, plus a new generation of readers, that persuaded me Jane's story should be reissued. The sad reality is that there is no sustained public outcry as criminal violence in the home continues to plague us and we seem to lack the political will to end it.

Two decades have passed but Jane Hurshman's words are still pertinent today: "Society needs to be educated and made more aware that domestic violence is an unacceptable criminal behaviour, punishable by law.

"My purpose in speaking out is to tell other battered women not to be silent screamers. Do not keep it behind closed doors. Come out and be heard. The more that come forward and speak out the sooner society's attitudes will change and there will be an end to this cycle of violence. Publicly tell your story no matter how shocking or unbelievable it may sound."

Pamela Cross, former legal director of the Ontario Women's Justice Network, says it's time "that the same media and political attention given to other victims of war be given to women killed by their partners. Perhaps then we would see that these women—who spend every day of their lives trying to outwit the enemy, stay one step ahead of him, protect the children, stay alive for one more day—are heroes as much as any soldier serving in a war."

Under those parameters, surviving five years with Billy Stafford, Jane Hurshman was certainly a hero who later tried her best to help other battered women.

At the time of Jane's death, Joyce Deveau Kennedy wrote in the *Halifax Daily News*: "She wanted to be the soldier who pulls others from the trenches and leads them back to safety."

CHAPTER 1
A BODY

Queens County lies midway between Halifax and Yarmouth in the Canadian province of Nova Scotia, jutting into the Atlantic Ocean like a giant jagged foot. The livelihood of its people depends largely on the changeable fortunes of the fishing, logging, and pulp-and-paper industries. The county's largest town is Liverpool, a seaport with a population of about four thousand. Much of the county's population lives in outlying towns and hamlets—places like Charleston, Greenfield, and Riverdale. These settlements are strung along the fast-flowing Medway River, which runs to the sea from its headwaters at Ponhook Lake near Greenfield. The churning Medway is famous for its trout and prized Atlantic salmon. Its shoreline is dotted with cottages, many owned by wealthy residents from Halifax, the province's capital and its largest city.

People raised in the hamlets along the river have a unique way of speaking. To outsiders, their accent seems barbed with a hillbilly twang. The hamlets on the west bank of the river are accessible only by River Road, which twists and winds along the Medway.

Other than Harry Freeman's family-run sawmill at Greenfield, in 1982 the only work available along the river was at Teleglobe Canada, a satellite tracking and relay station built in the 1960s near Charleston. Teleglobe provided work for fifty people and sent satellite TV signals and telephone calls from Europe and other parts of the world to the rest of Canada. Locals knew Teleglobe as simply "the satellite station."

River Road was paved as far as Teleglobe. The remainder, running about ten miles north to the hamlet of Bangs Falls, had never been paved. With the spring thaw it became a treacherous stretch of washouts, muck, and potholes.

A strong stone's throw from the satellite station was a faded, ramshackle frame house and small barn owned by Carl Croft. The place could have been a set for a Ma and Pa Kettle movie. Croft lived there with his wife and teenage daughter. On March 12, 1982, a Friday, Croft was up as usual at four in the morning to feed the animals—a German shepherd, a horse, and a few sheep. Folding his arms against his chest to fight the chill, he entered the small living room and switched on the overhead light. The wood stove was lukewarm to his touch. He opened the door, jabbed at the embers with a poker until they began to glow, and added a few sticks of kindling and a log from the wood box beside the stove. Closing the door, he opened the draft halfway and watched as the kindling began to crackle. By the calendar, spring was a week and a half away, but Croft knew he'd be burning wood well into May.

Croft was the youngest in a family of six boys and three girls, all raised in the small house. Over the years, the others had moved away from home, but he continued to live there, staying on after his parents died. Now he was sixty-three and would be retiring from his labourer's job in the Liverpool dockyards. It was only at this time of the year, with the cold rains and the ground thawing, that he felt his age. Five days a week he left his house and walked along River Road, past the satellite station, to meet a ride in Charleston at the bridge over the Medway.

On this day, Croft left his house at 7:15 a.m. His ride to work was seldom late, regardless of the weather. He picked up his pace slightly, pulling the collar of his winter coat tight at the throat. It was cold and misty and he could smell the sea. As he approached the turnoff to the satellite station, he saw a half-ton Jeep pulled off to the side of the road. He thought the truck might belong to Chester Harlowe because it was near the entrance to the long driveway that led through the woods to Harlowe's place. Harlowe was a young commercial fisherman who operated his own boat out of Liverpool. Perhaps, reasoned Croft, he left the truck there because the driveway was too muddy. "But I get close to it and I see it wasn't Ches Harlowe's old truck there. I still didn't pay much attention to it, but I come along and got close to the truck and I see there's blood all over the door and I looked around the highway. I thought someone must have had an accident or something, but there was nothing tore up nowhere."

Moving closer, Croft saw a form lying inside the cab against the door on the driver's side. He noticed "a lot of blood and stuff. I looked at him and I knowed he wasn't all there. I know he wasn't living because he didn't move. So I run up to the next-door neighbour, up to John Babin, and I told him about it."

John Babin was a private person, a shorter, slighter version of British actor Michael York, with deep-set eyes, full sideburns, and a Beatles-style haircut. Years earlier he had left the isolated fishing village in the Gaspé where he was born. After travelling around the country working at a variety of jobs, he finally settled in Nova Scotia. In 1974, he and his wife, Colleen, moved into a frame bungalow on River Road.

The Babins lived an ordinary, uneventful life until August 1981, when their eldest son shot himself. Danny was sixteen and had been depressed for some time. He was to enter high school in the fall, leaving behind his grade-school sweetheart, who was a year behind him. "From December on, he tried to fail his year," recalled John Babin. "But he was an honour student and they told him even if he got zeros for the rest of the year he'd still pass."

Babin and his wife had spent much of the day of the shooting scraping the exterior of the house to prepare it for a coat of paint. "Danny was inside lying on the couch. We came in to make some coffee. He got up and went into the bathroom and then upstairs to his room. That's when we heard the shot. I ran up and found him there." Danny Babin had shot himself through the chest, just above the heart, with a .410 shotgun. John Babin was fully trained in first aid but there was nothing he could do. "He died in my arms as I carried him downstairs." He rushed the boy to the hospital in the family station wagon, but it was, as Babin knew, too late.

Danny had left notes for his girlfriend and for his family. He told his parents he loved them and asked to be buried in the village. John Babin wondered if his son really intended to kill himself or if it was a cry for help. But there'd been other teenage suicides in Queens County, including one of Danny's friends, and John Babin believed that may have influenced his son. "I don't think he would've thought about it without those others." Including Danny and his friend, there were six suicides in nineteen months in the county. The deaths had prompted Staff Sergeant Peter Williamson, in charge of the RCMP detachment, to arrange meetings with parents and teachers. "All I could tell them was to work at keeping lines of communication open with the kids. It was a frustrating thing."

When Carl Croft knocked on the Babins' door, eight months after Danny's death, John Babin was getting ready for work. Croft told him there was an accident "or something" and that somebody was hurt. Croft was clearly frightened, and they drove down in Babin's station wagon. Croft stayed in the wagon and Babin walked over to the half-ton. "I could see right away he was dead. I thought it might be a suicide. It was prime in my mind."

Babin stared at the bloodied, lifeless form in the truck. "I didn't recognize the truck. There was blood on the door. I didn't have a clue who it was. We went back to my place and called the police."

Rural Nova Scotia is policed by the RCMP and when Babin called the Liverpool detachment to report what he'd seen, he was automatically switched to Yarmouth, where officers are on duty twenty-four hours a day. The Liverpool switchboard would not be staffed until the detachment office opened shortly after 8 a.m. The dispatcher in Yarmouth checked his list to see who was on call for emergencies in Liverpool, and then telephoned Constables Archie Mason and Archie Doon. The two single men shared a house on School Street, just up the road from their new detachment. Awakened from their sleep, they were left with the impression that there had been a motor vehicle accident with possible injuries. In minutes they were rushing to the scene in their royal-blue RCMP cruiser with its familiar white markings. They radioed for an ambulance to meet them there. Mason and Doon got as far as Mill Village, about four miles from Charleston, when their cruiser blew its transmission.

"We'd broken down," recalled Mason. "We called for someone to take us to the scene, but the ambulance came by first and we flagged it down."

Babin, meanwhile, had returned to the truck and blocked the road with his station wagon while awaiting the police. "The ambulance came beatin' down the road and I thought, 'Isn't that the way, they get here before the police.' I was surprised to see the policemen get out of the ambulance. I told them there was a body in the truck—minus a head."

Archie Mason was a thirteen-year veteran of the RCMP. A glance inside the truck told him he was investigating a shooting, not an accident. He radioed for a coroner and a senior officer. A blood spot on the road near the truck was covered with a shovel and a yellow emergency blanket.

Constable Robert Hillier was next to arrive. He wrote in his notebook: "I arrived at the scene at 7:35 a.m. and observed a grey AMC motor vehicle, with Nova Scotia licence 52 47 7B, at the left side of the road approximately two hundred feet past the Satellite Road." He also recorded the arrival of the coroner, "and at 8:15 an unknown person seated in the vehicle was pronounced dead. The unknown male was seated in the cab of the pickup; he had been decapitated. It would appear to be some shotgun gauge due to the fact a piece of fibrous wad was laying on the seat. It was cold with misty rain and it was just early morning."

A police photographer noted later that the cab of the truck was splattered with blood, brain particles, lead, and wads of a firearm. "It was everywhere. It was just like an explosion in there." The keys were still in the ignition, and outside on the ground near the driver's door there was more brain matter and a set of false teeth.

The most precise report came later from pathologist Dr. Roland Perry: "In summary, this man died as a result of a gunshot wound to the head. The entrance wound being in front of the left ear approximately midway between the ear and the middle of the skull and upper face, extreme comminution of the skull bones and pulpification of most of the brain. It is my opinion that the muzzle/skull distance was probably within six inches. The slug fragments found indicated a single slug."

Corporal Howard Pike was thirty-five years old and a veteran of fifteen years with the RCMP, the last four at the Liverpool detachment. The raw-boned six-footer arrived at the scene shortly before 8:30 a.m., just as the employees of Teleglobe began arriving for work. Pike recognized the truck immediately and a licence check confirmed that it was registered to Billy Stafford, who lived ten miles up River Road in the tiny settlement of Bangs Falls. Pike peered into the cab of the half-ton. "There was no face to see, but the clothing and the size of the body made it obvious to me it was Billy Stafford. I'd seen him two or three days earlier up at Freeman's Lumber Mill at Greenfield. He was coming out in his truck when I was going in. He was wearing a light-brown sweater, same as was on the body." Corporal Pike had spoken to Billy Stafford only once, when he had pulled his truck over about a year earlier. "His wife was driving the truck. He was under the influence, but she was sober. He asked me why I was stopping him. I told him it was just routine and that was it."

Staff Sergeant Peter Williamson had a reputation for being a no-nonsense cop, and during his career had had more than his share of scraps with tough guys. A native of Bathurst, New Brunswick, he had joined the force in 1960. Married and with two sons, he had been transferred to Liverpool in July 1977. Now he headed the thirteen-member detachment and was responsible for policing the town as well as surrounding Queens County. The coroner had declared the man in the truck dead before Williamson arrived at 9 a.m., but nothing had been touched yet and there was still some doubt as to whether it was a murder or a suicide. "When they told me it was Billy Stafford," said Williamson later, "I admit I thought to myself, 'It couldn't have happened to a better guy.'"

Williamson walked around to the passenger side of the truck and opened the door. He was looking for a gun. "Okay, boys," he said after a careful look, "there's no gun. We've got a homicide here. No gun, no suicide. Call in a dog man. If someone threw the gun away a dog might be able to pick up the scent."

Williamson put Corporal Pike in charge of the investigation and returned to the detachment. "I advised my superiors in Halifax we had a homicide, and by the end of the day I had nine or ten men on the case. We didn't have a suspect. Knowing Billy Stafford, it could have been anybody. There were a lot of people who felt threatened by him. He intimidated most everyone he knew."

After making a note of the clothing Billy Stafford was wearing, Howie Pike and Constable Archie Mason decided to drive up to the Stafford residence in Bangs Falls. They stopped at every house along River Road, asking residents if they'd heard or seen anything unusual the night before. No one had. The drive to Bangs Falls was tortuous because of the washouts and mudholes brought on by the spring thaw. The Stafford house was on a gentle slope beyond a single-lane bridge that crosses the Medway River and joins River Road. A low, white, board fence flanked the long driveway leading to the yellow frame bungalow. Directly below the house, about halfway to the bridge, was a small, weathered barn with a sagging roof. It belonged to Margaret Joudrey, the Staffords' nearest neighbour. She lived in a trailer and used the barn for storage. Smoke was rising from the Stafford chimney when Pike and Mason drove across the narrow bridge. The driveway was too muddy for them to attempt in their cruiser. As they got out of the car they noticed a woman leaving Margaret Joudrey's trailer.

"That's her, that's Jane Stafford," said Pike. The woman was walking toward the house. She turned to the officers as they approached. She was a slim brunette of medium height with attractive, lightly freckled features. Pike did the talking. "Mrs. Stafford?"

"Yes?"

"I'm sorry to bother you, but I have a few questions to ask you." Jane Stafford nodded. "When did you last see your husband?"

"He left in his truck last night," she answered softly. Pike noticed her eyes seemed somewhat vacant, that she was staring off into the distance.

"You haven't seen him since?"

"No."

"Did he have a gold watch?" She nodded.

"Do you remember what he was wearing?"

"Blue jeans. A light-brown sweater."

"Work boots? A studded belt?" Again she nodded in agreement.

"Mrs. Stafford, I'm sorry to inform you, we found your husband deceased in his truck this morning."

Jane Stafford fainted.

CHAPTER 2
BILLY

Peter Williamson first met Billy Stafford in the summer of 1977, shortly after his transfer to Liverpool, and just before he took over the detachment as its staff sergeant. That summer he was working in a small office around a corner from the main public reception area. Two female stenographers were working at desks behind a counter set up for the public. Billy stormed into the office in an ugly mood, glaring at the frightened women across the counter. He stood slightly over six feet tall and weighed over 250 pounds. He was broad-faced, with protruding eyes and thick lips. His receding light-brown hair was slicked back, and his moustache and long sideburns were neatly trimmed.

"What in Christ is this notice you sent me suspending my licence?" he shouted.

"Do you wish to file a complaint?" asked one of the women politely.

"These bastards are always after me," said Billy, moving closer to the counter.

Williamson was out of sight of the counter but within earshot. "I could hear him mouthing off and yelling at the stenographers," he recalled. Williamson carried 220 pounds on a solid six-foot frame, and his reputation for toughness had followed him through his years with the RCMP. He was short-tempered and good with his fists. Billy Stafford was startled when Williamson appeared from around the corner and in one motion vaulted across the counter to face him toe to toe.

"You've got a bad mouth, mister," said Williamson, his square jaw inches from Billy.

"You've got no goddamn right suspending my licence again."

"You want to lodge a complaint—do it," said Williamson. "But you're going out of here fast or you're going to jail, and I don't need anyone to help me put you there."

Billy Stafford glowered at Williamson but backed away and turned for the door, cursing and swearing as he left. Williamson had been warned about Billy Stafford when he first arrived in Liverpool. "Over the years it became an involvement with him, almost on a regular basis. Mostly he'd be driving without a licence, or driving with too many points under the Motor Vehicle Act. He'd be suspended and then the boys would pick him up for driving when his suspension was in effect. He was well known and he was feared. He was an intimidating individual. He was a big man and he worked on that premise. He pretty well did what he wanted out there in Queens County. His neighbours feared him and they knew that if they went to the police, they'd have to go to court and then he might take some retribution later. He was very obnoxious and resented the law. When a summons was given to him, he'd just tear it up, leave it there, and then say, 'If I go, I go.' He never bothered me after that first confrontation and I had about seven big guys he stayed away from. We weren't afraid of Billy Stafford, but we were cautious. We enforced the law. He wasn't blatant enough to come up and threaten us. He knew that we'd take him to court. He was sort of a bully."

Williamson took Stafford very seriously when it came to the safety of his men. Whenever he sent them to deliver a summons he ordered them to go in pairs and armed. "I believe that Billy Stafford would be pushed to a certain point, or we would go out there sometime when he was under the influence of alcohol or whatever, and he would, no doubt in my mind, would have shot one of us. He was that type of individual. We knew he had a lot of loaded firearms."

Anyone who knew Stafford well was aware of his affinity for firearms. He had a reputation around Queens County as the ultimate "deer jacker"—a hunter who shoots deer out of season, or without a licence, or who exceeds the quota during the regulated deer season. Stafford was generous with his seemingly endless supply of illegal venison. It found its way to many a table and freezer in the county. The RCMP and the provincial Lands and Forest Department knew about his illegal activities, but he always managed to elude them. The one time he *was* charged for deer jacking, he persuaded a friend to go to court and take the blame for killing the animal. The friend perjured himself, and Billy was acquitted.

Some friends of Billy Stafford said he always had a mean streak; but others, such as Calvin, Timothy, and Leslie Anthony, said he was kind and generous. Billy was close to their parents, Allen and Leona Anthony. When the two separated, Billy lived for a time with Allen Anthony and his sons in Milton. When the boys moved in with their mother at Mill Village on River Road, Billy was a regular visitor. Timothy was about eight years old and Leslie twelve when they first met Billy Stafford, then in his early thirties. Billy worked on ships sailing out of Liverpool, and when he returned from sea, he gave the boys money, as Timothy recalled, "to buy clothes and cigarettes and stuff." As the boys got older, they often went hunting with Billy. Timothy said that as far back as he could remember, Billy Stafford nearly always carried and used drugs. Calvin Anthony said that Billy "used me pretty good" over the years—it was Calvin who lied in court to help get Billy acquitted on the charge of deer jacking.

Lamonte William "Billy" Stafford was born on Thursday, February 13, 1941. When he was older he would claim he was born on a Friday. He was the second-oldest of five children—three girls and two boys—in the family of Lamonte and Winnie Stafford. The couple later adopted a sixth child, a boy. They lived in a modest but comfortable home in Liverpool's upper end. Lamonte Stafford ran a successful scrap iron and junkyard business and eventually retired to a larger home in nearby Hunt's Point.

Alfie Warrington knew Billy from the time they were children. "Billy and I used to work for his dad in the junk-collecting business. His dad used to give me a few bucks for helping once in a while. His was the only junkyard and I think he did pretty good at it."

Warrington said that he and Billy were friends "but he's always been sadistic." He recalled an incident in their late teens when he and Billy were riding in the rear of Lamonte Stafford's truck. "We were helping his father who had bought a bunch of strands of guy-wire ends. Billy started whipping them across my legs. I told him to stop because it hurt, but he kept doing it. He didn't stop until I struck him with a piece of metal. After that he gave me a wide berth."

Billy Stafford had a strict upbringing. People who knew the family said that as he grew older, he became abusive toward his parents, particularly his father.

In 1962, when he was twenty-one, Billy Stafford married Pauline Oickle. She was pregnant by him at the time. Six years later, Pauline was granted a divorce on the grounds of cruelty.

Billy had begun beating her soon after they moved into a small, two-room apartment, and continued when they moved into her mother's home in Milton. "He was very cruel to me in the six years that I was married to him," recalled Pauline, who had moved to Ontario. "He beat me quite often with anything he could get a hold of—a beer bottle, broom handle...his fists mostly. I was really afraid of him, so I more or less kept my mouth shut unless I was spoken to. I treated him as well as I could—even with respect...even after the beatings I took and my children took. I always did everything that he wanted me to do because if I didn't I knew what was going to happen."

Pauline and Billy Stafford had five children during their short marriage. Pauline was pregnant with her third child in 1964 when Billy administered a particularly severe beating. Billy had been drinking with Pauline's mother when he suddenly went after Pauline and began beating her with his fists until her face was bloodied and badly bruised. It was during the winter. Somehow Pauline managed to free herself from Billy's grasp and ran out into the snow wearing only slippers and a nightgown. "I ran down to my uncle's house with no jacket or nothing. By the time I got there I was in shock and they had to take me right to the hospital. My face was all cut and black and blue. He kicked me so bad they thought I was going to lose the baby, but I didn't."

Pauline Stafford laid assault charges against her husband, and photographs of her injuries were taken as evidence. She agreed to drop the charges against Billy when his father assured her that Billy had signed a peace bond stating that he wouldn't beat her again. Billy Stafford came home, and two weeks later the beatings resumed. They became progressively worse. He once tried to drown Pauline by submerging her head in a bucket of water. And she credits her grandmother with once saving her life by pulling Billy off after he had choked her into unconsciousness. Pauline bore permanent scars on her body where Billy bit her. His violence became all too familiar to Pauline and her children—no matter how young—and the beatings came whether he was drunk or sober.

"He could be nice one minute," said Pauline, "and the next minute he'd turn right on you and just start beating you for no reason at all. He would really get wild-looking. His eyes would be just glaring and the spit would fly and froth from his mouth. He never treated the children with love at all. I'd say from the time they were about six months old, he started beating them. When you put them to bed at night, they didn't dare cry or he'd go up and beat them, right in the crib. I think he just hated them all, yet I kept having a child every eleven months because I was not allowed to do anything to keep from getting pregnant. He wouldn't allow me to take the pill or anything. I used to say to myself after every beating that I was going to leave. But I was always in pretty bad shape so I more or less just stayed hid in the house."

Billy Stafford's brutality against his wife and children continued until the spring of 1968, when Pauline's cousin, who lived in Ontario, returned to Nova Scotia for a visit. The cousin, who hadn't seen Pauline in fifteen years, immediately realized what was going on in the Stafford household and told Pauline she could always come to stay with her in Ontario if she ever decided to leave Billy. By then, Pauline was sickened by Billy's treatment of the children and knew she had to get out, but had no place to go. She had watched helplessly as Billy sat the children on a stairway leading to a bedroom. He would light up cigarettes, stick them in their mouths, and make them sit there until the tobacco burned away. Then he forced them to eat the butts. He was particularly brutal toward Elizabeth, their second-oldest daughter. Billy forced the child to stand against the house while he threw knives at her to see how close he could come without hitting her. "And he used to sit her out on the back porch in the dark at night," said Pauline. "Today she's still terrified in the dark. They were all terrified of him. As soon as he came home they all just went and sat. They had to sit there all day without moving. They couldn't even speak properly when they went to school."

One morning Billy prepared to leave for work on the fishing boats. Pauline watched, horrified, as he took their youngest daughter, Darlene, into the backyard and beat her with a wooden rocker from a rocking chair. The small girl was lying face down on the ground with Billy's foot on her back. "He beat her from the waist down until she messed herself." Without a word, Billy picked up his seaman's bag. Dutifully, Pauline went up to him and kissed him.

"Goodbye," she said. "I'll see you in two weeks."

Billy Stafford grunted and left. When he returned from sea his family was gone. Enraged, he beat Pauline's mother in an attempt to find out where they had gone. A year later, Pauline returned to Nova Scotia for a visit. Billy begged and pleaded with her to return to him. Pauline agreed to think it over. "But when I went back to Ontario, my cousin sat me down and talked to me. She said he would never change. So I just went out and started divorce proceedings." It was a decision she never regretted.

By 1971, Billy Stafford was living common law with another woman, Faith Hatt. Their relationship was to last two years. At first, Billy treated Faith well, and she saw no evidence of his dark side; but within a few months she became the victim of his unprovoked physical attacks. "For no apparent reason, he would take hold of me and pound me with his fists. You never knew. He could be good one minute and the next minute—snap! He actually frothed at the mouth when he came at me, like a mad dog. There were occasions that he beat me when he wasn't drinking, but most of the time it was when he was drinking."

Living with Billy Stafford's unpredictable moods was turning Faith Hatt into a nervous wreck. For her own sanity, she knew she had to get out. Then she discovered she was pregnant, and she wasn't sure what to do. The decision was made for her one night when Billy returned home from sea. He and Faith were staying in a cabin adjoining his parents' house. She was three months pregnant. Billy was drinking heavily and all evening he verbally pestered her, asking if there were something she'd forgotten to tell him, something she was withholding. Faith had no idea what he was talking about, but that didn't stop Billy. When they retired to the cabin, "he kept dwelling on this and finally he started pounding on me and then he grabbed hold of me and started choking me." She believed Billy would have killed her, but he was so drunk she managed to free herself and run from the house. He chased her down the street but she managed to elude him and stayed the night with a neighbour. The next day Faith's family scraped together enough money to pay her way out of town. "I knew I couldn't just break off with him and stay here in town because he probably would've haunted me to death." She moved all the way to Calgary and did not return to Liverpool until the summer of 1979—seven years later.

She stayed with her sister while looking for an apartment or house for her and her young son, Rodney. On a warm July day about two weeks after her arrival, Faith was driving out to look at a place she'd heard about in nearby Brooklyn. She was startled when Billy Stafford pulled up beside her in his truck. "He started talking to me, and he said he wanted to see Rodney. I really didn't want him to. But I was back in town and I planned on staying and I didn't want any more trouble. So I figured the best thing to do was to let him see him. He saw Rodney one time and that was it."

Billy Stafford was pleased to think that he was born on Friday the 13th, even though it wasn't true. He said it was lucky for him. He often bragged that he had been sent by the devil, or that he *was* the devil. He believed in astrology and horoscopes and kept a book handy to see what the stars held for him each day. One time, at a fair in the town of Bridgewater, Billy paid for a "personal" computerized handwriting analysis and horoscope reading. The computer told him he was well-adjusted mentally, easily influenced, secretive, idealistic, philosophical, and considerate. It described him as sarcastic and shrewd and as not easily discouraged. It also told him he had a magnetic personality with strong likes and dislikes. His dislike—hatred, really—of the RCMP was legendary in Queens County. "He was always on about them," remembered Alfie Warrington. "He'd chew the heads right off them. He used to tell me that if they ever stepped a foot in his house, it would be the last time they stepped anywhere."

By his thirty-third year, Billy Stafford had two broken relationships behind him and six children, none of whom he supported. He was a merchant seaman and looked the part. He was big and burly, with crude tattoos on each forearm just below the elbow. A lot of people went out of their way to avoid him. Those who drank with him said he could be considerate and good-natured one minute, and fly into a rage and take a swing at you the next. He had a reputation as a bully who preyed on those who feared him.

One man who feared Billy Stafford was young Jimmy LeBlanc, a Liverpool fisherman who died mysteriously in the winter of 1974 while at sea aboard the *Mersey Enterprise*, a fishing vessel. Billy Stafford was also on board on that trip. On

February 14, the day after Billy's thirty-third birthday, it was reported that Jimmy LeBlanc either fell or jumped overboard. He was twenty years old. Years later, Billy Stafford bragged that he had thrown the young seaman over the side following a heated argument. He claimed that after the argument LeBlanc went into the galley to make a mug of tea, and that he went in behind LeBlanc, dragged him out, and threw him overboard.

Jimmy LeBlanc was the second-oldest of the six children of Myrna LeBlanc. Jimmy was five-foot-seven and of medium build. His mother remembered him telling her he was afraid of two people "and one of them was Billy Stafford. Jimmy told me a lot of people were afraid of Billy Stafford. I know my son did not commit suicide or fall overboard. Jimmy didn't know how to swim a stroke. There have been so many different stories over the years—if only somebody would come forward and tell me the truth.

"The day I found out, a neighbour called and asked me if it was true about Jimmy's death. I had to call Mersey Seafoods and ask if he'd drowned. They told me it was true. I had nothing in writing from them. Even if I had a death certificate it would make it more real, even though in the back of your mind you know he's dead. I always think of him. He was quiet and shy and he would give you the shirt off his back. He was happy-go-lucky and he loved the woods and hunting. We've been a very poor family but we're a close family. I've always had a suspicion that Billy was involved in my son's death. When I heard about Billy's death, I looked up at Jimmy's picture on the wall. It was almost as if he was smiling—revenge at last."

CHAPTER 3
JANE

January 25, 1949. The unforgiving North Atlantic smashed against the rocky Nova Scotia coast. It was a bitterly cold afternoon. In the small coastal town of Brooklyn, a few miles from Liverpool, Gladys and Maurice Hurshman were welcoming their second child into the world. They were pleased it was a girl, a sister for Douglas Edward, born sixteen months earlier. They named their daughter Jane. Her first recollections of their house in Brooklyn were of its huge size, and how cold it was in winter. There was no bathroom and no running water. Her father, who worked in a nearby sawmill, carried wood home on his back each night in the cold months.

With the outbreak of the Korean War in June 1950, Maurice Hurshman joined the Canadian Army, and after basic training was sent to Korea to fight the Chinese and North Koreans. He served thirteen-month and six-month stints before returning home permanently in 1952. He decided to remain in the army, and because he liked to cook, became a chef. Two more children were born to the Hurshmans during their stay in Brooklyn—Mona Dianne in April 1953, and Sandra Rose ten months later.

When Jane was five years old, she witnessed her father behave in a way she had never seen before. The day began happily enough when her mother took her and Douglas to see their first movie. It featured the Three Stooges with their zany, make-believe violence. But what Jane saw that day when she left the movie house was not make-believe. "There was a commotion taking place outside. It was my father fighting with the town cops. They were trying to get him in their car to take him to jail. He'd been fighting in a restaurant. I'm sure that's when I had my first feelings of being a lost little girl—not knowing what to do or where to go. I was very frightened and confused. I didn't know who was hurting who. All I knew was that they were taking my daddy away."

Life in the Canadian Army usually meant a lot of moving around. It was no exception for Maurice Hurshman and his family. In May 1954 he was transferred to Truro in north-central Nova Scotia where they lived off base in a two-storey house with a spacious backyard. Jane's brother had his own bedroom while she and her younger sisters shared another. Jane remembered a wide staircase leading to the upstairs bedrooms. That staircase became her favourite place—her hideout.

Maurice Hurshman drank more heavily in Truro, and it made him irritable, unpredictable, and often mean. Soon he began beating his wife. He never physically abused his children, but Jane remembered: "He was very strict with us. We couldn't leave things lying around or out of place. At night I used to sit alone on the stairway, especially when they were fighting. I could see them but they couldn't see me. He would stay up all night drinking, go to work, do his job, and come home and start the vicious cycle again."

Whatever his faults, Maurice Hurshman saw to it that his family was never hungry or without proper clothing. With four children, money was tight—their clothing usually second-hand, purchased from a thrift shop. Gladys Hurshman was an accomplished seamstress and often made her children outfits from the second-hand clothing. Jane was tickled one day when her parents bought her a new blue dress and white knee stockings. She smiled about it all day. That night, she heard her parents fighting and came out to sit in her secret spot on the stairway. When the fighting and shouting ended, Jane went to bed, forgetting her new stockings on the stairs. Her father found them there later and burned them in the wood stove. He told Jane it was her fault for not putting them away.

Jane began her schooling in a two-room Truro schoolhouse where grades one to eight were taught. It was new and exciting, and she took to it immediately. She loved to read and study and wanted desperately to please her teacher—often volunteering to clean the boards and brushes after school. She liked the praise that came with the chore. It made her feel needed and loved. That feeling was short-lived. Jane was caught up in the anticipation that first-graders feel with the approach of Christmas when her teacher talked about decorating the classroom and then brought out a bundle of Christmas cards to be used for that purpose. That day, Jane stayed on after the bell rang to clean the boards and brushes as she usually did. The Christmas cards were lying invitingly on the teacher's desk, dazzling Jane with their bright colours. She wanted to display them, to share her pleasure with her fellow students, and, most important, to please the teacher. She noticed a bottle of glue on the teacher's desk and stuck all the cards to the blackboard. She was brimming with pride. She couldn't wait to see how happy everyone would be when they saw the cards the next morning. But nothing was said, and the teacher didn't look at all happy.

"Would whomever put these cards on the board please come up here," said the teacher, unsmiling. "I have something for you."

Jane, somewhat confused by the sombre mood, stood and walked to the front of the class.

"I did it. Aren't they beautiful?" she asked.

The teacher stared at her coldly, and without a word reached for the strap in her desk drawer. Six-year-old Jane was hurt and bewildered. "She never explained why I was being punished. I wouldn't cry. I just went back and took my seat and did my work. I never told my parents that I got a strapping. I vowed at that time that I'd never get another one, and I never did." Jane had the same teacher for three years, and for three years she tried to make up for a wrongdoing she didn't understand. She was an honour student, but she stopped trusting people and became quiet and withdrawn. Never again did she volunteer to help out around the school.

Jane cherished her few fond memories of the three years the family spent in Truro. "Mom used to take us picking blueberries. We would pick all day and then sell the berries. We were never given allowances, so the berries provided us with some spending money. Sometimes in the winter we helped make ice cream. Those were the nice times, but they were very scarce." She had no regrets when in 1957 the family was transferred again, this time to Camp Gagetown in New Brunswick. They moved into a three-bedroom brick bungalow with hardwood floors. Her mother kept it spotless and filled it with plants. What Jane liked best about the move was the army school on the base. It was much larger than the school in Truro, and each grade had its own teacher. There was even a gymnasium. Jane continued to get top grades, and she excelled in gym class. She became an avid reader and began studying French. There were even pluses in her home life. Her parents bought her her first bicycle, a solid second-hand one with a large frame. Jane was very proud of it.

About the same time, another army family moved in next door. They had a daughter, Valery, who was Jane's age. What Jane found unique about Valery's family was that her parents didn't drink, smoke, or fight. She loved visiting their house, and she and Valery became inseparable. Her friend's home became an oasis for Jane, a respite from the continuing violence and pain in the Hurshman household and in the homes of many of their friends and acquaintances. Drinking, arguing, and physical abuse were commonplace. "Except for Val's parents, it seemed everybody we knew lived that way. There were all-night drinking sessions and poker games with Dad and a group of men. There was always loud music playing."

During one poker game, a neighbour, obviously drunk, declared he was going out to get something to eat. He was killed instantly when his car slammed head-on into a truck. He left behind a wife and six children. Jane sensed the depth of the tragedy—the waste. "I was sad, yet I was secretly thinking, 'Now maybe Dad can see what drinking can do. Maybe he'll stop.' But he never did."

Jane never felt prouder of her parents than the night they dressed up in their finest clothes to attend a dance. They weren't arguing when they left the house, and Jane thought they were about the most beautiful couple she'd ever seen. But when she heard them come in a few hours later, her father was cursing in a loud voice. "They just got in the door and he ripped Mom's dress almost off. He pushed her to the floor and was cursing at her and hitting her." Gladys Hurshman pleaded with her husband to stop. She was crying and worried he would awaken the children.

"Fuck the kids!" shouted Maurice Hurshman, striking her again. Jane and her brother ran downstairs, pleading with their father to leave their mother alone.

"Get the hell in your beds where you belong!" he ordered. The children retreated to their rooms. Jane was ten or eleven at the time. She shared a double bed with her younger sisters. "I went in and they were crying, wanting to know what was happening. I held them and kissed them and sang to them." Usually when Jane's father abused her mother, she took her sisters to the basement. "I don't know why. It just seemed to be safe there. I never wanted them to see what was going on. So we sat in the basement. I held them and sang to them until there was no more fighting or noise."

Maurice Hurshman's violence wasn't restricted to his wife. Jane remembered seeing a military police van in the yard of their home at the Gagetown base one afternoon after school. The police were forcing her father into the van.

"Where are they taking you?" asked Jane.

Her father looked at her hesitantly. "Goodbye," he said with a sigh. Running into the house, Jane asked her mother what was happening.

"Your father is just going away on a scheme again for a while." "Scheme" meant manoeuvres, but Jane learned later her father had struck an officer in a fight. Sending him off on manoeuvres was his punishment. Seeing her father whisked away by police was traumatic for such a young girl. She felt a sense of loss, even though his absence meant temporary peace in the Hurshman household. Equally devastating for Jane was the departure of her best friend, Valery, whose father had been transferred to the Canadian Forces base at Hemer, West Germany. The two had been closer than sisters, sharing their innermost secrets; they had even found pleasure in New Brunswick's soft summer rains. "We'd get out our bathing suits and play in the rain. I can remember how nice it felt, hitting my hot skin. It made me feel new—all fresh and clean." After that, Jane always loved walking in the rain.

As it turned out, the loss of her friend was temporary. A month after Valery left, the Hurshmans found themselves on their way to the same Canadian base in Germany. The family sailed to Europe from Quebec. Jane had never been on a ship, but her excitement waned just hours out to sea. She took to her bed, severely seasick, and remained there for most of the eleven-day voyage. "The doctor gave me a needle every so often. We hit the tail end of a hurricane and I thought the boat would sink. Everything got thrown around and broken. It was then I realized how powerful the ocean is. I have great respect for it. It fascinates me." Jane didn't learn to swim and never went near another boat, large or small.

Arriving at the English port city of Southampton, the Hurshman family, carrying only their personal belongings, travelled by train to the Channel and then across France and into Germany. Their military housing complex at Hemer consisted of a long row of uniform grey cement buildings with each apartment identically laid out and furnished, right down to the curtains and bedding. Each unit had a balcony, small kitchen, dining room, living room, and three bedrooms.

The family had no television, no telephone, and no car—but for a drinking man the place was a godsend. Across the street was a pub where beer was cheaper than soft drinks, and to have beer delivered, Maurice Hurshman had only to place a card in the window. "The beer truck always stopped at our place," said Jane. "The card was a permanent fixture in our kitchen window." Servicemen were also issued ration cards entitling them to purchase liquor and cigarettes duty free on the base.

Jane was happy to find Valery living in the same complex. Having her friend close by also proved to be a bonus for Maurice Hurshman. Since Valery's parents didn't drink or smoke, they gave him their ration cards. His supply of tobacco and alcohol was virtually limitless. Jane remembered her father often being drunk, and he always had friends in drinking. He bought a floor-model stereo and played loud music constantly. When he wasn't drinking at home, he was drinking in the pub.

Like the pub, Jane's school was directly across the street from their apartment building. She remembered the place as "huge and beautiful," with a winding staircase leading up from the main entrance, its black wrought-iron railing festooned with plants. The Hurshmans stayed in Germany for three-and-a-half years, which for Jane meant grades seven through nine. Academically, she continued to excel, and she took up volleyball and basketball. But her favourite sport was cross-country running and she was good enough to win several ribbons and medals.

During one sports meet involving schools from Canadian bases at Hemer, Soest, and Werl, Jane's basketball team won a first-place ribbon; her volleyball team a second-place ribbon; and she won an individual medal for placing second against one hundred competitors in a seven-mile cross-country run. Jane started a diary, in which she kept her ribbons and medals and recorded her most personal thoughts. During the school year she picked up extra money by babysitting and by "washing heads" and cleaning floors and sinks at a hairdressing shop. Much of her income went for Elvis Presley and Beatles records, but she wasn't allowed to use her father's record player. On weekends, Jane and Valery often went into the record shop in Hemer, where they chose several records at a time, took them into a booth, put on earphones, and listened to their favourite songs.

Jane became fluent in German, and in the summers found light work in a factory. She and Valery spent a lot of time in a teen hangout called the Slop Shop. It was at the rear of a pub owned by a German family. As they got older, the inseparable friends began travelling on their own. "We used to catch a bus or train, with no specific destination in mind, and just go. We travelled all over Germany that way. We even went by bus to Holland several times, exploring old castles and caves." Friends who owned a car once took the Hurshman family on a day trip to a castle and huge dam. It was the only family outing Jane remembered.

While working at the hairdressing shop one day after school, Jane asked if she could have her hair done in lieu of pay. They back-combed her hair, which was the style then, and applied a touch of make-up. "They transformed me into a new person. I went home and went right into the bathroom, where I stood gazing at myself in the mirror and thinking how pretty I looked. Dad was drinking as usual. I could hear music and men talking. Mom was running around waiting on them hand and foot. I walked into the room hoping that someone would comment on how nice I looked." Her father looked at her.

"Who in hell do you think you are?" he yelled. "You made-up whore, get in that bathroom and wash that shit off your face and comb your hair."

Jane was fourteen. She was hurt and humiliated. Her mother had never used anything more than lipstick on her face, and after that incident, Jane seldom wore make-up, even into her twenties and thirties. "That's how much of an impression that day made on me."

A few days after that incident, Gladys Hurshman entered Jane's bedroom and handed her a brown paper bag. "Hide this in your closet," said her mother in a hushed voice. "You'll need it soon if you don't already."

"What is it?" asked Jane.

"You'll know someday."

Jane closed the door and opened the bag. Inside was a sanitary napkin and belt. "I didn't know what they were for, but I thought they must be bad because my mother told me to hide them." Several months later at Valery's house, Jane didn't feel well and she went into the bathroom. "When I saw all the blood I thought I had some disease and was going to die. I stuffed toilet paper in my panties and ran home." Lying on her bed she wondered what was wrong with her. The bleeding continued at school the next day. For the first time ever, she asked to be excused from gym class.

"You don't look very well," said her teacher. "Are you sick?"

"I'm bleeding, and I'm going to die."

Comforting her, the teacher explained what was happening.

The drinking and abuse continued unabated in the Hurshman household. Returning from school one afternoon, Jane heard her father shouting. She bent down and peered through the mail slot in the front door. "Dad was drunk and had vomited all over everything. He was yelling at Mom to 'clean up this Jesus mess.' Mom, as usual, did what he ordered." Jane sat outside on the steps praying silently: "Oh, Lord, please let it get better. I can't stand this." Moments later her father staggered out of the house and slumped down on the step beside her. Eyes glazed, he stared at Jane.

"I hate you!" he blurted.

Jane sat stunned. "I like to believe he was so drunk he didn't know who he was talking to or what he was saying. But at the time, and for years to come, it left an awful impact. I thought, 'If my own father hates me, then who will ever love me?'"

Maurice Hurshman had a younger brother, James, who had come to live with them during their stay in Gagetown. He was eight years Jane's senior. She looked up to him and thought of him as a big brother. He later joined the Canadian Army's Black

Watch. Jane hadn't seen him since the family left Canada. One night there was a knock at the door while she was babysitting her sisters and her parents were up the street partying at a neighbour's house. It was her uncle James in full uniform, including a kilt. "I opened the door and got the biggest hug…I was so happy to see him. He had a male friend with him." Jane allowed Sandy and Mona to get up and see their uncle.

When the girls returned to bed, James and his friend began drinking. She was shocked. She'd never seen Jim drink before. He seemed different. When he fell asleep, she joined her sisters in their room and locked the door. Before long, there was a knock on the bedroom door. It was Jim's friend, and he wanted in. He banged loudly on the door, and Sandy and Mona began crying. Jane quieted her sisters and told them to hide under the bed. She was terrified. Somehow she found the strength to push and pull a large wardrobe against the door. She told the girls she was going for help. Directly below the bedroom window was a stairway leading to the basement of the apartment building. Climbing out the window, Jane tried to balance herself on the thin steel railing around the stairwell. If she slipped, she would fall to the cement stairs below. Somehow in the darkness she managed to climb down and ran to the neighbours' apartment to get help.

"Dad was drinking. I told him what was happening and he left in a rage. The guy had the bedroom door open and was pushing his way into the room when Dad arrived. The kids were terrified, but they remained silent, still hiding under the bed. Dad grabbed hold of the guy and threw him down the apartment steps and out of the building. Dad was raving mad at Jim, who was awakened by the noise but didn't have a clue about what had happened." Jane snuggled into bed with Sandy and Mona. By this time, the party had moved to the

Hurshmans' apartment. Jane knew it was going to be another long night when she heard her father shout to her mother: "Get me a drink, squaw, and get some music playing."

Jane considered her mother to be the backbone of the family. Even though she seldom expressed outward affection, "it seems as if we knew she loved us. She made sure we went to Sunday school and church. She always had a strong belief in God, and she instilled that belief in us. I feel certain that God always had a special angel watching over my mother."

Returning from school one day, Jane found her mother in bed, which was most unusual. She was too ill to get up. Her body was hot and the bedclothes were soaked in blood. Maurice Hurshman arrived shortly after Jane.

"Jesus Christ!" he said. "What the hell happened?"

He rushed Gladys to the hospital. Jane stayed behind to look after her sisters and prepare supper. There was no telephone, so she had no way of checking on her mother's condition. She put Mona and Sandy to bed and waited, distraught and worried. Later in the evening she kept her mind occupied by reading to her sisters in bed. She heard a car pull up and her father's voice. Fearing he might be drunk, Jane stayed in the bedroom. She heard him talking and thought he'd brought someone with him. She listened intently but heard only his voice. It was then she realized Maurice Hurshman was praying. She never forgot his words: "Dear God, let Gladys live, please. I don't know what I'd do without her. I love her, and I'll never lay a hand on her again."

Gladys Hurshman had suffered a tubal pregnancy. The doctors were afraid the massive bleeding would induce shock and death. Later that night there was a knock on the Hurshman door. Jane heard a male voice urging her father to go immediately to the hospital. They didn't think his wife would live through the night. Jane stifled a sob and did her own praying as her father left the apartment for the hospital.

Gladys Hurshman recovered and was home in a few days. Jane never saw her father strike her mother again. The drinking, cursing, and arguing continued, but there was no more physical abuse.

Jane was fifteen when she left Germany. During her last eight months overseas she had a boyfriend, Joe, who was in the service and several years her senior. She met him at a Salvation Army recreation centre and restaurant set up for Canadian servicemen and their families. Joe had a motorcycle and a car. Jane was impressed. She wasn't supposed to date Joe but she did anyway. She loved riding with him on his motorcycle. It gave her a feeling of freedom. Joe was good-natured and made her happy. "We often drove—no place in particular. We walked in the rain, talked about anything and everything. He would hold my face in his hands and kiss me ever so gently, as if I might break." On Jane's fifteenth birthday, Joe threw a party for her at a pub, complete with birthday cake and candles. He gave her a delicate watch, which she cherished for the rest of her life. When Jane arrived home that evening she showed the watch to her mother.

"My boyfriend gave it to me," she said proudly.

"Don't tell your father."

Her father stormed into the room. "Don't tell your father what?" he demanded.

"Jane has a boyfriend and he just gave her a watch for her birthday."

Maurice Hurshman eyed his daughter.

"And what did you give him in return?" he asked curtly.

Jane didn't understand the question.

"We've got two more weeks over here," said her father. "Then we go back to Canada. You're grounded until we leave."

Jane was crushed. Joe was waiting for her the next day after school. "I told him what had happened. He was as heartbroken as I was. For the next three days I played hookey. Joe would pick me up in the afternoon and we just drove around on his motorcycle." When she came home for dinner on the third day, Jane knew she was in trouble. Her father was sitting at the table, her brother Douglas beside him.

"Just ask her, Dad," said her brother. "She hasn't been to school in the last three afternoons. I saw her get on that guy's motorcycle and drive away."

"Is it true?" asked her father sternly.

"Yes, it's true," said Jane.

Her father removed his belt. "That was the only time my dad beat me. I was so hurt. I felt so defeated but I wouldn't give him the satisfaction of crying."

When Joe arrived at school during noon break the next day, Jane explained what had happened. He was close to tears.

"I'll stay away," he said. "I don't want you to be punished for seeing me."

But Jane wanted to see Joe again, more than anything she'd ever wanted in her life. They made plans to meet the following Saturday night—her last night in Germany. "As usual, Dad was drinking that night. I put Sandy and Mona to bed early. I told them I was going to sneak out the window to see Joe. They agreed not to tell. Joe was waiting for me down the street. There was a heavy mist in the air, but it was warm." They drove into the country in his car, stopping on a deserted cobblestone road. They left the car and walked in silence. There were grassy fields on either side of the road. "So much was passing between us without a word being said. I asked him to hold me and kiss me. He lifted me right up in his arms and kissed me while he was still walking along." They stopped and stared into each other's eyes.

"Joe, will you make love to me?" asked Jane softly.

"Janey, you're so very special, so pure. I can't hurt you like that."

"Please, Joe, I want one good memory to last me forever."

Jane could feel her heart pounding when he laid her down in the damp, soft grass. They made love in the darkness. "I was a virgin. It wasn't what I expected it to be. It hurt a lot. I wanted to cry, but I didn't. I told him it was nice." Afterwards, Joe held her gently in his arms.

"I love you, Janey," he whispered. "I'll be returning to Canada in six months and we'll be together again."

"I can't wait for that day."

Arriving back home, Jane asked Joe to come in, not knowing what to expect. He agreed. "My dad was still drinking, but he appeared to be in a good mood. I was so happy that Dad didn't make a scene, I don't even remember the conversation. I was so proud to have Joe sitting beside me. My mind kept flashing back to what we'd done earlier. I wondered if anyone could tell by looking at me." Joe stayed about an hour, then Jane walked him to the door. He kissed her gently on the lips.

"Good night, my angel," he whispered. "I'll see you tomorrow before you leave."

On the morning of February 5, 1964, the Hurshman family's belongings were packed and ready to be loaded on the bus that would take them to the airport. There was no sign of Joe. Jane waited anxiously, but he wasn't there when the bus arrived. It was a cold, grey, rainy day. Jane felt deep sadness on the bus. "I didn't want to board that plane. It was going to take me away from the only person who ever said he loved me." There was a large crowd at the airport. Jane heard a voice calling her name. "I searched the faces and there stood Joe. I was so happy. We said our goodbyes in the rain, with Joe reassuring me that he would write and we'd be together again when he returned to Canada."

Maurice Hurshman's new posting was the Canadian Army base at Winnipeg, Manitoba. The family flew from Germany to Trenton, Ontario, where they were put up in a motel for two days before catching a train to Winnipeg. Jane remembered stuffing herself with treats that were unavailable in Germany. They ate a lot of ice cream, banana splits, and red licorice, and spent considerable time in front of the television set, where Jane saw *The Beverly Hillbillies* for the first time.

The train trip from Trenton to Winnipeg was a nightmare for the Hurshmans. The army bungled their reservations, and they were forced to share a single compartment. Jane was crushed between her brother and sisters and slept fitfully on the overnight journey. It was still dark when they arrived in Winnipeg. It was the heart of winter. The snow was deep and the temperature was forty below zero. Jane had never experienced such cold. "The air was so cold it hurt to take a breath. I thought I was going to die. We weren't prepared at all. We were dressed in spring clothing. The winters in Germany weren't near as cold."

There was no room for the family on the army base, and they were forced to live in a motel with housekeeping units for a month. There was no respite from the subzero temperatures, and Jane's breathing problems continued. "We all thought it was just the weather, until one morning I bent over to tie my shoe; the pain was more than I could stand. Mom took me to a clinic where they found I had three fractured ribs." The ribs had been fractured in the cramped compartment on the train nearly three weeks earlier. "They strapped my ribs up with tape, and I can remember the doctor saying, 'Young lady, you sure must have a high pain threshold.' At the time I didn't know what the doctor meant, but I was to find out in the years to come."

After a month of searching, Maurice Hurshman found a four-bedroom house for his family off the base in the city. Jane had her own bedroom for the first time. Although happy to have her own room, she missed the company of her younger sisters and the comfort they had provided one another at night for as long as she could remember. Jane wrote often to Joe in Germany, but until her family found a house and a permanent address, he couldn't respond. "When I sent him my new address, I got a beautiful letter from him and a pair of white leather boots. I had admired them once in a shop window in Germany. It made me so happy. But it was the first and last time I heard from Joe. I put his letter in my diary. I still wrote him but never got a reply. I figured he had just forgotten about me. I was very hurt."

In Winnipeg, Gladys Hurshman found a job doing housework. "It was the first time she ever had a job. It was different, coming home and Mom not being there. I used to make lunch for the kids and I'd have supper started by the time she got home. It must have been difficult for her, walking to and from work in all that cold."

Jane began feeling desperate and lonely. Because she lived off the army base she enrolled, midway through the year, in a civilian high school. Joe wasn't writing to her, and although her friend Valery had moved to Winnipeg when her family was also transferred from Germany, she lived and went to school on the base. "I didn't see much of her. For the first time ever I hated to go to school. I just didn't fit in. Everything just seemed so wrong, and I was so very lonely. Once again I started feeling like that lost little girl. I kept up my grades at school, but I never made any friends there. I knew my marks were good, so I never worried about passing. It was sure a shock and surprise when I got my report card in June 1964 and it said I failed. I couldn't believe it.

That was the last straw. I wasn't the only one who failed that year—they failed everyone who came back from Germany. They said they failed us because we were behind a year, according to their standards. To me it was just a feeble excuse."

Spring sunshine melted the snow and warmed winter-weary bones, but did nothing to soothe Jane's disappointment over failing. She felt trapped in an unhappy home life with no friends. She wanted to leave home, and when her chance came, she took it. "Some friends of Mom's and Dad's were being transferred to Nova Scotia, and I wanted very much to go. It was summer now, and the summer in Winnipeg was as hot as the winter was cold. Mom and Dad said I could go—at least for the summer. When Dad came to the train station to see me off, I knew in my heart I'd never return there to live."

The couple Jane travelled with had two young sons. She looked after them on the long trip to Nova Scotia, while their parents drank and fought. The husband was an alcoholic who often beat his wife. They went as far as Kentville, Nova Scotia, where Jane stayed with them a few days, "but it was just one big drunk with lots of physical abuse on the part of the husband to his wife. Eventually one of his relatives drove me to my grandmother's house in Liverpool. I remember thinking when I arrived, 'I'm in a safe place now.'"

CHAPTER 4

"YOU LOSE . . ."

Jane's "safe place" was the home of her paternal grandmother, Mildred Hurshman, known affectionately as Gramma Mill. She was an energetic, stocky woman who lived in a large house in Liverpool. A path from the house led down a gentle, tree-covered slope and across a rail line to the rocky shoreline, where the Mersey River emptied into the Atlantic Ocean. There, salt-water from the ocean mixed with the fresh river water, making children's bodies more buoyant when they jumped from the nearby train trestle during the warm summer months. Gramma Mill worked at a nursing home, usually in the evenings. She was separated from her husband and lived with a fisherman, big George Whynot, who operated his own boat out of Liverpool. Jane remembered George being more of a grand-father to her than her real grandfather. She had her own room in the house, and Gramma Mill, who loved to bake, always pre-pared hearty meals. Jane spent a lot of quiet moments sitting on the rocky shore watching the tide. Sometimes she walked along the shore to a small sandy cove.

Big George, Gramma Mill, and Jane lived downstairs in the house. Her uncle James, whom she hadn't seen since Germany, lived upstairs with his wife and young son. James was out of the service and worked on a Liverpool scallop dragger. The house was a gathering point for many of James's fishing and drinking buddies.

At one of her uncle's parties Jane met Milford "Milfie" Whynot. Nine years her senior, Milfie owned his own car and reminded Jane of Joe, the boyfriend she'd left behind in Germany. "He was a nice-looking, quietly spoken, very talented man. He filled a very lonely spot in my life. I needed him—needed someone. He happened to be the one to come along. He told me he cared. I'm sure I would've clung to anyone who showed interest or affection. I don't honestly know if I loved him or not. I was still a child myself. When I first went out with Milfie he took me to visit friends of his—a married couple. There was drinking, but it was a different kind of drinking. Everyone was happy and having a good time. There was no fighting, no hollering... no abuse of any kind. Milfie could play any kind of stringed instrument, and he could sing very well. It was all very nice. We went to a lot of house parties like that one. Milfie had a very placid nature. It wasn't in him to be violent or abusive. His grandparents raised him as if he was their own son. They were devoted to him and they catered to his every wish. When I started going with him he had a good job at the Power Commission. His grandmother was the real motherly type and I got along with her very well. She never drank or smoked. His grandfather had quit drinking years before, and they didn't allow any drinking in their house. That was a form of security for me. They had a big house which was well maintained but it had no bathroom or running water. It was heated by a wood stove. I loved going there. It was homey."

Jane began dating Milfie on a regular basis. The first time they had intercourse was in his car. He'd been drinking. When it was over, Milfie asked Jane if she had "come." She had no idea what he was talking about, "but I figured I was supposed to say 'yes,' so that's what I said."

There was a county fair that summer of 1964. It was at Caledonia, about twenty-five miles from Liverpool. Milfie asked Jane to go as his date. Jane asked Gramma Mill if she could go. She was shocked by the response: "No, you can't go. And I don't want you to see Milfie anymore. I'm going to write your parents and tell them you're being bad and I don't want you here anymore."

Jane promised not to see Milfie again. She didn't want to return to Winnipeg but she had no intention of keeping her promise and saw Milfie whenever she could. In September, she started back to school, repeating ninth grade.

"Mill knew I was still seeing Milfie. I came home one evening and went directly to my room. I'd been out with Milfie and we'd had sex. I didn't want to face anyone. When I entered my room, I saw my diary lying on top of my dresser. I knew someone had been at it. I was so very hurt. I felt I'd been violated. My diary was sacred to me, and now even that wasn't mine alone anymore. I couldn't accept that Mill had actually read my diary. But I knew it was her. My hurt turned to anger and I ripped up every page and threw them and my ribbons and medals from Germany into the garbage. When I went into the living room Mill was trying to get in touch with Mom and Dad by phone. I didn't say a word to her. I just went back to my room and packed up my belongings and hid them under the bed. Then I laid down and waited for morning to come."

Jane's maternal grandparents, George and Gertrude Westhaver, lived nearby, across the railway tracks. She arrived on their doorstep with her suitcase the next morning. "I told them what had happened and asked them if I could live there. They'd had hard times. My grandfather didn't work, and their house was small—it had no bathroom or running water. There were still four boys and a girl living at home, yet they said I could move in.

"My grandma was a tiny, very quiet, hard-working woman, much like my own mother. She would always do without to give to us kids. My grandpa, who I always called George, was a big man with a deep, loud voice. When he spoke, you listened. He drank a bottle of wine every day, but I never once saw him get violent or abusive. He would just drink his wine and go sleep it off. They were very poor, but they were good to me. Freddy was the youngest of their boys. He was six years younger than me, but we became very close. We played a sort of a game every day when we walked to school. We always asked each other what would be the first thing we'd do when we grew up. He always said he'd never eat bologna and I said I was going to have a padded toilet seat—no more rough boards or splinters in my bum. We'd always laugh, but Freddy doesn't eat bologna anymore, and when I got my first bathroom in 1980, the toilet had a padded seat."

The Westhavers didn't mind Jane dating Milfie. He was allowed to come to the house to pick her up for dates. On school nights she had to be in by 10 p.m. Milfie often brought a bottle of wine over for George, and the two of them would sit and talk while he drank it. Jane felt secure and content—part of the family.

Then came a surprising letter from her mother: Joe had returned from Germany and had come to Winnipeg to visit her. "He told Mom he hadn't written to me because he'd been involved in a serious motorcycle accident and was hospitalized for a long time. I don't know what I felt when I read that letter, but I knew I didn't want to go to Winnipeg ever again, and I was involved with Milfie. That was the last I ever heard about Joe. I still think of him every so often. I hope he has a happy life, wherever he is."

Other letters passed between Winnipeg and Halifax. Gramma Mill became vindictive toward Jane, even though she no longer lived with her. "She wrote my parents and told them I was running wild with an older man. She told some terrible lies about Milfie." Gramma Mill claimed Milfie had impregnated a fourteen-year-old girl and then abandoned her. She also claimed he had syphilis. "I got a letter from Mom telling me I had to come home because of what Mill had told her. I told Milfie what was going on and he was very hurt, very upset with Mill. He even went to a doctor to prove her wrong. It was all a pack of lies." Jane wrote her mother and assured her the stories were not true and that she had no intention of returning to Winnipeg.

Two months after her sixteenth birthday, a doctor confirmed that Jane was pregnant. She was shocked and worried how Milfie might react. His grandparents left that weekend to visit their daughter in Halifax. Milfie had asked Jane to spend the weekend with him. They were lying in his bed in the darkness on a Friday night.

"Milfie, I went to the doctor today and he said I'm going to have a baby." Jane couldn't see his face. He was silent for several minutes.

"Well, that's something, ain't it," he said finally. "I guess I have to marry you. When do you want to get married?"

"I don't know. When do you think we should?"

"I dunno either. Go to sleep now and I'll decide tomorrow."

Milfie fell immediately to sleep. Jane lay awake, thoughts and questions bombarding her mind. "How was I going to tell Mom and Dad? What would I do with a baby? Would I be a good mother? I knew I wanted this baby very much. It would be mine and I would love it."

In the morning, Jane called her mother. It was their first conversation since her departure from Winnipeg the previous summer. Her father wasn't home: he was on a six-month posting at the Canadian Forces base at Alert in the Northwest Territories, two hundred miles from the North Pole. "I told Mom I was pregnant and we were getting married. She said she'd write and tell Dad." Her mother asked when the wedding would take place. Milfie checked the calendar and decided on Saturday, April 24. She told her mother the date, and that was the end of the conversation. They broke the news to Milfie's grandparents when they returned from Halifax Sunday afternoon. They hugged her, and Milfie drove Jane home to tell her grandparents.

"Does your mother know?" asked her grandmother.

"Yes," Jane replied. "I called her and she said it was okay."

It was settled, and Jane was relieved. She went to school until the day before the wedding. "Milfie took care of everything. His sister loaned me a blue dress. Milfie bought me some flowers and my aunt Judy and her new husband stood up for us." They were married at 7 p.m. at the minister's house. Friends of Milfie gave them a small reception in their apartment. Jane didn't know most of the people, and she didn't remember who held the reception. Neither Milfie's grandparents nor Jane's parents attended the wedding, nor did they send gifts. Milfie got drunk at the reception. They went back to his grandparents' house and went to bed. Milfie vomited and immediately fell asleep. Jane lay in bed thinking about her life. She didn't really know what love was or what the future held. "I was pregnant. When you got pregnant, you got married. You make your bed; you lie in it and make the best of it. I didn't blame anyone. I was going to be a mother and Milfie a father."

Jane and Milfie moved in with his grandparents. The baby wasn't due until October. The next six months were uneventful and boring for Jane. Milfie's grandmother did everything for him; it was as if he didn't have a wife. She made up his lunchbox for work, and made his breakfast in the mornings, and even woke him to get ready for work. She did all the housework. Jane got up when Milfie did and made the bed. That was the extent of her chores. Milfie turned his paycheque over to his grandmother, who paid whatever bills he owed and gave him the rest. He didn't give Jane any money unless she asked for it, which she seldom did. "I really didn't need any. I had plenty to eat, clothes on my back, and a roof over my head. I felt I was just there as a convenience for Milfie—giving him sex whenever he wanted it." Jane centred her existence on her baby. She weighed only ninety-eight pounds the day she was married, but she didn't begin to show until her last two months. As her pregnancy progressed, Milfie ignored her more and more. Being married didn't change his lifestyle: he came and went as he pleased. Sometimes he asked Jane to go with him, but usually he went alone. When she asked him where he was going or who he had been with, Milfie would say, "It's none of your business."

Jane knew she would love her child, but she was also looking forward to the birth to end the monotony of her day-to-day existence. "I needed something to fill the growing void inside me. I didn't know anything about having babies, and I didn't know anybody I could ask about it. I didn't know what to expect when my time came." She awoke one morning, a few days after her due date, with a pain in her lower back. She'd never had a day of illness during her entire pregnancy. The pain persisted through the day. Milfie came home from work at 5:30 p.m., cleaned up, and ate supper.

"I'm going out," he announced.

"Can you drop me off at Mill's? I want to take a bath."

Milfie drove Jane to Gramma Mill's without a word.

"Where can I reach you if I need you?" she asked as he was about to leave.

"I don't know, but you can try the tavern."

Jane had a soothing hot bath, but the pains persisted. Gramma Mill made her a hearty snack. By 11:30 p.m. the pains had worsened considerably. She looked imploringly at Gramma Mill.

"I think I'm going to have my baby. The pains are really bad now."

"This is your first one, so it could take a while."

Jane sat back and gritted her teeth, and they both watched television. Shortly after midnight a severe contraction caused her to double up in pain. She jumped to her feet. "Call someone to take me to the hospital!"

Milfie was telephoned at the tavern. He wasn't there. A friend of Gramma Mill's drove Jane to the hospital. She was admitted shortly after 1 a.m. on October 9, 1965. She was alone and terrified. They prepared her for the delivery room and left her alone again in the cold, unfamiliar surroundings. Jane got up to go to the bathroom when her water broke. She didn't know what was happening. She yelled for the nurse, who appeared immediately. Jane apologized for making a mess. She was taken to the delivery room, and the doctor arrived shortly after. He did his best to put her at ease.

"It won't take long now, Jane," he said soothingly. "Do you want a boy or a girl?"

"I want a boy. I'm sure it will be a boy."

The pain got worse. The baby was coming. The doctor urged Jane to push harder. "I see the head now. Keep pushing." Jane pushed as hard as she could.

"It's a boy, Jane," announced the doctor. "You got your wish."

It was 5:05 a.m. Jane was drained but ecstatic. "Does he have all his fingers and toes and everything?" she asked.

"Hey, slow down," said the doctor with a smile. "Here, you can see for yourself."

He placed Jane's seven-pound, fifteen-ounce baby in her arms. "At that moment I was the happiest person alive. I felt so much love. There was a lot of pain, but I'd had a very easy delivery." Jane decided to name her son Allen. Milfie's sister had suggested the name to her months before. When she left the delivery room, Jane called Milfie to tell him the news. His grandmother answered the telephone. "Milfie is asleep and I don't want to wake him," she said.

"Well, tell him we have a son and ask him to bring my suitcase when he comes to visit us tonight. It's all packed under our bed."

"I'll do that. Good night."

Milfie arrived at the hospital after supper that day. He left Jane's suitcase at the nursing station "and he told them to tell me that he had a cold and couldn't come to see me or the baby. He never did come to visit us. Not once. Nor did I have any other visitors. Milfie's grandfather came to pick us up when we were ready to come home. It didn't matter how much I was ignored—I had my baby. I devoted all my time to him. I talked to him and sang to him right from the time he was born."

Milfie's grandparents now had a great-grandchild, and they doted on him. Jane never went anywhere without Allen. He became her whole world. Jane and Milfie lived with his grandparents for a year and a half after their wedding. The house was on the main highway in Milton, a town three miles from Liverpool. After Allen was born, Milfie and Jane began thinking about getting their own home. They bought a piece of vacant land a half-mile from his grandparents. When Allen was about six months old, Jane found a job at a Liverpool grocery store, where she worked every day but Sunday. It was a nine-to-five job except for Fridays, when she worked twelve hours, and earned her twenty-nine dollars a week—most of which went into a savings account for a new home. Either Milfie or his grandparents would drive Jane to and from work. Milfie's grandparents babysat for Allen when Jane worked.

When an old building was torn down, Milfie bought the lumber from a Liverpool dealer and used it to build a home on their vacant lot. It was a small, two-bedroom structure with grey-and-white siding. Jane remembered that the house was simple but comfortable. She left her job at the grocery store to spend more time with Allen and to decorate their home.

Jane didn't remember much of the next few years, except that Milfie was drinking more and more and that life was monotonous. He never abused her physically, but he was seldom at home, and when he was, he was usually half-drunk or asleep. They had sex at his whim. The act became mechanical for Jane. "One night I got enough nerve to ask him what he'd meant when he asked if I'd 'come' the first time we had sex."

"Good God," he replied, "you wasn't any virgin when I first had sex with you. You must know what 'come' means. You ain't really that stupid, are you?"

"Oh, I was just joking—never mind me," said Jane, embarrassed.

She remembered one night when they'd been married about three years. "It wasn't Milfie's usual on-and-off sort of sex. It lasted a long time. That was the first and only time in our ten-year marriage that I had a climax. It was different. It felt good. It was then that I knew what he meant when he asked, 'Did you come?'"

When Allen was old enough to go to school, Jane decided to upgrade her education. In September 1970, she enrolled in adult classes at a Liverpool school. She found it fulfilling, and attended classes regularly till the end of the school year in June 1971. She completed grade ten with straight As. Allen also did well in school.

That summer she took him with her to visit her parents, who were now living at the Camp Borden base in Ontario. Milfie refused to make the trip with them.

"After we came home from that visit, I got a letter containing a photograph of a nude woman. It was cut up in pieces and you had to put it together like a jigsaw puzzle. The face was missing. The letter said, 'Guess what Milfie was doing while you were away?' I asked him about the photo but he denied knowing anything about it. I didn't mention it again but I didn't dismiss it from my mind, either."

With the summer over and Allen back at school, Jane found herself with too much idle time. In January 1972 she enrolled in a typing course in nearby Bridgewater. Milfie was no longer working. He'd quit his job with the Power Commission for a better-paying one at the Bowater-Mersey Paper Company, but that ended in the summer of 1971, "because of his drinking," Jane remembered. "He was sick a lot. It was a vicious cycle for him. He'd get drunk, sober up, get sick, turn back to the booze, and the cycle went on. He went into hospital to dry out. He had major stomach surgery for bleeding ulcers—all due to booze—yet he kept on drinking." The family was living on unemployment insurance and the fifty dollars a week Jane began receiving from Canada Manpower when she enrolled in the typing course. She drove to and from school in Milfie's 1964 Ford Fairlane.

Shortly after she started the typing course, Jane discovered she was pregnant again. "I considered having an abortion, but when I thought about it seriously, I knew I couldn't. About two months before the baby was born I heard about a guy at the paper mill who had some pictures taken at our house while I was visiting my parents in Ontario the previous summer. I got the guy's name and address and went to his house. Apparently, when Milfie left his job at the paper mill he gave the pictures to him. Milfie had kept them hanging in his locker at the mill, thinking I would never find out about them. The guy's wife answered the door when I went there. I introduced myself and told them I knew about the pictures. I told them I wanted them and if they didn't give them to me I would call the police to come and get them. I told them it was illegal to have that type of picture in their possession. I didn't expect the reaction I got. They were scared. They told me to come back at 1 p.m. to get the pictures."

Jane returned and they handed over the photographs. Looking at them made her nauseous. "They were disgusting photos of a naked woman lying on my bed, in my bedroom, in my house. There was a bottle of wine between her legs with the neck shoved into her vagina. I couldn't believe Milfie had actually done this to me. I felt used and dirty. And here I was, seven months pregnant. My world was crushed."

Jane soon learned that Milfie was still seeing the woman in the photographs. He drove Jane to school one Friday afternoon and was supposed to pick her up at 10:30 p.m. "He never showed up. Here I was thirty miles from home and pregnant. I knew of no way to get home. I started walking and after about ten miles a car full of young guys stopped and offered me a ride. They drove me right to my door. It was around midnight. The house was in darkness. My first thought was, 'Oh, God, where's Allen?' I rushed next door to Milfie's brother and they had Allen. They told me Milfie was in jail. He'd been picked up for impaired driving after being with that woman."

Jane's second son, Jamie, was born October 17, 1972. Allen was seven years old at the time. It was an easy birth, but afterwards Jane began hemorrhaging and required blood transfusions. Only once did Milfie, with Allen in tow, come to the hospital to visit Jane and the new baby.

Jane was despondent about her marriage but resigned to her fate. She decided, because of the new baby, to stay and try to make a go of it. But by the time Jamie was three years old, she could take no more. Her father had been transferred once again by the army, this time to Cornwallis, Nova Scotia, only a hundred miles away. A few days after the New Year in 1976, Milfie came home half-drunk at about 10 p.m. and set a forty-ounce bottle of rum on the table. Jane had had enough. They'd shared nothing in their relationship for more than a year—not even sex. Jane eyed Milfie and the bottle.

"It's either me and the kids or that bottle," she said.

Milfie hesitated a moment, then picked up the bottle and kissed it. "I guess you lose," he said with a smirk.

Entering the bedroom, Jane threw her clothes and the children's clothes into a garbage bag. She woke Allen and Jamie and they left in the car for her parents' home. "It was very cold and it was snowing hard. The car broke down in the middle of nowhere. It was late and I was scared. I didn't know what to do. But it was so cold I knew I had to do something. You could see your breath when you talked, and frost was forming on the inside of the windows. I put the boys in the back seat and put the garbage bag of clothes over them. There was no traffic on the road and I didn't know which way would be shorter to go for help. My parents didn't know we were coming, so they wouldn't be expecting us, and Milfie would be too drunk by now to care about us. I left the boys in the car and gave them strict orders not to sleep or to get out of the car. There was about a foot of snow on the road. It was still coming down and blowing hard. I had no hat, gloves, or boots. It seemed like I walked forever. Then I saw a light in the distance and kept walking towards it. I couldn't feel the cold anymore. I heard dogs barking. There were two German shepherds, and they came at me. I was already too scared for my boys and myself to be frightened of them. I just walked right past them and pounded on the door of the house.

"An elderly man and woman opened the door and let me in. I was hysterical. I told them what happened and that my boys were still in the car in the cold. The man got dressed, went out on his snow machine, and brought my boys back. They were so very cold. The milk in Jamie's nursing bottle had frozen. He was crying and said, 'Look, Mommy, it don't work' as he held up his bottle. He'd wet himself, and his snowsuit and pants were frozen stiff. We were all so happy to be where it was warm. They gave me hot coffee and let us stay the night. The next day the man got my car going. It was so cold the gas line had frozen up. I thanked the people and we continued on to my parents'. As I drove I thanked the Lord for keeping us safe. I vowed I'd never go back to Milfie again."

Jane stayed a few days with her parents before driving back to Milton to have it out with Milfie. Allen was reluctant to leave his father until the school year was over. Jane agreed to let him stay with his dad during the week. He would stay with her on weekends and any other time he wanted to come to her. She and Jamie went to live with friends. Milfie begged her not to leave him, but her mind was set. Jane didn't expect—or ask for—any help from him. She went to the Queens County welfare office. She was told they couldn't help her unless she was legally separated or divorced. She wanted nothing less than a divorce. The welfare office set up an appointment for her with a legal aid lawyer. The welfare director told her she could leave Jamie with his secretary while she saw the lawyer. Returning from the lawyer's office, she discovered Milfie had taken Jamie.

"Well, since you don't have any dependents, we can't help you," said the director, shrugging.

Jane rushed back to the lawyer, who told her there was nothing she could do because Milfie had as much right to Jamie as she did. Jane was convinced the welfare director had set her up to save the county some money. She was shattered, frightened for her children, and very angry. "I went to Milfie's house, but no one was there. Then I went to his sister's house. I could hear Jamie crying, 'Mommy... Mommy,' but no one would answer when I pounded on the door. There was nothing I could do. There was no fight left in me. My boys were gone. I was falling apart." Jane was convinced Milfie had taken Jamie as a ploy to get her to return to him. Desperate, she returned again to the lawyer's office.

"Milfie doesn't want a divorce," said the lawyer. "And as far as I can see, you don't have grounds for one."

Jane was furious. She still had the photographs Milfie had taken of the woman in their bed, but she thought they were too disgusting to use as legal grounds for a divorce. They made her feel used and degraded. Thinking of the photographs made her more determined to be free of Milfie. She stared coldly at the lawyer. "I'll be back in a week," she declared. "And I'll give you grounds—grounds that will even make Milfie want to divorce me."

Leaving the welfare offices, Jane walked directly across the street to a doctor's office. He had a reputation for providing women with ready access to birth control pills. He prescribed Jane a three-month supply. "My own doctor wouldn't understand why I needed the pill unless I went into a long explanation, and I didn't want to do that. After Jamie's birth he advised me not to have any more children, and he was able to convince Milfie to have a vasectomy." Jane needed the pills because she had decided to have an affair to give Milfie grounds for a divorce. The man she had chosen for the affair was Billy Stafford, one of Milfie's many casual friends. Milfie had so many people in and out of the house that Jane didn't take much notice of any of them. But she did take notice of Billy Stafford, and she got to talk to him after a 1976 New Year's party. Milfie got drunk at the party and wanted to visit Jane's parents. He invited Billy Stafford to join them. Billy agreed and suggested they take his car. Jane did the driving. On the way there Milfie went to sleep. Jane and Billy got to talking. She told him she'd had enough and was going to leave Milfie. She was taken by Billy's engaging smile and found him to be a perfect gentleman.

"If you ever need any help or if there's anything I can ever do for you, just let me know," offered Billy.

Jane thanked him for being so kind and said she would call him if she needed anything. At her parents' place, Milfie drank while Jane and Billy talked. He seemed concerned, and she was very taken with him. They drove home the next day and a week later Jane left Milfie. She called Billy and reminded him of his offer to help.

"I remember, and the offer still stands," said Billy. "Is there some way I can help?"

"Well," said Jane, somewhat embarrassed, "if I slept with you and you were willing to testify in court, it would be grounds for Milfie to divorce me."

"I'll do whatever you want," said Billy.

By the end of January 1976, Jane and Billy Stafford were living together. Her divorce from Milfie was final by May. "I was full of hope for a new and better life when I went off with Bill. He was my knight in shining armour. He was always telling me he loved me."

"We'll have a good life together," promised Billy. "I will protect you always. You won't be hurt anymore."

CHAPTER 5

BLISS AND BRUTALITY

In the first weeks and months Jane was with Billy Stafford, he was charming and attentive. She felt safe and secure living with him, but there was a large void in her life. Her sons were still with their father. The question of custody didn't arise at the divorce hearing, and she believed that Milfie wouldn't want to bother with the children once the divorce was final. It didn't work out that way. She learned years later that Milfie didn't allow her name to be spoken in his house and ordered his sons to stay away from her. He would keep Jane's children from her as punishment for her leaving him. While she agonized over the loss of her sons, Billy reassured her over and over that she would eventually get them back.

"Don't be bothered about it," he would say. "Let them get used to the situation as it is. They'll have their fill soon enough. Let him see what it's like trying to raise two kids."

At first, Jane and Billy rented a comfortable bachelor apartment in Liverpool. Living with Billy exposed Jane to a lifestyle she had never imagined. When he wasn't out working on the fishing boats, he was always busy at something—going somewhere—and he always took Jane with him. He seemed to have an endless supply of friends to visit for drinking, card playing, or partying. "Even in my marriage to Milfie, I was never a person to go visiting. I knew a lot of people but I didn't have any special friends. Milfie's brother and his family lived next door to us for eight years, but I didn't go to visit them more than three or four times, and that was at Christmas, when it was appropriate. I was never like a lot of women who went around visiting—having tea and catching up on gossip. My mother never did those things either. But with Billy it seems we were always out visiting somebody."

In March 1976, while Billy was out on the fishing boats on a typical two-week run, Jane went to visit her parents. While driving back to her apartment in Billy's car, a 440 Dodge Monaco, she hit an icy spot and the car spun into a telephone pole, which snapped in two. The upper portion, including a transformer, crashed onto the car's roof. Jane was stunned but unhurt.

The car was totaled and Billy had no collision insurance. Jane went to the wharf to meet him when he returned from fishing. Before she could explain what happened, he reached out and hugged and kissed her.

"You wrecked my car, didn't you?" he asked with a smile.

"How did you know?"

"I had a feeling. Don't worry about it—I can always get another car, but never another you."

Billy picked up his pay packet and they went home. "He went out for a while and returned with a dozen roses—my first ever—and a beautiful pair of earrings with my birthstone set in them. I was just floating on cloud nine. I was really enjoying all this love and affection. We made love that night. It was the second time in my life that I reached a climax during sexual relations."

During a visit with friends of Billy in Charleston, a hamlet a few miles from Liverpool, Jane noticed a big vacant house. She asked Billy if he'd like to live there.

"No one has lived there for over twenty years," he laughed. "The people who own it won't rent it."

"Do you mind if I check into it?"

"I don't mind. If it makes you happy, do it."

Surprisingly, the woman who owned the house agreed to rent it to Jane for twenty-five dollars a month. She gave Jane the key and when Billy returned from fishing they went to see the place, which was old and filthy. Billy shook his head and laughed when he glanced over the interior. "Why, it's a wreck. You can never get this place fit to live in. They should pay us to live here."

But Jane was not discouraged. Billy stood back and watched as she wandered from room to room. She loved the house and believed it had potential and a lot of character. Billy could see her mind was made up. "All right, hon, I'll give you five hundred dollars to spend however you want. If you think you can fix it up while I'm out on my next trip, then fine, we'll move in."

Over the next two weeks Jane cleaned, painted, papered, laid floor coverings, hung drapes, and moved their furniture into the house. "No one, including Bill, could believe what I did. It was lovely and anyone would've been proud to live in it. Bill was very impressed with what I accomplished. I thought we would be very happy there."

Although her life with Billy was somewhat fulfilling, the guilt Jane felt about her sons gnawed at her continuously. "The emptiness from their loss was growing deeper and deeper. It was especially hard when Bill was out fishing. I longed to see them, to touch them, to hold them in my arms. I felt guilty about not seeing them, but there was nothing I could do. Several times I went up to Allen's school just to get a look at him." To help fill the void, Jane bought a miniature poodle. "She was coal-black. When I first got her she was so small I could hold her in the palm of my hand. When the sun shone on her she looked blue from the rays. So I named her Blue. She helped fill my time. I took her everywhere."

While they were still living in their first apartment Billy discovered Jane was on the pill. She kept them on the refrigerator beside the kitchen sink so she wouldn't forget to take them. "How long have you been taking these?" he asked.

"I started taking them when I knew I was going to go out with you."

"Why?"

"I didn't need them with Milfie because he had a vasectomy. I had complications after Jamie was born and I was advised not to get pregnant again."

"I wish you wouldn't take them, hon. Just let nature take its course. If you did get pregnant, wouldn't it be great? Wouldn't you like to have a little girl?"

"No. I don't know why, but I never wanted girls. I always wanted boys."

"Well, hon, you can't have a boy *or* a girl taking those things."

Jane was standing by the sink holding the pills in her hands. "Do I dare take the chance of getting pregnant?" she asked herself. "I was scared, but Bill wanted a baby. Bill reached out, took the pills, and dropped them in the garbage. They were never mentioned again, and as each month came and went, I breathed a sigh of relief." But she missed her period in August 1976. They were living in their big house in Charleston by then. "After a couple of months, the doctor confirmed I was pregnant. I wanted the baby very much, but I lived each day in fear, wondering what would happen to me and the unborn baby. I had myself believing something drastic was going to happen to us. I never expressed my fears to anyone, especially to Bill. I just figured because I didn't say much when he threw my pills away, now I had to suffer the consequences."

Because Jane had a rare blood type, she had to undergo regular blood checks in the latter part of her pregnancy to ensure she wasn't producing antibodies that would endanger the fetus. She also had an ultrasound examination of the baby. "It made me feel better. I could hear the baby's heart beating and feel it moving. It took my fears away for a short time, but they always returned. It seemed like I was always at the hospital getting poked with needles so they could examine my blood. The more I went to the hospital the more my fears grew." Jane also had problems controlling her bladder because of the pressure from the weight of the baby.

Overshadowing all of her health worries was a gradual, sinister change in Billy's attitude toward her. Although she and Billy didn't discuss marriage after her divorce from Milfie, Jane took his surname. She was Jane Stafford, and in Billy's mind, now that she was carrying his child, ownership was complete. Signs of his true self, the side that Jane didn't know existed, began to surface. She wouldn't learn of his penchant for physical violence until several months after the birth of their child. But as her pregnancy progressed, her gentle sympathetic and physically imposing protector and benefactor became threatening. Jane was confused and bewildered—this was, after all, the man who had promised she would be safe with him, the man who had promised she would never again be hurt as long as he was around. Jane couldn't understand Billy's resentment. It was Billy who had said time and again he wanted her to get pregnant. The more her pregnancy showed, the less he took her out. He spent more and more time away from home, drinking. When he was home he made snide remarks about how big she was getting. He called her a cow, and when he was drunk the verbal abuse escalated, particularly over her problem controlling her bladder.

"Jesus Christ!" he would shout. "I can't dress you up and take you anywhere. You piss wherever you sit. Can't you control yourself? It ain't bad enough you're big as a barrel, now you have to be like a dog and go around pissing on everything. Fuck you, I ain't taking you anywhere until you have that kid." Billy was true to his word.

Jane went into false labour on May 24, 1977. She was in the hospital for three days. Billy left on the boats the day after she was released. She went to his parents' to be near someone if the baby came while he was away. On May 30, Jane woke up at 3 a.m. with severe pains. Billy's father, Lamonte Stafford, drove her to the hospital. They took her to the maternity floor in a wheelchair. The nurses didn't have time to finish prepping Jane. She was only partially shaved when they wheeled her to the delivery room. An eight-pound, nine-and-a-half-ounce boy was delivered at 3:45 a.m. "I knew Bill wanted a girl, but I was happy it was a boy. After the birth I began to hemorrhage again, just as I did after Jamie's birth."

Jane's doctor advised her to have a tubal ligation within three months of the delivery. Her baby was born on a Wednesday. Two days later she went in for surgery, but hospital officials said her husband would have to sign a form approving the operation.

"He's out at sea," said Jane. "He'll sign the form when he comes to visit."

The operation went ahead. "I was secretly happy about the surgery. I knew I couldn't get pregnant ever again. Nine months of never-ending fear and worry was enough. I didn't ever want to go through that again."

Billy Stafford returned from fishing the day after the operation, but didn't come to visit Jane until the following day, a

Sunday. He didn't ask her how she felt, and he made no mention of the baby's health.

"Well, you got what you wanted, didn't you," he said sarcastically. "You got your boy." Jane was silent. "Well, old woman, you can damn well look after him. He's all yours. I've been on a party since I got in Saturday morning and now I'm going back to party some more."

"Before you go, you're supposed to sign a form for my surgery."

"Fuck that. You expect me to sign for an operation that makes you no fuckin' good anymore? No way, old woman, no way. Don't call me until you're ready to come home. And I'm sailing on Wednesday, so you make sure you're out by then."

After Billy's outburst at the hospital, Jane wasn't looking forward to going home, but she hoped he would feel differently once she arrived with the baby. That afternoon Billy's parents came to visit her. She asked them to help her choose a name for the baby. She couldn't decide between Jason and Darren.

"Call him Darren," said Billy's mother, Winnie. "Darren—Darren Edward. Edward is Lamonte's middle name." Jane agreed, and the baby was named Darren Edward Stafford.

The following Tuesday morning, Jane called Billy at his mother's house. He was in a surly mood when he came to pick up her and the baby, and it didn't change in the car. She told Billy: "Because of my surgery, they told me not to do any lifting or any strenuous work for six to eight weeks. I've still got my stitches in. Can the baby and I stay at your mother's for the next two weeks while you're out to sea?"

Billy stared at her incredulously. "To hell with that idea, old woman. It was you who agreed to that operation, not me. So you just get your ass home and get back to keeping house and looking after that bastard you got there in your arms."

Jane didn't dare speak again during the drive home. She was shocked at what she saw when she entered the house. "I am a spotless housekeeper and I couldn't believe the mess. The sink was stacked full of dirty dishes. There were booze bottles and cigarette butts all over the place. The ashtrays were filled to overflowing. Your feet stuck to the floor where booze and pop had been spilled. The bedroom smelled like a pigpen. Bill had been drunk-sick and vomited over the bed and floor and just left it there. In the bedroom was a bucket he'd used as a toilet. He'd been too drunk or too lazy to walk outside to the outhouse."

"Well, what the hell are you waiting for?" Billy sneered. "Can't you see all the work that needs doing around here? Put that little bastard in the crib and get busy."

There was no running water in the house. It had to be drawn from a well by bucket, carried to the house, and heated on the wood stove. There was no washing machine, and the laundry had to be done by hand.

"Can you please get me a few buckets of water so I can wash the bedclothes and do the dishes and floors?" asked Jane.

"What in fuck is wrong with you? Crippled or something? Get your own fucking water."

Jane was bewildered and hurt, but she sensed there was no point in arguing with him. Despite the pain, she drew the water and cleaned up the entire house. "Between doing all of that, I had to cook supper, prepare Darren's formula, and change his diapers. I finished about 10 p.m. I was so exhausted my whole body ached and my stitches hurt. Bill was already in bed when I crawled in. It seemed like I just got to sleep when it was time to get up to feed Darren. I was glad Bill was going on the boat. I needed the rest.

"A couple of days after Bill sailed, I went to visit his parents. I told them how Bill was acting towards me and Darren."

Lamonte Stafford was silent. "Janey dear," said Winnie, "you have to understand his side. He's had you all to himself for a year or more and now he has to share your time. Give him time, dear. Let him adjust to all the changes. He'll be just fine, you'll see."

Billy was at sea for two weeks. On his return, he demanded Jane have sex with him. Jane had been to the doctor to have her stitches removed, but she was in no condition to have intercourse. She had just finished feeding and bathing Darren when Billy came through the door.

"Go into the bedroom and strip," he demanded. "I want to screw you. I haven't touched you since you started getting big, and now I want it."

"But, Bill, it's too soon. I just got my stitches out."

"I don't want to hear none of that. Just get your ass into the bedroom."

Jane went into the bedroom and undressed. He came and stood there glaring at her. "Just look at you! What a hard-looking mess! A scar across your guts; stretch marks all over you, legs that look like two broom handles—the only good thing I got out of this is that your tits got bigger."

He reached out with both hands and squeezed Jane's breasts until they began to drip milk. "I'll get something that little bastard won't get. I'll just help myself to a little drink of this."

Jane stared in disbelief as Billy began suckling her breasts. She thought about his mother's advice: "Give him time, dear. Let him adjust to all the changes."

Billy pushed Jane to the bed and entered her roughly. "I thought I was being torn apart. He wasn't gentle, and since he'd been drinking, it took him longer. To me it seemed like forever. When he finished he just rolled over and went to sleep. I just lay there feeling used and dirty. I wished we had a bathtub so I could take a hot bath to soothe my hurting body and wash away the awful feeling."

Jane and Darren were home from the hospital less than a month when the woman who owned the house ordered them to leave so that her mother could move in. "We offered to buy the house but she refused to sell. I loved the house and it hurt to have to move out. I'd put so much work into it." Jane was despondent, but her situation wasn't entirely desperate. From her years with Milfie she had met a kindly woman, Margaret Joudrey, whose husband, Stan, was a longtime friend of Billy's. They lived in a house ten miles up River Road in Bangs Falls, and the couples often visited each other. The Joudreys came to visit Jane at the hospital when she had Darren, and when they learned they were being forced to move out of their Charleston home, they severed a piece of their land and gave it to Jane and Billy at no cost, other than surveyor fees. Billy bought a cabin for a thousand dollars and had it moved to the lot.

From the time they moved out of the Charleston house in June 1977 until the cabin was converted to a liveable house, Jane and Billy stayed with Lamonte and Winnie Stafford. "It was fine living there. His parents had a beautiful big home and I got along well with them. They loved Darren and they were very good to me. Lamonte never got abusive or violent. He would drink until he had enough and then go to bed. Winnie and I would sit and talk and have a few drinks."

Billy and Jane moved to Bangs Falls at the end of August 1977. Billy put the house in Jane's name because he owed considerable tax arrears and feared the government might take it from him. A few days after they moved in, Jane began working at the Hillsview Acres County Home for the elderly. "It was a good job, and it was close to home. I figured I would have my own money and I would be able to clothe Darren and buy whatever he needed. Bill didn't mind me getting the job there. The staff were all women, and the patients were all elderly." Jane was hired as a domestic, but within a month she was promoted to cook. "Right from the start, my wages bought groceries and paid bills. If I managed to have a few dollars left, Bill would steal it right out of my purse." The first time Jane confronted him, Billy went into a rage.

"Did you take some money from my purse?" she asked.

"No goddamn way!" he shouted.

"It's only you and me here in the house. Who else could take it?"

"I told you I didn't take it. Are you calling me a liar? You're so fucking stupid you probably spent it and you want to blame me for stealing it." Billy's face flushed and his eyes bulged as he raged, and Jane knew it was pointless to pursue the matter.

In eighteen months Jane had seen her common-law husband change from being kind and loving to verbally abusive. In November 1977, she would learn about his penchant for physical abuse. "Darren was six months old. It was my day off and I'd gone to town to do my shopping. There happened to be a photographer in town taking baby pictures. I had Darren's taken. On the way home I stopped to pick up some Kentucky Fried Chicken for supper. When I left the house Bill was installing some kitchen cabinets I'd purchased. He had a friend, Richard Coombs, helping him. It was late afternoon when I got home. I bought the chicken because we didn't have a stove—only a hot plate—and the guys were working in the kitchen. By buying supper I wouldn't be in their way."

Billy glared at Jane when she came through the door. "Where the hell were you all day?" he demanded. "I'm starving. Get me something to eat." Jane could see Billy had been drinking. She served the chicken. Billy didn't say anything until after

Richard left. By then, Jane had Darren in bed and had cleaned up the kitchen. It was a beautiful night. She went out and sat on the veranda. She was gazing at the stars when she heard Billy come out of the house behind her.

"Here, come and sit beside me and look at some of this beauty," she said. Billy walked over to her, put his hand on her head, and pulled her into the house by the hair.

"You fuckin' whore!" he shouted. "You slut! You tramp! I'll give you beauty. I saw you giving Richard the eyes. You just bought that chicken to impress him, didn't you?"

Jane struggled against the pressure of his grip on her hair.

"Answer me, you no-good whore. Didn't you?"

"I...I don't know what you're talking about. I just don't know."

Billy slapped her face and began punching and kicking her. "That was my first real beating, and I didn't know why."

Billy was sheepish the next morning at breakfast. "I'm sorry," he said. "I'll never do it again. I promise."

The beating planted a seed of fear and self-doubt in Jane. "Doubt about myself and whether it was my fault. I wondered: 'Did I look at Richard like he said I did?' Just maybe, I did. To me, no one got that angry or violent without a reason. So I must have been the reason. I prayed a silent prayer, 'Please, Lord, help me to be better so this doesn't happen again.' But it did happen, over and over again, and it always ended up being my fault. The scene was repeated every time a man came to the house after that. It got so I wouldn't even come out of the bedroom when he had male company, but he still accused me of the same thing and beat me for it."

About the time the Staffords moved into their home at Bangs Falls, Billy found himself blacklisted on Nova Scotia fishing boats. Details of the incident that caused the blacklisting are sketchy, but it resulted in Billy being charged with mutiny. He'd been hired for a trip aboard the scallop dragger *Kathy and Susie* out of Lunenburg. When he returned home, he told Jane he had been in an argument with the skipper and first mate. "He wanted them to turn the boat around and bring him home. He beat up the mate, held a knife to him, and said that if they didn't turn around, he would tear everything to hell on the boat. They did bring him in. He was blacklisted, and the Mounties charged him. Two of them came to the house and served him the papers. He slammed the door in their faces and told them to get out. While they were walking back to their car, which was parked by our picture window, Bill got a fully loaded automatic rifle and came to the window. He pointed it right at one of them as he was getting into the car. They ducked down and backed the car out of the driveway with the driver's door open so that they could see where they were going."

Billy, meanwhile, was into one of his patented rages. "You fucking pigs!" he screamed, thrusting his middle finger into the air. "I'll get you one day." He continued his diatribe long after the police cruiser was out of sight. No one would testify against him, and the charge against him was dropped. Jane said Billy "just laughed about it. He wasn't sorry. To him it was a big joke when it was all over. He just got his way again."

After he was blacklisted, Billy began collecting unemployment insurance. He stayed at home through the winter of 1977–78, and made it clear what he expected of Jane: "Well, old woman, you're working now, so I don't need to work. You can look after me. Besides, you're in debt to me for three thousand dollars."

"What do you mean?"

"You remember when you smashed up my car? Well, that's how much it was worth. Now start paying."

Billy taunted Jane about the car accident from then on. "He forever brought that up to me, and to his death he claimed I never paid that debt."

Although Jane worked, Billy adamantly refused to babysit Darren. But a retired couple, Marie and Morton Joudrey—no relation to Jane's close friend and neighbour Margaret Joudrey—lived nearby and agreed to babysit. Marie, perpetually good-humoured, was short and heavy-set with a broad face and laughing eyes. She loved playing bingo and continued to live in Bangs Falls after Morton died of cancer in August 1984.

"Marie and Morton were fantastic people," remembered Jane. "When I told Darren of Morton's death he cried for two days. He spoke very lovingly of Morton and always included him in his prayers at night. They looked after Darren from September 1977, when we moved to Bangs Falls. He was treated as if he were their very own. They loved him. He called Morton 'Daddy' and Marie 'Mommy Marie.' They had an adopted son and he and Darren were like brothers. In retrospect, I'm thankful that Billy wouldn't babysit Darren. According to psychiatrists, Darren's way of coping with a negative situation was helped very much by being put into a normal atmosphere every day. When I came home from work at 3 p.m., I'd stop to pick up him up at Marie and Morton's—but he didn't want to leave."

Marie Joudrey said Darren would often run and hide when it was time to go home. "He'd hide until Jane would say, 'You'd better come out, your father's waiting for us.' He was scared to death of Billy."

Jane said Darren's eyes filled with fear whenever she mentioned his father was waiting for him. "He would run and get his coat and hat, kiss Marie and Morton goodbye, and look at me as if to say, 'Well, Mommy, if we must go—let's go.'"

Why was Darren Stafford so frightened of his father? Jane said that as far as Billy was concerned, "Darren was just something to be abused and used and taught to make it through life as a man from the day his feet could touch the floor. He could laugh when he was told. He could talk when Bill told him to. Being a man, he couldn't cry. If you've gone through that from the time you were about six months old, it's like brainwashing. Through the middle of the night as any baby does, he would cry, and I would get up to feed him. Well, by the time he was six months old, I wasn't allowed to get up and go to him. Bill used to go to the crib, and I'd never hear another word. I used to wonder all night long, is he dead? There was never a sound came out of there. He didn't cry."

When Darren was about three years old, Jane was outside working in the garden when she heard Billy hollering. "Our bedroom was in the front of the house, and he just stuck the gun out the window and he fired a shot. It was close enough to me that it lifted the ground up beside me."

"Get in here, old woman!" shouted Billy. "You've got a mess to clean up!"

Jane went quickly into the house. Billy was standing in the kitchen, his face flushed. "It's in there," he said, pointing to the bedroom.

Jane entered the room. "It was like a nightmare. My little boy was lying on the bed naked and his body was covered in welts from his neck to his feet." Billy had broken a piece off a mop handle and used it to beat the child. Darren was trying unsuccessfully to stifle his sobs, his tiny body quivering like a wounded animal. He had defecated during the beating and there was blood and feces all over the bed and floor. Darren lay on the bed, quivering. Jane began weeping. Billy heard her, came into the bedroom, and punched her in the face.

"Get this fucking mess cleaned up, old woman. We're going out. And get the kid dressed. He's going, too."

Obediently, Jane cleaned up herself and Darren as best she could. They went out to the car and drove down to Margaret Joudrey's trailer. "We picked up Margaret and we all went for a drive. It was just as if nothing had happened."

In the winter of 1978–79, Billy Stafford found temporary employment on a Canada Works Program project at Buckfield, a few miles north of Bangs Falls. He couldn't get work on a fishing boat, but in 1980 he began sailing on the Irving Company's oil tankers—Kent Lines Limited—out of Saint John, New Brunswick. Later he worked on Irving's gypsum boats. The final trip he made was aboard the *SS Gypsum Countess* in the fall of 1981. He was supposed to stay for three months, but he quit after one month and came home. Jane said Billy got into some kind of trouble during that trip, either with the crew or with drugs. She said he came home with a large quantity of drugs. When he came through the door after that trip, he had an announcement for Jane.

"Old woman, I just quit. I'm not working any more." He also announced that an alcoholic friend of his, Ronald Wamboldt, who had known Billy for twenty-five years, was coming to live with them. Jane had no say in the matter. Wamboldt was also a wife beater. Alcohol had taken its toll on his body, and when he moved in with the Staffords he was a shell of a man and much smaller than Billy. Wamboldt's wife, at the urging of her children, had left him and moved to Toronto in August 1978. He failed to meet his mortgage payments, and the bank took his house in September 1981. He knew it wasn't wise to move in with Billy, but had nowhere else to go. Wamboldt was given a separate room—the room where Billy kept his guns. Billy often punched him and slapped him around. He usually called Wamboldt "dummy," and one time he shot at him, just missing. "He didn't shoot right at me... you see, if he did, he'd never miss because he was a good shot."

To earn his keep, Wamboldt did chores for Billy and helped with the various animals Billy kept on occasion. Wamboldt said that if he failed to follow Billy's orders, "I'd get another smash." He said it never entered his mind to go to the police after Billy's assaults because "I was afraid I might get more." Wamboldt often saw Billy beat Jane and Darren. He said Billy knocked her down many times and always referred to her as "old woman." Jane, he said, was "a beautiful mother. She worked hard and she was clean. Kept the house clean... clothes. And a good cook." Wamboldt remembered Darren being "very afraid and some nervous. It was unbelievable."

One evening Jane prepared dinner for herself, Darren, and Margaret Joudrey. Darren reached for something and fell off his chair, striking his mouth on another chair. It drove his top teeth through his lip. The cut bled profusely, and Darren cried aloud from the pain. He was two or three at the time. Jane tried to calm him, and Margaret Joudrey applied an ice pack. It was an hour before the pain subsided and he was able to sleep. His lips were swollen. Billy came home later that night. "The first thing he did was go in and wake Darren up," said Jane. "And when he saw his sore mouth he asked him if he cried."

"Yes, Daddy, I did cry," said Darren. Billy gave the child three sharp punches in the face. "Blood was flying everywhere," said Jane.

"Don't dare cry again or you'll get more of the same," warned Billy.

The next time Bill was away, Jane took Darren to the dentist. "He wouldn't touch him. He sent me to a children's hospital. They put him asleep and drilled the nerves out of his two front teeth and five others. They didn't want to pull them out at his age." Darren's two front baby teeth were black until he lost them.

Billy Stafford often picked his son up by the hair of the head and held him suspended off the floor. He once gave Darren three dollars, which the boy lost. Billy picked him up by the hair, put a butcher knife to his throat, and told him that if he ever lost any more money, he'd cut his gizzard out. At other times he held him upside down by the feet and pointed a loaded .30-.30 rifle to his head. He would warn the boy if he was bad, his brains would be splattered all over the place.

When Billy was home, mealtimes were traumatic for both Jane and Darren. "Darren couldn't even hold a cup in his hand without spilling it, he would shake so badly. Mealtime was just so full of hate at our table. Darren had to eat at the same speed as his father did, and lots of times he couldn't keep up. So Bill would take the spoon and just keep shoving it into his mouth. Darren would vomit right on the table, and Bill would just take Darren's plate and scrape the vomit into it and keep on feeding him until it was gone. It all had to be eaten. Nothing was ever left. Sometimes Bill would just reach out and hit Darren or myself on the side of the head for no reason at all. Or he might hit you over the head with a cup or knife, or whatever he had in his hand. If I complained about how he treated Darren, he would just knock me to the floor.

"Bill's parents were there for dinner one day with his sister Cathy, her boyfriend, and their two children. I had come home from work, and his mother had started supper already. Everything was ready to be served, and it was on the plates. For some reason Bill just went berserk. He got a gun and smashed the plates around. He took everybody's plate and scraped everything into the garbage. He hit Cathy's boyfriend on the side of the head with the gun. Her kids were screaming and crying, Cathy was crying, and everybody just got in their truck and left."

Although Darren had a lot of toys, he was never allowed to play with them when Billy was around. At Christmas, the boy wasn't even allowed to open his gifts. "Bill would open them for him. He'd pass them to Darren and put them back under the tree, where they had to stay. Darren could just look at them. He was never allowed to play with them. One time I bought Darren a battery-powered motorcycle, one you could really drive. Because Darren liked it so much, Bill gave it away to another little boy. Darren was heartbroken but couldn't show any emotion. If Bill happened to be away and I let Darren play with his toys, Bill would come home and throw them in the garbage or run over them with his truck. The only time Darren was happy was when Bill was away on the boats—but even then, he was always afraid of his father coming home. The only thing Bill ever taught Darren was to 'be a man'—to fight and hate. He didn't know how to play with other children. All he could do was show them his muscles and fight with them."

When Darren was two years old he became seriously ill. He had a deep cough, a high temperature, and trouble breathing. Jane asked Bill to drive him to the hospital. "Bill literally dropped us off at the door of the hospital. I stayed with Darren all night and sponge-bathed him to get his fever down. A bad infection in his ears caused the high temperature. About 10 a.m. the next day I called Bill to come and get us. He picked us up and we went back to his parents'. Darren was very irritable. Although he didn't cry, he whined a bit, which was understandable. Bill gave him a beating and put him to bed, all alone. Bill's mother, Winnie, didn't like what she'd seen."

"Don't do that, Billy," she said. "The baby is sick."

Billy glared at his mother.

"You just go about your work and mind your own goddamn business," he told her.

When Billy was away at sea, Jane often stayed with his parents on her days off. "It was nice. Lamonte would babysit for Darren, and Winnie and I would go to bingo. When we got home we would sit and talk and sometimes have a few drinks. It was nice and peaceful. No Bill around, yelling and hollering—just the peaceful sound of silence. It was like everyone became their normal selves when Billy wasn't there."

In October 1980, Jane's eldest son from her previous marriage, Allen, came to live with her and Billy in Bangs Falls. He was fifteen years old and had been in trouble with the law for breaking and entering. He was on probation at the time. While Billy was at sea in March 1981, Allen got into more trouble. As soon as Jane found out, she contacted his parole officer. "I was so scared that Bill would find out about this, and get off the boat and come home, that the worry of it nearly drove me crazy. I knew that if Bill found out he would kill him.

"During this period of stress, Margaret Joudrey asked me to take her to Bridgewater to do her shopping. We went that evening, and since I was there, I decided to get some Easter shopping done for the children. I was so worried about Allen I walked right out of the store with a shopping cart and everything in it. I didn't even realize it. The next thing I knew the man from the store had me by the arm and I was being arrested for shoplifting. The court took it easy on me and gave me fifty hours of community work and a year probation. I was worried about what Billy might do if he found out about Allen, and now with this happening I had all that much more to worry about. I went to a psychiatrist at the time. I told her I could never tell Bill what had happened, but I couldn't tell her why. I did my community service hours and I reported to my probation officer and on February 24, 1982, I appeared in court and got an absolute discharge. Billy never did find out about it. Allen was sent to the School for Boys in Shelburne, and he remained there until the end of August 1981. When he got out he went to live with his father."

In January 1982, the Social Services Department from Liverpool called Jane at work and asked if she and Billy would be willing to take Allen back again. Jane was against it because she feared how Billy might treat him, but Billy insisted he come and live with them. It was Allen's choice. He wasn't getting along with his father and decided to move in with Jane and Billy. He did pretty much as Billy told him to avoid his wrath. That strategy didn't always work. "I used to get hit all the time, like Ronny Wamboldt," said Allen. "It was normal. We just got used to that." Billy treated the two of them like his personal slaves. When they went to cut wood in the bush, Billy used the saw and Allen and Ronny did the carrying and loaded the truck. "He just did the easy stuff. Me and Ronny did the rest of it."

Allen remembered the night friends of his, who were also Billy's friends, came to the house at Bangs Falls. "They all sat at the table in the kitchen and I went over to talk to them to see what was going on in Liverpool and in Milton. Just like that, Bill hit me so hard that I didn't feel it at first and he said, 'Go sit on the chesterfield.' So I went over and sat on the chesterfield." Ronny Wamboldt said Billy treated Allen like he was ten or twelve years old, not sixteen. From time to time Billy gave Allen spending money or a marijuana joint. These small rewards didn't come close to compensating for the overriding fear that he, his mother, Darren, and Ronny Wamboldt were forced to live under.

Allen vividly recalled one of the mealtime episodes when Billy went berserk. "I used to eat my supper real fast. Well, my little brother, he couldn't eat very fast. So one day Billy started feeding it to him himself, spoonful after spoonful. Darren threw up and Bill just scraped it all back in the plate and made him eat it again. And then Mom said, 'You know he can't eat very fast, hon,' and Bill just got up and smashed all the plates and cracked me on the head and went over and started beating Ma with his fists. Then he went over and gave Darren a good beating. He said to my mother, 'When I'm talking to these fucking kids, I don't want your mouth to open.'"

Allen said Jane often called Billy "hon" or "dear" to calm him because she was afraid of him. He often saw Billy beat Jane, Darren, Ronny Wamboldt, and even their pets and other animals. He would beat Wamboldt "because Ronny wouldn't go to bed or he'd go to the washroom and miss the toilet. Bill kicked him in the stomach one night and put him outside. When Ronny woke up the next morning, he was in bed in the house. Bill told Ronny he fell outside on a cement brick but he kicked him in the stomach that night."

Because he was drunk much of the time, Wamboldt didn't remember many of the beatings he took from Billy Stafford. "I got hit," he said, "but I never hit back. There's a good many times he cracked me."

Billy was also cruel to Jane's dog, Blue. She had always been a house dog. But one day Billy decided to keep her outside. "She wasn't used to that," said Jane. "Then he started kicking her around and he'd hold her up by the back of the neck and bite her nose. It broke my heart to see this, but I knew not to say anything because if I did he would just do it all the more. If I acted as if I didn't care, he'd usually stop doing it."

At one time the family also had a St. Bernard, which became vicious because Billy mistreated it so often. "Bill used to grab him by the jaws and bite him on the nose or kick him under the chin," remembered Allen. "He was right crazy from being beat all the time. I took it for a walk one day and this old woman was coming down the road in her car down in Greenfield and he charged right up on her roof. He'd bite anybody. It was just craziness." In a small barn at the rear of the Stafford property they kept a horse and two cows. Allen said when he went out to feed the horse "it was right up on its hind legs. It was right wild from being kicked and whipped by Bill."

Billy Stafford's obsession with horoscopes, the devil, and astrology did much to determine what he would or would not do on any given day. He kept up-to-date horoscope books in the house and expected Jane to read the daily predictions for his zodiac sign.

"Okay, old woman, let's see what today holds in store for me," he would say. Jane would read his horoscope and Billy would sit back and think about it. He would smile smugly if the reading was positive. "Well, the old devil is going to be with me today. I can do as I please and nothing will happen to me." He would scowl darkly if the reading was negative. "The old devil gave me my warning. I'll be good today." Being good usually meant staying around the house getting drunk or high. Jane dreaded the negative readings because they meant she and Darren would be abused more than usual. "Being cruel to us gave him a sort of satisfaction or revenge for having to stay at home."

On one of those days that Billy Stafford stayed home, Jane was bent over putting wood in the stove when a shot rang out and struck the wall inches above her head. The stove was in direct line with the open bedroom door. Billy had fired a .22 bullet at her while lying in bed.

"Don't worry, old woman," he chuckled. "If I wanted to hit you, I wouldn't have missed."

Jane's heart was beating wildly. "If I had stood up, I'd be dead. I really thought I was going to have a heart attack."

Billy Stafford often said he'd never die. "I have the power—right from the devil."

Billy Stafford's use of the word "power" was appropriate. His definition of "power" meant absolute control over every aspect of Jane's life—her job, her household chores, the raising of children, her social life, and all of her contacts outside the home, including her parents, siblings, and friends.

Alcohol and drugs often play a facilitator role in spousal abuse, but they are not usually the root cause. In Billy Stafford's case, he beat Jane whether he was drunk or sober. And although abusive men typically suffer from low self-esteem and rely strongly on a duty-bound wife, Billy Stafford was *atypical*: low self-esteem did not seem to be a problem for him. Rather, he believed he was invincible—a power unto himself.

Jane Stafford had been optimistic when she and Billy moved into their own home in Bangs Falls. But her dream of a happy, normal, married life would not be realized and it would be in that house that Jane would begin to see the ugliness and brutality of Billy Stafford's true nature. "It was there," said Jane, "that all the fighting and abuse took place; where my children and I lived in fear; where Billy Stafford reigned over his kingdom like a dictator. I was very much like my mother, always having faith things would get better. For Mom it did. For me, it kept getting worse."

Billy Stafford's total income for the five years from 1977 to 1981 was only $22,000, and that included unemployment insurance payments. Everything that went into turning the Bangs Falls home from a cabin into a proper house came from Jane's wages. "And I did a lot of the actual work on the repairs, remodelling, and rebuilding, along with a friend of ours, Dempsey Hatt, who I hired to help me. That included a new roof, an addition to the house, and construction of our small barn. I worked harder than any man. We had no well, and until 1980 I brought water from where I worked or carried it from a spring half a mile from our house. I carried all the water for cleaning, cooking, and laundry. There was no stove in the house until I got a second-hand electric one at the end of 1979. We also got a wood stove about that time for heat. Before that, I cooked on a single-burner hot plate and did my baking at Margaret Joudrey's."

Jane loved her job at Hillsview Acres because it gave her precious time away from Billy and the home she had come to view as a torture chamber, made more miserable by Billy's slovenly personal habits. Often he purposely messed up the house because he knew it bothered Jane, who was a perfectionist. Drunk or sober, it was routine for Billy to get up several times during the night for a snack. He would bring the food into the bedroom, turn on the light, and sit on the bed smacking his lips and slurping loudly while he ate. He always made enough noise to keep Jane awake. If he ate grapes, apples, watermelons, or peaches, he spat the seeds and pits around the bedroom. Particularly revolting to Jane was Billy's habit of urinating in a pot he kept beside the bed. Sometimes he ignored the pot and simply wet the bed. "When that happened, he would start to hoot and holler until I got up and stripped the bed and changed the sheets. He knew I needed my sleep because I had to work. He slept all day while I worked, but he did his best to keep me awake at night. To get to work was a pleasure, tired or not. It was when I came home that my work really started."

In retrospect, the shot that Billy Stafford fired at Jane while she was filling the wood stove was a turning point in her life. It was the last time in their relationship she was able to voice anger, to rebel against his brutality. After the shock and fear subsided, Jane stared hatefully at him while he lay in bed laughing, the rifle across his thighs.

"I'm going to leave you," said Jane firmly.

"You can leave me anytime you want, old woman," said Billy, with a derisive laugh. "But I told you before I won't be a third-time loser. If you go, you'll be coming back, and you'll bring that little bastard with you because I'll start shooting that precious family of yours, one by one."

Jane's anger turned to fear, and she was overcome with deep despair. She felt there was no way out, no hope. "I realized I just couldn't stand any more. I totally withdrew from that point on. I built a protective wall around myself. I didn't have the strength or the will to deal with it. I resigned as a wife, a mother—a human being. I had always found the strength to deal with whatever came along. No more. I'd had it. The limit was reached. My mind went limp, blank, and drained of emotion. I became a robot and believed that only in death would I find peace."

The metamorphosis was now complete. Jane Stafford now perfectly fit the definition of a victim of "battered wife syndrome"—a woman blamed so often for the attacks against her that she comes to believe they are her own fault. She becomes passive and demoralized; she feels no self-worth and stays because she fears her husband will kill her, her children, or her family. She believes she is not worth saving, and her despair is exacerbated because she has no money and nowhere to go.

CHAPTER 6

BULLY OF THE COUNTY

Billy Stafford's reign of terror wasn't restricted to his Bangs Falls home. Many people around Queens County—friends, relatives, even strangers—experienced his wrath over the years. Marilyn Fisher met Billy in the fall of 1978. One day her dog came home bleeding from a bullet wound. The bullet had passed through the dog's neck. The dog survived, and Marilyn Fisher's son, Barry, followed the trail of blood across the river to the driveway leading to Billy Stafford's home. Marilyn took her dog to a veterinarian "and when I came home from there I went into the RCMP headquarters. That was on a Monday."

Billy Stafford showed up at her door the next afternoon. "There was a knock at my door. I can't remember the words that he used. He was standing there with both fists doubled up, shaking them at me. He was hollering about my husband, Cleveland, and my son, Barry." Several woman friends were visiting Marilyn Fisher at the time, and she was embarrassed and frightened.

"Are you Mr. Stafford?" she asked.

"You're goddamn right I am!" screamed Billy.

"Well, it wasn't my husband or my son who reported you to the Mounties. It was me."

"I didn't shoot your fucking dog. Why did you say I did?"

"My son followed the blood."

"How do you know Stan Joudrey didn't shoot it?"

"I know Stan well enough that he'd never do something like that."

Billy went into a rage and began screaming and cursing at her. "He looked like a wild man. His face was red; his eyeballs were bulging out of his head. He scared me. I was terrified, so I said, 'Goodbye, Mr. Stafford,' and shut the door in his face."

Marilyn Fisher's husband was furious when he learned about Billy's visit. "My husband talked to him and told him if he ever came near us again he'd kill him." Billy Stafford never bothered them again.

In the spring of 1979, Marsha Freeman was walking down the road near Greenfield, pushing her child ahead of her in a baby carriage. Billy Stafford was driving on the same road. He drove his car right at them, swerving at the last minute. "He gave me a good scare. I thought he was going to hit us with his car. And it was deliberate." Marsha Freeman reported Billy to the RCMP and he was taken to court, fined, and put on probation. At the time, Marsha and her husband, Kevin, were building a house directly across the river from Billy Stafford's place. They built as time and money permitted. It took them four years.

Before Billy tried to frighten Marsha with the car, the Freemans had hired a man to do some backhoe work. "The fellow left his backhoe in our yard with oil drums in the bucket, and it was facing the Stafford house," said Marsha Freeman. "When he came the next day there were bullet holes in the oil drums." The Freemans didn't call the police because "at the time we didn't know whether it was accidental or exactly how it happened. We just assumed that it was maybe some child had a gun." And at that time they had no reason to suspect Billy Stafford. But they later found a bullet hole in the house they were building. "We had no proof as to who did it, but it was from the direction of his [Billy's] house." The RCMP investigated that incident but nothing came of it. However, Jane's son Allen remembered Billy shooting at the Freeman house while it was under construction. "On New Year's Eve, he never used to shoot off his gun at twelve o'clock. He'd shoot it off about three o'clock in the morning. He used to shoot at a house that a fellow was building there."

One summer day in 1980, Allen was home when two of Jane's cousins, Victor Westhaver and Doug Parnell, dropped in to visit Jane and Billy. "I was watching TV and I don't know what happened. Dougie was talking to Ma or something. Bill had a forty-ouncer, and he was talking. Suddenly he jumped up and grabbed a hold of Dougie and threw him over against the sink." Victor Westhaver, who was sitting in a chair at the time, asked what was going on.

"Don't hold your head up to me or I'll put it down!" Billy shouted at Westhaver.

"It'll take a lot more than you to put it down," replied Westhaver.

Allen said Billy went for Westhaver and "just cracked him. His head hit the wall and when it come back he was all full of blood." Billy turned to Jane. "Get the gun, old woman. I'll get rid of them."

Obediently, Jane took a .22 from the gun rack and handed it to him. He aimed it at them. "Get the fuck out of here or you'll be carried out!" screamed Billy.

"Come on, let's go," said Westhaver to Doug Parnell as they rushed for the door. "I headed for my truck," said Westhaver, "and I heard a shot go off. I wasn't looking back to see if he was shooting at me, or up or down or where. But I heard the shot so I just jumped in my truck and Dougie jumped in the other side and we just drove off. I thought he was crazy." Allen was scared and ran from the house at the same time. He said Billy fired in Westhaver's direction "and parted his hair, I guess."

Ivan Higgins, from the small town of Brooklyn, near Liverpool, once sold Billy Stafford a wood stove. Billy invited him and his wife and two-year-old child to visit his house in Bangs Falls. "It wasn't any real party by any means," recalled Higgins. "We got there and Billy had just installed the new wood stove and we were sitting around talking to him. Maybe about an hour had gone by and the next thing you know, Billy was quite upset with me. I really didn't notice anything too different about him, but I had to be real careful what I said to him. Maybe he had a few too many beers or something, I don't know. Next thing you know, he turned on me. He was quite grumpy and gruff."

Higgins was not a big man. Suddenly he found himself sitting in a chair with the threatening form of Billy Stafford looming in front of him. Higgins got to his feet. "What's wrong, Billy?" he asked, backing away. Billy punched him in the mouth with no warning.

"I'm hardly a man to stand up to him," Higgins remembered. "After I realized he really intended to do some harm to me, I scooted out. Some people grabbed his arm. He was quite upset with me. I couldn't make out why or what. Somebody said I should just get out." The Higgins's child was asleep in another room. "I'll be grabbing the kid," said his wife. Higgins was sitting barefooted and didn't even have time to get his sneakers on. "A couple of friends just sort of kept him at bay and I zoomed out of there. He came in a few days later, very apologetic, saying such things as, 'I wouldn't be much of a man if I couldn't apologize for something like this.' Ever since that we got along fine, but I never went to any more parties of his."

Ronny Wamboldt's brother, Gene, was six feet tall and weighed about 210 pounds—not as big a man as Billy Stafford, but capable of handling himself. He once had a fight with Billy, and it ended in a draw. He knew Billy for about twenty years and considered him his friend. "Well, if you stood up to him, you didn't have any trouble with him," he said. "But if he thought you were scared of him, he'd keep it that way. He had an awful temper. He'd fly off the handle some quick. It grew worse as he got older." Gene Wamboldt saw Billy once in a while when he went out to Bangs Falls to see his brother. He noticed Billy was smoking a lot of dope, and he warned Ronny Wamboldt that if he stayed he would get into trouble.

Billy was using a lot of dope, and the RCMP suspected him of buying and selling it. At first, he used mostly marijuana, but as he travelled to ports in Europe, Jamaica, and Mexico he began bringing home hash and acid. Jane said that when he came home from his last trip "he brought some kind of pills and he made me and Ronny a pot of tea and put some of them in it. I was in another world for a couple of days and Ronny almost went crazy."

Her son Allen was watching TV and saw Ronny's reaction. "I think it was acid or something. About an hour later Ronny said he saw a truck with no wheels on it going around out in the yard. And he saw a duck lay a golden egg on the floor, and he was like that for three days. Bill just sat back and had a good laugh."

But Billy Stafford wasn't laughing when he mixed acid and alcohol. "It was bad enough when he drank," said Jane, "but when he did both at the same time, you could see murder in his eyes. He had a spell for three nights in a row where he brought one of the wooden kitchen chairs into the bedroom and used two of his belts to strap me to it. He would load up the shotgun and lay on the bed with it pointing at me. Those were three long nights. I didn't know if I was going to see daylight or not. He just raved on and on through those nights. When the alarm went off, he'd get up, unstrap me, and tell me to get ready for work." Before freeing Jane on one of those mornings, Billy Stafford urinated over her head.

Ronny Wamboldt's estranged wife, Andrea, had a pleasant face that hid a lot of bad memories. She was married to Wamboldt for twenty-one years, before leaving at her children's urging. Ronny was drunk most of the time, and he used to beat her. Andrea grew up with Billy Stafford's first wife, Pauline, and went to school with Billy in Liverpool. She and Jane Stafford got to know each other—and became best friends—through their husbands. Andrea lived with Ronny in a house in Milton before she left him and moved to Toronto. They saw Jane and Billy at least once a week. Andrea also worked with Jane at Hillsview Acres for three years. She remembered visiting the Staffords in 1978 or 1979. Margaret Joudrey was also there. "Billy and Ron were drinking and suddenly Billy got up and started beating Jane around the head and face. He was calling her 'Pauline' and beating on her. I had to holler at him. I said, 'That's not Pauline,' and he snapped right out of it." Andrea knew Billy had mistreated Pauline, but at first she didn't know Jane well enough to warn her about him. "Billy and Jane got along well when they first started living together, but things changed after Darren was born. I saw him beat her up many a time."

Andrea never thought about going to the police to complain about Billy's treatment of Jane, or of Pauline before her. She herself was being beaten at home, and "if I went to the police, what would Billy have done to Pauline and Jane? He would have killed the pair of them. He threatened to a good many times. There's no protection. There's no protection whatsoever for women that are being beaten. Pauline had to leave or he would have ended up killing her. But he told Jane, I heard him say it many times, 'Old woman, get it out of your head. Don't think you're leaving me, because I'll kill you. I'll find you and kill you.' He never got over Pauline leaving him, which is why he threatened Jane. Telling a woman to leave a situation is easier said than done. You've got a lot of things to think about. You're scared. You've got kids to look after. You don't know where you're going to go, who's going to look after you. And Jane was *really* afraid of Billy. She was scared of Billy. Really frightened. She wanted out of that situation. Every other week she had bruises—on her face, on her body. I didn't like Billy. I was very scared of him. When Pauline took her kids to Ontario, they couldn't talk. They had to get speech therapy, he had them so scared."

When Andrea Wamboldt returned from Toronto on her vacation in February 1980, she went to Hillsview Acres to surprise Jane and her other former workmates. It was a Wednesday, and Jane was off for the next two days. Andrea agreed to stay with her in Bangs Falls while she was off. On Thursday they went into town and bought a quart of rum to celebrate their reunion. Billy was home quietly drinking and went to bed shortly after Darren and Allen went to bed. The women sat up, talking about old times. At about 2 a.m., Billy suddenly appeared in the bedroom doorway with a .30-.30 rifle. He pointed it at Andrea Wamboldt's head.

"You're just like Pauline," he sneered. "Leaving your husband like that. You never should have left Ron." He turned to Jane and began beating her on the head and face with the gun.

"Don't get it in your head to leave me, old woman!" he

screamed. Billy grabbed both women by the throat, ripping the neck of Andrea's sweater and glaring at her.

"Now get the fuck out of here or I'll blow your fucking head off."

Andrea fled the house without her coat. It was dark and windy and the temperature was below zero. She walked three miles in the cold to Hillsview Acres, where she called her brother, who drove out to pick her up. "Jane brought my coat in the next day and apologized for what happened. She wanted me to come back out for supper that night because Billy wanted to apologize to me. I said, 'No way.' I never saw Billy after that."

After Andrea left the house the night before, Billy had continued beating Jane with the gun until she was unconscious. It was daylight when she came to, lying on the kitchen floor. Her clothes were wet. Allen heard the beating but waited until Billy was snoring before checking on his mother's condition. "When I found her she wouldn't wake up." He didn't dare turn on a light for fear of waking Billy. In the dark, Allen felt his way to the kitchen, filled a cup with water, and poured it on his mother's face. "And I shook her a few times but still couldn't wake her. She just laid there. I was nervous about Billy, so I just went back to bed. By the time I got up the next morning, Ma was in bed and there was no water on the floor, or anything." Several days later, Allen told his mother he thought she was dead that night because he couldn't rouse her.

Jane Stafford's parents moved to Danesville, about a half-hour's drive from Bangs Falls, when her father retired from the armed forces in 1977. It was the same year Jane moved in with Billy. Maurice Hurshman quit drinking in 1980. Jane hadn't been close to her family, but now they began visiting back and forth and socializing from time to time. Before he gave up alcohol, Maurice sometimes drank with Billy Stafford. "He wasn't too bad a fellow when he was sober. You could sit down and talk to him and joke and carry on. But if you was having a drink with him, you had to be very careful what you said because he'd get very violent."

He saw an extreme example of that violence one day and avoided Billy Stafford after that. The Hurshmans lived in a spacious trailer home on a landscaped lot with trees and flowers. Jane and Billy were visiting one evening. "We were having a few drinks," recalled Maurice, "and I don't know what I said, something jokingly. He thought I called his house a shack or something and he really went into one. He went just like he was crazy, like a madman. He frothed from the mouth and went right into a rage, just that quick."

Maurice Hurshman wore glasses. His complexion was ruddy, and his thick, steel-grey hair was combed back off his forehead. At five feet, eleven inches and two hundred pounds he wasn't in bad shape for his age. He kept in condition after his retirement by hiring on as a crew member for fishing boats sailing out of local harbours. But he was no match for Billy Stafford. "He hit me, knocked the window out of the house. He kicked the door. Drove a hole through it. Broke the latch off the outside aluminum door. There was nothing I could do. He knocked me down. Gladys and Jane jumped in between. Billy struck Jane and knocked her back against the wall. Then he said, 'Come on, woman, we're going home,' and they left. After I saw what Billy was like, I never came around them that much. He'd come down to the house after that sometimes, and I'd be scared just to hear him come in the yard."

Maurice Hurshman didn't know the extent of the abuse his daughter was suffering at Billy Stafford's hands. "Jane never mentioned it to me. I guess if it would have got out, well... he'd probably have killed her for sure. Jane used to wear dark glasses, but I didn't know this was going on. If she had a bruise or something, I'd say, 'How'd you do that, Jane?' She'd tell me she bumped it or something."

Billy was a wild, reckless driver, and Jane was terrified when she was with him. "He was a maniac. You took your life in your hands when you got in a vehicle with him. He was a speed freak. He had to pass everything on the highway. He'd drive as fast as he could. It didn't matter what the weather conditions were or whether he was drunk, sober, or stoned. He had more accidents than you can count on your fingers and toes. I had to take the blame for several of them because he was drunk. He forced me to say I was driving. He lost his licence several times for motor vehicle offences like speeding and reckless driving. He was a real hazard on the highway. It's a miracle he didn't kill someone or seriously injure them."

Billy usually had a gun with him in his truck when he drove around Queens County, and if he saw a deer, he shot it. It didn't matter what time of year it was—whether it was hunting season or not. During the 1981 deer-hunting season, Billy didn't have to worry about bagging his quota of one—he had shot nine deer before the season even opened. He gave some of them away because his freezers were full. It is difficult to understand why he thought the police were picking on him. He was buying, using, and probably selling drugs. He was a deer jacker par excellence. He was often drunk while driving. He disobeyed most traffic laws. And he let it be known on countless occasions that he hated the police.

If it had been publicly known how he treated his animals, he could have been charged under animal welfare laws as well. One of his two cows died after Billy abused it. Jane and others saw him push a shovel handle up the cow's rectum. "One morning after I'd seen him do that, he went out to feed the cow and it was dead. He couldn't get it out of the barn, so he tied a rope around its back and hooked the rope to his truck. He got the cow out and put it on the back of the truck. About that time a friend from Buckfield came by. He knew cattle and he took a look at the cow. He thought it must have had a heart attack, but he didn't know what really had happened. Bill took the cow way back into the woods and dumped it off the truck and left it."

Billy Stafford hated the RCMP in general and Constable Gary Grant in particular. Grant first met Billy in 1977, shortly after he was transferred to Liverpool from a small town in rural Newfoundland. Grant later slimmed down considerably, but in his three years in Liverpool he carried 250 pounds on his six-foot-three frame. Grant was affable, with dimpled cheeks, receding light-brown hair, and a neatly trimmed moustache. From a distance, he seemed to have a permanent smile, courtesy of the lines at the corners of his mouth. Grant had a quick wit but could also be tough when he had to be. "I spent five-and-a-half years in a small Newfoundland town. On Friday nights we put on old clothes because we knew we'd be out breaking up fights. We had five clubs to police and there were only two of us."

Grant's baptism of fire in Newfoundland was a slugfest at the scene of an accident with half the town watching. His opponent was a local tough, a big man who was drunk. Grant finally got the better of him. It wasn't until he was putting the cuffs on the drunk that a man in the crowd stepped forward to help. When Grant and his partner were called to a club to break up a fight "we always put the sirens on a half-mile away" to give the participants fair warning they were coming. "If they were still at it when we arrived we always took one of them away or they'd be back at it as soon as we left. They knew we meant business, but they knew we were fair. If there was a crowd around the fight, they always cleared a path for us. We were both a good size, but we had to be. We had no backup for sixty miles."

By the time Gary Grant arrived in Liverpool, everyone knew about Billy Stafford. "We were warned about him. He was a person we had to keep an eye on. There was nobody like him. Two or three months after I got there, I stopped him to size him up. I wanted to know about him and I wanted him to know I was in town. I was friendly that first time, but even though I'd never met him, he was totally hostile. He was one of those guys you would look into his eyes and see the hate, like he wanted to tear your face off. There wasn't even an attempt to cover his hostility. He was the kind of guy you'd never let think you were afraid of for a second. You had to have that approach with him or you'd lose. If he thought you were intimidated, he'd own you. You never knew with Billy Stafford. He was helter-skelter. The people who lived out there couldn't really enjoy the place knowing he was around. I used to stop him every two or three months. He never crossed the line, but he always went right to it. He knew the police were looking at him and we took verbal abuse every time."

Grant and two other officers were once sent out to Billy's house to search for illegal venison. "My role was to take care of Billy Stafford and let them do the search. I was half thinking, maybe today was the day I'd find out what the guy was made of. I was prepared. Let's get at her—pitter, patter."

The Mounties parked their cruiser at the foot of the driveway and strolled toward the house. They weren't in any rush. It was deer meat they were after, and it would be difficult to conceal quickly. Grant knocked on the outside door. There were a few chickens squawking in the yard.

"What the fuck do you want?" shouted Billy from behind the door.

"These hens are all virgins," said Grant, trying to ease the tension.

"You're wrong—I fucked them all," yelled Billy. "What do you want?"

"We've got a search warrant here to look for deer meat."

Billy opened the door a few inches. "There's no fucking deer meat here. You guys are always trying to get me. You fucking assholes."

Gary Grant was contemplating citing Billy for obstruction of justice when suddenly the door opened fully.

"Fuck it, come in," said Billy. "You want to come in and fucking look, come in and look."

Grant went to the centre of the living room "because I figured that's where we'd have it out if there was going to be a problem." The other officers began searching the house. "They were looking for illegal deer meat and we wanted to see what weapons and ammunition he had around. Billy came within two feet of me and came out with a string of obscenities. He was bugged that he couldn't keep his eyes on all three of us at once. He'd stare at me and then glance quickly over to the other two." One of them opened a dresser drawer.

"What the fuck are you looking for in there? Panties?" shouted Billy. "Why don't you sniff them?"

Grant moved toward Billy when he started cursing at the officer. "Why don't you grow up and start acting like a man," said Grant.

Billy became even more incensed. "He just went on and on," said Grant. "I got in about ten words. His eyes bugged out. He was red as a beet and started frothing at the mouth. He looked very intimidating. I'd dealt with mental cases in the past, and when they explode they become very strong. I thought, 'If he explodes, he's going to be totally awesome to deal with.' I made up my mind: If he made a move for me, I'd kick him in the testicles. I was half scared so I was looking for the quickest way to end it. His spit was hitting me in the face. It was just flying all over. He was like a demon. He never moved more than a foot away from me the whole time."

"You rotten cocksucker," screamed Billy. "One of these days you're going to push me too far!"

Billy didn't complete a single sentence without an obscenity. "He was totally enraged," said Grant. "We'd violated him. We were in his domain. This was his fortress, and we were inside. He continued to abuse us as we left. We looked around outside for power cords in case he had a buried freezer somewhere. We didn't find anything. It was the most distractive search I've ever been on. I never met anyone like Billy Stafford."

Jane Stafford had sat quietly during the search listening to Billy rant at the police. He kept it up when they left, stomping through the house hollering and bellowing about Gary Grant. "He hated all cops with a passion, but he especially hated Grant," Jane said.

"One of these days I'll get that fucking Grant!" shrieked Billy. "I'll get him alone somewhere and I guarantee you, only one of us will be coming out alive. I killed one man already and got away with it. It would be a real thrill to kill that cocksucker."

"What do you mean, you killed one man already?" asked Jane, frightened but curious.

"Do you remember Jimmy LeBlanc? He supposedly jumped overboard a few years back... Well, he never jumped. I threw him overboard. He made me mad and I threw him over the side. And I'm going to kill Grant when I get him alone—no witnesses—just the same as with Jimmy."

Jane sat stunned. "That really put the fear in me."

Jane was a good worker and well thought of at Hillsview Acres. Her bosses promoted her to chef after only one month at the home, and in June 1981 they approached her and asked if she was interested in attending a cooking workshop in Truro, Nova Scotia, all expenses paid. "My bosses, Raymond and Debbie Fiske, gave me all the information about the workshop and we talked about it all one afternoon. I wanted badly to go. It would have been an interesting learning venture, and Lord knows I needed it. I'd been with Billy for five years at that point and my mind had become stagnant. I still had a secret desire for learning, and I wanted this so much. I told them I'd give them an answer by the end of the week. That gave me four days to catch Bill in a good mood and get his approval. Deep inside I knew it was no good to get my hopes up, but I wanted to go so badly. When I got home that day, Bill appeared to be in a good mood. He wasn't working at the time but he'd received his unemployment insurance cheque that day so he was all set with his booze and his drugs. He didn't yell at me or hit me when I came through the door, and that was a good sign. I never talked unless I was spoken to, so I just walked in and smiled and started about my work. We got through our usual suppertime ordeal and I got Darren settled in bed."

Billy sensed something was on Jane's mind. "Okay, old woman, what is it? You've been going around here like a dog shining razor blades ever since you got home, so spit it out."

"Well, there's this cooking workshop in Truro from June 30 until July 3. I've been asked to attend on behalf of Hillsview Acres. It's all expenses paid. I'd really like to go. It sounds very interesting and I'd learn a lot."

Jane realized immediately she had made a mistake, telling Billy how important it was to her. "For the next four days he played cat and mouse with me. One minute he'd tell me I could go and I would get excited and happy. Then he'd tell me I couldn't go." Jane was off, as usual, on Thursday and Friday. Billy gave her a black eye during that time. When she was leaving for work Billy told her she could go to the workshop, but she knew he was just toying with her. "When I got to work I told Raymond Fiske I couldn't go because I had too much to do at home." When she arrived home from work Billy met her at the door.

"I made up my mind," he gloated, "you ain't going to no fucking workshop. I may have said this morning you could go, but now I say you can't. And that's the end of it. Now run down to Margaret's and phone that bastard boss of yours and tell him you ain't going."

"I already told him I wasn't going," said Jane.

Billy stared at her, his anger rising. "You think you are some fuckin' smart now, don't you. You old bag. Well, I'll tell you something, old woman—you think you can out-think me, eh? It will be one fucking foggy day when you get one step ahead of me. You'll never live long enough to out-think me. I've been sent by the devil. I have the power. And that old grey-whiskered prick up there [Billy pointed to the heavens] can't help you." He began pounding on the table with his closed fist.

Suddenly he was on his feet, punching Jane about the head and chest. "Then he started choking me, squeezing my throat. As I started to pass out I heard him saying, 'I am sent by the devil.' When I came to, he was snoring in the bedroom. I picked myself up and I remember thinking, 'I hate you, Stafford. I hate you—and I had never hated anyone in my life.' Yet there was also a different feeling. I thought about what Bill had said about my never getting one step ahead of him, and I knew I had done just that. It was some sort of a small victory."

Billy didn't allow Jane to go anywhere alone, except to work or to run an errand for him. If she went to town there was a time limit. “When I went anywhere, I avoided talking to anyone. I was terrified if someone spoke to me. When that happened I told Bill as soon as I got home. I was that paranoid. Bill was a very jealous man, although he never had any reason to be. As a couple we never went anywhere in public; never to a movie, a restaurant, a dance, or a tavern. When we did go out it was to someone’s house to drink or smoke dope. The only entertainment I knew was work, work, work. I wasn’t even allowed to attend church or speak of the Lord. I wasn’t allowed to have a Bible, and I wasn’t even allowed to have any pictures of any members of my family in the house.”

CHAPTER 7
DEGRADATION

In the first months that Jane lived with Billy Stafford, their sex life was normal. But that changed after Darren's birth. Jane's pubic hair had been shaved off for Darren's delivery, and Billy liked it that way. It sexually stimulated him. From then on he periodically shaved Jane. It got worse for Jane when he began sailing on the gypsum boats to ports in Norway, Holland, Mexico, Portugal, Bermuda, and the United States. "When he started on the boats he would come home and tie me to a chair and pluck out the hair with a pair of tweezers. He always used to say, 'You won't have to worry, because when I get done with you no man will ever want you.' He would tie me to a chair and pull out each hair one at a time. My legs were spread apart. It was very embarrassing and painful. When he went away on those boats, he would buy me all kinds of weird underwear—things in white, gold, silver, black, and red. And fancy garter belts, silk stockings, and panties without crotches." He also arrived with half-cup bras, perfumes, sheer nighties, and stacks of pornographic magazines. Jane believed they incited Billy to engage her in increasingly degrading and painful sexual rituals. "Usually he came home off the boats in the middle of the night. He would wake Darren up, show him what he bought him, give him a beating, and put him back to bed. Then he'd stand me in the middle of the room, rip my nightgown off me, and throw it in the garbage. He'd examine me from head to foot to see if I had any marks or bruises on me, and if I had any, I had to explain how I got them. He would call me every dirty name he could think of, put the stereo on full blast, and run my bath water."

After Jane bathed, Billy would douse her with perfume and dress her up in whatever new underwear he had brought home with him. "He would lay down on the bed and order me to undress him. While I was doing that he would bite my breasts and pinch the insides of my thighs. It was very painful." Billy would then hurl Jane to the bed on her stomach and tie her wrists to the bed rail with heavy string or fishing line. Then he would force her to her knees and administer a vicious spanking that left her buttocks bruised and burning. His "games" would vary, but eventually he would untie Jane from the bed rail and retie her with her wrists together. Then he would force her to masturbate while he watched from above. Later, he would tie her hands behind her back and force her to her knees and enter her from the rear. After a few minutes of vaginal intercourse, he would switch to anal sex. "The pain was always so awful. It was like being torn apart." It was apparently painful for Billy, too, because about the third or fourth time he performed that ritual, he went out to the barn and returned with a piece of solid plastic plumbing pipe, an inch in diameter and four or five inches long.

"This'll fix it so you get used to it," he declared as he greased the pipe with petroleum jelly and pushed it into Jane's rectum. He forced her to leave the pipe inside her whenever he was home. She was allowed to remove it only when she went to work or when Billy wanted sex. The entire ritual was repeated for several months.

One day Jane arrived home from work to discover that Billy had returned from a trip to Mexico. He was sitting at the table drinking. He had brought Darren a beautiful Mexican hat. "Have you been a good boy while Daddy was gone?" asked Billy.

"Yes, Daddy."

"Then this is for you," said Billy. Darren tried on the hat.

"Okay, now put it away and get to bed," Billy ordered, cuffing the boy.

Billy was on his feet the second Darren's door closed. "He came over to me and slapped me across the face several times," said Jane. "He ripped my clothes off and examined me. As usual, he tied me to a chair and plucked out my hairs, and as usual, it was painful, disgusting, and humiliating. When I was naked and bathed and perfumed, he tied my hands behind my back and put a dog collar around my neck. It had a leash. He led me around the house on my hands and knees, examining me. We finally went into the bedroom, where he made me lay across his knees and he beat me with a hard-bristled hairbrush until I started to cry and begged him to stop." Billy then forced Jane to masturbate while he photographed her with a Polaroid camera. "When he tired of that he said he had a surprise for me." He went to his sea bag and returned with an artificial penis and a vibrator.

"You won't have to masturbate with your hand anymore," said Billy. "This will be better." He plugged in the vibrator and ordered Jane to use it on herself. "My hands were now tied in front of me and I was lying on my back. He had my feet tied to the bed rails with my legs spread apart. He took the artificial penis and kept shoving it in and out of my mouth."

"You're such a good cocksucker," said Billy. Jane bit down on the artificial penis to stop the pain. That made Billy angry.

"You'll have to pay for that," he declared. "I'll have to wash your mouth out with something bad." Jane watched as he urinated in a glass. Grabbing her by the hair, he forced her to drink it. The degradation continued. Tying all of her limbs to the bed, he penetrated her with the vibrator and artificial penis. Later he forced her to perform oral sex on him and ejaculated on her face. Billy fell asleep while Jane lay there wondering what further depravity she would be subjected to. Three hours later he woke up and began pummelling her about the head and shoulders. Dragging her by the breasts into the bathroom, he forced her to her hands and knees in the tub as it filled with hot water. Forcing her douche syringe in and out of her anus, he screamed obscenities at her and beat her. When she screamed in pain he took a pair of soiled panties from a laundry hamper and pushed them into her mouth. Dragging her back to the bedroom, he again tied her up, abused her with his "toys," and forced her to have anal sex. That scenario would be repeated many times. But the worst was still to come.

Jane was menstruating when Billy arrived home from the boats one afternoon. After the usual bathing and perfuming ritual, he ordered her to mount him. Jane was bleeding heavily and he forced her to lick the blood from his body. Then he brought in their St. Bernard dog and tried to force her to fellate the animal. When Jane vomited, Billy forced her to clean up the mess and then fellate him while simultaneously copulating with the dog.

It is difficult to understand how an innocent young teenager who sought love in a soft, grassy field in Germany, could eventually find herself being battered and sexually tortured by a monster. That she was able to somehow cope and survive seems miraculous in itself. "To me, I was violated in the most degrading ways possible," she said much later. "Courage is often a matter of learning that you can survive doing things that frighten and hurt you. Do it often enough and the fear gets somewhat tamed, but it's always there, gnawing away at you."

CHAPTER 8
ALONE

Jane Stafford felt trapped, isolated, and alone. Only she knew the full extent of Billy Stafford's growing depravity. Others around her were probably aware that Billy beat her from time to time—but wives getting slapped around was not all that unusual. With Billy not working, her only respites were her job at Hillsview Acres and her quiet moments with Darren and Allen when Billy was away from the house. Besides beating her and sexually humiliating and degrading her, Billy was constantly denigrating, threatening, and verbally abusing her. "You hear it so often, that everything is your own fault," she said, "that you're always wrong, you begin to believe it." What Jane Stafford didn't realize was that as bad as her life with Billy was, thousands of other women were living similar hells across the country. Nor did she realize that about half a million Canadian women each year were being threatened, punched, kicked, knifed, or shot. She didn't know that calls to domestic disputes—a euphemism for criminal assaults against women—were the largest category of requests to police for help, even though less than 10 per cent of such incidents were reported to police.

Jane never went to the police about Billy Stafford. She didn't dare. She had seen how he manipulated the law and forced others to take the blame for his crimes.

In a very real way, Jane Stafford was a victim of society's patriarchal institutions, including the legal system and religion, both of which had for centuries entrenched acceptance of violence against wives. At that time in Jane's life, the feminist movement, spurred by the increasing participation of married women in the work force, was beginning a final push to get spousal abuse out of the closet. Despite that effort, however, religion and the legal system continued to perpetuate battering by tacitly supporting the preservation of the family unit over the safety of women. Even judges encouraged the belief that if a domestic assault was treated as a crime, it would break up the family. Better to treat it lightly—to do whatever is necessary to keep the family together.

When police did respond to domestic disputes, and did not actually witness an assault, and the woman wasn't seriously injured—no broken bones or bloodied face—no charges were laid. More often than not, the police would tell the woman to get a lawyer, or to see a justice of the peace and lay a charge and go to court herself. Crown attorneys seemed to give spousal assault cases a low priority, viewing the problem as less serious than an assault between strangers. And when cases actually went to court, judges rarely imposed jail terms or even fines. Typically, they handed out suspended sentences, probation orders, or absolute or conditional discharges. This, despite the fact that at the time, 20 per cent of all homicides in Canada were spouse slayings, and that of 222 women murdered in Canada in 1982, more than half were killed by their spouse or ex-spouse.

Jane Stafford's desperation was compounded by the fact that Billy's two previous wives had fled the province to get away from him. She believed that his threats to kill members of her family if she left were real. She concluded that either she or Billy would die in their house in Bangs Falls. "The older he got, the worse he got. I can remember twice waking up through the night and getting out of bed and getting the shotgun and loading it and putting it to his head when he was asleep. The only thing that kept me from pulling the trigger was the fact that Darren would wake up to see what a mess his father would be in. That is the only reason I never pulled the trigger."

Jane also contemplated suicide, but discarded the idea. Leaving Darren to grow up alone under Billy's roof was out of the question. On one occasion Jane drove with Darren to a curve on a highway where cars and trucks would be unable to stop when suddenly confronted by a parked vehicle in the middle of the road. There was heavy truck traffic on that particular road, and Jane figured she and Darren would be killed instantly if one hit them. "I considered that and then I said, 'Hell, no,' maybe I could do it for myself, but not for Darren. My son was the only thing that kept me from death and from losing my sanity. He was my strength, my gift from God, my whole instinct to survive."

Billy had beaten Jane into unconsciousness more than once. She believed the time would come when she wouldn't wake up. Her desperation and her instinct for survival led her to start thinking of hiring someone, an outsider, to kill Billy. The man she chose for the job was Beverly Taylor, from the coastal town of Riverport, on the LaHave River about an hour's drive away. Taylor was a fisherman who later got a job on an oil rig. He came to the Stafford house in Bangs Falls around Christmas of 1981. "He arrived with a friend of Bill's and they were talking about some dope deals and he mentioned about having a gun and talk along that line. I thought he might be able to help me."

Over the next couple of weeks, Jane thought about how to approach Taylor. Fellow workers at Hillsview Acres noticed that Jane was more withdrawn than usual, and that she was losing weight noticeably. "It seemed like something was bothering her, but I didn't know what," recalled Gail Brewster, who worked with Jane at the home for three years. Sometime around Christmas she noticed a bruise on Jane's arm and another under her left eye, "but she covered it with makeup." In January, Jane approached Gail and asked her to telephone Beverly Taylor in Riverport.

"I'm having something made for Bill's birthday," explained Jane. "I don't want him to know about it. Call Bev Taylor and ask him to call me at work between seven and three."

Gail Brewster tried for a week to reach Taylor. "I finally got him on a Saturday morning before I went to work."

Eventually Jane talked to Taylor and asked him to visit her at Hillsview Acres. "She didn't really specify why," he said. "She just said it meant a great deal of money." After two more calls from Jane, he agreed to meet her. He arrived on a Sunday morning shortly after breakfast. The home's assistant matron, Muriel Oliver, answered the door. "I came out to see what he wanted and Jane said, 'This is for me,' so I went back inside." Jane met Taylor at the back door. It was snowing heavily outside. For privacy, they went to a small room at the rear of the home.

"What did you want to see me about?" asked Taylor.

"I want to hire somebody to hit Billy. To kill him."

"Why did you pick me?"

"You look like a guy that would help a person out of a bad situation."

"Why do you want him killed?"

"I've got good reason."

"Does he beat you?"

Jane nodded. "He's driving my little boy crazy and he threatened to kill my mother and father if I ever left him."

Taylor saw the desperation in Jane's eyes. "What's in it for me?"

"Twenty thousand dollars," replied Jane. "It's Bill's life insurance policy. You can have it all."

Taylor was silent for a moment. "I'm not interested in anything to do with killing Billy," he said. "Why not phone a lawyer or something?"

"There wouldn't be any purpose in that. He'd get revenge on me, or hurt my mother and father. I could never run far enough to get away from him."

"What about the police?"

"They can't do anything."

Jane's mind was in turmoil. She felt that an opportunity to do away with Billy was slipping through her fingers. "Billy jacks a lot of deer," she said. "He's always hunting in the bush. You could do it there and leave him. Nobody would ever know who to suspect because he's got so many enemies."

"I can't do that. But Billy trucks dope back and forth on the gypsum boats. Why don't you set him up and have him put away for a couple of years?"

Jane pondered the idea for a few moments. She thought it might work. She told Taylor she would be in touch with him about it.

When Taylor left Hillsview, he felt uneasy. "I wasn't really sure whether she was serious or not at the time. I thought it might have been Billy putting her up to it for some reason, so I just went down and paid Billy a visit and talked to him. Billy was involved in drugs to the best of my knowledge, and that's the only thing I could figure. And when I talked to a few of Billy's friends later, they said that's pretty well something he might very well do."

A day or two later, Taylor telephoned Jane. "He asked me for three hundred dollars so he could get enough dope to set

Bill up. I said no because somehow, someway, Bill would have got out of that. One of us—me, Ronny, somebody—would have taken the blame for it."

Jane did not give up on Beverly Taylor. She telephoned him two or three more times to see if he would help her by hiring someone else to kill Billy. "She also asked me to get her poison. I said no, and after a while she just stopped calling and that was the end of it."

That was the end of it for Beverly Taylor, but not for Jane Stafford. "I wanted him dead. I hated him. He was a maniac."

CHAPTER 9
"GET THE GUN . . ."

Billy Stafford was all business when he awoke on the morning of March 11, 1982. He had a project under way and he wanted to get at it. By daybreak, he was in his truck, with Allen and Ronny Wamboldt, headed up River Road to Freeman's Sawmill to pick up a load of sawdust. He planned to make three or four runs before lunchtime. He intended to use the sawdust as fill behind the barn, where he was planning to build a pigpen. Chuckling, he recounted his confrontation with Margaret Joudrey the night before, when he had informed her he planned to raise pigs. She complained that the stink would be awful. Billy told her he could do as he pleased, because none of the land really belonged to her. Her common-law husband Stan Joudrey had died, and Billy often told her that Stan had owned the land, and because they had never married, the land wasn't hers. This infuriated Joudrey, who insisted she owned the land. Sometime after Stan Joudrey's death, a male friend, Roger Manthorne, had moved into the trailer with Margaret. Billy loved to bring up the land issue in front of Manthorne because he knew it further upset Margaret. Manthorne was frightened of Billy Stafford and sat silently as the argument progressed.

"Old lady, I'd like to burn you out," said Billy as he left the trailer.

About the time Billy's truck pulled into Freeman's Sawmill, Jane Stafford was at home doing the laundry. It was her day off, but she got up to do the washing early, because according to the forecast the bright sunshine was to give way to fog and rain by early afternoon. "I had to get the laundry done, hung out, and dried before the rain started. They got done hauling sawdust about mid-morning and I made them tea and a sandwich. My laundry was all finished and on the line and the kids were outside. Whenever Bill ate he would lie down and sleep for a while." Ronny Wamboldt went out to the shed Billy had built near the barn. It had a stove and a bed in it. He was asleep in minutes. Jane was in the kitchen when Billy called to her from the bedroom.

"Come in here and give me a backrub," he demanded. Jane went immediately to the bedroom.

"Shut the door and strip," ordered Billy. "I want to screw ya."

As Jane undressed, she glanced over her body. Ugly bruises and welts were visible on her upper left arm between the shoulder and the elbow, and on her left leg from her hip to her ankle. She shivered involuntarily, remembering the beating she'd received several days earlier. She'd been in bed and Billy had the stereo playing full blast, making sleep impossible. Between songs she called out to him politely: "Hon, could you please turn the stereo down a bit?"

Billy peered into the bedroom. "What's the matter? Is the music bothering you? Is it keeping you awake?"

"Yes, hon, it is."

"Just a minute, I'll fix that."

Seconds later, Jane looked up to see Billy enter the bedroom with the metal portion of a vacuum cleaner hose. Cringing, she lay on her right side against the wall. When the first blow landed, she put her left arm up to protect her head. He struck her over and over with the pipe.

"Don't tell me what to do in my fucking house, you tramp!" he shouted. "I'll kill you. I'll give you something to complain about, and it won't be music."

Jane could not shake the image of that beating as she got into bed with Billy. She prayed he wouldn't take long. He climaxed quickly, rolled off her, and pushed her away. "Get the fuck up, old woman, you've got work to do."

Jane dressed and went outside to check the clothes on the line. They were dry. She brought them in and had begun ironing them when Margaret Joudrey came to the door.

"Hi, honey. Is Billy home?"

Jane pointed to the bedroom. Margaret Joudrey walked over and looked in. "Bill, are you awake?" she asked.

"Yeah. What the fuck do you want?"

"You really hurt me by what you said to me in front of Roger last evening, and I want you to know that. I can't fight you alone, so this morning I called Stan's people in the States and they're going to help me fight you. And I called the police and reported you for shooting at my trailer, and they're investigating it."

Billy Stafford jumped up from the bed. "Get the fuck out of my house and don't ever step foot in here again!" he shouted. "You fuckin' old bag, you don't scare me one little bit!"

Margaret Joudrey turned quickly and left the house with Billy yelling after her. "You'd better have a good day, you old cunt, because you'll never live to see another one."

Jane Stafford saw the telltale signs: the flushed face, the bulging eyes, and the foam forming at the sides of his mouth. She went over to the table and sat down. Allen and Darren were lying down. Ronny Wamboldt came into the house. Billy told him to get ready to go into town and looked over at Jane.

"Give me some money, old woman, I'm going to town."

"I can't give you any, hon, I've only got enough to pay the truck insurance when it comes due at the end of the month."

Billy stared at her fiercely. "What's the matter with you? Sitting there with nothing to do, eh?" Billy reached for a pile of clean laundry, carried it outside, and threw it in the dirt and mud. He carried the clothes back into the house and threw them around the kitchen floor. "There now, you fuckin' slut, that should give you enough to do until I get back."

Jane felt nauseated as Billy approached, slapped her across the face, and spat on her. Without a word, he went to her purse on the kitchen cupboard and opened it. "He took whatever money was in it, and they were gone. I just sat there and looked at the mess all around me. The kids got up as soon as Bill left. They were hungry, so I made them something to eat. They looked so sad and pleading. I got out the washing machine and began washing all those dirty, muddy clothes all over again. By then, it was cloudy and rainy and I was a nervous wreck, wondering when they would be home and what shape they'd be in."

Ronny Wamboldt remembered he and Billy stopping in Milton to pick up a quart of rum at the liquor store. They had finished most of the bottle and a marijuana joint by the time they returned to Bangs Falls in time for supper. They drank the rum straight from the bottle without mix, or as Ronny described it, "raw" and "that alone." It was about 6:30 p.m. when they arrived back at the house. Jane heard the truck's stereo before they came into view. "I could hear it playing full blast. Even before I saw them, I knew they were drinking. I don't remember if they ate supper or not. I know they had one drink each to finish off the bottle of rum." Jane did the dishes while Billy and Ronny sat at the table.

"Did you put that can of gas in the shed, dummy?" asked Billy.

"Yes, sure did," answered Wamboldt.

"I got the truck filled up and I got five extra gallons," Billy said to Jane. "I charged them at Myles Whynot's garage. You can pay for it when you go into town tomorrow."

Jane noticed Billy seemed contented.

"Well, old woman, see what my horoscope is for today." Jane looked it up in the book he kept. Billy was pleased when she told him it said it was his lucky day. She was also an Aquarian, but she thought that it certainly hadn't been her lucky day.

"Get ready, old woman," declared Billy, "you're going to drive Ron and me down to Leona's."

Jane later remembered it was raining and foggy when the three of them went out to the truck. Billy noticed that the five-gallon can of gas was still in the back of the truck.

"Lookit, dummy, the gas is still on the truck."

Wamboldt got out of the cab and took the gas to the shed. Leona Anthony lived about five miles from the Staffords on the River Road toward Charleston. The road was a mess. The frost was coming out of the ground, and with all the rain, it made driving very difficult. Billy had the stereo wide open, so loud they couldn't hear each other talk.

A mile or two along the road, Billy, who was sitting in the middle of the cab, nudged Jane with his elbow. "Pull over!" he shouted above the music. "I want to smoke a joint!"

Jane sat silent as Billy and Wamboldt shared the marijuana. She felt like she was in a deep well that she could never climb out of. The image of her sons' pleading eyes was imprinted in her mind. "I just kept seeing them in front of me and my thoughts drifted back to the previous spring. Bill was on the boats at sea. Allen had a girlfriend who lived just over the road from where we lived. Her father didn't want Allen around because of Bill's reputation. One Saturday night she told Allen she couldn't see him anymore. Allen came home about 10:30 p.m. He was fifteen years old then. I was already in bed because I had to work in the morning. Allen hollered in at me, 'Good night, Mom. I love you.' Next thing I heard was the alarm. I got up and got Darren and myself ready to go. When we went out I was astonished to see my car was gone. I ran back into the house to tell Allen that someone had stolen my car. I was even more shocked to find Allen was also gone. I went over to Marie and Morton's and I called my boss and asked him if he could come and pick me up. He did. When I got to work I called the RCMP and asked if they knew anything about Allen or my car. Constable Buchanan said he would come out to work and pick me up and take me to get my car. It was a party line and that's all he would say on the phone. He came and picked me up."

"Mrs. Stafford, we picked up Allen driving your car," said the policeman. "He was drinking and wouldn't tell us anything, so we put him in jail for the night. We were hoping you would get in touch with us this morning. I think your son has a problem, but he won't talk."

The RCMP turned Jane's car keys over to her and let Allen out of jail. On the drive home, the boy was quiet and sullen.

"Why did you take my car?" asked Jane softly. "Where were you going?"

Allen looked her in the eyes with the same pleading look she was to see again and again. "Mom," he said quietly, "I took your car and I was driving to Liverpool to the wharfs. I was going to put the pedal to the metal and drive right off the wharf, into the ocean, and just die."

Jane felt tears welling in her eyes. She wanted to reach out and hug her son.

"Mom, we aren't living. We aren't alive. We're just like robots—we just exist."

Jane knew her son was right, and felt panic and frustration as she sat in the cab of the truck at the side of the road in the rain with the stereo blaring while Billy and Wamboldt passed a joint back and forth. "I couldn't deny what Allen said back then, any more than I could deny the look on his face when we left the house earlier that evening. Well, we got to Leona's. Ron was drunk and stoned by that time. Leona was at home with her sons, Leslie and Timmy. I think we played cards but I can't really remember. They drank beer. I had one—I didn't finish it. They also smoked some dope and I had a puff or two when they passed it to me." Billy did much of the talking, mostly about deer hunting and animals. At about 8:30 p.m., he declared it was time to go home. Ronny Wamboldt staggered into the truck. Again, Billy sat in the centre and Jane drove. "From the time we got into the truck Bill never shut up. The stereo was playing full blast and he was ranting and raving above the noise." The focus of Billy's abuse was Margaret Joudrey.

"When Margaret turns her lights off down there tonight, it'll be lights off for her, for good!" he shouted. "I got five gallons of gas in town today and I'm going to dump it all around that fucking trailer and watch them burn. They'll never get out. Can't you just see Margaret with her game leg and Roger with his bad heart, running around trying to get out. They won't have a chance." Jane stared straight ahead, trying to manage the wheel on the treacherous road while Billy went into a fit of laughter, which she described as "his evil laugh." He stopped laughing abruptly and stared directly at Jane.

"And I'll deal with that son of yours at the same time. I've waited a long time to deal with him. I might as well clean them all up at one time."

"He went on like that the whole way home, and just before we pulled into the driveway, he fell asleep. He could fall asleep any time, any place, at the drop of a hat. All he had to do was close his eyes and he was asleep."

Allen had sat down to watch television after Jane and Billy left in the truck. "I watched *Fame*," he recalled, "and when that was over, figure skating was on. I didn't watch that. I went to bed." Darren had watched some television with Allen, but was sound asleep when Jane pulled into the driveway. Allen woke up when he heard the truck. Outside it was foggy and raining and very dark. Ronny Wamboldt staggered from the truck into the house and passed out. Allen heard him come in and went back to sleep.

Billy, meanwhile, was asleep or passed out in the truck, with Jane behind the wheel beside him. A tape continued to play on the stereo in the cab of the truck. Jane stared straight ahead. It was one of Billy's rules that she had to remain in the truck until he woke up and gave her permission to enter the house. The beatings and the mental anguish, which had become more intense in the previous months, had taken their toll on her body and her mind. Her nerves were frayed, and her weight, normally 140 pounds, was hovering just above one hundred pounds. Her eyes seemed blank and distant and had a haunted look. Because of the weight loss, her clothes no longer fit properly. Her self-esteem was nonexistent. She could see no future. "I just sat there and the words... everything that he had been saying, just started sinking in... Margaret... Allen. What was he going to do? I just said, 'To hell with it, I'm not going to live like this anymore.'"

Jane Hurshman

Jane at age fifteen.

Brian Vallée

Maurice and Gladys Hurshman at the kitchen table of their Danesville home.

Brian Vallée

The Stafford house at Bangs Falls.

Jane Hurshman

Jane and Billy in happier days.

Jane with Darren when he was a few months old.

Billy with Darren.

Jane Hurshman

Ronny Wamboldt and Billy Stafford asleep in the Stafford living room after heavy drinking.

Brian Vallée

Margaret Joudrey was like a mother to Jane Stafford until Billy's death.

rcmp

Billy's truck with his body in the cab.

rcmp

Billy's decapitated body slouched against the driver's door.

Brian Vallée

Gary Grant, the RCMP constable Billy Stafford hated the most.

Brian Vallée

Nova Scotia lawyer Alan Ferrier, who defended Jane Stafford.

Brian Vallée

Prosecutor Blaine Allaby.

cbc

The Liverpool courthouse where Jane was sentenced to six months in prison after pleading guilty to manslaughter.

cbc

Jane, days before she went back to court for sentencing in February 1984.

Brian Vallée

Darren, in front of his grandparents' house in early summer 1985.

Jane beeped the horn. Allen heard it but ignored it. He thought Billy might be fighting with his mother, so that one of them hit the horn accidentally. When he heard a second beep, he got out of bed and went to the door. Opening the door, he peered out, saw his mother, and approached the truck. It was raining, and the truck was parked about ten feet from the door to the house. The driver's window was rolled down.

"Get the gun and load it," said his mother simply.

Allen shrugged and returned to the house. He chose a twelve-gauge, single-shot shotgun, one of seven guns Billy kept on a rack in Ronny Wamboldt's bedroom. He also kept a box full of rifle ammunition under the bed. Shotgun shells were kept in a belt hanging on the gun rack. Allen wasn't certain it was his mother who wanted the gun. He thought it might be Billy who wanted it. "A lot of times they told me to get a gun if Bill saw a deer or something on the way home." He put a shell in the shotgun, slid it under his bed, and returned to the truck to determine whether they really wanted the gun. His mother was standing outside the truck. He couldn't see Billy.

"Bring me the gun," repeated Jane.

Allen went into the house and brought it out to her.

"Go back to the house," she ordered.

Jane approached the open window on the driver's side of the truck and put the barrel in. Turning her head away, she pulled the trigger.

Allen wasn't sure what was happening. He paced around the house a bit and was standing by the kitchen sink when he heard the shot. He waited twenty or thirty seconds and went outside. He saw his mother standing beside the truck with the gun in her hand.

"Here, take this," said Jane, handing the gun to Allen. He took the gun and placed it on the floor of the back porch.

"Get me some clean clothes," instructed Jane, "and put them in a garbage bag."

Allen went to his mother's bedroom and brought out a blouse and a pair of slacks. When he got outside, Jane was sitting in the truck. He put the garbage bag in the rear of the truck. "Take the gun down to Margaret's," said Jane nervously. "Roger will help you get rid of it. And call your grandfather and tell him to meet me down by the satellite station."

Jane said her only thought was to get the truck away from the house so that Darren wouldn't see anything. "I told Allen to clean the place and get rid of the gun, and that Roger would help him, and to tell Margaret that everything would be all right, that he wouldn't hurt her no more. I didn't know if Bill was dead or not, because I never once looked at him. It was just a big mess. I was covered with blood and stuff. I left the house and just drove. I don't know how I drove that road, it was in such bad shape. It was so rough and bumpy I couldn't tell if Bill was moving or not."

Jane drove the seven miles along the River Road in the rain and fog with the full weight of Billy's upper torso leaning against her. She looked straight ahead, her mind in a turmoil. She stopped the truck just before the gravel portion ended at the entrance to the satellite station road. "I stopped, pulled over to the side of the road, and put the truck in reverse. I backed up until I couldn't back up any more. Then I shut the motor off and got out and got my clothes out of the back."

The television was on in Margaret Joudrey's trailer, and she and Roger Manthorne were playing cards, as they did most evenings. They heard a knock on their window and looked up to see Allen.

"Well, go let him in," Margaret said to Manthorne, who went to the porch that had been built onto the trailer and opened the door for Allen, who placed the shotgun on the porch floor.

"Ma did it," the boy said. "I've got to use the phone."

Allen called his grandparents in nearby Danesville. Gladys Hurshman answered. "I told her not to ask no questions because it was a party line and somebody might be listening. I told her to just go down and pick my mother up by the satellite station." When Allen got off the telephone he turned to Manthorne.

"What should we do with the gun?"

"We'll break it down first and throw it in the river," replied Manthorne. They broke the gun down into three pieces, walked the hundred yards or so to the bridge over the Medway River, and tossed the pieces over the railing.

"Is there a mess up at the house?" asked Manthorne when they returned to the trailer.

"Yes," replied Allen. "There's a lot of dots and stuff on the house."

Allen went back up to the house and used a rag to clean blood and brain particles from the outside wall. He put the rag in a plastic garbage bag along with several bloody stones from the ground near the porch. About half an hour later he returned to Joudrey's trailer with the garbage bag in hand. "What am I going to do with it?" he asked Manthorne.

"I don't know."

"Will you come with me while I throw it in the river?"

Manthorne refused, and Allen carried the garbage bag to the bridge and threw it over the railing into the Medway. He returned to the trailer to await his mother's return.

Maurice and Gladys Hurshman's trailer home in Danesville was no more than a ten-minute drive from the satellite station. They arrived at the turnoff but saw no sign of Jane. Hurshman parked his car on the satellite road just off River Road. He turned out his headlights but left his parking lights on. They were there about ten minutes when they saw the lights of a car approaching from the direction of Charleston. Driving the car was Ronald Harlowe, who lived along River Road past the satellite station. He was returning home from Liverpool. "I took the 103 Highway and swung off on the River Road. When I got close to home just before the satellite road I noticed a car parked with just parking lights on. When he seen me coming, he shut his parking lights off and drove by me with no lights on." Harlowe recognized Hurshman's car and "I just thought it was odd that he drove by me with no lights on."

Jane Stafford, with Billy's body in the cab beside her, hadn't yet passed by, and Harlowe saw no other vehicles. He knew Billy Stafford and would have recognized the truck. He had once stopped working on a scallop dragger because of an altercation with Billy.

Maurice Hurshman didn't realize it was Ronald Harlowe's car that had passed him on River Road. "When I got abreast of the car I realized that I didn't have my lights on, so I pulled them on." He drove into Charleston as far as the fire hall, where he turned and went back to the satellite road to wait for Jane. He waited a few minutes and began moving slowly back toward River Road.

By that time, Jane had left the truck and was walking along the side of the road. "I saw the car coming from down the satellite road and I knew it was Mom. I knew the car. They stopped near the stop sign and I came up and got in the back on the passenger side."

"What's wrong, Janey?" asked Maurice Hurshman. "Why did you want us to pick you up out here? Did you have a fight or something?"

"Don't ask me anything," replied Jane. "Just leave me alone and please take me to your place so I can get cleaned up."

They drove in silence to the Hurshman home in Danesville. Jane could hear her parents' dogs, Zimby and Tina, barking when they pulled into the driveway. "Mom left the lights on in the trailer for the dogs. I told her to turn them off. Dad got out of the car, but stayed outside the trailer. I went into the trailer in the dark and went right to the bathroom. I took the clean clothes from the green garbage bag. Then I undressed and had a bath. I cleaned up everything and put all of the stuff back into the same bag, including the towel and the facecloth. When I came out, the lights were on."

"Please take me home now," said Jane to her mother.

"I wish you would tell me what's wrong."

"I just don't want to talk about it." Jane again sat in the rear seat with her parents in front.

"River Road is too bad to drive," said Jane. "Take me around the pavement instead." They drove along Highway 3 east through the town of Brooklyn, skirting Liverpool, and along Highway 8, which follows the Mersey River past the town of Milton. They turned off the highway to 210 East, which took them to the Bangs Falls cutoff, at that time of year an almost impassable dirt road. It was several hundred yards from the cutoff to the rear of the Stafford house. Maurice Hurshman made the turn to the cutoff, but Jane insisted he stop.

"I'll take you right to your door, Janey," he said.

"No. I'll get out right here."

Jane waited until her father turned around and drove off before she started walking. It was dark, and the rain continued to come down in a steady drizzle. The road was full of ruts. "I could feel the mud up to my ankles. I didn't have any boots on. I tried to follow the tire tracks but I couldn't see in the dark and I kept slipping into the muck. I walked along until I could see the light from Mr. and Mrs. Wood's place, and then I cut through the bush." The Woods were an elderly, retired couple. Jane did not want to chance them seeing her. It left her a nightmarish struggle through three hundred feet of dense, wet bush. Branches sprayed her with rainwater and scratched her face and hands when she brushed against them in the dark. She also had to contend with isolated patches of snow, which were crusty on top and sometimes couldn't bear her weight.

Jane came out of the woods behind the Stafford barn and entered the house. On the kitchen table there was a note from Allen saying he was down in Margaret Joudrey's trailer. Jane went into her bedroom and flicked her light on and off. "Margaret knew when the light went on and off that I wanted her for something. It was a signal we had used for years."

Margaret Joudrey, Manthorne, and Allen came up to the house together. Margaret and Jane hugged each other. "Don't worry, everything will be all right," said Margaret. Manthorne and Allen both noticed Jane seemed pretty shaken up.

"It's all over," said Jane. "I won't have to put up with it anymore. I blew his fucking brains out."

Jane still had the garbage bag with her bloodied clothing, towel, and facecloth. Allen burned them in the wood stove, along with her purse, which had been in the cab of the truck when Billy was shot. They sat around the table talking in whispered tones for a time.

"We broke the gun down into three pieces and threw it into the river," said Manthorne.

Allen told his mother about cleaning off the side of the house and throwing the rags and bloodied rocks into the river. Manthorne had a cup of tea before he and Margaret left shortly before midnight. Jane put on her housecoat and sat on the edge of her bed. Allen came in and lay down on the bed.

"I don't know what's going to happen from here on in," said Jane softly. "I left the truck off the side of the road down by the satellite station."

Allen eventually fell asleep, dozing off and on through the night. Jane didn't sleep at all. "I didn't really believe Bill was dead. When I got out of the truck, I left the keys in the ignition. To me, he was going to drive back home. I sat there all night, just sat there. I knew he should be dead, with all the blood and everything, but I didn't really believe it. I just waited for that truck to come up the driveway."

In the morning, Jane woke up Ronny Wamboldt with the first light of day. "Do you know where Billy is?" she asked.

"No, I don't know where he could have went," replied Wamboldt. "He must have gone somewhere through the night." He washed up in the bathroom. After a cup of tea, he went out to the shed and started drinking.

Jane wandered around the house in a daze. She drank tea and smoked cigarette after cigarette. She was also taking Valium. "It was like a weird dream. Finally I got dressed and went down to visit with Margaret. I was just coming back from there when the police arrived. When they told me Bill was actually dead, I passed out. At that moment I really knew that he couldn't hurt any of us anymore. I must have passed out from sheer exhaustion and relief. Just the fact that he was gone. That he wouldn't be there anymore."

CHAPTER 10
CHARGES

By the end of the first day of the investigation, Staff Sergeant Peter Williamson had assigned ten officers to the Billy Stafford case. As the day wore on, the evidence increasingly pointed to Billy's common-law wife, Jane Stafford. There was Billy's mistreatment of her and rumours of attempts to hire a hit man and of a twenty-thousand-dollar life insurance policy. In the early evening of March 12, 1982, Williamson sent Corporal Howard Pike and Constable Archie Mason back out to the Stafford residence in Bangs Falls. Jane's memories of the events immediately following Billy Stafford's death were blurred. The heavy doses of Valium she was taking added to her confusion. She couldn't concentrate, and her thoughts were disconnected. But she clearly remembered closing the truck door with Billy's body propped against it inside. "It was foggy, cold, and raining. I remember the rain hitting my face. I always loved the rain. As I walked the short distance across the road, a warm feeling came over me. I felt like I was being anointed with warm oil. As if I was being forgiven for what I'd done."

Jane also remembered fainting when Howie Pike told her Billy was dead. She remembered waking up on the sofa and telling Allen she didn't want to go to jail and leave Darren alone. She told Allen she would try to hide her role in Billy's death by telling the police he was involved in drug deals and that Mafia hit men probably shot him. That's what she told Pike and Mason when they returned to her house that night. According to Pike, he and Mason talked to Jane for about an hour that evening. She appeared to be drugged, "almost as if she was in a daze, more or less, staring off into the distance."

The next day, a Friday, Lamonte Stafford drove Jane to the hospital, where a doctor prescribed Valium for her. Meanwhile, the police were picking up further leads pointing to Jane as the prime suspect. Most important were comments by friends of Beverly Taylor. Taylor was at sea the night Billy Stafford was killed. When he landed two days later, he contacted the RCMP when he learned they wanted to talk to him.

By the night of March 13, Peter Williamson had decided it was time to bring Jane Stafford into the Liverpool detachment for questioning. Armed with a search warrant, Archie Mason and five other RCMP officers arrived at the Stafford house shortly after midnight. "I don't know how many Valium I had consumed at that point," said Jane. "I don't know what all took place that night."

With Mason were Constable Robert Hillier, who was continuing to secure exhibits in the case; Auxiliary Constable Andrew Baker, who was to stand guard at the house through the night; Constable Susan Ivany, from the RCMP Bridgewater detachment; Corporal Ron Pond, a veteran officer brought in from the Yarmouth detachment to aid in the investigation; and Constable Blair McKnight. Pond and McKnight were to interrogate Jane. Mason's job was to introduce them to her.

"Corporal Pond and Constable McKnight want to ask you some questions," said Mason. "And they might want you to return to the Liverpool detachment with them. I also have a search warrant to search your residence."

Constable Susan Ivany noticed that Jane "seemed to be in a state of some remorse, or she was very subdued. She wasn't very energetic or vital." Corporal Pond remembered that Jane was wearing a blue housecoat and was asleep on the sofa when they arrived. Susan Ivany, who was in uniform, accompanied Jane to her bedroom, where she dressed in a brown plaid shirt, blue slacks, and a brown corduroy jacket. Pond and McKnight, who were not in uniform, accompanied Jane to an unmarked cruiser. When Jane walked past Constable Hillier, he noticed she was "solemn, sedentary. As she walked past me her head was down and she didn't say anything to anybody that I heard. She seemed very quiet."

Susan Ivany sat with Jane in the back seat. Pond was driving the cruiser, and McKnight sat beside him. McKnight turned to Jane when she entered the car and read her the standard caution: "You need not say anything. You have nothing to hope for, any promise or favour, and nothing to fear from any threat whether or not you say anything. Anything you do say may be used as evidence. Do you understand what I've said?"

"Yes," mumbled Jane, nodding.

"We'd rather not engage in any conversation until we get to the office," advised McKnight.

"Can I smoke?" asked Jane.

"Yes."

They drove Jane to the Liverpool detachment. With them was a bottle of Valium seized from the house. Jane was taken to a small interview room, about ten by twelve feet with an eight-foot ceiling. The walls were covered with white Styrofoam, and there was a green filing cabinet in one corner, a solid wood table in the centre, and two wood chairs. There were no pictures on the walls. The Styrofoam reduced echoes and outside noises. It was 12:35 on Sunday morning when Jane entered the room with Susan Ivany. They engaged in small talk for about fifteen minutes, until Blair McKnight entered and told Ivany to leave. He and Jane lit up cigarettes. He later said that she answered his questions slowly and didn't seem very alert. He thought she might be on tranquillizers. McKnight questioned Jane until 2:15 a.m. She stuck to her Mafia story. Susan Ivany came back into the room when McKnight left. She had a camera with her and wanted to check for bruises on Jane's body. "She wasn't unkempt," said Ivany. "She just seemed quite expressionless." Jane said that Ivany told her to strip from the waist up so she could photograph her.

"Why don't I strip completely," said Jane defensively. "Then you can photograph all of me."

"That won't be necessary." Ivany photographed a large bruise on Jane's left arm. Jane said that no photographs were taken of the left side of her body, which was still black and blue from the beating Billy had administered with the vacuum cleaner hose. The photograph Ivany took did not turn out. Ivany left the room. Minutes later, at 2:38 a.m., Corporal Pond, dressed in a business suit, entered and questioned Jane for more than two hours. "I was actually very sympathetic with her. I was obviously trying to get at the truth, but I was trying to be as gentle as I could to her under the circumstances." He said he was sympathetic because he had heard a lot of stories about Billy Stafford "and possible motive for this incident."

Pond told Jane that the police knew of her attempt to hire Beverly Taylor to kill Billy. Jane was not swayed. Pond gave up at 4:50 a.m. At 5:05 a.m. it was Blair McKnight's turn again. He was with her almost two hours, until Pond returned at 6:55 a.m. Soon after, both Pond and McKnight entered the room. At no time was

Jane told she was a suspect or under arrest. She declined when they asked her if she wanted a lawyer, insisting instead that she be allowed to see Lamonte Stafford. Throughout the ordeal she stuck to her story and said she wanted to go home because she feared that the men who shot Billy might return and shoot her children.

Pond and McKnight spent about ten minutes together in the room with Jane, urging her to tell the truth. They believed that with the two of them telling her they didn't believe her, she might tell them what really happened. "No heavy tactics, nothing like that," said Pond. But Jane Stafford saw it differently. She remembered feeling drained and tired through the night, sometimes dozing off with her bead resting on her hand between visits from the two police officers. She believed they were engaging in a game of "good cop–bad cop," with one being sympathetic to her and the other being aggressive and stern. She remembered dozing off when Constable McKnight entered the room to repeat that the police were aware of her attempt to hire someone to kill Billy. When she didn't respond, he dropped a copy of the Criminal Code on the table.

"Here, read that," he said. "You can be locked up for fourteen years as an accomplice."

"I want to see Lamonte," said Jane.

"Look," said McKnight, frustrated, "I'm getting tired, you're getting tired, we're all getting tired. So why don't you tell us the truth so we can all go home?"

Jane was silent.

"Do you know what the people are doing out around Greenfield tonight?" he asked. "They're celebrating. Celebrating Stafford's death. Why don't you confess so you can go home and celebrate, too?"

"I want to see Lamonte," repeated Jane. She felt close to Billy's father and believed he had the right to hear from her that she killed his son. She would tell him before anyone else. She hadn't done much talking during the years under Billy Stafford's reign of fear. She'd been beaten into unconsciousness, shot at at close range with a high-powered rifle, had a knife held to her throat, and been degraded and humiliated. She thought it ironic that the police thought they could cajole her into talking. Their tactics steeled her resolve to remain silent.

Jane's throat was dry. "Can I have a drink of water?" she asked McKnight.

"You wouldn't want to drink the water in this station," he said, smiling. He brought Jane a cold orange drink instead, and at 8:30 a.m. he brought her coffee and breakfast. At 8:40 a.m. Corporal Howard Pike drove to Hunt's Point to pick up Lamonte Stafford, who was working outdoors when Pike arrived. Lamonte cleaned up and changed his clothes before they left for Liverpool. They arrived at about 9:15 a.m. Jane asked to go to the washroom to clean up before meeting Lamonte. She didn't know it at the time, but her own father was already at the station. Maurice Hurshman had been picked up at his home and had spent the night sleeping in a cell waiting to see his daughter.

Jane met with Lamonte for about twenty minutes in the interview room, and then her father joined them for another ten minutes. Staff Sergeant Williamson, meanwhile, had arrived at the detachment. Lamonte Stafford, Maurice Hurshman, and Jane emerged from the interview room and went into a large coffee room. Williamson followed them in and closed the door behind him. At that point, Jane was still sticking to her Mafia story. The four of them sat around a table, with Williamson directly across from Jane.

"What can you tell us about this matter?" asked Williamson somewhat gruffly.

Lamonte Stafford jumped to his feet. "She's had enough of that garbage," he said. "If you want her to talk to you, then you talk right to her."

Lamonte sat down and turned to Jane. "Did you kill Bill?" he asked.

"Yes," replied Jane.

Williamson sat back and listened while Jane described all of the abuse that Billy Stafford had subjected her to. He interjected from time to time "to keep the flow of the conversation going." Jane's shoulders sagged with relief when she completed her story.

"I feel a great weight has been lifted from me," she said.

Williamson gave her the standard police caution, and had her repeat her story as he took it down. He left out her descriptions of Billy's abuses.

That oversight prevented the statement from being introduced in subsequent court proceedings. Lamonte Stafford remembered that Jane "seemed to be in quite a dopey state, like she'd been taking a lot of tranquillizers or some darn thing." He held Jane's hand while Williamson took down her statement, and he consoled her when she wept at its conclusion. Williamson noticed that Lamonte didn't seem angry or upset with Jane when she admitted to killing Billy.

In her statement to Williamson, Jane Stafford took sole blame for the death of her husband. She said she went into the house, loaded the shotgun, and went out to the truck and shot Billy. She said she drove the body to the spot where it was found and walked the seven miles home along River Road. She said she threw the gun in the river and burned her clothes after cleaning up and changing. She made no mention of the actions of Allen or Roger Manthorne, nor did she tell of her parents' role in picking her up and later driving her to the Bangs Falls turnoff. Jane was relieved it was over and that she had protected her family and friends. Peter Williamson was also relieved. He had a confession, but he also felt a lot of sympathy for Jane Stafford. Jane was sipping a cup of coffee when she overheard him talking to fellow officers in the outer office.

"She deserves a medal," said Williamson. "She probably saved a couple of our officers' lives. He always had loaded guns. I'm sure we would have gone out there one day and he would have shot one of us."

Shortly after 11 a.m., Corporal Pike and Lamonte Stafford helped Jane out to a police cruiser. She wanted only one thing—sleep. But first they drove her to the scene of the crime, to the satellite station, and back to Liverpool to reconstruct the events of the night Billy died. Corporal Stan Clarke was waiting with two divers when Jane arrived at the Bangs Falls bridge at 12:30 p.m. She walked from the car and pointed to a spot in the river where she claimed she had thrown the shotgun.

"Finally I got to go home," said Jane. "It was cold in the house and there was a real mess, with mud and dirt everywhere. I guess it was from the police searching the place. Everything was torn apart. The attic, the dresser drawers, the beds, the closets, and the cupboards—everything was a mess. I didn't know what had happened, and I didn't care. I walked through the mess, picked up a blanket, and lay on the bare mattress. I was totally exhausted."

A few minutes later, Darren came into the bedroom and stared at his mother. Jane lifted the blanket and without a word he crawled in beside her. Jane held him close.

"Your father is dead," she said softly. "I killed him. He won't be coming home anymore."

Darren sat up and looked at her. "He won't do this to you anymore?" he asked, flicking his hand back and forth as if slapping her face. "He won't hurt us anymore?"

"No, baby."

"He's really gone, Mommy? Is he really gone forever?"

"Yes, baby, he's gone forever."

Darren wrapped his tiny arms around his mother's neck, and hugged her. "I'm glad, Mommy. I'm glad. Are you glad?"

On March 16, 1982, an information was sworn by Corporal Howard Pike charging Jane Marie Stafford with first-degree murder in the shooting death of her common-law husband, William Lamonte Stafford. Jane was not arrested or jailed. Staff Sergeant Peter Williamson was convinced he had the whole story. His men were continuing their investigations, and Jane Stafford wasn't about to go anywhere. Jane remained heavily sedated, and her recollections of the next two weeks are minimal. "I don't know who came or went or how long I slept. I don't know what kind of a state I was in. Someone cleaned the house up and took care of things because I certainly wasn't capable." She vaguely remembered the arrival of her sister Mona from Barrie, Ontario, and of her sister Sandy from Ottawa. She also remembered seeking the services of a lawyer. The one she chose was Alan Ferrier, who worked in the Bridgewater office of Nova Scotia Legal Aid. She had met Ferrier several months earlier, when she was seeking advice on another matter. "A friend of mine recommended him and set up an appointment for me. He handed me a form to fill out to see if I qualified for legal aid." At the time, Ferrier told her that her income was too high to qualify for legal aid.

"Gee, I never thought of getting your services without paying," said Jane. "I'm quite willing to pay."

"I can't do that," explained Ferrier. "Under the law, I can only handle clients who qualify for legal aid. I can recommend someone who can handle this for you." He had arranged an appointment with another lawyer. But Jane had been impressed by his forthright manner, and now, facing a charge of first-degree murder, she decided he was the one she wanted.

Alan Ferrier was thirty-one when Jane Stafford came to see him in March 1982. Even with a thick moustache, he could have passed for twenty-four or twenty-five. He was born in Edinburgh, Scotland. His father, an insurance salesman, immigrated to Canada when Alan was nine months old. Alan was raised in Dartmouth, Nova Scotia, across the harbour from Halifax. He was a good student and spent his sixth, seventh, and eighth grades at Dartmouth Academy, then an exclusive school for boys. Most of the teachers at the academy were either English or Scottish. Parents loved to send their children to the academy because it was a throwback to the private schools in the old country.

Ferrier enrolled at Dalhousie University when he was sixteen, and graduated in 1970 with a degree in commerce. He was five-feet-two when he started at Dalhousie and didn't have his first date for two-and-a-half years "because I looked more like fourteen." His commerce degree wasn't much good to him because at nineteen, he wasn't old enough to sign legal documents or contracts, so he decided to go on to law school. He graduated at age twenty-three, the second-youngest in his class. He spent two months articling at the Kentville office of Nova Scotia Legal Aid before moving to the Yarmouth office, where "I ended up with a murder and an indecent assault right off." When his boss moved to Ontario to open a civil litigation practice, Alan Ferrier, an articling student, was left virtually in charge of legal aid for three counties. The year was 1974, and he was earning $700 a month. "I was thrown into a lot of trials. It was a wonderful time. I learned a whole shitload of law." In the spring of 1975, he was admitted to the Nova Scotia bar. He moved to Bridgewater legal aid in January 1979.

Under Nova Scotia law, Jane Stafford had an option of using the legal aid offices or a private lawyer of her choice. She wanted Alan Ferrier.

"Well, I think I qualify for legal aid now," said Jane when she met Ferrier again. "The police say I need a lawyer, and I would like you to handle my case. Will you do it?"

Alan Ferrier leaned back in his chair and half-smiled.

"Yes, you sure do need a lawyer. Now do you want to tell me about it?"

Jane forgot much of the conversation that followed "except that he stopped me and asked, 'Are you on anything now?' I reached in my pocket and took out the pills from the doctor. He read the container and counted the pills. That's all I remember of that meeting."

It was obvious to Alan Ferrier that Jane Stafford was still distraught and very confused. He arranged for her to see a psychiatrist. "I don't even remember his name," said Jane. "I was really right out of it. I know he was in Halifax and I know my uncle Jimmy and my sister Mona drove me there. I really didn't want to go. It was just like on TV. There were fancy dressed women in his office with lots of jewellery. They probably had nothing better to do with their time or money. I had to wait there with them. I had on blue jeans, and the sides were out of my sneakers. The fact that he was a man really put me off. When I was called in, the room was very dim. He told me to sit in a chair, but I refused. He had a couch across the room and asked me to go there. That did it. I couldn't stand it. I left. I think I might have told him I thought he was crazier than me. I was still heavily drugged. I don't know if that was it or not."

Jane's thoughts were swirling when she left the psychiatrist's office. She couldn't understand what was happening to her. Billy was dead. Everybody, including the police, was sympathetic toward her, yet she was still facing a charge of first-degree murder. She feared she would be locked up for life and separated from Darren. She decided to make a new confession to the police. She would say that her son Allen shot Billy Stafford while he was pummeling her in the cab of the truck. Allen would have been defending her. She would be free to be with Darren. Jane told her sister Mona she was changing her confession. Mona called Allen to tell him of his mother's plans. When the police came for him later at his grandfather's house, he told them he shot Billy Stafford. "I figured that's what Ma wanted," he said later.

On March 25, 1982, Jane Stafford, in the company of her lawyer, went to Staff Sergeant Peter Williamson's office at the RCMP's Liverpool detachment. There she signed a statement in which she said her son Allen had shot Billy Stafford after "he started beating me on the head. He kept pounding me on the head and my head was down by the steering wheel and somehow the horn blew. He was still beating on me when the next thing I remember was a gun blast."

Jane Stafford and her son were arraigned on first-degree murder charges the next day. She was placed in a cell in the Queens County Jail in Liverpool. Later that night, Cyril Page, the diminutive High Sheriff for Queens County, picked up Jane at the Liverpool detachment to transport her to the women's section of the Halifax Correctional Centre. Page's wife, Pearl, accompanied him, as she always did when he was transporting female prisoners. It was a two-hour drive to the corrections centre.

"Cyril, do you mind if I take my shoes off and try to rest some?" asked Jane.

"Suit yourself," replied Page. "You got the whole back seat. There's a blanket back there. If you want to make a pillow out of it, go right ahead."

Jane mentioned that Darren was going to Ontario to be with her sister. Then she fell asleep. "I believe Jane slept pretty near the whole way to the Halifax Correctional Centre," said Page. "It was a terribly foggy night going to Halifax, and I was much more concerned with my driving than I was with really talking that night."

The Halifax Correctional Centre was a dreary red-brick building on the outskirts of Bedford, just north of Halifax. It housed about 150 male prisoners and 24 women. The women were housed in A Block.

Cyril Page turned Jane over to a prison matron, who escorted her through the drab foyer and the narrow visitors' corridor, with its facing orange vinyl couches, to the women's section. Jane was quickly processed, issued prison clothing, and locked in a cell. Most women prisoners were confined to one of two dormitory rooms, but troublemakers, newcomers, and those whom authorities believed might be threatened in the general population were placed in the cells.

There were eight cells, four on each side of a horseshoe-shaped room, with a guard station at the base. The room itself had brick end walls, painted a dismal green, and a cement floor, painted grey. The cells had individual steel doors. There was a common shower room, and each cell had its own toilet and metal bed. From her cell Jane could see four inmates playing cards on a table in front of the cells.

"What are you in for?" asked one of the women.

"I killed somebody," replied Jane softly.

The four continued playing cards and joking with each other, and seemed to ignore Jane for a time. Then one of them turned to Jane. "How did you do it?" she asked.

"I shot somebody."

"What did you shoot him with?"

"A shotgun."

The four women studied Jane for a moment. Her weight, normally 140 pounds, had fallen to just one hundred pounds in her last brutal months with Billy Stafford.

"You don't look big enough to hold a gun, let alone pull the trigger," said one of the inmates. They began joking among themselves again and then sang a song. The chorus included the words, "She didn't know the gun was loaded…"

The police were not satisfied with Jane Stafford's latest version of Billy's death. The physical evidence proved conclusively that she could not have been in the cab of the truck when Billy Stafford was shot. They were relieved when Jane agreed to take a lie detector test. On Saturday afternoon, the day after Jane's arrival at the Halifax Correctional Centre, Corporal Howie Pike arrived to take her to the Halifax RCMP headquarters, a squat, five-storey brick building. Jane smoked a cigarette as she sat on a chair near the commissionaire's desk at the front entrance while Pike went upstairs to see if the polygraph operator was ready for her. In the ten minutes or so that Pike was gone, Jane felt sad when she overheard a police radio call about a dead baby found abandoned in a sleeping bag on the side of the road. The baby had died of exposure.

The RCMP always had two qualified polygraph operators available from provincial headquarters in Halifax. The day Jane arrived, Michael Innes, whose territory included the western part of the province, was on duty. At the time Jane Stafford was brought in for testing, Innes, a twenty-one-year veteran of the RCMP, had been a certified polygraph examiner for three years. He had administered polygraph tests in Nova Scotia, New Brunswick, Prince Edward Island, and Newfoundland. He had been trained at the Canadian Police College in Ottawa and had been upgrading himself at seminars in the United States and Canada. There is a saying in the polygraph trade: "The instrument is only as reliable as the examiner who operates it." Michael Innes was considered one of the best.

Jane didn't know it, but Innes had earlier spent sixteen hours in Liverpool, where he had talked to her mother and had given her father a polygraph test, which indicated that Maurice Hurshman had nothing to do with Billy Stafford's death. Corporal Pike talked to Innes for a few minutes, and the two of them took the elevator down to the main entrance. Jane would remember Innes as "an easy-speaking man with a very nice smile." Jane accompanied him to the polygraph suite, where they spent almost three hours together. "We mostly talked about me and my life," Jane remembered. "Then he took me into a room full of all sorts of weird-looking equipment." Innes saw that Jane was quite nervous, and he did his best to set her mind at ease during his pretest interview.

"When people speak to the police they normally don't tell all they know, perhaps because of our uniform," he explained to Jane. "At times people become scared when they see a uniform. And maybe they forget to tell the police the truth."

"I hope I don't detect some suspicion from you, because I'm getting fed up with this," said Jane. "I came in here today to show you that I'm telling the truth. The rest of those guys didn't believe me."

"Look, I'm sorry, Mrs. Stafford, but my job here today is just to show you are in fact telling the truth, or if you're not telling the truth, to show you're telling a lie, so I'm very sorry if you're misunderstanding anything from what I've said."

The carpeted polygraph suite was about ten feet square. During a test, the drapes were drawn, and the door was closed to prevent interruption. The only sound, other than the voices of the examiner and the person being interviewed, came from a heater by the window that kept the temperature at seventy-two degrees Fahrenheit—the ideal temperature for accurate testing.

Jane arrived in the polygraph suite around 2:30 p.m. The first test commenced two hours later. Innes explained how the polygraph worked and motioned her to sit in the chair, which had padded arms for comfort. "He began hooking wires and belts on me, and he told me I had to keep very still. I was terrified. He assured me it wouldn't hurt, but deep inside I didn't believe him. I remember thinking this must be what it's like when they put you in the electric chair. I thought this is what they're eventually going to do to me." The wires and belts included a standard blood-pressure belt or cuff, which was attached to Jane's left arm and would measure blood pressure and heartbeat accelerations. There were also tubes around the upper and lower chest, to measure breathing or internal movement. The tubes were placed over her clothing. Two small plates were attached to Jane's right hand to record sweating or "galvanic skin response."

The polygraph instrument itself was set up behind Jane to prevent her from seeing any tracings that might upset her or affect her concentration. Innes told Jane she didn't have to take the test, gave her the standard police warning, and asked her if she wanted to have her lawyer present. He also had her fill out a form outlining her personal and medical history.

"It's my understanding, Mrs. Stafford, that you're here because on the night of March 11, 1982, your common-law husband, William Stafford, was found shot to death," intoned Innes. "As a result of that you're suspected by the police as possibly being involved. That's why you are here to take this test—to clear up whether you are involved or not involved."

Innes ran four tests on Jane; each had ten questions. "Three are crime questions," Innes later explained. "We call those relevant questions. We ask three other questions, which are known lies or probably lies. We refer to them as control questions. And then we ask them four other questions—is your name so-and-so, and so on..."

Upon completion of the tests, Innes took the results to another room to review and score them. He concluded that Jane had lied to him about who had pulled the trigger on the gun that killed Billy Stafford. He returned to the polygraph room to confront her.

"When you came in here today you knew the truth and the good Lord above knew the truth," he said. "I didn't know what the truth was. Unfortunately, as a result of my polygraph test, I now know you haven't been completely truthful with me. You did pull the trigger on the gun that killed Stafford, didn't you?"

"Yes, I did it," said Jane. "I'm glad it's over. You wouldn't believe how bad he was to me."

"If I get Howie, will you give him a statement now?"

"Yes," said Jane softly. Minutes later, Innes returned with Pike. Innes handed him a card with a printed police warning. Before leaving the polygraph suite, Jane grasped Innes by the hand. "She looked me in the eye and just held my hand for a while, and she thanked me very much and left. I thought she looked relieved."

Pike escorted Jane to the elevator. "I'm sorry for all the trouble I caused everybody," she said. They went to a small office on one side of the main detachment office and sat at a table. Jane began weeping.

"Are you all right?" asked Pike.

Jane nodded and lit a cigarette. Pike waited while she composed herself before reading her her rights.

"I understand," said Jane. "I killed Billy. Everything I said earlier was the truth except that it was me who shot Bill—not Allen." She gave a detailed statement, which Pike wrote down and which she signed. They left the building and began the drive back to the Halifax Corrections Centre in Pike's unmarked steel-grey Ford.

"Would you like to stop for something to eat or drink?" asked Pike.

"No thanks. I don't want anything. Just take me back to jail, where I can lie down and be alone in peace and quiet."

It was Saturday afternoon, March 27, 1982. Two days later she was freed after a bail hearing at which her father posted a $5,000 bond. Her son, Allen, still charged with first-degree murder along with his mother, was also freed on a $5,000 bond, his posted by Jane's uncle, James Hurshman.

As she waited for her case to go to the courts, Jane attempted as best she could to put her life back together. "After all that had happened, I stayed at Mom's for a while and then I decided I had to come home to Bangs Falls. It was something I had to do. I had to deal with it. And I did. I came home and I made a big fire in the fireplace outside. And everything that was here that was his or anything that I shared with him, I burned. That bed got burned just the same as everything else. I just burned and burned and burned... it seemed like forever. My neighbour Margaret Joudrey stayed with me that first night. I didn't know what kind of feelings I would have after coming back here for the first time. Sometime through the night I woke up. It was still dark, but it was coming on to morning. I can remember I was sweating, but I was cold at the same time. It was just awful. At that point I just didn't know... I wanted to be able to deal with everything. I wanted to be able to handle it inside, in my own way. I spent a lot of time praying and just sort of talking to myself. After a while there was a feeling of comfort, a real nice feeling. Whatever happened that night—I'm not sure. But there was a different feeling in that house from then on—peaceful. And I didn't find it hard to live there after that."

Jane resigned herself to whatever might lie ahead. "I just figured I'd probably go to prison. Whatever they decided they were going to do, they were going to do. And I didn't think about what was going to happen tomorrow. All I knew was that Bill wasn't going to be there. Prison couldn't be worse than the way I lived. When I went to the correctional centre for those few days it was almost like being in a motel. Somebody served you something to eat. You didn't have to get up. You had nobody telling you to do anything. Nothing could have been worse than when I lived with him."

On June 7, 1982, following a preliminary inquiry before judge W.A.D. Gunn of the Provincial Magistrates Court in Liverpool, Jane Stafford was committed to stand trial at the next sittings of the Trial Division of the Supreme Court of Nova Scotia at Liverpool. At the June inquiry, charges against Allen were dropped.

It galled Jane's lawyer, Alan Ferrier, that there would be any trial at all. He was prepared to enter a plea of guilty to manslaughter on her behalf, and then let a judge decide what her punishment should be after hearing about the life she was forced to lead. Ferrier was certain that the local RCMP and Crown prosecutor were in favour of accepting the manslaughter plea, but the provincial attorney general's office was against it because Billy Stafford was asleep when Jane shot him.

Ferrier believed that the decision to proceed with a charge of first-degree murder was absurd, considering Staff Sergeant Williamson's remarks after he learned of the abuse Jane had suffered: "He commented to his officers that she deserved a medal, and that she'd probably saved at least two police officers' lives. In the context of that kind of reaction, it's not surprising that he would accede to a suggestion of a manslaughter plea, because obviously he knew what Jane was up against. They appreciated Billy probably far better than most people did, and I think that the Crown on the local level and the police were prepared to be fair. Accepting the plea of manslaughter would allow some flexibility in the question of sentencing, and it would leave it for the trial judge to decide on the basis of all the evidence what would be an appropriate sentence. The difficulty with first- and second-degree murder is that the minimums are established and the judge has no control over that. Jane was charged with first-degree murder. She was looking at twenty-five years without parole. It's absolutely absurd to consider that kind of a punishment for her reaction to an enduring life of violence over five years that none of us would tolerate for five seconds. I think it's an irony that in telling the truth, she ended up creating great difficulties for herself. And I think that's an indication of how she was not thinking things out, as the Crown originally contended when they laid a charge of first-degree murder. Clearly she hadn't thought things out or she wouldn't have said Billy was asleep when she shot him. She could easily have lied or made up a situation, and it's doubtful that anybody would have disbelieved her in light of his character and the way he had treated her in the past."

In the weeks and months before her trial, Jane Stafford put her complete trust in Alan Ferrier. "My trust in him just grew and grew as time passed. To me, he was God-sent. He always laid everything on the line. I knew he would do his best for me." She was convinced she had the right lawyer at her bail hearing, when she saw him in action in court for the first time.

In a back room in the courthouse, while awaiting a decision, they talked quietly.

"Jane, are you suicidal?" asked Ferrier.

The question surprised Jane. "Are you asking me if I'm considering killing myself?"

"Yes, that's what I'm asking you."

"Hell, no. Maybe I was when I was with Bill, but no one is going to hurt me anymore—so why would I want to do that?"

Jane was smiling. Ferrier smiled and reached out and hugged her.

"I knew at that moment that he really cared about what happened to me. At that point I put everything in his hands."

CHAPTER 11

PROSECUTION

The quaint frame courthouse in downtown Liverpool, where Jane was to stand trial, was built in 1854. Except for its black doors and grey veranda along the front, the single-storey building was gleaming white. Its four evenly spaced columns abutted the sidewalk. The elegant, low-peaked building seemed to belong on the quiet residential street one block from Liverpool's main thoroughfare.

Inside, the judge's bench, with its high-backed, carved oak chair, sat in an alcove looking out over the courtroom. Matching jury boxes were to the right and left of the bench. The door to the jury room was to the left of the judge, and tables for the court clerk and recorder were directly in front of the bench. Behind them was a long table for Crown and defence counsel. Directly behind the counsel's table was the much smaller press table. At the rear of the courtroom, seventy-five plywood and metal stacking chairs were set up for the public. The simple chairs detracted from the carved oak furniture and railings at the front.

Jane Stafford's trial, which would last eighteen days, attracted nationwide attention and the courtroom was filled to capacity every day. Beginning on November 2, 1982, the private woman who had lived an isolated existence for so many years would find it an ordeal to run a daily gauntlet of well-wishers and television and newspaper reporters scrambling for a quote. "Reporters were always waiting for me to arrive in the morning and again when I left at night. Thank God Alan was there to reassure me. He told me just to say 'no comment,' and that's what I did, day after day." The public and media attention were there not only because there was widespread sympathy for Jane Stafford in the community, which knew what Billy Stafford had been like, but also because her case had become a national symbol in the struggle against male oppression and spousal abuse.

The task of the young aggressive Crown attorney, Blaine Allaby, was to convince the jury that Jane Stafford had no right to kill Billy simply because she was in a tough situation, and that the murder was planned and deliberate beyond a reasonable doubt.

Jane Stafford's case wasn't the only one on the docket when the Supreme Court session opened on Tuesday morning, November 2. The first order of business was to select a grand jury. That process moved quickly, and the grand jury retired to consider whether there was enough evidence to proceed against Jane Stafford. The jury took less than two hours to decide there was enough evidence, which didn't surprise anyone. The Supreme Court session in Liverpool was scheduled to last two weeks. Ferrier, Allaby, and the presiding judge, Mr. Justice D. Burchell, quickly agreed that the Stafford trial would take at least that long. In the afternoon, a twelve-member jury was chosen from the hundred or so people summoned for jury duty. However, the trial proceeded with only eleven jurors when Doris Whynot stepped down after it was revealed that she knew Jane Stafford and might not be impartial.

After selection of the jury, Jane Stafford was arraigned on the charge of first-degree murder. She pleaded not guilty. It was to be Friday, the fourth day of the trial, before the jury got to hear any evidence in the case: Wednesday and Thursday were taken up with *voir dire* matters, in which Allaby and Ferrier argued about what evidence was admissible. The public was allowed to listen to those arguments but not the jury. As well, the media were restricted from publishing evidence or arguments put forward in the *voir dire* sessions. Alan Ferrier won a victory of sorts when he successfully argued against the admission of Jane Stafford's first statement to police, given to Staff Sergeant Williamson in the presence of Lamonte Stafford and her father. Ferrier argued: "The course of the evening was in fact designed to tire and frustrate a woman who is obviously very placid and quiet, who was under the influence of drugs, and it was a design on their part to create an atmosphere of sympathy, to give Mrs. Stafford the impression that they understood her. She was almost constantly with one police officer or another for a period of nine hours, one o'clock in the morning until approximately ten. How would the average citizen react to that, far less a person who is on tranquillizers?"

Mr. Justice Burchell noted that the conduct of the police "does raise some questions in my mind. It has not been explained, for example, why it was necessary to take the accused into custody in the middle of the night. The question is... whether the police deliberately set about to deprive the accused of sleep so as to make her compliant under interrogation." He concluded: "I'm unable to say that the methods employed by the police affected the operating mind of the accused, nor am I able to say that of themselves they offend standards of decency or offend the integrity of the judicial process." However, he accepted another of Ferrier's arguments—that Staff Sergeant Williamson had chosen not to include Jane's description of the brutalities Billy Stafford inflicted on her in the statement he took from her. Williamson testified that he excluded the beatings from the statement because he felt they had nothing to do with the event, since they occurred in the past.

"I take a serious view of the question of whether the statement that has been reduced to writing was a complete statement of the disclosures of the accused," stated Burchell. "If the prosecution decides to induce a confession it must take the whole of it together and cannot select one part and leave another. On that ground, rather than on the issue of freeness and voluntariness, I conclude that the statement should not be admitted."

The jury was finally returned to open court on Friday morning, November 5. Allaby's first witness was Beverly Taylor, the Riverport seaman, who told his story of Jane approaching him to kill Billy Stafford in return for the proceeds from the $20,000 family insurance policy. Taylor told Ferrier during cross-examination that he never once considered killing Billy Stafford.

After Taylor, two women who worked with Jane at Hillsview Acres testified that Jane wasn't herself and had lost considerable weight in the months prior to Billy Stafford's death. Both remembered seeing Beverly Taylor visit Jane at work.

Allaby next called Ronald Wamboldt, who was an ineffective witness for the Crown. An admitted alcoholic, Wamboldt remembered nothing of the events of the day of the shooting beyond mid-afternoon. The last thing he remembered was driving toward the Bangs Falls house in Billy's truck. If it was the Crown's intention to show benevolence on Billy's part in that he had invited Wamboldt to come and live in his house, the strategy backfired. Wamboldt said he accepted Billy's invitation to live at the house because he had no other place to go. He admitted under Ferrier's cross-examination that Billy often slapped and punched him and ordered him to do odd jobs around the house and in the yard and woods.

Wamboldt's testimony gave the jury its first glimpse into how Billy Stafford ran the lives of the people around him. Wamboldt told Ferrier that Billy often pointed loaded guns at him.

FERRIER: And did you ever give him good reason to point a gun at you?

WAMBOLDT: Never.

FERRIER: Because you wouldn't have said boo to him?

WAMBOLDT: No.

FERRIER: Has he fired shots at you?

WAMBOLDT: Not right at me, no. You see, if he did he'd never miss me because he was a good shot.

FERRIER: So he knew how to tantalize you and scare you?

WAMBOLDT: Right.

Wamboldt also testified that Billy used his fists on him long before he moved into the Stafford home.

FERRIER: For a man that was your friend, he never really called you Ronny very much, did he?

WAMBOLDT: Not too often.

FERRIER: He called you dummy?

WAMBOLDT: Dummy.

FERRIER: So you were aware of his behaviour towards you but you went to live with him anyway?

WAMBOLDT: Yeah—stupidity.

FERRIER: If he told you to do a job around the house, you did it?

WAMBOLDT: Right.

FERRIER: What would likely happen if you didn't do it?

WAMBOLDT: I'd get another smash.

Wamboldt testified that Billy Stafford was particularly cruel to four-year-old Darren, punching or hitting him "at least five times a day," sometimes with his fist. Asked how hard Billy hit his son, Wamboldt replied: "Well you could hear it...it wouldn't knock him out, but you could hear it."

Wamboldt said Darren was a nervous child and "very afraid" of Billy Stafford. He said Billy often cuffed the boy at the dinner table, and that he witnessed Billy force-feeding him several times.

FERRIER: To the point where he threw up?

WAMBOLDT: Right.

FERRIER: Into the bowl that he was eating out of?

WAMBOLDT: Yes.

FERRIER: And then be made to eat that thrown-up food again?

WAMBOLDT: Yes, he did.

During cross-examination, Wamboldt also told Ferrier about the punishment Jane took from Billy, even while playing cards.

FERRIER: And Billy wouldn't like the card that she played?

WAMBOLDT: Oh, yes, that's right.

FERRIER: And he'd cuff her?

WAMBOLDT: Right.

FERRIER: Punch her? With the back of his hand, is that what you're indicating?

WAMBOLDT: Like that, yes.

FERRIER: Knock her right off her chair?

WAMBOLDT: Right.

FERRIER: What happened to her? Did she get back up and keep playing cards?

WAMBOLDT: Yes.

FERRIER: Did she complain?

WAMBOLDT: No.

FERRIER: What would happen if she complained?

WAMBOLDT: She'd get it again. I imagine.

At the preliminary inquiry in June, Ronald Wamboldt had

testified that Billy Stafford often argued with his neighbour Margaret Joudrey and that he had threatened, the day before he died, that "if she didn't straighten her ways up and mind her own business, that he'd take and burn her out...or blow her friggin' head off." But at Jane's trial five months later, Wamboldt couldn't remember making the statement. Under questioning by Ferrier, he said he had managed to quit drinking from shortly after Billy's death until he testified at the preliminary inquiry.

FERRIER: Would you say to this court that your ability to recall events on June 4th would have been better than it is today?

WAMBOLDT: Yes, quite a bit better.

FERRIER: Partly because it was closer to the events?

WAMBOLDT: Partly, yes.

FERRIER: And partly because you had stopped drinking?

WAMBOLDT: Yes.

FERRIER: Do you often get blackout spells when you're drinking?

WAMBOLDT: Yeah, I pass right out, yeah, quite often.

He said he had been drinking quite heavily since the preliminary inquiry and was now living alone in the woods.

Crown witness Timothy Anthony, an eighteen-year-old who'd known Billy for ten years, testified that on the evening of March 11, Billy, Jane, and Ronny Wamboldt arrived at Timothy's mother's house on River Road. He said Billy brought a case of beer with him and they sat around drinking and talking about animals. Billy also produced a marijuana joint, which was passed around. Anthony said he liked Billy, who gave him money and drugs from time to time and sometimes hunted with him. As far back as he could remember, Billy always had drugs with him, he said.

Allaby's final witness for the day was Jane's son, Allen. He recounted the day of the killing and how he brought the shotgun out to his mother and later broke it down with Roger Manthorne and threw it in the Medway River. Allaby asked him if he realized what had happened after hearing the shot and coming back out of the house.

ALLEN: I didn't know exactly what happened, but I mean, I was sixteen, I had a good idea what happened.

ALLABY: Could you see the truck or see into the cab of the truck?

ALLEN: I imagine I didn't. You wouldn't have paid me enough to look in the truck.

Allaby asked him if his mother ever discussed the problems she was having with Billy. Allen remembered one conversation about a month before Billy's death. "One night, Bill and Ronny was to town and I was sitting watching TV and Ma was taking the curlers out of her hair or something. And I looked at her for about fifteen minutes and just kind of thought about her and I said, 'Ma, you don't look good.' She said, 'I just can't live this way no more, it's getting to me.'" Allen said that he and his mother never talked about his taking the blame for shooting Billy.

ALLABY: Why did you do that?

ALLEN: I don't know. I figured that's what Ma wanted.

ALLABY: Had you discussed with her that you were going to do this?

ALLEN: No. The Mounties just come down when I was down to my grandfather's and said, "You're under arrest for first-degree murder." I said, "All right."

ALLABY: So what did you tell them about your involvement at that point?

ALLEN: I just said I went in and got the gun, Ma told me to get the gun, and I went in and got it, and I come out and Ma told me to shoot him and I shot him.

ALLABY: But you hadn't discussed doing this with your mother at all?

ALLEN: No.

Under cross-examination, Allen told the court about Billy's abusive treatment of him, Wamboldt, Jane, and Darren. Allen said Billy didn't allow him to go down to Margaret Joudrey's trailer. "Sometimes I'd go down anyways, when Bill wasn't home, and have a game of cards with Margaret and Roger. She always had a gun laying on the table with a shell laying on the bed...I asked her what she had it there for and she said, 'If that fool ever comes down here causing trouble, he won't be walking back.' I didn't say no more."

The trial was recessed for the weekend. Roger Manthorne was the first witness called when it resumed the following Monday morning. He told how he helped Allen break down the gun and dispose of it in the river, and added that he and Margaret went up to the Stafford house to comfort Jane when she returned home. He said that he didn't realize at the time that he was covering up evidence when he helped destroy the gun (which had blood on the barrel), and that he didn't say anything to the police until two weeks later because no one asked him. Manthorne, who had a heart condition, said he was afraid of Billy. During cross-examination by Ferrier, he said he had witnessed Billy arguing with Margaret Joudrey.

FERRIER: Now those arguments were over the property?

MANTHORNE: Yes.

FERRIER: And you heard Mr. Stafford get into an argument with her, not very long before he died, about the property?

MANTHORNE: Yes.

FERRIER: Wherein Mr. Stafford said at one point, "You old lady, I'd like to burn you out"?

MANTHORNE: Yes, sir, he said that, yeah.

During re-examination, Allaby asked Manthorne if Margaret Joudrey was upset by Billy's threats. "Yes, sir, she was," he replied. All of that was crucial evidence for the defence, because the prosecution's next witness was Margaret Joudrey, and she had turned hostile toward Jane Stafford from the moment she was ordered to give evidence at the June preliminary inquiry. It was a shock for Jane to see the woman "who'd been my friend and mother for six years, get on that stand and turn against me. I just hurt so bad inside." She listened as Margaret Joudrey told the court that Jane had been like a daughter to her and that she got along well with her and Billy. She admitted having arguments with Billy but passed them off as "just foolishness."

ALLABY: Now do you recall shortly before he died there was an argument that you had with him?

JOUDREY: Oh, yeah, we had a little argument.

ALLABY: What was that about?

JOUDREY: Not much. Well, he was going to put pigs up there, a pig yard, and I didn't want the pigs up there.

ALLABY: And why didn't you want them there?

JOUDREY: Because they stink.

ALLABY: And what about the title of property lines? Was there an argument with him over that?

JOUDREY: Well, sometimes he used to go over the line and I used to go up. He made a big cement thing to put a tree or something in and I said well if anything happened and somebody else got the land, you know, he couldn't put it there.

ALLABY: So where did he put this with respect to his own land?

JOUDREY: Still put it there.

ALLABY: But you felt it wasn't on his land?

JOUDREY: It wasn't on his land. It was down below the mark.

Margaret Joudrey painted Billy Stafford as an overgrown loudmouth whom she liked to argue with and had no fear of. She said Billy sometimes gave Darren a slap on the buttocks but "I never seen a mark on Darren from Bill." When Joudrey said she once saw Jane beat Darren with a broomstick after he had run away, Jane was stunned. Images of Billy Stafford breaking a mop handle in two and beating Darren until he was covered with welts filled her mind. That was the day Billy shot at her while she was out in the yard, ordered her to come in and clean up the mess, and punched her when she began to cry after seeing Darren lying in his own blood and feces. After that, they had picked up Margaret Joudrey and had gone for a ride as if nothing had happened. Now, in the courtroom, she stared in disbelief at her neighbour, who said she couldn't remember all the details but "she took that stick and she laid it on his little bum and I was afraid. And he had black and blue spots for quite a while afterwards. But I've never seen none from Bill."

ALLABY: What about Jane? Have you ever seen her with any black and blue spots?

JOUDREY: No, only her eyes, and that's natural because I think that's the way she is.

ALLABY: Did she ever complain to you about any treatment from Bill?

JOUDREY: Oh, yes, she complained but I didn't pay any attention to her. I heard so many lies that...

ALLABY: What type of thing would she complain about?

JOUDREY: Oh, Bill done this and Bill done that.

ALLABY: What do you mean by this and that?

JOUDREY: I didn't pay any attention to her.

Jane said she had never touched Darren with anything other than her hand, and that the only time she spanked him in front of Margaret Joudrey was when, at age two or three, she found him down by the river. "He'd run off and taken all his clothes off. I was scared he could have drowned. I put him over my knee and spanked him. That was it. I'd never hurt my child."

Under cross-examination by Ferrier, Margaret Joudrey became belligerent and several times had to be ordered by Justice Burchell to answer Ferrier's questions.

FERRIER: The biggest problem you had at your place was the fact that Mr. Stafford always objected to your ownership of the property?

JOUDREY: Well, I don't know what that's got to do with this. I ain't going to answer that.

FERRIER: Mrs. Joudrey, you'll answer that question.

BURCHELL: Yes, you have to answer any questions that are put to you, Mrs. Joudrey.

FERRIER: The biggest problems between you and Mr. Stafford were that he told you you didn't own the property you were living on?

JOUDREY: No, not necessarily.

FERRIER: That's what he told you, Mrs. Joudrey. Isn't it?

JOUDREY: Oh, yes, but what in the heck is that?

FERRIER: And is it not true that the man that owned that property was Stanley Joudrey?

JOUDREY: That's right.

FERRIER: The man you lived common-law with?

JOUDREY: That I ain't going to answer. I don't have to.

FERRIER: My Lordship?

BURCHELL: Yes, you have to answer that, Mrs. Joudrey.

JOUDREY: Okay, yes.

FERRIER: Stanley died without a will, isn't that correct?

JOUDREY: That's right.

FERRIER: So in fact you do not own, legally, that property? You do not have legal title...

JOUDREY: I own it. Sure I own it.

FERRIER: You do not have a legal paper to that title?

JOUDREY: That's right.

FERRIER: And that's what Mr. Stafford used to rub in your face all the time.

JOUDREY: No, he didn't...

Joudrey said she didn't think details of her common-law marriage or the property where she lived were any of Ferrier's business. Justice Burchell immediately rebuked her. "Well, it's the business of this court and the business of the jury, Mrs. Joudrey. It's not for you to say."

Contrary to Roger Manthorne's testimony, Margaret Joudrey said she wasn't crying when she hugged and comforted Jane Stafford the night Billy was shot.

FERRIER: So if Roger Manthorne said you were crying, he'd be lying?

JOUDREY: Well, I don't know why he'd say I was crying, because I wasn't crying.

She also disputed Manthorne's testimony that she was upset by Billy Stafford's threat to burn her out. "So if Roger Manthorne told this court that you were upset by the remarks that Billy Stafford made to you, he'd be lying about that, too?" asked Ferrier.

JOUDREY: No, I don't think he'd be lying too much about that because Roger doesn't know too much.

FERRIER: Roger lives there?

JOUDREY: Sure he stays there.

FERRIER: He's got two eyes in his head?

JOUDREY: I know he's got two eyes. He'd be a funny-looking thing if he didn't.

FERRIER: He can see what's going on, can't he, Margaret?

JOUDREY: Roger don't pay any attention to what's going on.

Ferrier asked Joudrey why "you say all these wrong things about Jane and nothing about Billy." She said her feelings toward Jane "ain't the same as what it used to be." She said her feelings changed after she had to testify at the preliminary inquiry.

FERRIER: Things have changed now, haven't they?

JOUDREY: That's correct, because she got me mixed up in this and there's no need of it.

FERRIER: How did she get you mixed up in it?

JOUDREY: Well, she's got me here, ain't she?

FERRIER: Now what you're telling this court is that now, today, you don't feel anything for that woman?

JOUDREY: That's right.

FERRIER: But on the night that Billy Stafford was shot, Mrs. Joudrey, that woman was still your daughter, like a daughter to you?

JOUDREY: Well, yeah, I still liked her.

She told Ferrier she was mad at Jane "because I'm at an age now where I shouldn't be mixed up in anything. I've never been in the law before." She said she hadn't talked to Jane after the June 4 preliminary. "I never had no more to do with her after that because I don't want to get in no more trouble. I'm in thick enough now."

Joudrey insisted that she and Billy Stafford were great friends who had occasional arguments. "We played cards," she said, "and I learned him to play Yammy and we played that. Then they say Bill and I didn't get along. Well, heck, we was together mostly all the time, he was down home or I was up there."

FERRIER: So why would he do these things to your property? Why would he deliberately put something on your side of the property?

JOUDREY: Well, she knew the line as well as he did.

FERRIER: But Billy put it there. Billy was the head of the household, right?

JOUDREY: I suppose so. In fact, I'd say so.

FERRIER: And your idea is that when there's a man, he should be the head of the household?

JOUDREY: That's right.

FERRIER: And Billy made the decision to put something on your property line—and did it?

JOUDREY: That's right. He wasn't hurting nothing.

Joudrey told Ferrier that Jane once told her she hated Billy. Under re-examination, Blaine Allaby asked her when Jane made that statement. "Oh, Lord. I don't know. I'm a woman, I don't keep run of the time, and I don't keep run of the days, and I don't keep run of the months."

ALLABY: Would it be weeks, months, or years?

JOUDREY: Oh, it wasn't years, maybe months.

On the afternoon of Monday, November 8, Jane Stafford's mother and father were called to testify. Like other Crown witnesses, they had been banned from attending the trial until it was their turn to testify.

Maurice Hurshman said his daughter seemed to be in shock when he picked her up near the satellite station on the night of the shooting and brought her to their trailer home in Danesville to clean up. He said she wouldn't tell him what was wrong and that he didn't learn about Billy's death until the next day. Hurshman told Ferrier during cross-examination that he hadn't seen much of Jane after she left home in Winnipeg as a teenager.

FERRIER: Is it fair to say that your relationship with your daughter was not all that close?

HURSHMAN: That's right, yeah... We never got to see each other that much, only if she'd phone sometimes and see how things were.

Both Maurice and Gladys said they had no idea how serious Jane's situation with Billy Stafford was. Both said they were frightened of Billy after he attacked Maurice Hurshman and damaged their home. Gladys Hurshman said Billy "jumped up and plowed him one in the face and knocked him back against the window and broke the window out and kicked the door in and hauled it off the hinges, and then Jane stepped in and he doubled up his fists and plowed her back against the wall." She said they didn't see much of Jane after that incident. She denied that she had any problems early in her own marriage.

Following Gladys Hurshman to the stand was Constable Robert Hillier, the first of seventeen police and medical witnesses to be called by the Crown. Hillier, from the RCMP Liverpool detachment, was in charge of exhibits during the investigation into Billy Stafford's death. His duties included accompanying the body from the scene of the shooting to Queens General Hospital, where at 3:15 on the afternoon of March 12, 1982, he placed it in a cooler in the basement. He secured the hinged door of the cooler with two padlocks until the following morning, when he transferred the body to the morgue at Victoria General Hospital for an autopsy. Hillier also helped gather exhibits from the Stafford residence. He was there with several other officers the night Jane was taken into custody for questioning the first time. "When Mrs. Stafford was leaving the living room, walking through the kitchen, her younger son was seated at the table and she walked over to him and picked him up and gave him a hug before she left."

Corporal Philip Campbell, a forensic firearms examiner with the RCMP Crime Detection Laboratory in Halifax, presented considerable technical evidence about the workings of the type of gun that killed Billy Stafford. He concluded that the Coey model 840 twelve-gauge, manufactured in Cobourg, Ontario, had been held at a range of less than six inches "and it could have been contact." He added that the slug would have had a velocity of sixteen hundred feet per second as it left the muzzle of the gun. "And if one has a contained vessel such as the skull, it would cause the skull to explode. The flesh around the wound would be burned. The flesh in that area would exhibit what's called a monoxide pink appearance. The oxygen is taken out of the blood and the tissue, in the combustion of the powder, and forms monoxide colour, a very characteristic colour."

Corporal Ron Pond, one of the two RCMP officers who interrogated Jane through the night of March 14, said she was picked up around midnight because "things started to come together throughout that day and up until an hour or so before midnight. We sat down and went over what we had, and with my experience with anything serious, it's best to keep going when you are hot on the trail. Things were on a roll, so we thought we better keep pushing at it trying to get to the bottom, or to the truth."

When the trial resumed on the morning of November 10, a Wednesday, Alan Ferrier asked to speak to Mr. Justice Burchell before the jury was brought in. He was upset by reports in the local media. Ferrier said he didn't want to overreact, but there were a number of inaccuracies in the reporting. He was particularly concerned about a report on the local radio station, CKBW, and in the *Halifax Chronicle-Herald*, that linked the evidence of the bruise on Jane Stafford's left arm to the effects of the recoil of a shotgun. Justice Burchell agreed with Ferrier that there had been "no connection in the evidence. When I read it I twitched, reacting the same way you are to it." Ferrier asked the judge to caution the press, but warned he would seek a publication ban if that type of reporting continued. "I accept his comments as being significant," said Burchell, "and I think the caution he has requested should be given by me at this time, and I do so."

Jane Stafford, who was wearing blue slacks, a sweater, and a light-brown jacket, looked up as the jury filed into the courtroom to listen to its fourth full day of testimony. The first witness was Constable Blair McKnight, one of her interrogators in the early morning hours of March 14. He was followed by Staff Sergeant Peter Williamson, who read the statement given to him by Jane on March 25 when she said her son shot Billy. During cross-examination, Williamson outlined his dealings with Billy Stafford over the years:

WILLIAMSON: He was a violent man.

FERRIER: And were other members of your detachment advised to deal with him carefully?

WILLIAMSON: Yes, I left instructions that if we were ever to respond to a complaint at Billy Stafford's that they were to go armed.

FERRIER: And were you aware that he had some propensity towards guns himself?

WILLIAMSON: Yes, he had made threats against several of my members.

FERRIER: And when did he do that?

WILLIAMSON: Over the ensuing years, depending on which member had come in contact with him.

FERRIER: What was his general attitude towards the police?

WILLIAMSON: He hated us.

FERRIER: Were you aware of any specific prosecutions against him?

WILLIAMSON: I remember he was charged with mutiny in Lunenburg. I know he'd been charged with several charges under the Lands and Forests Act for jacking deer. We investigated him on a number of occasions for intimidation of his neighbours out in that area. We suspected that he was dealing with drugs, that he was using drugs, and that he was pushing drugs. Over the years we keep track of all the complaints that come in on an individual, and I would say that the average person would probably have three or four entries on a card, and that's over a period of maybe twenty years. He had three full cards.

Ferrier asked Williamson if he was sympathetic to Mrs. Stafford.

WILLIAMSON: I made some comments that I sympathized with the way she was living.

FERRIER: And you had become aware of alleged abuse?

WILLIAMSON: Oh, I was aware of it.

FERRIER: And did you not in fact say to her that she deserved a medal?

WILLIAMSON: No, I didn't say that to her because that would be condoning the action that she took. But I made that statement to other policemen.

FERRIER: And you're sure, absolutely sure, that she may not have heard that comment?

WILLIAMSON: She may have heard it, but it wasn't directed at her.

FERRIER: All right. Now at that particular point did you also say she probably saved at least a couple of police officers' lives?

WILLIAMSON: Yes. That man had threatened many of our members, and from our investigation we went into the house and checked his guns and each one of the guns were loaded and hanging on the wall.

FERRIER: And you didn't believe at that point that your feelings about Mrs. Stafford were unfounded?

WILLIAMSON: No, they were really founded.

FERRIER: And you weren't really surprised to hear all of the personal abuse that Mrs. Stafford had undergone?

WILLIAMSON: No, not in the least.

FERRIER: I realize, and I'm not suggesting to you that you condoned it, that you condoned anything, but you did have a considerable amount of sympathy for Mrs. Stafford at that point?

WILLIAMSON: I did.

The Crown's final witness was Corporal Howard Pike. He identified the barrel of the shotgun used to shoot Billy Stafford. It had been retrieved from the Medway River on June 3, the day before the preliminary inquiry. Divers had been unable to retrieve it before that. "At the time in March the river itself was quite high from the spring flooding and the current was too strong for the divers to stay in the fast current. We had to wait until the water level went down in the river." Pike described his dealings with Jane Stafford from the time he and Archie Mason informed her of Billy's death to his taking of her signed statement after meeting Sergeant Michael Innes for the polygraph test. Pike read the statement to the court.

At the end of the morning session on Wednesday, November 10, the Crown rested its case. The trial was adjourned to 2 p.m. the following Tuesday.

CHAPTER 12
DEFENCE

When the trial resumed, Alan Ferrier briefly addressed the jury and then called Gladys Hurshman as his first witness. Jurors and spectators were surprised to see her take the stand, since she had already testified.

FERRIER: You've given evidence previously in respect to this matter?

HURSHMAN: Yes.

FERRIER: And at that point in time in the trial you gave evidence with respect to questions by me regarding your relationship with your husband?

HURSHMAN: Yes.

FERRIER: In respect to that, can you now tell the court whether or not there was a period of time in your marriage that was tumultuous?

HURSHMAN: Yes... when Jane was growing up we were in New Brunswick, like we moved around a lot... Winnipeg and Germany.

FERRIER: And can you tell the court what kind of problems you had in your marriage at that point in time?

HURSHMAN: There was a lot of drinking problems and fighting and things like that.

FERRIER: And how severe was the drinking problem at that point in time?

HURSHMAN: Quite a bit. Quite a lot.

FERRIER: And who had the problem?

HURSHMAN: My husband.

FERRIER: And how did he treat you during these times of heavy drinking?

HURSHMAN: There was some rough times, fights... well, just more or less slapped around.

FERRIER: Now can you tell the court whether or not this would take place in front of the children?

HURSHMAN: Yes, oh, yes.

FERRIER: And do you recall specifically how Jane would react to those incidents?

HURSHMAN: Well, sometimes if it got too bad she'd take the two smaller ones out, out in the room or somewhere around.

FERRIER: Why did you not indicate to the court that there was these problems between you and your husband when you were on the stand previously?

HURSHMAN: Well, I didn't want to cause any trouble between my husband and myself. I mean, he's not... he don't drink now.

FERRIER: And how would you characterize your relationship now with your husband?

HURSHMAN: Good.

Under cross-examination by Blaine Allaby, Gladys Hurshman insisted that the reason she didn't admit to marital problems in her previous testimony was to protect her marriage. "I didn't want to cause any trouble between my husband and me."

ALLABY: What made you change your mind?

HURSHMAN: I just figured I might as well tell.
ALLABY: Did anybody tell you you should tell?
HURSHMAN: No.
ALLABY: Did you feel it might help Jane's position if you...
HURSHMAN: ...Yes.
ALLABY: So that was the main reason you've changed your story? Because you feel it will help Jane?
HURSHMAN: Yes.

The courtroom went very quiet when Alan Ferrier called his next witness: the accused, Jane Marie Stafford. She had dreaded this moment for weeks. The fear intensified after the trial began. Although she was closer to her parents than ever before, and her sisters Sandy and Mona were in town to provide moral support, Jane often felt alone and depressed. "I couldn't think, and my sanity was wearing very thin. I just drifted from day to day waiting and wondering when it would all end. There were times I was so frightened I didn't think I'd make it through the coming day."

To help make it through the trial, Jane kept to a structured routine. Allen and Darren were living with her at home, and in the mornings she was up early to make their breakfast. Allen caught his bus by 8 a.m. Jane took Darren the short distance to Marie and Morton Joudrey's at 8:30, on her way to the courthouse. After school, Darren stayed with the Joudreys until Allen or Jane arrived home.

"When we were all home," recalled Jane, "I'd make supper and the three of us would discuss our day. All I would say about court was whether I thought it was a good or bad day. In the evening I bathed Darren and let him play or watch TV until 7:30 p.m. When he was in bed I did my daily household chores. I don't care much for television, so I read a lot and listened to music when the house was quiet in the late evenings. Sometimes Mom and Dad or my sisters would visit for a while. On Saturdays and Sundays or other days when there was no court I would drive to the beach alone and walk for hours. Sometimes I went to Mom and Dad's for supper and then I'd go home to my music and my quiet."

While her life was being dissected in front of the media and the public, she received encouragement from friends and strangers, who packed the courtroom each day. She said they helped her hold herself together. During the morning and afternoon recesses she drank coffee and smoked cigarettes in a back room, often in the company of Alan Ferrier. She ate lunch with her friend Andrea Wamboldt or at Gramma Mill's house. Always in the back of her mind was the knowledge that it would soon be her turn to take the witness stand. As the day approached she began having nightmares. She lost more weight, and her pale-blue eyes were ringed with dark circles. "I was terrified. I had two main fears—that they would show me pictures of Bill's body. That was the main fear. I didn't know until I read it in the newspaper, after my preliminary, that he was decapitated. I never knew where I shot him and I never asked. The other fear was that I would get a mental block and just sit there and forget everything I had to say. I wasn't really frightened by all the people in the courtroom. They helped me get through each day."

Alan Ferrier did his best to ease Jane's fear about taking the witness stand. "You've got to pretend the only people in the courtroom are you, me, and the prosecutor," he told her over coffee. "Just tune everyone else right out."

Jane was a religious person, and she believed it helped her. "I know I had God inside me. Only people who have felt His presence can understand what I mean by that. I can't express it in words, I just know that He was constantly with me."

Jane approached the witness stand with her head bowed. She appeared frail and vulnerable. Even with the hush in the courtroom she could barely be heard as she spoke in a sometimes inaudible monotone. Several times during her testimony, Justice Burchell asked her to speak up. Slowly, Ferrier guided her through her early years and her first marriage. Jane characterized those years as rough ones.

"Dad drank a lot," she said. "Most of the time he was drunk. He went to work that way and came home that way... fighting... hollering." Her first husband drank a lot but wasn't violent. "He lost his work and everything through drinking. The last three or four years I was with him he didn't work." Jurors and spectators craned to hear her words when Jane related the horrors of her life with Billy Stafford.

FERRIER: What did you do about these assaults, anything?

JANE: No, I didn't. I just carried on about my business. He would tell me it was my fault, anyway. Whenever I did get a beating he would always tell me it was my fault. I was the one who started it—you hear it so much, after a while you begin to believe it.

For more than two full hours Jane recounted the physical and mental abuse that Billy inflicted on her and other members of the Stafford household. The jury also heard how Jane was sexually abused and forced into bestiality and how, when she dared complain, Billy beat her and on one occasion forced her to drink a glass of his urine. Jane told about her unsuccessful attempt to hire Beverly Taylor to kill Billy Stafford.

FERRIER: At that point in time, Mrs. Stafford, can you tell the court whether or not you wanted Mr. Stafford dead?

JANE: Yes, I wanted him dead. I hated him. He was a maniac.

FERRIER: Why didn't you leave him?

JANE: There was no leaving him in my mind. I told him once

before that I was going to leave him and he said he was never going to be a third-time loser.

Jane testified about Billy's threats to kill her parents and her sisters, one at a time, until she returned. "So there was no way, no way." She was still on the stand at 4:45 p.m., when the court adjourned for the day. Justice Burchell instructed her not to discuss the case with anyone until court resumed in the morning at 9:30. That instruction would seem reasonable and logical to any observer, but for Jane it was devastating. "I had to leave the courtroom without seeing Alan Ferrier before I left. I was not allowed to talk to anyone because I was still under oath. I still don't understand that. I felt awful—deserted. I had to go home and think all night about having to come back in the morning and take that stand again. My nerves were like live wires. When I arrived the next morning, it was as if Alan was reading my thoughts. He looked around and for a brief moment we made eye contact. He smiled to reassure me and I knew by his eyes he was saying, 'You can do it, Jane, I know you can.' I was on the stand another two-and-a-half hours."

Jane testified that Billy's treatment of her and others got worse as time went on, and that the worst time of the day was suppertime. "It was just an ordeal to have supper."

FERRIER: Who prepared supper?

JANE: I did, when I came home from work.

FERRIER: Now during this time what would Mr. Stafford be doing when you came home from work? What would he be up to?

JANE: I'd say three-quarters of the time he was drunk or smoked up, sitting around hooting and hollering. He was usually hollering before I got in the door. Just anything that came into his head. He was always ranting and raving. Always had money to drive around, go places, do things.

FERRIER: Whose money was he using during this time period?

JANE: Oh, whenever I had any left he would take that, but that wasn't usually very much.

FERRIER: So where did he usually get his money?

JANE: Selling dope.

FERRIER: Are you personally aware of that?

JANE: Yes, I know that.

Ferrier asked Jane what kind of a relationship she had with Margaret Joudrey.

JANE: A very good one. She knew everything that was going on for the last five years that I lived there. She was the same as a mother to me.

FERRIER: And what kind of things would you confide in her?

JANE: Everything. She was the only one that I had any contact with. We lived out there, and except for Margaret and where I took Darren to the babysitters, I never visited anybody's house.

FERRIER: When you did have contact with people, was it alone or with Mr. Stafford?

JANE: He was generally with me. One day a week I would get to come to town, to do errands, to pick up groceries and such, go out and visit his mother and father. Had a certain time to do everything and had to be home by a certain time.

FERRIER: And going back to Mrs. Joudrey, how did she appear to you to be reacting to Mr. Stafford's accusations about the land?

JANE: She was as scared of Bill as everybody else out around there. She probably hated him more than I did.

FERRIER: You've heard her give evidence in this matter?

JANE: Yes, I have.

FERRIER: What do you think of the position that she's taken now?

JANE: Well, until we had the preliminary I didn't know that she'd be like that. She was the last person I ever expected to go like that.

FERRIER: Why do you think she's not supportive of you now?

JANE: Oh, she figures I can get her in some kind of trouble or take her land. I don't really know what reason she's thinking. I don't know.

Ferrier asked Jane to compare the relationship she had with Mrs. Joudrey to the relationship she had with her own parents. Jane said her relationship with Margaret Joudrey was much closer. "I didn't have much contact with Mom and Dad. Margaret was about the only one around that I talked to. At that time she was closer than my own mother."

Jane testified that on the night she shot Billy he was hollering and very angry on the way to visit Leona Anthony's. She said he called Margaret Joudrey an old bag, and added that she was worried that last night. "He said her light was on all night. He said she won't have to worry about seeing the light shine down there no more after tonight. He said he was going to burn her out. And he kept this up pretty well the whole way." Jane said that after leaving the Anthony house, "he started right in on the way back. He told me about the Mounties being out to visit Allen. He said when he got done with Margaret he would deal with him, too, might as well clean everything up in one night."

Ferrier asked Jane about the statement she made to Sergeant Williamson, claiming that her son had shot Billy Stafford. "Why did you lie at that point, obviously to me and to Sergeant Williamson?"

JANE: The RCMP and all the people seemed good and sympathetic and they talked like they understood, but I was still charged with first-degree murder. And I didn't really think anybody would believe just how we lived in that house. How bad it really was. I was still at that point taking the tranquillizers or nerve pills. I wasn't even thinking... when I come in and told all of this, I didn't even think to tell Allen the story I was going to tell. I didn't even know I was going to tell it at that point. I didn't want to go to jail. I didn't want to be away from Darren.

FERRIER: Now what made you think that Allen was going to give the same story as that?

JANE: I don't know. I didn't even consider that fact.

Under cross-examination, Jane admitted to Allaby that besides attempting to hire Beverly Taylor to kill Billy and twice considering shooting him herself, she once asked Billy's eldest daughter, Sharon, from his first marriage, to help her kill him. Sharon Stafford had moved to Nova Scotia from Ontario to live for a time.

ALLABY: Do you remember talking to Sharon Stafford about getting some chemical?

JANE: Yes.

ALLABY: What was that about?

JANE: I asked her to get me some dope or something.

ALLABY: What for?

JANE: That would kill a person.

ALLABY: And why did you want it?

JANE: Well, I figured I could give it to Bill.

ALLABY: How many times did you mention it to Sharon?

JANE: I think I asked her on a couple of occasions.

ALLABY: What did you tell her you wanted it for?

JANE: She knew what I wanted it for. I told her—for her father.

Jane testified that she wasn't aware that a shelter for battered wives existed in Halifax.

ALLABY: You never inquired about any way the situation could be relieved other than by killing Billy?

JANE: If I'd have left there would have been a lot more people killed than Bill.

ALLABY: That was your feeling?

JANE: That I knew.

Alan Ferrier, during re-examination, asked Jane "whether or not on the 11th of March of 1982 that you had any thoughts of killing Mr. Stafford prior to the time that you were in the truck?"

JANE: No, I didn't. I didn't think I had guts enough to do it.

Ferrier also asked Jane if Billy ever told her anything about killing anybody. "Yes, he did. He told me he couldn't fish out of Liverpool. That's when he went to Lunenburg. When the boat went out, the *Enterprise*, the crew was aboard, and he said how Jimmy LeBlanc and him had argued. He said Jimmy went into the galley to make a mug up, and he said, shortly after, he went in behind him and he threw him overboard. And nobody on that boat would talk either. It was the same as the mutiny, nobody would talk. They knew he done it."

Jane's body sagged with relief when Justice Burchell thanked her and told her to step down from the witness stand. "I was finally finished but I was drained." Her greatest fear, throughout Allaby's cross-examination, had proved unfounded. "It never left my mind—at what minute are they going to make me look at those pictures." As for Allaby's questions, Ferrier had prepared her well. "He told me to take my time and think of my answers before I spoke. Sometimes I thought so long, I couldn't remember the question. He also told me if I couldn't remember an answer or didn't know it, to tell them so. I tried so very hard to do everything right. I know the judge and the Crown kept telling me to speak up, over and over again. But to me it seemed like everything I said had an echo. I could hear myself well. The questions seemed to be nonstop. They just kept coming at me. Sometimes I never had time to finish one before they asked me another."

Ferrier next called three experts to the stand to talk about her mental condition. The first was Dr. Rosemary Sampson, a clinical psychologist from Halifax, who had interviewed and tested Jane six weeks before the trial. She had tested her for verbal, general, and performance IQ and found all three scores "within the normal range of intelligence. Considering her educational level, her occupational status, the time that she has been away from school, she answered and dealt with the test quite well." Dr. Sampson said she found Jane to be extremely depressed, "with many defences. In other words, she has ways of keeping herself pretty well encased as it were." She also saw herself as a victim and had "an extremely low self-concept. She's an extremely anxious person, very guilt-ridden. I think she's an emotionally immature woman whose life history reflects poor interpersonal, particularly heterosexual, relationships. She presents a pattern of anger which has continually been internalized, which eats away at the person. I think that type of a person would very often think of suicide, but she had a moral strength in her that would not act upon that, unless really pushed to the extreme."

As Jane was subjected to increasing stress, said Dr. Sampson, "her ability to deal with situations lessens, but I would surmise that her planning ability, even in the best of times, is problematic... she would maybe start out thinking on something and then not really see what the end point was going to be." Dr. Sampson told the court that when she presented Jane with material she could identify with, "the stress made her thinking, her way of acting, more fuzzy—more illogical."

Under cross-examination, Dr. Sampson told Allaby she thought Jane was aware of what she was doing when she pulled the trigger and killed Billy Stafford. Allaby also questioned Jane's motives in implicating her son Allen in her second statement to the RCMP.

ALLABY: Does it surprise you that she would try to indicate that her son was responsible for what she had in fact done?

SAMPSON: I think it's pretty much in keeping with the extreme stress that she was under, and afterwards the extreme shock...

ALLABY: ...But is there not a protective maternal instinct that would say to her, "No, you don't do this, you don't blame it on your son, your child"?

SAMPSON: Her confusion was to the point where she was amnesiac, she doesn't remember certain things. She was sort of at the ultimate of her stress level and her thinking became more confused, more fuzzy, and she wasn't thinking properly.

ALLABY: Is what she did consistent with her personality, killing Billy Stafford?

SAMPSON: I don't believe so.

ALLABY: Once he was dead, and she realized he was dead, would there be a reaction, perhaps relief, almost an elation?

SAMPSON: I wouldn't predict that to be so. I think she would just be so disbelieving of what was going on, and I think her confusion level would be even increased.

Dr. Carol Abbott, a Halifax medical doctor specializing in psychiatry, testified that she had assessed Jane after three meetings with her in May and June. She said Jane appeared to be older than her stated age and "she was extremely nervous and tense. I described her affect as being flat rather than depressed, though I think one could call it depressed as well... The situation that she'd been in for the last five years of her marriage had been one of overwhelming stress, both physical and mental... I think it affected her in terms of her passivity, which we see to the alleged abuse... She could never predict when he was going to react the way he was, and I think it's this unpredictability that made it difficult for her to feel that she could do anything to control the situation."

Dr. Abbott said Jane told her she initially trusted Billy Stafford, "and I don't think she looked beyond that... I think outwardly she was compliant. I think outwardly she went along with him, and I don't think that she felt at any time that she could express any of her feelings towards him because of the risk of provoking him, and I think this was constantly there. Even when he was away I think that she felt it even then—there was the fear that it would get back to him. So that although she suppressed or repressed or denied her feelings, these were the defence mechanisms with which she dealt with the stress at that time."

FERRIER: Can you tell us whether or not she has any aggressive tendencies in her personality?

ABBOTT: I can't think of any that come to mind. I think that there is no history, to my knowledge, of violent behaviour in her personality... in fact it was the opposite, her behaviour was far more likely to be compliant and passive.

FERRIER: How did you assess her ability to put thoughts together in a structured way?

ABBOTT: That's a difficult question to answer. I think that she can put thoughts together. I think she reacts to situations as they come up. I think that she does not look at the consequences and in this respect her judgement is limited, it's limited to the effects of her immediate reactions.

FERRIER: You've heard her evidence with respect to the events of the night in question. Can you tell us whether or not it appears to be consistent with, or inconsistent with, a well-thought-out plan of deliberate, cold-blooded murder?

ABBOTT: No, I think it's quite inconsistent with a deliberate plan that is well thought out and what you call cold-blooded murder.

Dr. Abbott said she thought Jane was protective of both Darren and Allen. When she implicated Allen in one of her statements to police, it was "an example of the fact that she had no idea of the consequences of her action, and hadn't realized the implications of it for both herself and for other people close to her." She said she didn't think Jane had ever been close to her parents, and that Margaret Joudrey "was probably one of the only resources that she had in terms of someone that she could share some little amount of feeling with."

FERRIER: Did you note whether or not there was suicidal tendencies in terms of your examination of her?

ABBOTT: Yes, she told me that she had considered suicide at times during the last years that she spent with her husband. She told me that she never carried out anything about it because of her fear of leaving her small son to suffer further abuse.

When Ferrier asked Dr. Abbott if she thought Jane was strong-willed or weak-willed, she said, "In some ways one could say that she's been a strong person to stay in such a situation for as long as she did, which I think most people would consider not endurable. I think to stay in a situation that is such a bad one involves having pretty strong defences to be able to withstand it, so in some ways one can say that she has strength. Well, there are weaknesses, too. I mean her weaknesses in terms of her passivity, in terms of her inability to exercise judgement beyond the immediate situation, inability to see other ways out of this situation, to see other resources that might be available."

Dr. Abbott said she had to qualify her analysis because Jane's situation was so unusual in that she felt totally blocked because of Billy's intimidation and believed "that this man had the ability to carry out his intimidation. So I think in one way, one can see these as weaknesses, but that should be qualified because there were very good reasons why this lady couldn't get out of the situation she was in."

FERRIER: Are you saying that she did not have the strength to get out of it, but she had the strength to endure it?

ABBOTT: Initially she thought that maybe the situation would improve. I think that as the years went by she lost hope of the situation improving, and I think, increasingly felt a sense of hopelessness and helplessness about it. Along with that goes difficulty feeling that there is any future, an inability to see that things can be any better for herself. I think she suffered a tremendous amount of loss of self-esteem, loss of any kind of personal integrity in this situation. We've heard some of the abuse that she talked about, and I would think it would be extremely hard to maintain any kind of sense of personal integrity, any sense of one's own effectiveness in that situation.

FERRIER: Would there be a similarity in the sense of being psychologically imprisoned?

ABBOTT: I think that's one way of putting it. I think that's a very good way of putting it, of feeling, as I think someone has already used the term, "encased," shut in without being able to see any escape.

The stress on Jane Stafford was at its peak the night she shot Billy, said Dr. Abbott, and when it became no longer endurable she saw only one way out. "I think she felt there was a threat to the lives of people that were very dear to her and I don't think that she had much doubt that there was a very, very high chance of her husband carrying through his threats. She knew he had the ability to do that and had made the plans to do it."

Alan Ferrier's final medical witness, Dr. John Dimock, was an expert in forensic and child psychiatry from the Royal Ottawa Hospital, where he was director of the Family Court Clinic section. Dimock was also an assistant professor of psychiatry at the University of Ottawa and had an extensive background in child abuse cases. He was also a member of the Ottawa Committee on Battered Wives. He concluded that Darren had been subjected to a moderate degree of "emotional if not physical abuse. I asked him to reproduce some diagrams that I drew and he did two or three of them fairly successfully, but then it came to the diamond and he did not complete that successfully, and he reflexively and immediately flinched away from me, taking sort of evasive action. And I was most amazed by seeing that, and I obviously asked him why he had done that and he quite spontaneously, without any provoking on my part, said he wasn't allowed to get things wrong or else his father would give him a clip or would strike him."

Dimock had interviewed Darren in Ottawa in the summer of 1982, while the boy was staying with Jane's sister, Sandy. Darren played with the toys the doctor had in his office. One was a toy truck that Darren said was like his father's truck. The boy told him his father was always hollering at him or hitting him, on one occasion hitting him in the mouth. On another occasion he pointed a gun at him. Darren was five years old at the time he was interviewed. Dimock testified that he asked Darren what three magic wishes he would like to make, "and he would tend to talk to me about wishing to be like me, and wishing to have all the toys that I had, and that kind of response. He asked for some toys very much like mine. He asked for some paper and pencils because there were paper and pencils there and we were drawing...and then his third wish was that he was big and his father was small and that he could have hit his father. He seemed quite pleased with that last wish and smiled to himself afterwards."

Dimock said that as Darren relaxed in his presence over ensuing visits, he seemed to become quite aggressive. "I see that often in children who are subject to emotional problems, who will show aggressiveness as really an expression of their sadness, of their depression." He recommended Darren receive further psychiatric care.

He had also interviewed Jane and was familiar with the abuses she'd been subjected to. He said it wasn't unusual that she didn't know about the existence of the home for battered wives in Halifax, "and anyway these institutions are underfunded and overcrowded."

FERRIER: Is your evidence indicating in your experience with battered wives that there tends to be a self-isolation about the problem?

DIMOCK: There's a lot of shame, a lot of fear, a lot of personality traits in the wife herself, which all associate themselves with that particular syndrome. I believe it is a syndrome. It's certainly different in some cases than others, [there are] different reasons for staying in a marital situation. But certainly these wives, the wives that I've seen, tend to isolate themselves, will keep things secret for many years in some kind of almost unreal hope that things will improve, which they sometimes do, you know, if maybe the alcohol abuse ceases or...

FERRIER: How important would it be to Mrs. Stafford that her mother had been subjected to abuse by her husband and stuck it out and survived?

DIMOCK: There's certainly an aspect of learned behaviour. She'd seen a similar kind of thing occurring. Really, she used to sort of shepherd the other kids away into another room perhaps when things were getting hot. And this kind of reaction to abuse again is sort of quiet acceptance because of the hopelessness of the situation. That certainly explains to me a lot of what was going on even in their own marriage.

Dimock said that the sexual abuse Jane was subjected to was not unusual in terms of bondage and the use of an artificial penis and vibrators. "The bestiality aspect, the use of the dog, I've seen on occasion, but I think when that kind of behaviour is involved, then one is really involved in a very serious sadistic type of a relationship."

Under cross-examination, Dimock said he believed Jane was trying to remove Billy's body as far away from Darren as she could when she drove it down River Road the night of the shooting. He didn't believe she did it to avoid detection.

Following Dimock's testimony, the court recessed for twenty-five minutes. Jane Stafford felt uneasy as she listened to the evidence from the three doctors. She didn't understand some of the terminology, but she felt that much of it was negative. Her spirits lifted when she went to a back room off the main courtroom and saw Alan Ferrier smiling. He was proud of the job she had done on the witness stand. He hugged her. "I know how hard that was for you, but you did it," he said.

Jane sat down and lit up a cigarette. "I left out so much that I should have said."

"You did just fine."

"I had trouble keeping my train of thought."

"It was okay. It was okay. We're almost there."

"I'm so scared, Alan, I'm so scared."

Jane went back into the courtroom and sat, head bowed, as she had through most of the testimony. Ferrier's next five witnesses were neighbours or acquaintances of the Staffords from the Bangs Falls area. Marsha Freeman told of finding a bullet hole in her home after Billy Stafford was fined and put on probation when she complained to police that he had tried to run her down while she was walking down a road with her baby in a carriage. Another neighbour, Marilyn Fisher, testified about Billy threatening her at her home after she complained to police that her dog had been shot. "He looked like a wild man. His face was red. His eyeballs was bulging out of his head. Like I said, he scared me." Victor Westhaver testified about his visit to the Stafford residence when Billy punched him and then shot at him and a friend as they fled his house. Calvin Anthony told the court he perjured himself at a trial in which Billy Stafford was charged with jacking deer.

FERRIER: And as a result of the evidence that you gave at that time, can you tell us whether or not Mr. Stafford was acquitted or convicted?

ANTHONY: Acquitted.

Ivan Higgins described Billy's unprovoked attack on him when he was invited with his wife and child to the Stafford house by Billy, who had purchased a wood-burning stove from him. He told of running from the house in his bare feet after Billy struck him for no reason. The court then adjourned until the next day, when Ferrier would wrap up the case for the defence.

His first witness in the morning was Leona Anthony, who testified that she once saw Billy hit Jane with his fist in an unprovoked attack while she was visiting them. And she verified that Billy, Jane, and Ronny Wamboldt came to visit her the night Billy was shot. She said she saw Jane with bruises "different times."

Ronny Wamboldt's brother, Gene, testified that he'd known Billy for twenty years and "he had an awful temper, he'd fly off the handle some quick." He said he warned his brother not to stay with Billy Stafford because he was going to get himself in trouble. He agreed with Allaby that Billy Stafford was a bully—but if you stood up to him, he would leave you alone.

Andrea Wamboldt, Ronny's estranged wife, said she witnessed Billy abuse and physically assault Jane many times, and described the night Billy went into a rage and put a gun to her head in the Stafford kitchen when she came to visit Jane from Ontario. "He just come running out of the bedroom with the gun and pointed it right at me, right between my eyes." Andrea also testified that Margaret Joudrey witnessed many of the abuses she saw Billy inflict on Jane. "I say Margaret Joudrey knows pretty well everything that went on. She pretty well done everything Billy told her to do. I think she was scared of Billy." Allaby asked her if she was aware how Billy treated Ronny Wamboldt.

ANDREA: Yes.

ALLABY: Did that upset you?

ANDREA: No, because Ron always hated him. I don't know why he even bothered with him.

ALLABY: But it didn't bother you the way that Billy treated him?

ANDREA: No, because I figured he should have stayed away from him.

The last two witnesses Ferrier proposed to call were Billy's first wife, Pauline Stafford, and previous common-law wife, Faith Hatt. The Crown objected to their testimony, and the jury was sent out while the matter was argued before Justice Burchell. After some deliberation, he ruled in favour of the defence and had the jury called back into the courtroom.

"Mr. Foreman, members of the jury, in this case, the accused has admitted firing the shot that killed her husband," said Burchell. "One of the matters in issue is the state of mind of the accused at the time in question. You've heard evidence to the effect that her state of mind was affected by abuse she had suffered at the hands of the late Mr. Stafford. Some doubt as to the veracity of her evidence on the matter of abuse has been raised and in particular by the testimony of Margaret Joudrey. The defence now proposes to introduce evidence as to Mr. Stafford's treatment of several other persons with whom he, in the past, has lived in a marital relationship. The purpose of that evidence is to show that it was the habit of Mr. Stafford to abuse women with whom he had such a relationship. It will be suggested by the defence that if the deceased had a disposition to abuse his legal wife and a former common-law wife, then evidence of such a disposition should be viewed as corroborating the testimony of the accused as to abuse suffered by her. It is therefore in relation to the question of whether evidence of the accused as to abuse suffered by her was truthful that the evidence you are about to hear is being allowed to come before you. You must not lose sight of the fact that the real issue is the state of mind of the accused at the time in question, and you must not lose sight of the fact that it is the accused and not Mr. Stafford who is on trial."

Faith Hatt, who lived common law with Billy for two years, said she became a nervous wreck because of his unpredictability, and fled to Calgary when she was three months pregnant. She said Billy was "like a mad dog…He actually frothed at the mouth when he'd come after me."

Billy's first wife, Pauline, said she was with Billy from 1962 to 1968 and had five children by him. "He beat me quite often with anything he could get a hold of. A beer bottle, broom handle, his fists mostly." She also described how he abused the children from the time they were babies. She told of fleeing to a cousin's home in Ontario with her children while Billy was out on the boats.

The defence rested its case, and the court adjourned until 2 p.m., at which time Alan Ferrier addressed the jury. He made reference to section 31 of the Criminal Code, which outlined self-defence: "Everyone is justified in using force to defend himself or anyone under his protection from assault if he uses no more force than is necessary to prevent the assault or the repetition of it. Nothing in this section shall be deemed to justify the wilful infliction of any hurt or mischief that is excessive having regards to the nature of the assault that the force used was intended to prevent."

Ferrier said that section of the code "may be a relevant consideration for you to deal with in this matter. We have a situation where the deceased had indicated to Mrs. Stafford an intention to burn out Mrs. Joudrey and to deal with her son Allen. The consequences of that action, of course, could be just property damage, or bodily harm, or perhaps even death. Her view of that particular threat at that point was that it was serious and real, and that it could, in fact, be carried out when Mr. Stafford woke up. You will have to consider whether or not her actions at that point were more forceful than what was necessary under those circumstances. You will have to assess whether or not you believe at this stage that he was indeed going to carry out that very intended act."

But Ferrier's main argument was directed at convincing the jury to bring in a verdict of guilty of manslaughter rather than first-degree murder. He quoted section 215 of the Criminal Code: "Culpable homicide that otherwise would be murder may be reduced to manslaughter if the person who committed it did so in the heat of passion caused by sudden provocation.

A wrongful act or insult that is of such a nature as to be sufficient to deprive an ordinary person of the power of self-control is provocation for the purposes of this section if the accused acted upon it on the sudden and before there was time for his passion to cool."

Ferrier told the jury that Jane shot Billy Stafford as an impulsive reaction to what he said to her. "If you were thinking about a deliberate and planned murder and you wanted to get rid of the body, would you drive it down the road and stop it on the side of the road where it would definitely be found the next morning?" he asked. "Would you allow the gun belt to stay on the wall of your own home with the one slug missing for three days until the police finally came to your house and it was still there in the same condition it was before? How much thought went into this? I suggest to you, not very much. In fact, her actions are consistent with not thinking at all. Her only thought was to get rid of this mess. Get rid of this body, and then I'll go home. Those actions are much more consistent with somebody who was just simply acting on the sudden, at the moment, hasn't carefully planned it out. Hasn't carefully thought out the consequences of what she has done. She reacted out of a protective nature which has been described to you by the psychiatrist—her feeling of responsibility towards the people who were around her and to Mrs. Joudrey."

Ferrier said Margaret Joudrey admitted she was upset with Jane because she had to testify in court. "She doesn't like Jane anymore. From a woman who was like a mother to an enemy, just like that. Her motives, quite frankly, make her a suspect witness. I would suggest to you that her evidence is absolutely useless."

Billy Stafford's first two wives, said Ferrier, lived terrible lives with him, but they were able to escape. Billy, meanwhile, was getting worse and worse, "more violent and more unpredictable as time went on. So we had a man that was even worse, if that can be possible, than the kind of man that those two women had to deal with years ago. His basic makeup, his basic personality, never changed, he just got worse, and worse, and worse. This case generally requires you to consider the syndrome of a battered wife. That feeling of putting up with incredible abuse but staying for reasons that made absolutely no sense to a person who was outside of that relationship. It's easy for us to say, 'Well, we wouldn't be imprisoned under those circumstances,' but first of all we are not Jane Stafford. *She* is Jane Stafford. And we are not Billy Stafford, either. And we don't know what it was like to live in that household. We don't know what it was like to be subjected to the kind of violence and abuse and sadomasochistic sexual practices that would drive anybody over the wall. And that evidence is a plain reflection of the kind of man he was. He liked to abuse people that he could control.

"I would suggest to you very, very strongly that the issue of provocation is substantial enough in this case to raise a doubt, and I want you to know that the law is that the Crown must disprove provocation. It is not for the defence to prove it. The Crown must establish that this murder happened and, without any doubt, without provocation. If you have any doubt whatsoever about provocation, you must exercise that in favour of Mrs. Stafford, and as a result it is acquittal on the charge of murder and a guilty finding on manslaughter. I urge that on you in the strongest way after hearing all of the evidence that you have heard.

"Jane Stafford was a prisoner in that home. If you were unlawfully imprisoned under those circumstances, if you were, if I might use the example, if you were a Jew in Auschwitz and you saw the boys coming to take your mother away to the oven and you had a chance to stop it, no matter what the consequences to yourself, you would react immediately, promptly, and you would do what you could to help without the thought of consequences to yourself. That's how she reacted that night.

"I would ask you to consider all of the evidence very, very carefully... and bring in a verdict of manslaughter only."

In his summation to the jury, Blaine Allaby said the Stafford case was important from the point of view of the law and "from the point of view of a lot of women out there who are considered battered wives. It is a problem which is much in the news in our society today and it's a problem which you are confronted with very directly. I am not going to stand here and suggest to you that Billy Stafford was a saint. In fact, I think on a scale of one to ten, he'd be on the lower end. He was not a nice person. He was a difficult person. He was a bully and I think the evidence clearly establishes that, but Billy Stafford, unfortunately, perhaps, is not the one who is on trial. It is Jane Stafford who is on trial, and Jane Stafford is on trial for first-degree murder.

"My learned friend and the psychiatrists perhaps suggest that Jane Stafford was not mentally capable of formulating a foolproof plan, but anybody who commits murder and is charged has not had a foolproof plan because they were charged. If the plan was foolproof, nobody would know about it. First she was going to get somebody else to do it for her and he wouldn't. Then rather than actually perform the act herself directly, she was going to do it by chemical poisoning, and finally she realized that if this was going to be done she had to do it herself. The Crown is suggesting that she waited for the opportunity and on March 11th the opportunity arose. He was passed out in the truck, he was asleep, she could get the gun, she could kill Billy Stafford, which she wanted to do. She indicated in her own evidence she hated him, she wanted him dead, and I think the evidence establishes perhaps that that feeling had been there for at least a year and a half. She had it in her mind that she was going to kill Billy Stafford at some point.

"The whole thing may not have been a perfect plan, but as I say, perfect plans don't end up in court. The Crown is suggesting that she was waiting for her chance and she took it on this particular night and what she did was planned and what she did was deliberate.

"I don't think anybody is questioning the fact that she had one hell of a life with that man, but she is also a very interested party and some aspects of her evidence are corroborated, others aren't. Really there are only two people who know what happened in the truck that night on the way home. Was the story about burning out Margaret true? Those are things that you have to decide and make your determination on.

"The Crown is suggesting to you that first-degree murder is what this was. We may sympathize with Jane Stafford in her situation, but the law is the law, and what do we say to people out there? I would submit that in this case we have to say we sympathize but what you did was planned and deliberate, was not provoked, and was first-degree murder."

The trial was adjourned for the day. It resumed the next morning, a Friday, with Justice Burchell's charge to the jury. He lived up to his reputation for meticulously reviewing the testimony of the witnesses. In this trial there were forty-six witnesses, and his charge, including an explanation of the law, took seven-and-a-half hours. His discussion of the law included a look at section 37, the defence of self-defence. After reading the section he said the jury would have to decide whether for the "purpose of defending those under her protection, the killing of Mr. Stafford was objectively or actually a matter of necessity. So you must look at the means employed in self-defence and decide whether those means were necessary. In addressing that question, of course, you may take into account what you know about the character and disposition of Mr. Stafford... You should understand that the law of self-defence proceeds from necessity, from the instinctive and the intuitive necessity to preserve oneself. Under no circumstances may that defence be raised as a cloak for retaliation or revenge. The use of force in self-defence should come as a matter of last resort. It's justified only where there are no other reasonable means to prevent the assault. If you have any reasonable doubt as to whether the accused acted in self-defence as I've defined it, you will find the accused not guilty of murder or of any other offence because if that is your finding or if you have a doubt, a reasonable doubt, as to self-defence, then the Crown will have failed to prove that the homicide was culpable, because a homicide committed in self-defence is not a culpable homicide."

He told the jury it could return one of four verdicts: guilty of first-degree murder; guilty of second-degree murder; guilty of manslaughter; or not guilty. He explained in detail how each verdict could be reached. It was 5:30 p.m. when he completed his charge.

The jury retired to begin deliberations. They took time off for dinner at 6:30 p.m. and continued deliberating until shortly after midnight. During the evening, they requested that the testimony of Jane's son Allen be played back to them. The jury was sequestered in a hotel overnight, and returned to continue deliberations the next day.

Jane Stafford had arrived in the courtroom at 9 a.m. Friday morning. She was tense and her heart raced as she watched the jurors file into the jury room that afternoon, closing the door behind them. "Alan Ferrier talked to me for a while, telling me to keep cool. But my whole life was being determined behind that closed door. The courtroom was filled wall to wall with people. There was noise and confusion all around me. I'd walk around a bit, sit a bit, and smoke one cigarette after another. I kept thinking of what Alan had told me: 'The longer the jury is out, the worse things look.' I didn't leave that courtroom until 12:45 a.m. I was exhausted. My head was pounding. I couldn't concentrate on anything. When I came out of the courtroom Mom and Dad were waiting outside." Jane went to them and hugged them.

"Is it over for tonight?" asked Maurice Hurshman.

"Yes, it's over for tonight."

"Can you come home with us now, Janey?"

"I can go home, but I'm not. I have to remain in town, where I can get to the courthouse quickly if a verdict is reached before 9 a.m. tomorrow morning."

Jane said her father "was hurt and couldn't understand why I didn't want to go home. I didn't even try to explain. I walked away and got into my car with my sister Mona and my friend Andrea. I thought back to when the court had adjourned the night before, on Thursday. Everything that could be done had been done. The rest was just legal talk. As I was getting ready to leave the courtroom that evening, Alan took me aside and said, 'Well, Jane, it's done. There is no more we can do. When you come to court tomorrow, bring your bag with you. You may need it. Say your goodbyes before you come tomorrow.' I never told Alan, but my bag had been packed and in my car since day one of the trial. Well, on Friday morning I said my goodbyes to Darren, to Allen, to my family. I told Darren, 'I might not be home anymore, so you be a good boy and you grow up and be as proud of your mommy as she is of you. I love you, babe.' And I sent him off to school. I said to Allen, 'I love you dearly—

please always know that and please forgive me all the hurts that I've caused you. Don't worry about anything. Grampy has a letter and he knows everything that I want done. You will all be looked after.' I just could not go back to Dad's that Friday night. My mind couldn't handle any more hurt. Saying goodbye to everyone again in the morning was just too much for me. I wanted to go where there was no talk of tomorrow, no sad faces, no nothing…"

Jane, Mona, and Andrea Wamboldt went to Sid Tollimore's house in Liverpool. "He's a good friend of Andrea's. Mona drove us there. I didn't want to talk to anybody. Mona could sense it, and she decided to drive home to Dad's for the night."

"I'll be here to pick you up in the morning," said Mona as she was leaving.

"I love you, sis," said Jane, hugging her. "Thanks for understanding. Now go home and try to make Dad understand."

When Mona left, Jane poured herself a drink, went into the living room, and switched on the stereo. "I put on the earphones and let the world pass on by. I fell asleep there on the floor. I was awake very early—waiting for Mona to come."

The next morning, Mona picked up Jane and Andrea, and they were back at the courthouse by 9 a.m. The jury filed in and resumed its deliberations at 9:30. Jane's mother and father were sitting in their car when she arrived with Mona. Jane went over to them. They wanted to be with her in the courtroom when the jury returned its verdict.

"Is it all right for us to go in?" asked Maurice Hurshman.

"I'll check to see if you're allowed," said Jane.

She returned moments later and told them they could be in the courtroom. They walked in together. "There were already a lot of people gathered. The news media were setting up their equipment outside, and everyone was hustling around. I didn't know what to do with myself. People kept coming up and wishing me luck and making comments as people do when they are trying to be nice but don't quite know what's appropriate to say. I smoked and smoked. Mona was like my shadow. She was with me through it all. Besides being my sister, she is one hell of a friend. Alan wasn't in the courtroom when I arrived that morning. He told me he wouldn't be back until the jury reached a verdict. He was within five minutes of the courthouse and would come as soon as they called him to say there was a verdict."

The jury again interrupted its deliberations to ask Justice Burchell to clarify pertinent sections of the Criminal Code. Jane was frightened. She was facing twenty-five years without parole if they found her guilty of first-degree murder. She glanced at her watch over and over, counting the minutes, and the hours. "They were out too long. I was sure I was going to prison for the rest of my life. By 11 a.m. Saturday morning it had been seventeen-and-a-half hours since the jury first began its deliberations. At 11:30 a.m. the jury announced it had reached a verdict.

"For nearly three weeks I dragged myself in and out of that courtroom," said Jane. "I was terribly thin and run down. I didn't have any clothes that fit me properly, and I had no urge to buy any. In fact, I had no urge to do anything. Nothing really mattered. I was mentally and physically exhausted. I often forgot when I last ate or when I had more than a couple of hours' sleep at a time. Yet when court was called to order for that last time, for that crucial moment, every fibre of my being came alive. I sat in my usual spot about four feet from Alan, but this time he reached out and pulled my chair close to him and put his arm around me."

"Hang in there, Jane," he said. "It's almost over."

Jane showed no outward emotion. "I sat there like a statue. My heart was pounding so hard I thought that everyone else could hear it. The jury filed in. I looked at each of their faces as they took their seats. I had no idea what they were thinking."

The court clerk rose from his chair in front of the judge.

"Mr. Foreman, have you reached a verdict?" he asked.

"Yes, we have."

"Do you have your indictment?"

"Yes, I do."

"Would you hand it to me, please?"

"Oh, I'm sorry," said the jury foreman. "We didn't fill it out ourselves. We thought that was to be done here."

"No, you must write it inside and bring it to me."

"I didn't... do you need all the jurors for that?"

"Perhaps you should," said Justice Burchell.

The jury filed out of the courtroom. Alan Ferrier got up from his chair and paced across the floor and back. Jane Stafford sat motionless. "I said a silent prayer: 'Please, Lord, no more delays. Let all this end.' I couldn't take any more."

The jury returned to the courtroom within minutes. "Mr. Foreman, have you reached a verdict?" asked the clerk.

"Yes, we have."

"Would you pass me the indictment, please?"

The foreman passed the folded paper to the clerk.

"Mr. Foreman, what was your verdict?" asked the clerk.

"Not guilty."

Jane's legs nearly gave out when she heard the verdict. All around her was laughter, shouts of 'Praise the Lord,' and tears of joy. "Every emotion possible was felt in that courtroom at that moment, yet I couldn't move. I was in shock. I said to myself, 'Thank you, Lord, for the miracle you just performed.' I couldn't believe the verdict. Alan had prepared me for the worst. I didn't know how to accept the best. I'd never once allowed myself to believe the verdict might be 'not guilty.' I killed someone and they were telling me I was free to go. I didn't know how to react. Then everyone was around me, hugging me, shaking hands. It was too much."

Alan Ferrier guided Jane into the back room where they had spent so many breaks during the trial. There were papers to be signed. Jane could see he was happy with the verdict, but she sensed something was troubling him.

"You should seriously consider packing up and moving away from here," said Ferrier. "Start a new life." He paused a moment, and looked at Jane. "There is a possibility that this verdict may be appealed."

"If it is, does that mean I have to go through all this again?"

"Yes, it probably does."

Jane was devastated. "If there is an appeal, I could never go through all this again—I won't."

"Slow down," said Ferrier. "I'm only assuming there might be an appeal. If it does happen, I'll do everything possible to prevent you going through this agony again."

"What should I do?"

"I think you should go to Ontario, like you talked about."

"All right, I'll do it."

They walked back into the courtroom. There were still a lot of people milling about. Jane sat down. Alan Ferrier approached her.

"Well, lady, what are you waiting for?" he said. "You're free to go."

Jane looked up at him and smiled. "Look, mister, I walked in this courtroom with you, and by golly, I'm leaving the same way."

They walked out together to face a barrage of reporters. "When they asked me how I felt, I answered in one word, 'Super.' But in the back of my mind I felt it wasn't over yet."

Juror Daniel Smart, who worked for a Liverpool hardware store, said after the trial that the jurors found the Stafford case to be very emotional. "When she was on the stand it was very hard to sit and listen to, because she said some things that people shouldn't have to say to other people. And it was hard for her. I was relieved when it was over, and I felt we came to the best decision that we could. Did she plan to murder him? That was the question. First-degree murder. There was no way it was proved to us that she actually planned it. There was no way we could come to that decision without any doubts at all."

Alan Ferrier believed that the single piece of evidence that affected the jury the most concerned Billy Stafford's treatment of Darren at the dinner table. "Many people say a woman deserves it. Many people say if she doesn't like it, she can get out. But when it comes to a child being abused, I think that's where they draw the line. And certainly in this case, the single most gruesome particular was that Billy force-fed this young fellow to eat at the same rate he did... And I recall that perhaps that was the only time during the trial in which the jury reacted with just a sickening response, and everybody in the courtroom did. I think that one single gesture was an indication of how brutal a man he could be."

Ferrier said there was no question that Billy Stafford's character was of key importance in the case. "I don't think anybody would dispute that. Some people say that's wrong, that the victim's character shouldn't be on trial. But in some cases it's necessary, and in some cases it's obviously more important than the character of your client, because even if your client is charged with shooting—as Jane was in this case—her individual act of violence paled by comparison with the continuous acts of violence that this man perpetrated against her and her child."

Some feminist organizations heralded the jury's verdict as a legal breakthrough for battered women. They saw it as a victory in the campaign against spousal abuse and as a sign of changing public attitudes toward battered women. Others hoped the decision would prompt other battered women to speak out. Dr. Christine Simmons of Women Against Violence Against Women, a national feminist group, thought the case was perhaps a confirmation that the legal system was finally prepared to protect women from battery.

Alan Ferrier didn't see the Jane Stafford verdict as setting any sort of precedent. "I don't see this verdict having consequences for other cases. Jury trials are not precedents for anything. It doesn't even set a social precedent. Battered women don't have a licence to blow the heads off the men who abuse them just because Jane Stafford got off. You simply won't find many situations in which a jury will say it was okay for a person to kill someone. This was a special case. And I think the verdict does show that our system of punishments isn't flexible enough to take into consideration abuse like this."

There were other reactions to the verdict. Local reporter Vernon Oickle, who covered the Stafford case for the *Liverpool Advance*, said that a lot of people thought she was a heroine. But Wayne MacKay, a professor of criminology at Dalhousie University, took a different view. "Some people have applauded the Stafford jury victory as a successful quest for justice," he wrote in the February 1983 issue of *Atlantic Insight*. "Few people would suggest that Jane Stafford deserved a severe criminal penalty. She was clearly a victim of her tragic circumstances and did not have many realistic options. However, those factors would normally relate to the severity of her sentence, not to establishing whether she committed the crime. Is the moral of the Stafford case that an abused wife can kill her abusing husband (even when he is not immediately threatening), without engaging in the crime of murder?...It's hard to find much sympathy for Billy Stafford. But are such people fair targets for vigilante justice at a local level? There is obviously a place for the jury in our criminal system. It gives flexibility to the law. However, in its quest for justice in the individual case, a jury should not be permitted to distort principles. Whatever one thinks of the result in the Stafford case, it is difficult to support on the basis of principle. The meaning of this morality play is at best confusing and at worst disturbing. Jane Stafford was the person on trial, but it was Billy Stafford who was found guilty."

CHAPTER 13
APPEAL

When Jane Stafford and her sister Mona left the Liverpool courtroom shortly before noon on November 20, 1982, they were speechless. "We just stared at each other," said Jane. "No words were appropriate. Then as she drove a ways we said a prayer together. It was one my sister Sandy wrote for me after Bill's death: 'May we ever have grateful appreciation of our blessings and opportunities; strength and courage for whatever the day may bring; wisdom for our problems and decisions; faith for our disappointments and sorrows; no annoying regrets of yesterday; no undue concern for tomorrow; kindness, patience, and sane cheerfulness and unselfishness; in all things—to all people, Amen.'" They drove to their parents' Danesville home. When the car pulled into the yard, Darren ran out to meet them. He jumped into Jane's lap before she could get out of the car.

"Mommy, I heard about you on the radio. You don't have to go to jail. You can stay home with me and be my mommy forever."

The telephone rang continually with well-wishers offering congratulations. "Finally I had to go and lie down, I was so tired. That evening Mona and I went to a tavern to celebrate. A lot of people who attended the trial were there, and we had a nice time." The next day, Sunday, Mona returned to Ontario. Jane, Darren, and Allen would be following in two weeks' time.

"After we came home from the airport," Jane remembered, "I had supper with Mom and Dad, and then Darren, Allen, and I went home. I wanted to spend a quiet evening with them, like a family. The next day Darren and Allen went to school. I was busy answering the telephone all day. Friends, strangers, everyone called. I got fed up with it all and jumped in the car and went to the beach for some peace and quiet. I sat wondering about the future. I realized I was free, really free for the first time in my whole life. It was all new to me. The questions kept going around and around in my head. What was I supposed to do now? I didn't want to go back to my old job. How was I going to support myself and the boys? Here I was, free, and I didn't have a clue what to do about it. Then I started thinking about the things I used to dream about. Ever since I was a little girl I wanted to be a nurse or an interior decorator. I decided on nursing. At that point they were just thoughts and dreams. I also thought about the move to Ontario. I was so confused. I never had to think for myself before. I really didn't know how. It was astonishing how many things I didn't know how to do. Mom and Dad came to visit that evening, and we decided I would pack up and move away. I'd leave the first week in December. From then on I didn't have time to think, to reason things out."

On December 2, 1982, less than two weeks after Jane was found not guilty, she, Allen, and Darren left by train for Ontario. Mona met them at Union Station in Toronto and drove them to her home in Barrie, sixty miles north of Toronto. The house was small and had only one bedroom. "Mona and her husband, Ed, were very good to us. But they weren't used to having kids around, especially on a permanent basis. The boys and I slept on a mattress on the floor in what was their dining room. It was very crowded. I got the boys enrolled in school and I went to the local college to inquire about a nursing course. I couldn't get in right away. As the days went by I got more and more depressed. I was in a whole new world. I didn't know anyone, and I didn't know the area. I was scared and confused. I had many mixed feelings. Everything was happening too fast, and I didn't know how to cope. I couldn't adjust, and I was withdrawing inside myself."

It got worse on December 15 when Alan Ferrier telephoned to say that the Crown had launched an appeal in her case. "Be prepared to be served papers by the RCMP," said Ferrier. "Send them to me by registered mail as soon as you receive them. It's not necessary for you to come back here at this time. I'll let you know when it's necessary."

Jane's depression deepened as she envisioned going through another long trial and possibly being sentenced to years in jail. The day after Ferrier's call, an RCMP officer delivered the notice of appeal to Jane. He was dressed in street clothes and drove an unmarked car. He introduced himself and handed Jane the papers. "I'm really sorry to have to give this to you," said the officer. "I can't see what they hope to gain. Every officer across the country has followed this case, and it should have ended when you were acquitted."

Jane thanked the officer, and he left. "I just stood there staring at the piece of paper in my hand. I couldn't believe it was all happening again. I couldn't handle another trial. I hadn't even had time to recover from the first one. My mind was like an overloaded circuit. I wanted to go home. I felt like I had to run away. I didn't want to be in Ontario anymore. I wanted to be home where I knew what was happening. I telephoned Alan, but he told me he didn't want me to come back yet. Then I called Mom and Dad. They wanted me to do whatever Alan advised. Mona wanted me to stay, but everything inside me was screaming, 'Go back!' Again I felt like a lost little girl, not knowing which way to go or where to turn. It was total confusion. I felt deserted."

Life brightened for Jane when she and the boys travelled to Ottawa to celebrate Christmas with her sister Sandy. Mona and her husband also made the trip. "It was the first Christmas I'd spent with my sisters in eighteen years and the only one I can really remember. After Christmas, I made up my own mind: I was going home, and no one was going to tell me I couldn't. In the second week of January I moved back to Nova Scotia."

Jane's house in Bangs Falls had been up for sale since the previous April. "I went back to the house and stayed there, even though it was still for sale. I was more at peace with myself, and Darren was happier. He'd had trouble adjusting in Ontario."

Jane went to see Alan Ferrier about the appeal. He told her it could drag on for a long time and suggested she get on with her life. Jane did just that. She upgraded her high-school education and prepared to enter a nursing course at the nearby Lunenburg Regional Vocational School in Bridgewater. She tried not to think about the upcoming appeal of her case.

Spring turned to summer and summer to fall as Jane waited for word of the appeal of her verdict. In September, she enrolled in a nurse's aide course. Finally, the word came down: the appeal would be heard in Halifax on October 20, 1983, in the Appeal Division of the Supreme Court of Nova Scotia. Jane had known it was coming, but with a date set, it became more real, and she felt very depressed.

At the appeal, Alan Ferrier argued on behalf of Jane Stafford, and Blaine Allaby and Kenneth W.F. Fiske on behalf of the prosecution. The court reserved its decision, which wasn't announced until six weeks later, on November 30, 1983. The Crown won this round: the verdict of the jury was set aside, and a new trial was ordered for Jane Stafford.

The written decision came from Supreme Court Justice J.A. Hart and was endorsed by four other judges. Hart said that both the prosecution and the defence had brought out a lot of evidence about the character of Billy Stafford. "Much of this was unnecessary and indeed inadmissible unless it was relevant to a defence that could properly be put to the jury. It served only to create sympathy for the respondent and for this reason should have been excluded."

On section 37, the defence of self-defence, Hart wrote that Burchell's instructions to the jury "were broad enough to say that a person is justified in killing anyone who has threatened them and is likely to carry out such a threat. I do not believe that Parliament intended such an interpretation of the section." He went on to say that there was no assault actively under way against Jane Stafford when she shot Billy Stafford, who was "passed out or sleeping in the truck... In my opinion no person has the right in anticipation of an assault that may or may not happen, to apply force to prevent the imaginary assault. The jury should not have been permitted to consider a possible assault as a justification of her deed, and section 37 of the code should not have been left with them. Since the jury was improperly instructed on the law relating to the offence alleged against the respondent and since that improper instruction may well have permitted them to reach a conclusion that would not otherwise be open to them, I would allow the appeal, set aside the verdict of the jury, and order a new trial upon the original indictment."

News of the decision received national attention. Alan Ferrier told the *Globe and Mail* that "the Crown went after her for first-degree murder, the penalty being twenty-five years without parole, yet its own agents said on the stand that she should get a medal." He said he initially advised Jane Stafford to plead guilty to manslaughter; if she had, the punishment would have been determined by the judge, who would have heard evidence of the abuse she had been subjected to and psychiatric evidence about the state of her mind. "She was prepared to go to jail for a couple of years. But the attorney general's office evidently did not want to be seen to be engaging in plea bargaining on a murder trial, and they made the decision to go for first-degree murder and to let the jury decide. Now they're not too pleased with what the jury decided."

Ferrier hadn't realistically expected Jane to be acquitted. "Reasonably, I think we expected that the best we could do would be to have a manslaughter verdict. The fact we got more than we expected, in hindsight, may have caused more problems than it solved. The use of the self-defence argument in the case was borderline. It was a situation where a man was asleep, and generally the courts have not accepted that anyone is acting in self-defence if somebody's immobile when you act." Another problem, said Ferrier, was "a reaction at the time of the acquittal that this somehow was a licence for women to go out and kill their husbands and then allege years of abuse or whatever."

Less than three weeks after Jane Stafford was acquitted, a woman in neighbouring New Brunswick shot her forty-four-year-old husband in the head. The woman was charged with second-degree murder. During the trial her husband was described as an introvert with a serious drinking problem who repeatedly beat his wife and children. It took the jury slightly more than an hour to find the woman not guilty. That case was also appealed.

Exactly two months after Jane Stafford used a shotgun to put an end to her years of humiliation and abuse, many male Liberal and Conservative members of Parliament laughed and guffawed loudly in the House of Commons when they were told that one out of ten women in Canada are battered by their husbands. When New Democrat MP Margaret Mitchell asked about the report there were gales of laughter, amid which one unidentified MP joked, "I don't beat my wife. Do you beat yours?" The laughter outraged women across the country, prompting many of them to complain bitterly to their MPs about their lack of response to women's issues.

"I thought it was absolutely disgusting that the men MPs would be laughing and almost condoning the fact that men can beat their wives," said Mitchell. "If I had asked about a man beating up another man they wouldn't have laughed at all. That's what the laughter meant to me."

Judy Erola, then minister responsible for the status of women, was quick to respond to the laughter. "I do not find it amusing. Neither do the women of Canada."

Lucie Pepin, president of the Advisory Council on the Status of Women, immediately wrote to every member of Parliament, enclosing a fact sheet on battered wives. "I'm really appalled they consider violence among 52 per cent of the population a laughing matter," she said.

Three days after the incident, on the third attempt, MPs gave unanimous consent to a motion assuring women that they considered the issue of family violence to be extremely grave. Conservative MP James McGrath said his party "very much regrets what happened in the House. We believe family violence is a very serious problem in the country, probably more widespread than is generally believed."

The incident underscored what a lot of feminists had been saying for years: that wife battering was considered a joke by much of society. As insensitive as it was, the laughter of the MPS did have some positive fallout. Government money was soon being found for emergency shelters and transition houses, and the legal system slowly began to harden its attitude toward wife batterers. In Ontario, $4 million was pumped into shelters for battered women, and a message came down from the attorney general's office urging police and Crown prosecutors to crack down on wife beaters. And more reports came out and more studies were ordered.

One working paper, "The Criminal Justice System Response to Wife Assault," showed with cold statistics and unemotional language the depth of the problem and the uncaring attitude of the legal system. It stated that domestic calls were the largest category of requests to police for help, even though less than 10 per cent of incidents were reported to police. Also, that between 40 and 70 per cent of all violent crimes in North America involved married couples or those living common law. It found that Canadian courts were extremely lenient with convicted wife beaters, and that jail terms were rare: typically, the court either suspended sentence and released the offender on probation, or gave him an absolute or conditional discharge.

The report also found that although police were more willing than before to answer domestic abuse calls, arrest rates were still too low for men who assaulted their spouses. Crown attorneys still seemed to give a low priority to cases of wife assault, viewing the problem as less serious than assault between strangers; and judges seldom sent men to jail because they were loath to break up families.

Whatever progress was being made to help abused women, it was too late for Jane Stafford. During her years with Billy

Stafford, there was no help available that she knew about, and now she was facing a second trial for his murder. Christmas 1983 came and went, and still no date had been set for her new trial. Her life had become relatively normal. She was taking her nursing courses in Bridgewater and doing well. Darren was doing well in school, and no longer lived in fear.

Finally, the word came down from Halifax. The date for Jane's new trial was February 14, 1984—Valentine's Day, and a month short of two years since Billy Stafford had been killed.

Alan Ferrier knew that Jane Stafford did not want another lengthy trial. He also knew that the Crown would now find it difficult not to accept a plea of guilty to manslaughter. He reasoned that a judge accepting that plea would not be able to ignore the jury's verdict of not guilty in her first trial. "The jury's decision was important because it was a statement to the effect that we don't want to see her punished—that we have empathy for what she had to live through. The judge would have to be mindful of the fact that these people sat through the trial and saw all the evidence and their decision shouldn't be ignored. Their decision can only be represented now in terms of leniency, in terms of understanding and giving her a sentence that gives her an opportunity to start her life over again, to fulfill some of the goals that she has now."

Ferrier's instincts proved correct. The Crown this time readily agreed to accept Jane Stafford's plea of guilty to manslaughter. Explaining the change of heart, Crown prosecutor Blaine Allaby said that facts apparent before Jane's trial had warranted a charge of first-degree murder. Her act had been planned and deliberate. But as the evidence unfolded during the trial, it became apparent that perhaps manslaughter would have been the proper charge. Jane was relieved that she wouldn't have to go through another lengthy trial, but now she faced the uncertainty of the sentencing. The only certainty was that she wouldn't be receiving twenty-five years with no prospect of parole.

The night before her court appearance, Jane packed her small bag as she had done so many times before and did her best to explain to six-year-old Darren that she might not see him again for a long, long time. It was a Monday. Her court appearance was Tuesday, and she had an exam scheduled for Wednesday at her school. "I knew they were either going to lock me up or let me go. I wanted to write that exam on Wednesday. I'd done very well at school since the day I started in September. I studied hard and put everything I had into that course. Being able to concentrate so hard on something was great. I didn't have to think about all this legal stuff. The next day was just another date I had to meet. I'd deal with it when it happened."

Jane's friend Andrea Wamboldt stayed overnight with her in Bangs Falls. The next morning Jane sent Darren off to school and they headed for Liverpool. They arrived at Andrea's apartment above Tompkins Market at about 8:15 a.m. and decided to have a cup of tea before going to the courthouse. Andrea's eleven-year-old daughter, Tammy, was getting ready for school. Jane asked Tammy if she would go down to the store for her and pick up some Halls cough drops and a package of cigarettes. The girl returned with the cigarettes but no cough drops.

"Jim didn't have any Halls; I didn't get you any cough drops," said Tammy.

"Thanks anyway, Tammy," said Jane. "They don't have to be Halls, but I'll pick some up when we leave."

Tammy left for school, and about fifteen minutes later Jane and Andrea left the apartment and went down the covered exterior stairway at the side of the white building. Andrea was walking in front of Jane. "Don't forget I want to get some cough drops at the store first," said Jane.

"I'll get them," said Andrea, turning toward the door of the store.

Jim Tompkins was related to Andrea Wamboldt by marriage. He was in his mid-thirties and operated the store with his wife. As usual, he had arrived at work first. His wife would join him later, after tending to their two young children. When Andrea entered the store she looked to the rear, near the meat counter, where Jim Tompkins could usually be found at that time of day. She couldn't see him, and he didn't respond when she called his name. As she turned to check along another aisle, her foot struck something. She looked down. It was Jim Tompkins' hand. He was lying on his back, dead. A rifle lay across his body. He had shot himself while in a sitting position on the floor.

Andrea ran quickly from the store just as Jane was approaching. She quickly closed the door. Jane didn't understand the look of panic on Andrea's face.

"Don't go in there!" said Andrea. "Jim is on the floor, dead. He shot himself."

The two of them ran from the store. Jane was terrified. "All I could hear was 'dead—shot.' I thought, 'Oh God, what's happening?'"

"Go upstairs and wait!" Jane shouted to Andrea. "I'll send the police. Don't do anything. Just stay in your apartment. I'll send someone right up."

Jane jumped into her car and sped away. "I went right down Main Street like a maniac, not stopping for stop signs or anything. I kept thinking over and over in my mind, 'Oh Lord, this isn't real. This can't be happening to me.' Here I was on my way to court for murder and I find a dead man. How would I explain this one? It was like a bad movie."

Jane was ashen-faced when she pulled up in front of the old Liverpool courthouse. A small crowd had already gathered, and newsmen and television cameras were waiting for her arrival. She ignored their questions.

"Are there any policemen here yet?" she asked a journalist.

"I don't know."

Jane ran into the courthouse. It was empty except for Deputy Sheriff Michael Smith.

"Jim Tompkins just shot himself," she said to the startled Smith. "He's at his store, lying on the floor, dead. Andrea is waiting in her apartment for the police to come. Hurry and send someone right over."

Jane sat down and tried to calm herself. "I was a total ball of nerves. I was shaking so bad my chair was shaking. I prayed I wouldn't get mixed up in it." She spoke for a while with Alan Ferrier and was calm by the time the proceedings began.

The courtroom was packed with spectators, including Jane's parents, when the clerk called the court to order and Mr. Justice Merlin Nunn took his seat on the bench. Jane's plea of guilty to manslaughter was quickly accepted. All that remained were the sentencing arguments, from Allaby for the Crown and Ferrier for the defence. All the players were aware that the case was being watched with interest across the country. It was still being cited by women's groups, and Progressive Conservative MP Jennifer Cossitt had even tried to get the federal government to intervene to ensure that Jane Stafford wouldn't have to go back to court. Before the date for a new trial was set, Cossitt made her view clear that the decision by the Nova Scotia attorney general's office to appeal the jury's acquittal was horrendous. She told the House of Commons that Jane Stafford had "already received enough punishment—five long years of painful mental and physical punishment—and it appears that the department of the attorney general of Nova Scotia wants to punish her further. I believe, and I am sure everyone in this chamber would agree, this lady was more than justified in her actions to protect herself and her son from this terrifying onslaught of repeated assault."

Allaby called for a jail term to discourage others from taking the law into their own hands. Ferrier called one witness—Darren's longtime babysitter Marie Joudrey, who said she often saw bruises on both Jane and Darren. She said the boy was terrified of his father and would often run and hide when it was time to go home if he knew his father was there.

In his address, Ferrier said that Jane would carry the mental scars of Billy's abuse for the rest of her life. He asked for a suspended sentence and cited a Sudbury, Ontario, case as precedent. In that case, from 1980, a woman was charged with murder after shooting her husband in his sleep. At her trial, the judge and jury heard of the beatings and degradation she and her children had suffered at the hands of her husband. Before the case went to the jury, the woman pleaded guilty to the lesser offence of manslaughter, and the judge imposed a suspended sentence. Ferrier told Mr. Justice Nunn that the cases were almost identical and that the Sudbury defendant had "felt entrapped in much the same way as Mrs. Stafford."

Ferrier reviewed some of the sexual humiliations Jane had been subjected to. "This was not a man. He was an animal. He indicated his power came from the devil." He said it was ironic that Jane was working in a nursing home, helping others, while being battered at home. Even the father of the victim was prepared to be bondsman for her. And the police had said to one another: "This woman deserves a medal and has saved at least two police officers' lives." It had been extremely difficult for his client during her long trial to spell out from the witness stand her degrading and humiliating experiences. The acquittal and courtroom applause, said Ferrier, cannot be forgotten.

Mr. Justice Nunn said that Jane had lived a tragic life, and that Billy Stafford had been a man on the outer fringes of the definition of humanity, but a human nevertheless. He said he did not subscribe to Staff Sergeant Peter Williamson's view that Jane should receive a medal for what she had done. He said that Jane had been "judge, jury, and executioner." He said that Jane was doing well in her certified nursing assistant's course, was well on the road to rehabilitating her life, and was not a danger to society. But he said there must be deterrence in the law and protection of society as a whole: "Wives don't have the right to take the lives of their husbands." The case, he concluded, did not warrant a suspended sentence. He sentenced her to six months in jail and two years' probation with a recommendation that she be allowed to commute from jail to attend her classes and complete her nursing course.

Jane Stafford, who sat impassively during the hearing, felt only tremendous relief when Nunn announced her sentence. "It was finally over after two years of waiting—wondering—with my life, my future on hold." Under Canadian law, Jane's six-month sentence meant that she could be out of jail in two months. "And I could finish my nursing course. It was super."

She and Ferrier met in the back room of the courthouse for the last time. Ferrier had tears in his eyes as they hugged each other.

"Do you want me to appeal this sentence?" he asked.

Jane looked at him and smiled. "Hey, smile, it's all over. Hell, no, I don't want you to appeal it. Just let me do my time and put all of this behind me forever. I'm so happy it's over."

Blaine Allaby was satisfied with Nunn's sentence. "She did take another human being's life. As the judge said, she acted as judge, jury, and executioner. I think in those circumstances a person has got to know if they're going to act in that way, then there has to be some price. Jane has paid a heavy price over the last two years and certainly well before that in the life she led with him. But the route she took is not the answer. I think what the judge was saying is that you will be shown compassion by the courts, but there also has to be a price involved if that's the route you're going to take."

A lot of people around Liverpool took a different view, perhaps best summed up in an editorial by Jock Inglis in the *Liverpool Advance*. It read in part:

> The Crown got its pound of flesh through the incarceration of Ms. Stafford, but at what cost to our judicial system? Obviously, the Crown was either afraid of losing the case the second time around, or like most who heard the evidence, felt that though she did take her husband's life, she had already suffered sufficiently. Otherwise they would not have plea-bargained. So Ms. Stafford was forced to go through another year of waiting, wondering whether she would spend the next ten years of her life in an Ontario penitentiary, only to find that the Crown would settle for the smallest of sentences. There are those of us who felt that the jury was the pillar of our judicial system, that once we were found to be innocent by a group of our fellow citizens we were free to go about our business. We know now that this is not so. We also wonder how, in the future, the Crown can expect we citizens to do our duty as jurors—to sit hour after hour, day after day, studying the testimony and finally to be told, once our verdict has been rendered, that no, our opinion was not really wanted after all, only that of the lawyers. What did the Crown really accomplish through this exercise? Did they prove to the citizens of Queens County, beyond

> a reasonable doubt, that Ms. Stafford committed a crime against our society? Did they show society that she deserved to be punished? Will the sentence stop others from protecting themselves from physical or emotional violence perpetrated by their mates? Did our society derive any meaningful benefit from the second trial? We think not.

Two weeks after Jane Stafford was sentenced to six months, Michele Jewell, a twenty-five-year-old nurse in Winnipeg, was killed—her throat slit by a knife—just hours before she was to appear in divorce court. Her husband, Michael, was charged with second-degree murder. At the time of her death, Michele had been granted a restraining order against her husband. In a sworn statement, she spoke of her fear that her husband might harm her. He had threatened her just as Billy Stafford had threatened Jane. Michele cited physical and mental cruelty as her grounds for divorce. She said that reconciliation was impossible because of her husband's "abhorrent behaviour." Michele's dismembered body was found on February 29, 1984. It had been packed into garbage bags and dumped on a farm in northwestern Ontario owned by her husband's brother. As wife abuse goes, the case wasn't all that unusual. When there is death in "domestic disputes," more than 90 per cent of the time it's the woman who dies. Michele Jewell took the legal way out. It didn't work. Death usually comes to a battered wife after one beating too many, one punch or one kick too many. Often the husband pleads guilty to manslaughter or second-degree murder, and the court accepts.

CHAPTER 14
FREEDOM

Jane Stafford was not afraid of jail. She considered it just another place to live. After saying her goodbyes to Alan Ferrier and her family, she was escorted to Sheriff Cyril Page's car, which was waiting in front of the courthouse. Page and his wife drove Jane to the now-familiar Halifax Correctional Centre. Page drove to the rear of the building and escorted Jane into the guard's station, where he handed the matron a commitment form. After Page left, Jane was taken into the matron's office for processing. She was issued a pair of jeans, a blouse, a sweater, and underwear, as well as bedding, a towel, a facecloth, soap, and toothpaste. The matron filled out a card with Jane's medical history for the prison doctor, and then an Inmates' Effects List. Her jewellery, cash, and wallet were put into an envelope. From there she moved through the guard station to the cell area. "My cell was about six feet by eight feet. It had a steel bed on the wall, a sink, and a toilet. Meals were brought in, and you had to keep your own cell clean. There was no privacy at all."

Jane stayed in the cells for four days before being placed with the general prison population. From their glassed-in post, guards controlled the shower, which was turned on in the cell area for a short period each night. On her first night in jail, Jane was taking her turn in the shower with the curtain drawn.

"You Jane Stafford?" said a gruff voice directly behind the curtain. Jane didn't have time to respond. "I'd like to know who the fuck you know or who the fuck you blew to get only six months for what you did."

Jane was frightened—she didn't know who was waiting for her behind that shower curtain. She didn't know what to say or how to react. Then she remembered some advice from a friend who had been in prison. "He told me they would test me and that I had to stand up for myself or I'd be used and abused the whole time I was inside." Jane took a deep breath and yanked the curtain back.

"And just who the fuck wants to know?" shouted Jane, surprised at her own outburst. Judging by the voice, Jane expected to see a big woman. Instead, she had to look down at a frail ninety-pounder with curly red hair. They stood staring at each other, and then the woman started to laugh.

"I'm Pearl," she said. "I was just sentenced to ten years for shooting my old man. I was just wondering how come you got only six months for the same thing."

Jane had trouble to keep from laughing. Pearl was spending thirty days at the correction centre, awaiting transfer to an Ontario penitentiary. "That was my one and only unfriendly encounter all the time I was in jail," Jane would remember.

Back in her cell, Jane settled in for the night. The cell next to her was vacant, but there was a woman in the cell beyond that. She was attractive, with long, dark hair. Jane guessed her to be in her late twenties. She was reading a book, but looked over to Jane a couple of times. Pearl was wandering around outside her cell.

"You don't talk to her," Pearl said to Jane. "She's a fucking baby-killer." The young woman was Colleen Gottchall, who had killed a young boy she had been babysitting. Some said it was the worst case of child beating ever seen in the Maritimes. When other prisoners were around, Gottchall was kept locked in her cell for her own protection. She had been sentenced to twenty-five years without parole, but had won an appeal and was waiting to go back to court. Jane noticed that the woman seemed to ignore Pearl's comments. Jane decided to talk to her.

"Did you really do what Pearl said?" asked Jane.

There was no response. Jane repeated the question. There was silence for a time. Jane was startled when the woman suddenly spoke to her.

"Do you like to read?" she asked.

"Yes," replied Jane.

"I've got lots of books here if you want to borrow one."

"No thanks. I don't feel much like reading right now."

"Baby-killer!" shouted Pearl from her cell on the other side of Jane.

Gottchall ignored Pearl and continued talking to Jane, mostly about lawyers and how she didn't think too much of hers.

"Did you find it awful going in and out of the courtroom?" she asked Jane.

"What do you mean?"

"They took me in in handcuffs and people were saying awful things to me. I had to have guards all around me."

"The courtroom I was in was small and I didn't have to wear handcuffs or anything like that," said Jane.

"It was terrible..." said Gottchall, her voice trailing off.

Jane had arrived at the jail on Tuesday. On Thursday she was permitted to drive to Bridgewater to attend classes and write her exam, a day later than scheduled. From then on she was permitted to attend her classes regularly. It meant four hours of driving each day. When she returned from school on Friday, she was moved into the general prison population. Including those in the cells, there were about twenty inmates in the women's block. Jane was assigned to the dormitories. One of these had six beds, the other seven. Three additional beds had been set up in the medical room.

Shawna, a heavy-set black woman with reddish hair and light freckles, fancied herself the boss among the inmates, and nobody was about to argue with her. She weighed about 170 pounds and sported short, Afro-style hair. She and another inmate shared the medical room. Several Cape Bretoners were in Jane's dormitory. They constantly argued or engaged in horseplay, making it difficult for her to study. On the Monday night following her first weekend in prison, Shawna told Jane to sit beside her in the dining room, a sign that she was accepted by the others, and more important, by the boss. Later, Shawna and some of her friends asked Jane to teach them to play Scrabble. Jane learned a lot of new words, most of them not to be found in any dictionary.

Shawna was serving time for assaulting a pregnant woman, who lost her child as a result of the beating. Despite her tough demeanor, Shawna had a compassionate side. When she saw Jane was having a difficult time trying to study in the dormitory, she offered to trade places with her so she could do her homework in the relative peace and quiet of the medical room. Jane gratefully accepted. Now she had only one roommate—a pregnant teenager who was serving time for break and entry.

Jane was up every morning at 6 a.m. and on her way to school an hour later. She was too early for breakfast, but managed to down a cup of tea after making her bed. At school, she bought her lunch at the cafeteria. By the time she got back to jail in the evening, supper was all over with. "But the guards were good to me. They always saved some food for me. It was cold, but at least I got something to eat."

The women's section of the prison included a drab but clean common room, cement-block walls painted green and white, and vinyl lounge chairs, a pool table, a small library, a record player, and a television with a VCR. Every second week a video was brought in. Jane watched only one during her stay in the prison. It was a B-grade feature about a prison island where male and female inmates were left to fend for themselves. "You talk about sex and violence," said Jane. "I couldn't figure it. They're supposed to be rehabilitating people and they show them trash like that."

Jane was subjected to a strip search each day when she left for school and again when she returned in the evening. Her prison garb was usually a pair of jeans and a pyjama top. Each night she washed her school clothes in the laundry room. Jane's purse was also searched daily, and if she needed money for food, or to purchase something for Darren, she had to sign for it. When she wasn't studying in the evening she was writing, usually poetry.

Jane discouraged friends and family from visiting her in prison. She found it stressful to carry on a conversation through a screen. Other than inmates, guards, and schoolmates, Jane saw more of her father than anybody. He usually drove to her school or to the hospital when she began on-the-job training. He always brought lunch, which they shared in the car as they chatted. Jane enjoyed the visits from her father. Sometimes he brought along Darren, or Jamie, or her mom.

Jane was assigned to train at Queens General Hospital in Liverpool, but one of her classmates, Jocelyn Priddle, agreed to switch, allowing her to train at Fisherman's Memorial Hospital in Lunenburg, forty-five miles closer to the prison. Jane completed her shift at 3:30 p.m., which meant she had two hours to get back to prison or face the possibility of her privileges being revoked. Not once was she late.

Jane's training included two weeks at a rehabilitation centre for psychiatric patients. While there, she gained some insight into Billy Stafford's behaviour. She had carried the guilt of his death for two years, during which she saw four psychiatrists but received no satisfactory answers. Jane admired her instructor, a psychiatric nurse who was aware of her background. By the end of her first week at the centre, Jane found some answers in her study of sociopathic personality disturbances. There were eleven indicators to help identify antisocial personalities, and Jane believed that all of them related to Billy.

- Little or no conscience.
- Self-centred, poor judgement, and lack of restraint.
- Failure to learn from experience.
- Lack of patience.
- Ability to impress and exploit others.
- Impaired interpersonal relationships.
- Low tolerance for stress.
- Rejection of authority.
- Lies easily, rationalizes, and projects guilt.
- Irritates, disappoints, and distresses others.
- Lacks ability to understand and accept ethical values.

"I could relate to all of these in Bill's personality," said Jane. "All during class I kept silent. I just sat there absorbing it all. I felt like someone had just given me a million dollars."

Jane couldn't wait to get back to prison to think out all she had learned. It was raining heavily when she left the rehabilitation centre. She was so excited, she took a wrong turn, ending up on a toll bridge heading for the city of Halifax. Trapped in traffic and unable to turn around, Jane was panicking at the prospect of losing her privileges and her school year. At the toll booth, she explained her plight to a sympathetic attendant, who called for a bridge patrolman. Traffic was stopped in both directions on the bridge to allow Jane to turn around. Driving faster than usual, she was able to make up the time she had lost, and arrived at the prison before her deadline.

"I spent the whole weekend putting all I learned into logical order," said Jane. "I finally came to the realization that I didn't have to carry all that guilt around inside me. I was finally able to put a label on Billy Stafford and bury him once and for all. It took me two years to do that. The guilt is gone, but the terror of how I lived will remain forever in my memory."

On April 14, 1984, Jane Stafford, eligible for parole after serving one-third of her sentence, returned to prison from her classes. It was a rainy, overcast day. She was told by prison authorities that her release papers had come through. "I just had to sign them, pick up my belongings, and I could go," said Jane. "I ran out of there, still in my nurse's uniform with the rain hitting my face. I ran to the gate. It seemed like I waited forever for it to open for the last time."

Jane looked back to the guardhouse, wondering if the officer on duty had forgotten she was there. The guard was waving to her and smiling from behind the glass. He pressed the button to open the gate, and Jane heard his voice over the speaker: "Good luck, Jane, be happy."

CHAPTER 15
STARTING OVER

Upon her release from prison on April 14, 1984, Jane Stafford had no illusions about what lay ahead of her. Her relief that she would never again have to face the daily, all-consuming fear of Billy Stafford's irrational anger and unpredictable brutality was tempered by her knowledge that her emotional scars would never completely heal, and that forgetting the horrors she had lived through would be impossible.

She knew that she and six-year-old Darren would need long-term therapy if they were to even begin to recover from the years of trauma and abuse. Therapy, Jane understood, must be her number-one priority. There were three others—find a job, reunite her family, and help other abused women. Her first step was to legally shed the Stafford name. She and Darren were now Hurshmans. Jane Stafford was no more.

In June 1984, it was thirty-five-year-old Jane Hurshman who graduated as a fully qualified nursing assistant. She was awarded a gold pin as the best in that job at Fisherman's Memorial Hospital. Two months later she was released from parole. All that remained was a year of probation.

Jane and Darren lived for a time in Ontario, but in the fall of 1984 she was offered a job as a nursing assistant at the Halifax

County Regional Rehabilitation Centre, in Cole Harbour, Nova Scotia. The job, working with aged patients with behavioural problems, was rewarding, and Jane was paid well. At her request, she was scheduled on permanent night shift. As was typical of women who had suffered severe sexual and physical abuse, she found it difficult to sleep at night. She also preferred the night shift because it gave her time to herself.

"I like the night for its quiet peacefulness," Jane often said. "For most of my life, nighttime was a living hell. The night shift works out very well, because I sleep much better in the daytime."

The story of Jane's shotgun killing of Billy Stafford and her subsequent journey through the Canadian legal system gained the attention of the media nationwide. Her case was the subject of a CBC *fifth estate* documentary, and she agreed, in 1984, to collaborate on a book, *Life With Billy.*

Even before the book, she began speaking to women's groups, gradually gaining confidence and self-esteem. "I am sure that as far back as I can remember, I was conditioned to be a victim. My mother always said that someday things will change—someday things will get better. For her, after many years, they did. For me, this is the first time I can honestly say that life is looking good. I survived hell and I feel as if I'm a totally different person. I want to live, and I am trying hard with each passing day to find out how. I am so much more aware of life's gifts than I ever was before. I guess I just *feel* more than I ever did."

Wendy Annand, Jane's parole officer after her release from prison, saw the gradual transformation. "I really liked her. She was always so natural, with a bright, shining disposition. Knowing a bit of the background and the horror that she'd been through, and seeing what a positive outlook she had on life, was just a treat."

Annand was a slim, wiry woman who spoke forcefully, and often, against family violence. By the time her supervision of Jane ended in August 1984, they had become good friends. "Jane's basic personality never changed the whole time I knew her, but her public persona certainly became more polished, and her ability to analyze was amazing. She picked things up almost by osmosis. She wouldn't sit down and read a feminist tome on wife battering, and she wouldn't necessarily label her ideas, but just by being around people who held certain views—they came out that way."

Annand had helped set up a transition house in the town of Bridgewater, near Bangs Falls. "The number of crisis calls we got from women who were being battered is unbelievable," said Annand. "And many of them end up having to go back to their abusive husbands because of the financial reality. The welfare system down here is the pits. To leave a husband when you have children and you're worried about their future and you know you can't even feed them properly—it's a dead end.

"The daycare system is terrible, and the kind of work available to women who do leave is menial at best. People ask, 'Why do they go back?' My response is, what choice do they have?"

Jane knew exactly what these women were going through, and she moved to Halifax-Dartmouth with a promise to herself that she would do whatever she could to help them. Wendy Annand encouraged her by inviting her to participate in workshops and conferences on abuse and related topics. "Sometimes I'd ask her to come and do a presentation or sometimes to just attend. She loved it."

Annand was aware that Jane had healing of her own to do and recommended that she contact Ann Keith, executive director of Services for Sexual Assault Victims, or SSAV, in Halifax.

Keith, a soft-spoken, compassionate woman, had been a social worker since the 1960s. SSAV began in 1983 when several women at Dalhousie University received a $70,000 grant to start a program to help victims of sexual abuse. They asked Ann Keith to develop and run it. "The heart of this place is the volunteers," said Keith. About sixty handled the organization's crisis telephone lines; a dozen more were on the board of directors; and several others helped out in the office. The centre was helping about two hundred women a month.

Keith said SSAV couldn't offer long-term counselling "because our volunteers would be burned out. If women who call in have been severely damaged, we refer them to other agencies or support groups. What we do is the emotional support. If a woman has been raped, for example, we go to the hospital with her, help her deal with the police, and go through the courts with her if it comes to that."

Ann Keith remembered vividly her first meeting with Jane Hurshman in early 1985. "I didn't know who she was, but I was certainly going to talk to her." Jane explained that she had served time for killing Billy Stafford. "We just sort of talked," said Keith. "And I guess because it was a sexual assault centre, she decided to concentrate on the sexual abuse she had been subjected to.

"When she started talking about things that really bothered her, I'll never forget her eyes—they were humongous. She would almost dissociate herself. I remember thinking to myself—it was like looking into the pits of hell. What she was carrying around was incredible."

Keith's impression of Jane in that first meeting was that she was like a little girl crying out for help. "She had lost her self-worth and sense of who she was—her identity. From there we established a real comfortable, easy relationship and worked on trying to get her back. I remember one time telling her, 'I'll know you're getting better when your eyes start looking normal.'"

Ann Keith's counselling sessions with Jane were unstructured and informal, with many sessions taking place over coffee or lunch.

"Now that I am seeing Ann and communicating on a one-to-one basis," Jane wrote at the time, "I am able to get objective feedback, and I like the feeling. I don't ever remember having a person that I trusted enough to confide in. As I think back, I wonder how long ago it was that I lost my ability to trust. Ann is very compassionate and easy to talk to. My therapy sessions are usually anywhere from two to four hours—but they are helping me a great deal."

Sometimes, however, Jane asked Keith to cancel her sessions.

"I asked not to have any this month, as they leave me feeling very drained—and a bit on the depressed side," she wrote. "But all will end up well."

Keith said there were times "when I felt like I couldn't really help her, that it was getting over my head." But the counselling would go on for five years, until Keith referred Jane to a local psychiatrist for more advanced help.

Ann Keith and Jane Hurshman became good friends and continued to see each other socially. On occasion, Jane would talk to battered women who called SSAV seeking support. Also, she sometimes spoke out on behalf of SSAV at events such as the International Women's Day rally.

"We used to go to the movies once in a while and go out for dinner—as friends more than anything else," recalled Keith. "Jane had a great sense of humour and we had some good laughs together."

Jane was gradually meeting the goals she had set for herself. She was gainfully employed, she was receiving therapy, and she was helping other abused women. Her other priority—to reunite her family—also became a reality when she and Darren moved into an apartment on Cole Harbour Road, in Dartmouth. They were joined by her sons Jamie and Allen, from her first marriage. Jamie, by then thirteen, had been living with his father in the town of Milton, near Liverpool. Allen, twenty, had been living on his own.

Jane had also resolved her negative feelings toward her parents. This healing began after she killed Billy. She wrote about it later: "The first time my parents ever told me they loved me was when I was arrested and spent the weekend in jail in Halifax. When I came to court from the jail, my dad was there to take me home. He put his arms around me and held me. 'I love you, Janey,' he said. 'Come now, I'm taking you home.' It was while I was staying with them at that time that my mother first said the same three magic words, 'I love you.' I waited thirty-three years to hear my parents tell me that. It's terrible to think that I had to kill someone to get the love from my parents that I always wanted."

Although Jane felt closer to her parents than ever before, she was still feeling a lot of anger and hurt from the earlier years of emotional abuse, particularly from her father.

During counselling sessions in 1987, Jane talked to Ann Keith about confronting her parents. "Jane never did anything without thinking about it first. I knew it was really important for her. I said, 'Okay, Jane, if you want to confront them, that's fine.'"

Jane drove down to Danesville and spoke first with her mother in the kitchen and then with her father. "I took my father into the garage. I made sure something was wrong with the car, so he couldn't get out of there. I sat him down and talked to him and he cried."

From that day on, Jane felt an enduring closeness to her parents, and she enjoyed visiting them on holidays and on her days off. The quiet time Jane spent with her parents was particularly important to Maurice, because it allowed him to make up for the lost years while his children were growing up, when he was an abusive heavy drinker.

"It was so hard for him," said Jane's sister, Mona. "I thought a lot about it, and you know, a person, to a degree, is a product of their environment. When he was eleven, he built a little addition on the side of the house. It wasn't much, but it was his spot and that's where he used to live. He was thirteen when he left home. The things that he went through as a child weren't very pleasant, and sometimes people don't know the whole story as to why a person becomes what they become."

Mona said that Maurice Hurshman worked from the time he was thirteen just to survive. He was married at the age of seventeen—a year older than Jane was when she married Milfie Whynot.

"You have four children, you're in the service, and believe me, they don't discourage drinking—unfortunately for him," said Mona. She said he had not smoked or drank in years "and certainly much longer than that since he hit my mother... I remember one time when I was at university and I had come home to visit them, and he said how life could have been so different for everybody and how sorry he was for all the pain he had caused because of the drinking. He realized how much he'd missed and how much was lost. At least he made an attempt to change his life—and did change his life."

Jane wrote around that time that her healing was far from complete and that she still had hurts and some wounds that would never heal, but that life was improving for her. "I was always so dominated—first by my father, then by my first husband, but mostly by Bill. There didn't seem to be any way that I could break away from it. Now I am finding I can talk about it, then walk away from it. I am not detached—I still hurt—but I am not controlled by it anymore. I cannot rewrite my past and I cannot forget, but I can get on with the rest of my life."

Carrie Rafuse felt uncomfortable the first time she met Jane Hurshman, in 1983. It was after Jane had returned to Nova Scotia from Ontario to await a new trial. Both women were enrolled in a government-sponsored job readiness training (JRT) program in Bridgewater. Jane was upgrading her education, completing grade twelve so that she could enrol in a nursing course.

Since 1988, Carrie Rafuse had been a crisis counsellor at Harbour House, a Bridgewater transition shelter for battered women. "The JRT course is supposed to help you get back into the work force," she said in a 1993 interview at the kitchen table in her Bridgewater home, where she lived with her two grown daughters.

Carrie is outgoing, with a cheerful disposition. She likes people and couldn't understand her negative feelings toward Jane when they first met. "I had a funny feeling about her. It was like she was looking through me... I could sense something about her. She always talked to me, and seemed to like me, and I was nice to her, but there was something about her...

"Then one morning I had the radio on and was getting ready for school when I heard on the news—'Jane Marie Stafford' and her second trial coming up. And all of a sudden—that's Jane! No wonder I'd been getting weird vibes. I realized then, she had a lot on her mind."

Jane did have a lot on her mind. In a radio interview three years later, she said the JRT course helped "build up some self-esteem and some confidence. That's when I started to realize that I was a human being. But I was still carrying all the guilt around and I felt like I wore a sign on my head that said, 'You're a murderer.'"

The day Carrie Rafuse heard the radio report, she told Jane about it at school. They talked for a while, and their friendship grew from that day. A short time later, Carrie, a Seventh-day Adventist, invited Jane to attend a church meeting in Liverpool to hear a visiting preacher.

"She said she'd love to," recalled Carrie. "We had dinner first and after the church meeting we chatted and chatted, and that was it—we just hit it off."

Like Jane, Carrie was pregnant in her mid-teens and married the father. The marriage was an unhappy one, and she and her husband separated in January 1975, three weeks after her second child was born. Like Billy Stafford, Carrie's husband was a scallop fisherman, and in 1976 he died in a storm at sea.

"Jane could relate to me," said Carrie. "Maybe because Bill and my husband were both dead. We became very close friends. And between her first and second trials, I'd go out to Bangs Falls where she was living and we often sat up talking and having tea until three or four in the morning."

One night, Carrie surprised a burglar in the trailer where she lived. He was wearing a mask, and he screamed and charged at her, but she fended him off with a lamp and he ran out the door. "I think he was frightened and he just wanted to get out of there." Carrie told Jane she was scared, and Jane offered to come down with Darren and stay with her for the weekend. "The first night I suddenly realized, here I am worried about a burglar and yet I'm sleeping beside someone who killed somebody. It took me two years to tell Jane about that, but we had a great laugh."

Carrie Rafuse was in the Liverpool courtroom in 1984 when Jane was sentenced to six months in prison for manslaughter.

Jane was ready to go to jail, but her main concern was the nursing exam she was scheduled to write the next day.

"After she was sentenced," said Carrie, "they took her into the back of the courtroom and she asked if I could come back to see her for a moment. Here she was going to jail for six months and all she was worried about was her books."

"Carrie, you've got to get me my damn books," said Jane. "I've got a test tomorrow."

Jane wrote her exam a day late and passed with high marks.

"I wanted to visit her [in prison], but it wasn't good at all," said Carrie. "It made her feel really bad. It was an awful place. So we decided to meet after school whenever we could. We'd have about ten minutes to talk. She loved Big Turk chocolate bars. She was addicted to them and I always took them to her."

Carrie became tearful when she recalled a conversation she had with Jane about a year after the church service in Liverpool.

"That night in the church," Jane told her, "I was looking at you and I decided, 'I want to be just like her—friendly, open, and nice. And she's got lots of friends and she knows where she's going.'"

Jane's comments surprised and saddened Carrie.

"You know, Jane," she replied, "you don't have to be like anybody. Just be yourself—you're great."

Like Jane's other friends, Carrie witnessed her friend's self-esteem and self-confidence blossom after she was released from prison and began speaking out on behalf of other abused women.

"She had no identity before, and now, all of a sudden, she became this person," said Carrie.

CHAPTER 16
ROAD TO BRYONY

As the staff at any shelter for battered women could attest, Jane Hurshman's suffering at the hands of Billy Stafford was not unusual in the netherworld of spousal abuse. And horror stories of domestic violence can be found in police reports in any North American city or town.

Jane felt a special kinship with those other women caught in the same web of despair, degradation, and depravity that had entrapped her and driven her to kill Billy. Jane wanted to help in any way she could.

At an August 13, 1985, meeting of the Queens County Council, six of eleven councillors voted against providing a $6,400 grant for a proposed transition house to aid battered women in Queens County and adjoining Lunenburg County. Two male councillors were particularly vocal in their opposition. Councillor Joe Rogers said he couldn't see a need for such a facility and that shelters become vacation spots for some women and entice them away from their homes and families. And Councillor Laurie Smith said that women bring on their own troubles. He added that what some women need today "is a good kick in the backside."

The local newspaper, *The Advance*, published in Liverpool, supported the transition house in its editorials. And reporting about the August 13 meeting brought a spate of angry letters to the editor deploring the actions of council. One of the letters was from Jane Hurshman, who was especially appalled by the remarks of Councillor Smith:

> Unless this man has himself lived in an environment of domestic violence I don't think that he has the right to say that "in some cases all they simply need is a kick in their backsides." If this man had any idea of what he was talking about he would know that once a woman takes that first kick it is the start of an act of violence against her will. It is a terrible way to have to live; a life of suspense and fear, when you wonder at all times when the next act of violence is going to occur…
>
> I think that the councillors who are against this should be ashamed of themselves. I do not know how many thousands of dollars my trial cost the taxpayers, but I am sure that most of the public in Queens County would be in favour of this transition house…I pray that in the near future these same councillors who now oppose this motion will have a change of heart and realize just how desperately this transition house is needed.

Councillor Laurie Smith did recant, and a month later backed a motion to provide funds for the transition house, which opened in 1986. Other communities, including the town of Liverpool, supported the transition house and were ready to proceed with it without participation by the Queens County Council. Councillor Joe Rogers retired from politics and did not run in the 1985 municipal elections. Councillor Laurie Smith ran again but was defeated.

In late November of 1986, shortly after her first visit to Bryony House, a Halifax shelter for battered women, Jane met a terrified woman who was to become one of her closest friends. (Pseudonyms are used in this account to protect the woman's identity and that of her children.)

Donna Smith grew up in a medium-sized Ontario city. Her father was abusive, and she was six when her mother left home after a brutal beating, never to return. Donna, her younger brother, and her older sister were left with their father.

"I know now that she didn't hate us," said Donna, in her mid-thirties in 1993. "I used to blame her a lot for not taking us with her. But she couldn't have supported us, and if she had taken us, he would have found her. I don't know if she's alive or dead."

Donna's father turned to his daughters for sexual gratification. "He started with my older sister. He used to beat her and abuse her sexually. She became a runaway and left for good at the age of thirteen."

On Donna's tenth birthday, her father sent one of his male friends into her bedroom. "This guy raped me with my father out in the kitchen laughing," said Donna, anger choking her voice. "All my life he said I owed him this and that because he could have sent us to Children's Aid when my mother left. He and his friends sexually abused me from age ten to seventeen."

One night in 1977, Donna was waiting for a bus on a main downtown street when a man dragged her down an alley at knifepoint and punched and kicked her before raping her. "People heard me screaming but nobody tried to help me." The rapist was eventually arrested when he attempted to attack another woman.

Every day for two weeks after the rape, Donna's father forced her to go with him to the scene of the attack. There, he verbally abused her, blaming her for the rape. Donna tried to kill herself, swallowing a deadly mix of pills. She was taken to hospital, where her stomach was pumped out. "I told them that if I was forced to go home, I'd do it again," she said. She stayed with friends for six months until her father found her and forced her to return home. His sexual assaults, however, ceased.

It was at this point that Robert came into her life. He was nineteen years old and in the military. She found a good job at a local hospital, where she worked for five years. She and Robert were inseparable, and they were married in the summer of 1982. She was twenty-three and he was twenty-four. That fall they moved to military housing on a Canadian Forces base in Ontario.

Using words chillingly similar to those Jane Hurshman once used to describe her first months with Billy Stafford, Donna described Robert as "my knight in shining armour." He had rescued her from an abusive father, just as Jane believed Billy had saved her from a bleak, monotonous marriage to an alcoholic.

Robert, like Billy, also had a dark, violent past: in his mid-teens he had been sent to a correctional centre after trying to kill his parents. "Everybody was terrified of him," said Donna. "But in those first five years I was with him, I never saw any of this."

For both Jane and Donna, pregnancy triggered the end of the fairy tale. Billy Stafford's verbal and emotional abuse of Jane increased throughout her pregnancy. The physical abuse came later, after Darren was born. Robert didn't wait that long. He first struck Donna when she was six months pregnant. "He had wanted me to bring him a chocolate bar, but he didn't tell me that, and because I didn't read his mind he kicked me down the stairs when I came back from the store. I didn't say anything when I went to the hospital. I just told them I fell."

To those familiar with the dynamics of violence against women, the conduct of Billy and Robert wasn't surprising: 40 per cent of abusive husbands begin hitting their spouses during a first pregnancy.

Donna spent three days in hospital after the assault. Like most first-time abusers, Robert offered a tearful apology and promised it would never happen again. His promise was hollow—the usual pattern for batterers. The abuse continued, escalating in frequency and severity.

Mary, Donna's first-born, was a breech birth delivered by Caesarean section. On her first night home, Donna was exhausted and bleeding after two weeks in hospital. When Robert had to get up with the baby at 3 a.m., he called her "that fucking little bitch." And when Donna tried to leave three months later, Robert threatened to kill Mary.

At five-foot-two and 110 pounds, Donna was no match for her husband, who was a shade under six feet and over two hundred pounds. And she was angry that the military police on the base did nothing to help her. "The first time I called them he told them, 'Get the fuck out. It's none of your goddamn business,' and they never came back after that. They were afraid of him. So I would end up in the hospital, covering up, lying."

When Mary was six months old, Robert tied her to her crib and threatened to sexually abuse her if Donna didn't agree to participate in degrading sexual acts with him. Donna, terrified for her daughter, went along. From then on bondage and beatings became routine, with Donna as the victim. This pattern paralleled the sexual abuse that Jane Hurshman was subjected to by Billy Stafford.

"That's when I got addicted to Valium—to get through it," said Donna. "My doctor knew what was going on. He didn't report it or anything, just gave me Valium."

Donna was four months pregnant with their second child when Robert was transferred to a Canadian Forces base in Nova Scotia in the spring of 1985. "I almost lost Bobby," said Donna.

"I was in the hospital for two-and-a-half months before I had him because Robert kicked me so hard."

One night, three weeks before the baby's due date, Robert arrived drunk at the hospital. "I'm going to make sure that fucking kid won't be born alive," he said, lashing out with a punch that left Donna with a black eye. She screamed, and the nurses called security to remove him. The trauma caused Donna to go into labour that night. Bobby was born twenty-three months after Mary.

Donna was now living the robotic existence of many battered women—cowering in fear of the man she once loved, her senses dulled by excessive use of tranquillizers. Indiscriminate beatings and sexual assaults had become commonplace. Her self-esteem was non-existent, and her only reason for living was to protect her children as best she could.

Robert, like Billy, was prone to fits of rage for no apparent reason. Also like Billy, his face would redden and his eyes would bulge. Robert kicked Donna so often she eventually required arthroscopic surgery on one of her knees. After the operation, he came home from an evening of drinking to find her sitting with her leg propped up on a table. "You bitch!" he sneered, raising his foot and stomping down on her knee with so much force that it snapped. Donna fell to the floor screaming in agony and had to crawl to the telephone to call for an ambulance.

"At the hospital, I lied and told them that I fell," she said. Because of that injury, further operations were required, and she was left with bone chips floating under her kneecap.

At one point an army social worker from the base's Family Support Services visited Donna. "He left crying," she said. "He handed me some money to get groceries and said he couldn't do anything."

Young Bobby had a chronic respiratory problem, and in November 1986 it led to their escape from the torture chamber they called home. Jean (a pseudonym), a friend and neighbour who was aware that Donna and her children were being abused, accompanied her and the boy to the hospital. Bobby was admitted, and the two women went to a private office, where a doctor began asking Donna routine questions.

"What does your husband do for a living?" he asked.

Jean jumped to her feet. "He beats her!" she exclaimed. "He beats her and he rapes her! Look at the marks on her arms and neck."

Donna and the children were kept at the hospital for a week. Social workers were brought in, and she was given an ultimatum—either enter a battered wives' shelter or be forced to give up her children.

Donna wasn't about to give up her children, and she reluctantly agreed to move into Bryony House, a Halifax shelter for battered women. Donna was fearful and uneasy when she and her children arrived at the transition house.

"The counsellors were excellent, but I didn't trust anybody and I wouldn't talk to them. I kept to myself. I was forced to be there, but I was sure I'd be going back home. I believed I had no place else to go."

She was certain Robert would find her and come after her as her father had done years before. That fear was magnified when Robert began telephoning the next day. The staff refused to acknowledge Donna's presence to him.

The location of Bryony House (and of all shelters and transition homes) is supposed to be confidential, but within a day or two, Robert was parked across the street. The police were aware of his presence, but he was on public property and there was nothing they could do. There were no laws against stalking at that time. Robert continued telephoning, asking first for Donna and then for Mary. "I know my kids are there," he would say angrily.

Donna remained totally withdrawn. Her father had cursed her and cut her off from the rest of the family when she told him she was in a shelter. She seldom slept and spent most of her time on a couch in the living room at the shelter. She didn't realize it, but she was also suffering from Valium withdrawal. "Every doctor I went to prescribed it. At Bryony House they lock up all your drugs and give them to you only as prescribed on the bottle. They were giving me two or three a day, while I was used to fifteen or twenty a day. I was shaking and my nerves were shot. I never slept."

At the end of Donna's second week at the shelter, Jane Hurshman happened to drop in to see the place for the first time. She didn't see Donna on that visit, but the counsellors told Jane about her, and Jane left her phone number.

"I didn't know anything about her," said Donna. "I wasn't from Nova Scotia and I hadn't read *Life With Billy*. It took me about an hour to get up the courage to call. Jane told me she had been through an abusive situation somewhat like mine and maybe she could help me. She asked if we could possibly get together and I agreed. After I hung up they told me who she was and that she had killed her husband."

Jane returned to Bryony House the next day, and the two women went into a private room to talk. "It was amazing," said Donna. "I didn't have to say anything at first. She talked and it was as if she was reading my mind. It was the first time that anybody understood how I really felt. She wasn't judgmental. If I told other people about my life they would be shocked, or start crying, or feel sorry for me, or start saying something stupid like, 'If my husband ever hit me just once it would be the last time he ever hit me.' You just want to take them and shake them when they talk like that."

Jane was stylishly dressed, and Donna was impressed by her composure and self-confidence. "She just knew how to express herself and she made me feel so comfortable and at ease."

"You're worried that there's not enough protection—that Bryony House isn't safe, aren't you?" asked Jane. Donna nodded.

"Don't worry," said Jane. "It will be okay. They didn't have safe houses when I was with Billy. At least none I knew about."

Jane talked about Billy and some of the abuse she had gone through. "See, I came out of it," she said. "You can do the same. You *do* have a chance."

"You don't even know me," said Donna.

"I have a feeling we're going to become really good friends," said Jane.

When the two women came out of the room, Donna was smiling. It was the first time counsellors and residents at Bryony House had seen her smile.

Despite the abuse that Donna had suffered, Robert had a legal right to see his children. A lawyer was arranged for Donna, and she went to court to seek interim custody until a final hearing could be scheduled. Donna was terrified at the thought of being in the same courtroom as Robert.

"Do you think he'd bring a gun in with him?" asked her lawyer on the way to the hearing. His question deepened her panic.

"I just froze on the witness stand," said Donna. "I couldn't even talk. The judge said he'd never seen such fear in a woman." He awarded her interim custody of the children.

Robert always went to bed at night with a pistol on his bedside table, and his gun collection outdid that of Billy Stafford. He had at least a dozen guns, including pistols, rifles, and shotguns. He also kept a large collection of knives.

With the custody hearing behind her, Donna was feeling much better, but shortly after, she was confronted by a new crisis. One of the two child care workers at Bryony House came upon three-year-old Mary masturbating in a loft in the basement playroom. The child told the counsellor, "Daddy does that to me." Donna suffered an emotional breakdown when she was told about Mary.

"It was absolutely devastating because I thought I had protected her by doing everything he asked me to do," she said.

Because of Donna's emotional state, it was decided to put the children into temporary foster care. The thought of her baby daughter being sexually molested was unbearable, and Donna contemplated suicide. Bryony House counsellors found twelve bottles of extra-strength sleeping pills that she had hidden.

Jane was informed of Donna's condition and spent as much time with her as she could. *Life With Billy* had been released a few months before, and Jane was caught up in a flurry of promotion events and interviews.

"She had to go to Yarmouth to do a book signing and radio interviews," said Donna. "She got special permission from Bryony House for me to go with her."

The two women left Halifax in Jane's car before 8 a.m. On the 190-mile trip to Yarmouth, they listened to music "and talked and talked and talked," recalled Donna. "It was just great."

They were to stay overnight in a private home. "The location of the house was supposed to be a secret," said Donna. "But when we arrived the woman who lived there was frightened and told us a man had called and threatened Jane. He told her he was going to do to Jane what Jane had done to Billy. I got really scared. Nobody could figure out how he knew we would be staying there."

An RCMP officer was assigned to stay overnight in the house with the women. "He and Jane started joking around," said Donna. "He said maybe Jane should be protecting *us*, because she probably had better aim than him. They both laughed. At first I couldn't believe they would joke about something like that, but then I realized it made us feel at ease."

The Mountie stayed on the main floor while the women slept upstairs. There were only two bedrooms, and Jane and Donna had to share a bed. Before they went to sleep, Jane told the story about staying with her friend Carrie Rafuse, who had been worried about a burglar but who suddenly realized she was sleeping in the same bed as a murderer.

"We laughed about that," said Donna, "but then it made me think—I'm in the same bed as a murderer too."

During their stay, a newspaper reporter interviewed Jane and the women visited Juniper House, a Yarmouth shelter for battered women. At the shelter, Donna was asked to introduce herself, and Jane gave a short address to the staff and residents.

The round-the-clock police protection continued. There were two officers with them when they went to a bookstore at a small downtown shopping centre.

"They set up two white wicker chairs for us and there were flowers on each side," said Donna. "People must have wondered who I was."

There was a steady line-up and Jane signed books for two or three hours. "It was non-stop," Donna remembered. "It was mostly women, but there were some men. Most of them wished her well."

From the bookstore, Jane went to a local television station for an interview.

On the drive back to Halifax, Donna thought about the anonymous threat. It would not be the last time she heard about Jane's life being threatened.

CHAPTER 17
SPEAKING OUT

During and after her trial, and before the publication of *Life With Billy* in the summer of 1986, Jane Hurshman was subjected to intense media attention. After living such an isolated, tortured existence with Billy Stafford, she found it overwhelming.

In a thirteen-page self-analysis written in 1985, three years after Billy's death, Jane wrestled with her feelings about her privacy. Many of the same themes would resurface later in her public speeches:

> In the days, weeks, and months following Bill's death, the world felt different. I was guilty! The world looked and sounded uglier and more cruel than it was before. The reporters and others wanting stories—demanding. I felt invaded, harassed, and used. Why was anyone interested? Why did they care? Why didn't they leave me alone? I was bewildered and frightened.
>
> An ache began in my chest—and it didn't go away. I had never sought the limelight. My past is always present. Bill's life was as violent as his death. Mine had been one tragedy after another. I've lived a life of pain that has left

Brian Vallée

Jane's middle son, Jamie Whynot (*left*), with Anita Bruce, and his brother Allen Whynot.

Brian Vallée

Jane's oldest son, Allen, and his wife, Charlene. Their daughter, Haley Dawn, was born on Valentine's Day, 1993. She would have been Jane's first grandchild.

Mona Donnelly

Jane's "pride and joy," her youngest son, Darren.

Carrie Rafuse

Jane with her husband, Joel Corkum, on their honeymoon in October 1991.

Ann Keith

Ann Keith, executive director of Services for Sexual Assault Victims, was counsellor and friend to Jane.

Liz Forestell

Liz Forestell, executive director of the Elizabeth Fry Society in Halifax, appointed Jane to her board of directors. Both women were appointed to a committee to study the needs of incarcerated women.

Annette Bushen

Jane with her friend Annette Bushen, who worked with her at the Halifax County Regional Rehabilitation Centre.

Halifax Chronicle-Herald

Jane and Darlene Darrington, victim of the "motorcycle rapist," comfort each other at an event marking the second anniversary of the killing of fourteen women in Montreal.

Mona Donnelly

Jane, after her wedding in Mahone Bay, with her sisters Mona (*centre*) and Sandy.

Jo Sheridan

Jane's "pen friend," Jo Sheridan, from British Columbia, considered Jane "a most remarkable woman."

Valery Cromwell

Jane and her childhood friend, Valery Cromwell, celebrate the 1987 New Year in Bermuda. "It was to celebrate my freedom... and a new life," said Jane.

Carrie Rafuse

Jane with Carrie Rafuse, one of her best friends.

James Tynes

Jane with James Tynes, whom she dated for more than four years.

Corporal Peter Astephen, the veteran Halifax officer who led the investigation into Jane's death.

Brian Vallée

Stu Ducklow / Halifax *Daily News*

On March 2, 1992, about 300 people lit candles at St. John's United Church in memory of Jane.

many scars. Often I still cry within and a knot forms in my throat. The public exposure took a physical as well as an emotional toll: At times, I couldn't believe it was really me all of this was happening to. I wasn't me anymore. I was somebody I didn't know, somebody lost and scared; somebody whose life seemed to have no focus. I just couldn't believe it. I felt like I was falling apart right before everyone's eyes and nobody noticed.

I was unable to sleep and barely able to eat. I was still frightened and scared. I felt cut off from everyone—the outside world, my family, myself. The only thing that had changed was that Bill was dead.

When I was told that Bill was dead, I was in my own world. I heard no noise—the world was soundless. I felt like I was floating, my head somewhere near the ceiling. No turning back. I kept going, fighting to hold on to the rational me, trying to let everything sink in. Bill was really dead. Maybe now there would be peace. I couldn't cry. I don't know if I wanted to, but I couldn't.

When Bill died, I thought it would be over. It wasn't over—it's still not over. It keeps coming back at me. I am a private person. I need my privacy. It was very rough and still is.

In the document, it becomes obvious that Jane Hurshman's desire for privacy was in conflict with her determination to help other battered women. But it was a problem she was working through:

Success has a new meaning to me. Personal accomplishment, doing well in school or business, used to be important to me. It's not anymore. Making a positive

> difference in the lives of other people is now the way I define accomplishment. That's what makes me go.

Some of Jane's friends and family were opposed to her collaboration on a book about her life. In the document, she addressed those concerns:

> I have told them, to me, it is necessary. And hopefully, some day, they will understand why. I used to be so dominated by Bill, there was no way I could break away from it. Now I can talk about him and walk away from it. I am not detached, but I'm not controlled by it anymore.

When Jane began to speak out against family violence, she and others were surprised at how good she was. Her voice didn't waver, and she spoke with a forceful passion that held her audience. It was her parole officer, Wendy Annand, who encouraged her to speak out. Her first address was to a criminal justice workshop in Lunenburg County in February 1985. Jane was on a victims' panel, and Annand was the moderator.

"There were about seventy-five people there," said Annand, "and a lot of them were very impressed with Jane. There were a lot of teary eyes. She was nervous at first, but once she got into it she was just fine."

It was particularly emotional when Jane talked about the scars she and her sons, particularly Darren, had been left with after the brutal years with Billy Stafford. "Not too long ago," she said, "Darren, who was then seven, came into the house and said something sassy to me. Without thinking, I turned and slapped him. With eyes as big as saucers, he looked at me and said, 'Mom, don't you think I've had enough of that?' I reached out and I hugged him and I said, 'I'm sorry, babe, I'm sorry.' So you see, that one slap brought back years of painful memories—memories that are his for life."

Jane told the workshop that she believed Billy was jealous of his son. "Taking Darren to the sitter and me going to work was our only refuge from this monster. From the time Darren began walking at a year old he was not allowed to cry. As Bill said, 'You're a man now—men don't cry.' If Darren cried, he was beaten. He was beaten until he lay there and didn't make a sound... What kind of memories does that child have?"

Jane did not have kind words for psychiatrists. "Darren and I saw a psychiatrist for two years," she said, "and for me, I don't think it helped. It was like sitting and talking to a brick wall. They're cold—there is no emotion. Sometimes you get a yes, sometimes a no, or maybe just a grunt. There was no feedback. I needed somebody to respond to me. I was guilty. I carried that guilt for two years before I even started to get any answers."

Jane described her state of mind when she fired the shot that killed Billy Stafford. "At that point there was no past, no present, no future—only the moment. I just stuck the gun in the window and pulled the trigger. I can look back on it all now, three years later, and I can say I'm sorry it ended the way it did, because no one has the right to take another person's life, no matter what. But I will *never* be sorry that Stafford is dead."

"I was very, very nervous when I spoke to all those professionals," wrote Jane later. "When I got done, I really felt I got my point across, because as I looked out at my audience, I knew I touched their hearts. I knew for a moment in time, that each and every one there felt a bit of my hurt. I knew it as I watched tears run down their faces—even the men."

On the evening of Jane's address to the workshop, there was a dinner at which the provincial attorney general, Harry How, was the guest speaker. "He is the same guy who ordered my appeal," Jane wrote to a friend. "I had no idea he was going to speak. When he stood up and introduced himself, I got up from my table and walked out."

At about 10 p.m., a woman from the provincial parole service telephoned Jane in her room and asked her if she could go to the hotel's main entrance to meet Attorney General How, who wanted to talk to her before he left. Jane hesitated a minute and then agreed. How introduced himself, and apologized for granting the appeal in her case, but said he had no choice.

How had listened to the taped evidence from Jane's trial several times, and once told a reporter: "The provocation was absolutely inconceivable in its brutality and degradation." How said he was advised that he had to go ahead with the appeal of the jury's verdict: "Self-defence only covers an immediate action or confrontation. It doesn't take into account the accumulation of provocation. I searched in vain for any precedent in Canadian or British law. The law hadn't caught up with the growing phenomenon of wife abuse. Society's attitude in Liverpool was that this lady had suffered enough—beyond human endurance—but the law provided no defence."

Jane would write that when she met How they talked for a time, "and then, right out of the blue, How said: 'Now, Jane—off the record—I want to say, that cocksucker should have been shot a long time ago.'"

Jane would write to a friend that those were How's exact words, and that she was "shocked, amazed, and flattered... It gave me a new outlook on things."

(How went on to become chief provincial court judge, retiring in 1988.)

With the publication of *Life With Billy* in 1986, Jane Hurshman became as much a celebrity as she was an activist against domestic violence. She appeared on *The Journal* and *Front Page Challenge* on CBC television, and on CBC's national radio show *Morningside*. She also did dozens of interviews with television, radio, and print media and was in demand as a speaker.

Jane soon discovered that the people she felt most comfortable speaking to were battered women. Her favourite venues were the shelters that offered them refuge. "It is therapeutic for me to be with others who have suffered what I suffered," she said. "When I'm with them, I don't feel like a freak anymore. We don't shock each other. We don't get embarrassed. We don't feel set apart. We feel safe enough to share, to cry, to laugh. We don't just sit around airing our grief. We also reaffirm life. We say that we are ready to live again and what we want is to find out how."

In a speech at Hestia House, a shelter for battered women in Saint John, New Brunswick, Jane said she had to learn to communicate "in order to get past my fears, my hurts, my injuries, and my insecurities."

"I am a survivor," she announced proudly. "I want all of you to be aware that you have a trap door that is on hinges, and if you choose to draw that door shut, then no one can get inside. I am here to open those doors and to allow other women in violent situations to realize that they are not alone. It is wrong to ignore battering, thinking it will go away. That does not work. If you ignore it, it continues to spread like a cancer.

"By relating my feelings I hope to help other battered women realize they are victims and they are not alone and they don't have to blame themselves. It was a long time after Stafford's death before I began to realize I was a victim, and even longer to understand that I was not to blame, nor did I have to carry the guilt for his actions. I knew nothing of transition houses or support groups. I felt totally isolated and trusted no one. In my community, everyone knew I was being abused, yet no one acknowledged the fact. No one spoke about it out loud.

"Battering isn't the taboo—talking about it is. And it can only continue if we keep silent. I was born in a period when people did not reveal their personal problems, everything was kept secret, as though if you spoke out about it, then it would be a negative reflection on you and the family.

"We all keep up appearances and tell our social lies—that's deep-rooted, early conditioning. As time goes on, and the abuse continues, bitterness piles up and emotions turn to hate. *You* feel like an outcast. *You* feel like the criminal.

"In my opinion, I was a hostage in my own home, living with the threat that others than myself would be killed unless I obeyed my captor. Stafford was my captor and he used guns, knives, and fists to control my every move, to isolate me, to degrade me, and to keep me totally captive and eventually destroy me.

"If society would accept domestic violence for what it is—a crime—then I am sure my life would have turned out differently. Instead, it is accepted behaviour."

The one question that Jane was most often asked was why she stayed all that time with Billy Stafford. Other severely battered women knew the answer, but even when she spoke in shelters such as Hestia House she felt compelled to repeat it. "The first and foremost reason women stay is fear. I lived in a world where fear was my reality. It was fear that immobilized me and ruled my every thought and decision. My guts and my mind were so full of fear that I was incapable of feeling anything else. I want you to understand that in the mind of anyone who has been severely beaten, fear blots out all reasoning.

"Also, my fear of not being believed kept me in my situation. My own personal story is shocking and unbelievable, yet it's so very, very true. When you are a victim, each day of existence takes its toll. I became an empty shell. I was like a terminally ill patient waiting for death, yet hoping for a magic cure, always thinking as long as I stayed alive, there might be a slight chance of survival for my sons and myself.

"Women in violent situations are in a state of helplessness which incapacitates them. You're in total isolation. I felt—as I know other battered women feel—that I was the only person in the world living like this. Battered women need to know that they are the victims and they are not the cause of the abuse, nor do they have to stay and put up with it. Domestic violence is not a sickness, nor a symptom of a problematic marriage—it is a crime."

In a speech to Bryony House residents and staff in late 1986, Jane said that some women stayed in abusive relationships because "they want to make the marriage work and they hope things can improve. Others stay because they experience deep shame which makes them feel like an outcast, or because they fear the unknown. Being on your own is scary, and when choosing between two evils, you usually choose the devil you know, not the one you don't know. Others stay because they don't have the money or the means to leave, and repeated beatings are like electric shocks, they take away your ability to respond to any form of stimuli or to think clearly.

"There are a lot more *Janes* out there—too many. When I pulled that trigger, it was too late for me to turn back, but it will never be too late for me to reach out and help others."

Jane warned the women that healing takes time and that some scars would never disappear. "I still have my down times, and not so long ago while feeling down I took a drive. During my drive, I saw a farmer and his horse ploughing up his field. Most people looking at this scene would have thought, 'My, what a peaceful setting.' But when I looked at it, I saw my life in front of me, I saw that the horse had blinders on and the purpose of blinders was to ensure that the horse moved straight ahead without seeing what was happening around him. As I watched, I realized that my whole life had been lived with blinders on. I had been able to move in only one direction, because someone else had always been in control and made my decisions for me.

"Now, for the first time, I do not have blinders on. I am in control of my life. I can make my own decisions. I do have a choice and I want all of you to take your blinders off and open that trap door and give all of us victims the right to have a choice. Help us to have a life without violence.

"I know that by my reaching out and trying to help other victims, I am also helping myself heal. My emotional scars are very deep. Eventually, with time, my feelings of fear and anger and powerlessness have lessened and a sense of purpose has replaced them."

Society's role in the healing process, Jane believed, must be to provide safe haven and solid, timely support when battered women decide to break from an abusive mate. "For somebody abused over a long period of time, it's usually a spur-of-the-moment decision to leave, and they need the help right then and there—not two hours from now, not tomorrow, not next week. When they make that decision, they are ready to go, they've made up their mind, they need the help from the outside from that point on."

That help and support, she said, must extend to the legal system. "A courtroom is a very cold, intimidating place, it is scary and its people—the judges and lawyers and the Crown—are very dominating and powerful. Victims need courtroom support."

In a 1987 radio interview, Jane was asked if witnessing her father abuse her mother had affected her later in her life. "It was a major factor," she replied. "Girls seeing that in a home generally become passive and submissive, and that's exactly what I was, with the thought in the back of my head that, you know, someday this might get better. In the meantime you just sort of put up with it and live with it. It's what my mother did. She put up with it and lived with it, and she said that someday things would get better. Well, for her they did. But in my case, and in most cases, it never does, it just goes from bad to worse.

"You're conditioned to be a victim, vulnerable to this sort of thing. On the male side, it's a learned behaviour also, except the male usually comes out the aggressor and the female, passive and submissive."

Over and over, in her interviews and speeches, Jane urged women not to be "silent screamers behind closed doors. You're worthy of being heard." She urged women to leave the first time they are assaulted. "If it's a just-starting situation, pack your bag and leave—get out."

In a radio interview with Kelly Ryan of *Maritime* magazine after *Life With Billy* was published, Jane admitted that collaborating on the book had been very difficult for her. "I had to go back into the situation and relive everything. There were times when I didn't think I was going to get through it at all. Until I got the book in my hands about two weeks ago when the courier delivered it, I'd never seen it. I was just so overwhelmed when I held it in my hands. And I opened it and I read it through from cover to finish and I just closed it up and I was still looking at it and I thought, 'It's really over—it's really over—it's somebody I used to know,' and it was such a nice, nice feeling. In the end, the heartaches I went through were worth it—it was the best therapy I could have had."

Carrie Rafuse noticed a change in Jane about the time she began collaborating on the book. And after it was published, she glimpsed, for the first time, her friend's troubling dark side. "I know she was pleased with the book. But after it was finished she told me she didn't want to live."

"I feel like a kid on Christmas Eve," Jane told her. "You're all excited and waiting. But after the gifts are opened and dinner is over, there's a let-down. That's how I feel."

It would not be the last time Jane told Carrie she didn't want to live.

CHAPTER 18
ROMANCE

Jane Hurshman worried that after the physical and sexual abuse she had suffered, a normal relationship with a man might be impossible. "The abuse was very humiliating and disgusting," she wrote to a friend. "I felt very used and degraded in the worst possible way. Those are memories that I will have to carry the rest of my life. I have been sexually abused, hurt, and raped, and I hate men. I doubt if I will ever again trust any man enough to have a physical or sexual relationship."

The letter was written in Ontario when Jane was staying with her sister Mona after her release from prison. In it she also said she was bored and homesick, even though she had found work two weeks previously. "I got myself a steady job and I started on the 10th," she wrote. "I work permanent nights at an old folks' home. It works out with Darren, as I am home in time to get him up and off to school. I sleep all day and have the evenings with him and then he is well in bed before I go to work—so he doesn't even realize I'm even gone."

Jane told her friend that Darren had no kids his own age to play with and that she had been inquiring about a nursing job in the Halifax area.

She also talked about a male friend from Bangs Falls whom she had been dating between her trials. He had been calling and writing to her in Ontario.

"I miss him and I want to be with him," said Jane. "Yet I get scared when I think of getting seriously involved with a man. It was all right when I was seeing him before because I didn't think there was any future for us."

Within a month of writing that letter, Jane was offered the job at the Halifax County Regional Rehabilitation Centre, in Cole Harbour, and she and Darren returned to Nova Scotia. Annette Bushen, her friend and former nursing classmate, who had been hired by the centre three months earlier, said Jane never once talked about the man she had been dating in Bangs Falls. "It seems when Jane got close to any male person, she got scared, and you can't blame her."

But soon after Jane started working at the rehab centre, she met fellow worker Ken Ackles, an orderly, who was immediately attracted to her. Jane was living in her apartment on Cole Harbour Road when Ackles took a job as superintendent of a low-rise apartment complex on nearby Merricmac Drive. He invited Jane to move in with him, and she accepted. Allen Whynot, her oldest son, decided to get his own apartment with friends in Halifax, but Darren and Jamie went with their mother.

"Ken was quite a bit older than Jane," said Carrie Rafuse. "But he was pleasant and very kind to her."

In a letter to a friend, Jane described Ackles as "a really nice guy. He is older (fifty-five), but we have been seeing quite a bit of each other. We get along well and I am comfortable with him."

Writing to the same friend seven months later, in August 1985, Jane said: "For me there are only two things that are permanent—my parents and my sons. Other than that, anything can change. I like Ken very much and I respect him, but I don't honestly know if I could say I love him."

Five weeks later she wrote: "I do not want anyone to feel that they need me, and Ken does give me that feeling. His is more a need to possess and that bothers me. I have told him, yet he keeps on. I think that maybe what I am after is a form of companionship. Whatever, each event in our life is a learning experience and as long as we learn and grow, it is well worth it. I think too, that perhaps love isn't the big deal that it is cracked up to be."

Her son Allen said that Ken Ackles "really loved Mom. But she didn't feel ready or he was a lot older, I don't know what it was."

Eventually, Jane moved into her own apartment in the same building and she and Ackles stopped dating.

Carrie Rafuse believed that Jane found Ken "too smothering" at a time when she needed space. "He was all over her. He would say, 'If you need a car, let me buy you one,' or, 'Let me buy you a ring.' That just wasn't Jane. She wasn't impressed with that stuff. I think it was too mushy-mushy for her. She liked Ken, but he wasn't really significant in her life."

About a year after Jane left Ken, he died suddenly while in hospital for an operation.

Jane's childhood friend, Valery Cromwell, had eventually settled in Toronto. After Jane left Winnipeg, Valery visited her in Nova Scotia "from time to time, until 1976 when she was breaking up with Milfie. I met Billy that year but I only saw him for a few minutes and I didn't really have an opinion of him, except that he was a big man."

After that, Valery lost contact with Jane. Six years later, in 1982, she read about Billy Stafford's death. "I was reading the paper and I said, 'I know this person,' and I phoned home right away and I found Jane's mother and she gave me her number. Then I went home and saw her. We were really happy to see each other, but she didn't say a lot about Billy's death."

Jane was still living with Ken Ackles when Valery came to visit her in 1984. "He was much older than Jane. I think he was more of a father figure to her." When Valery returned for a visit the next year, Jane had been on her own for several months. Valery's family was originally from Weymouth, Nova Scotia, on the Fundy side of the province. One of the cousins she grew up with, James Tynes, was living in the Halifax area when she came to visit Jane in 1985.

"Valery called me and I went out to see her at Jane's place on Merricmac," recalled Tynes, a heavy equipment operator from Lawrencetown, a few miles from Dartmouth. He was a divorced father of four.

"Now don't you be a stranger when Valery goes back to Toronto," Jane said as he was leaving after their first meeting. After Valery returned to Toronto, Jane called Tynes. She said she had a couple of tickets to a hockey game and asked him to go with her. He went to the game and they were soon dating. It was a relationship that would last, off and on, for more than four years. Tynes moved in with Jane and Darren at the Merricmac apartment and later to a rented townhouse on nearby Arklow Drive.

"Jane was a beautiful person with a great sense of humour," said Tynes. "We didn't do a whole lot because she was working nights. Once in a while we'd go down and visit her parents. Mostly, though, we liked going for walks in the woods. She loved the woods. She knew a lot about animals. She studied them and she told me a lot about their habits."

When they had quiet time together, he and Jane would often "just get a bottle of wine, listen to music, and carry on. We did a lot of that. We would talk for hours about real deep things."

Jane's relationship with Tynes was deeper and more romantic than her relationship with Ken Ackles, and she was feeling good about herself. On New Year's Day 1986, she was even able to kick her long-time, two-pack-a-day smoking habit. "I asked Darren what he wanted for Christmas and he looked at me with his big brown eyes and said, 'Mom, the best thing you can give me is to quit smoking. If you keep smoking you'll die and I want you to be my mommy forever.' So you see, that's what it took to break my smoking habit."

Tynes said that he and Jane never argued, and that the major problem in their relationship was that "she never really trusted that I loved her. She wouldn't confide in me. I would leave for a while and then we'd get back together again and laugh about how crazy it was. But I felt there was so much I didn't know about her."

Carrie Rafuse said she felt uncomfortable around Tynes. "I didn't know him that well, but he just didn't seem very warm. I know that Jane did tell me that he felt she wasn't sharing everything with him and that she wasn't close enough to him. Maybe he resented me because I was close to her and she wouldn't let him get close to her. Or maybe I just misunderstood him. Other friends of Jane have told me he was a really nice guy."

Tynes was also troubled by the number of speeches she was making. "I didn't want her to do any more of those talks. I felt it brought back too many memories. About a week before every talk, she would break out with a cold sore—from stress. I asked her not to do it anymore. She did stop for a while, but people kept calling and she got back into it.

"She was doing a whole lot more than I knew about. I told her I felt almost like an outsider. I wanted us to be best friends.

I wanted her to be able to come and talk to me about anything—any problem."

Tynes and Jane separated for good in early 1990. "After we broke up, she sent me letters, made me music tapes, and left cards and notes on my door. She said at different times she wanted us to get back together, but I felt it probably wouldn't work." He worried that she was helping other battered women to heal but not taking the time necessary to heal herself.

Tynes' view was shared by Victoria Jones, a nurse who retired from the rehabilitation centre and went to live with Jane in January of 1989. The two women had become friends at the rehab centre, and Jane was sad to see her retire at the age of sixty-two and move to Montreal to live with one of her two sons.

"I figured I was going to Montreal to live for good but it didn't work out," said Jones. "Jane and I kept in touch while I was there, and I phoned her one day and she said, 'Why don't you come and stay with me?' So I did."

Like Tynes, Jones urged Jane to quit speaking out because it was making her relive her life with Billy over and over. "My husband was an alcoholic who usually drank until he passed out and was nasty and hateful when he was sober," Jones told Jane. "After he choked on his own vomit and died, people said I should go to Al-Anon because the scars remain for the family and blah, blah, blah... I says no, my problem is dead and buried now and that's where it's going to stay. I mean, what's the good of resurrecting all the misery?"

Jones wanted Jane to adopt a lower profile because so many people were hounding her, even total strangers. One of them, an abused woman who lived nearby, came to Jane's door for help. After the woman left, Jones told Jane, "You had to cope with what happened to you, let them cope with what's happening to them. They know there are shelters for women to go to now—so let them go."

There were periods when Jane didn't want to speak to anyone, and Jones would tell callers she was out. "I saw that a lot of them didn't get to her. But a lot of them did."

CHAPTER 19
FRIENDS IN NEED

Jane Hurshman and Valery Cromwell celebrated the 1987 New Year in Bermuda. Jane said it was a trip they had planned for more than two years, "to celebrate my freedom—to mark the beginning of a new year and a new life for Jane Hurshman."

Before they left, she visited Donna Smith, who had been admitted to the detoxification centre at the Nova Scotia Hospital, a psychiatric care facility in Dartmouth. Jane was worried about her friend, and while she was in Bermuda, James Tynes visited Donna regularly at the detox centre. It took about two weeks for Donna to break her Valium addiction.

Donna was back in Bryony House shortly after Jane returned from her vacation. In late January 1987, the transition house placed Donna and her children in its Second Stage program, which provided her with an apartment in a secure building in Dartmouth. The building included six apartments with heavy-duty locks, and police responded promptly to any calls for help.

Robert continued to stalk and harass Donna, who was embroiled in divorce and visitation-rights proceedings with him. At the same time, Donna was seeking treatment for her daughter, whom Robert had sexually abused.

"I had fifteen different people telling me what I could or could not do," she said. "There were therapists, Children's Aid people, doctors, lawyers, counsellors... I kept saying, 'Leave me alone, I can't take it anymore.'"

One day in February, Donna was to drop Mary and Bobby off at a supermarket, where their father would pick them up for a two-hour visit, from 6 to 8 p.m. She always had someone accompany her when she was meeting Robert, but on this day, no one was available. The experience traumatized her.

"I shouldn't have taken the kids over by myself," she said. "I don't even remember coming home."

When she returned to her basement apartment, Donna locked the door and swallowed eighty sleeping pills. "I don't remember taking anything. I think I must have dissociated. I was told later that my family doctor called and she could tell something was strange. She must have called Jane because I remember talking on the phone and Jane saying, 'Don't go anywhere.'"

Jane rushed over to Donna's apartment with James Tynes, who had to break down the door. They found Donna unconscious. When Jane took Donna's pulse, she realized there was no time to call an ambulance. They carried her to their car and rushed her to Dartmouth General Hospital.

"Jane stayed with me the whole night," said Donna. "I remember seeing my doctor there. I guess I became terrified of her and the only person I would listen to was Jane. All I remember is Jane talking to me while they tried to pump my stomach out."

"Why did you stop me?" she asked Jane.

"I care about you and I don't want you dying on me," Jane replied.

By the summer of 1988, Donna and her children had their own apartment, not associated with Bryony House. Jane had grown close to the children and did what she could to help.

"My kids grew up with Jane," remembered Donna. "Mary had a lot of temper tantrums and she took one when we were over at Jane's one day. I'll never forget it. Jane held her for over an hour until she calmed down. If you didn't hold her, she would go right out of it and hurt herself or others. She has attacked babysitters, teachers, and other children.

"That day at Jane's, Mary was being held and she was ripping at the oilcloth table cover with her teeth. She was spitting and trying to kick out—it was pure, pure anger. But Jane just held her and rocked her in her arms until she finally calmed down. I explained to Mary that Jane loved her and that's why she was holding her—so she wouldn't hurt herself." The frequency and intensity of Mary's rages gradually diminished.

Donna's divorce from her husband became final in March of 1990. Two months later she learned that Bobby too had been sexually abused by his father. Despite the allegations of abuse, Robert forced another court hearing as he sought access to the children. Donna feared that an unsympathetic judge would grant further visiting rights. That fear, coupled with Robert's propensity for violence, convinced Jane that Donna and her children should go underground. An underground network for women and children seeking to escape their abusers did exist in Canada, but it was secret and seldom acknowledged. There are no figures on how many women and children are in hiding within the network, but the number is small. It is difficult to gain access to the underground network because most mainstream women's shelters are not involved in it. Jane knew the network existed, and through her connections paved the way for Donna and her children to go into hiding.

At first, Donna cooperated, but after getting rid of her apartment and most of her furniture, she changed her mind.

"What they didn't tell me is you lose all your identity when you go underground. They cut and dyed my hair, changed my name, and gave me sunglasses." The children's looks were also altered, and their names were changed.

"The kids would have had no birth certificates and we would have to move from one safe house to another for at least a year," said Donna. "I wouldn't be able to work, and the children wouldn't be in school. And I had to worry about Bobby's chronic respiratory problem. If I ever had to take him to a hospital, we'd get caught right away."

She and the children spent several days in hiding on the South Shore as they made their preparations. They were to take a train to Calgary. "The tickets were bought for me," said Donna. "They were in my hand, but I decided not to go. I decided I was going to stay and fight—I'd had it."

Counsellors preparing Donna and her children to go underground understood when she changed her mind, but Jane was angry. "I called Jane to tell her, and she was very, very upset with me. She couldn't see why I changed my mind. She thought somebody had influenced me and that I didn't have a mind of my own. The others couldn't believe it when I told them Jane was really, really mad. I can understand it. She did a lot of the preparation, and then to see me back out..."

Donna and the children returned to Dartmouth the day before the court hearing. Despite the evidence of sexual abuse, the family court judge allowed Robert supervised access to the children. Donna was shocked by his decision. "When I heard that, I wished to God I had gone to Calgary."

Donna did not hear from Jane for a month, and Jane would not return her phone calls. "Then one day, Jane walked in out of the blue. She said 'I'm back' and gave me a great big hug."

Their friendship endured, and when Donna and a friend started a crisis line to help other battered women, Jane was one of the first to volunteer her time to the project.

James Tynes was still living with Jane when she offered to help out with Donna's crisis line. He was not pleased. "They started this hotline to help other women, but they needed help themselves."

Jane's friend from work, Annette Bushen, said that Jane tried to recruit her, but she turned her down. "I said, 'Jane, I'm not strong enough.' I couldn't listen to stories of abuse over and over and over again. I don't know how she could do it. Every time she talked to someone, her own memories had to flash back."

According to Tynes, Jane told some of her friends that listening to the stories of abuse "was almost like living with Billy again."

Jane did cut back on her speaking schedule, but she was profoundly affected when, on December 6, 1989, a young man named Marc Lepine shot fourteen students, all of them women, at the École Polytechnique in Montreal. Jane wept uncontrollably when she heard about the massacre. "She would be driving along and suddenly burst into tears," said one friend.

"She really got into it after those women in Quebec got killed," said Tynes. "That really bothered her. I was still with her at the time but we broke up shortly after."

On the second anniversary of the massacre, Jane gave a stirring speech in which she attacked the Queens County Council for initially refusing to recognize the tragedy by lowering the municipal flag to half-mast. "I am a very real victim of domestic violence, and I come from Queens County," she told a gathering of two hundred in Halifax. She stated that the county's original decision did nothing to discourage abuse and demonstrated how much work was yet to be done to educate the public about violence against women. "Being a woman shouldn't make any difference to whether you live or die, or what kind of life you lead. But, unfortunately, the headlines and the statistics show that it does."

The next day, the *Halifax Daily News* ran a poignant photograph of a sombre young woman comforting Jane after her address. The woman was Darlene Darrington, and she was wearing a name tag with the letters S.O.S.A.—Survivor of Sexual Assault. She was one of at least seven victims of John Arthur O'Brien, dubbed "the motorcycle rapist."

In an interview in a small, quiet room at Ann Keith's Services for Sexual Assault Victims, Darrington described how her life had been shattered by the attack and how Jane Hurshman had inspired her to face the tragedy and begin speaking out. Darrington was thirty years old, married, and the mother of an eleven-year-old son when O'Brien attacked her on the night of September 18, 1988, while she was out for a walk. "He was driving along on his motorcycle and he must have gone ahead of me and parked it. As I walked by, he jumped me from behind and dragged me into the woods."

O'Brien forced Darrington to perform oral sex, threatening to stab her if she didn't. "And if you go to the police, I'll kill you," he warned. "Don't forget, I know who you are and I'll come back and kill you."

Darrington began to scream hysterically after O'Brien left. A family friend heard her and found her in the woods. "He was the one who took me home and he called the police because I was afraid to."

Two male RCMP officers from the Halifax County detachment came to her house. It was an experience she wasn't prepared for. Beechville, where Darrington lives, is an integrated community of blacks and whites, and Darrington, who is white, had a black husband. "And one of the first things they asked me was, 'Was it a black man that assaulted you?' They didn't ask me to describe him—they asked if he was black. It really upset me."

At the police station the next day, Darrington again found it disturbing that she had to relate her story to two male officers instead of a female. "I had to go into full detail of the assault, and then they wanted to know why I didn't give all the details the night before. I told them I was in shock and describing what he made me do was not something I wanted to blurt out to two male officers."

Darrington said the attack nearly destroyed her life. She quit her job as an evening cleaner at the Halifax Infirmary because she was afraid to be outside at night, and she turned to alcohol and tranquillizers. "It was my way of coping with the nightmares that I was having constantly. I kept reliving the attack over and over again."

O'Brien was eventually arrested, and seven victims testified against him. "I was very frightened when I saw him in the courtroom," said Darrington. "But I was also angry for what he had taken away from me. I was out on my own since the age of fifteen. I had worked all my life and I was very independent. He took all that away from me. And I'm still living in fear that he will come after me for revenge when he gets out."

O'Brien was sentenced to thirty-seven years. He lost an appeal of his conviction in November 1992. Under Canadian law he will likely serve no more than one-third of that time. Darrington is as angry at the parole board as she is at O'Brien: he had been convicted of forty-two crimes since the age of sixteen and was on parole for a previous sex crime during the year he was terrorizing women in Nova Scotia. "If it wasn't for the parole board letting him out, none of us would have been assaulted," said Darrington. "I'm very angry."

She credited Jane Hurshman with encouraging her to vent that anger publicly. "I heard Jane speak out and she really inspired me. She had so much courage and she gave me the strength to speak out."

Before Jane spoke on the 1991 anniversary of the Montreal massacre, she and Darrington talked together at the SSAV offices.

"Do you ever get used to speaking out in public?" Darrington asked.

"No," said Jane. "Every time I do, it brings back all the bad memories. You do it because you want to make a change—to stop the violence."

Darrington said it was Jane who made her realize she didn't have to stay at home and hide from the world. "She made me see I had nothing to feel ashamed or guilty about. Society tries to make you feel that way by saying, 'If you didn't wear a miniskirt or you weren't walking at night, this wouldn't have happened to you.' Well, that attitude is wrong and I have the right to be treated with respect."

For Darrington, the downside to speaking out was that she lost some of her friends. "It's like they're ashamed, and you should keep things like that quiet. They don't understand that we need to speak about it in order to get on with our healing."

Darrington decried the lack of services available for sexual assault victims, citing the example of the woman who was forced to travel seventy miles each way from Kentville, Nova Scotia, for once-a-week therapy at SSAV in Halifax. "There's nothing down there," she said. "There's nowhere else to go. And when the woman was taken to the hospital in Kentville, they didn't have any special team to deal with sexual assault. A male police officer was in the room as she was being examined, and a male doctor did the examination. You don't need any of this after a man has just sexually assaulted you. You need a woman who understands what you're going through. There are not enough female officers on our police forces. There should be more of them, and they should be trained to deal with sexual assaults."

Ann Keith said that besides speaking out publicly, Jane Hurshman privately helped many other women in one-on-one meetings or in telephone conversations. "If a woman called who had been battered but not sexually abused, we would refer them to other agencies, but sometimes I would give Jane their number," she said. "I wouldn't follow up on it. That was up to Jane, if she felt like it or not. She helped a lot of women."

In 1991, SSAV presented Jane with an award and a certificate for being one of the organization's outstanding volunteers. They took her out to dinner and presented her with a silver chain.

Many women who didn't meet Jane in person read about her and wrote or called her. One of those was Sara (a pseudonym), a woman in her early twenties. She was the youngest of nine children in a small town about a hundred miles from Halifax. She admired Jane and collected articles about her in a scrapbook. Eventually she gathered the courage to write to Jane.

"I was suicidal and it was Jane who kept me going," said Sara, who had seen unimaginable tragedy and abuse in her life. From the age of six, after the death of her mother from a brain tumour, she was physically and sexually abused by her father, two brothers, a cousin, a brother-in-law, and an uncle.

Sara would never forget the first night she was forced to sleep with her father. "I was six, pretty near seven. Dad said he wanted to break me in and make me into a woman. He laid on top of me and had intercourse with me. I was crying from the pain. Then he started telling me I was a whore."

A few days later, Sara discovered her father having intercourse with her eight-year-old sister. "I then took it to be something every father does to his daughter. I didn't know it was wrong."

She was on drugs by the age of eight, began running away from home in her early teens, and married at sixteen to escape the abuse at home. But her husband also physically and sexually abused her, as did a man she lived with after that.

Sara returned to her husband in March 1987, and the two of them entered a detox program. The abuse stopped, and they became drug free. She began seeing a psychiatrist in early 1990, hoping to find a way to heal and forgive. "Sometimes when I'm feeling depressed, I think of Jane or read her letters and it helps," she said. In one letter, Jane urged Sara to go back to school. "It can only help you," she wrote. "Don't ever give up and don't ever stop learning."

Jane also recommended that Sara consider helping others as a healing tool. "I have kept very busy, very involved, with women and women's issues—and I probably always will be," Jane wrote. "It is great to be able to help others."

CHAPTER 20
BEHIND BARS

In December 1989, Liz Forestell was hired to run the Elizabeth Fry Society in Halifax. She arrived armed with bulldog determination, a master's degree in sociology, and several years' experience fighting for the rights of the disabled and disenfranchised.

At the time, there were nineteen Elizabeth Fry societies across Canada, each of them autonomous. The Halifax organization was ten years old when it hired Forestell as its first executive director.

The society, which is named after a nineteenth-century prison reformer, fights to improve conditions for women in prison. It provides therapy and counselling, as well as recreation and education programs. It also seeks to educate the public about the economic discrimination that leads to nonviolent crime, which is the kind for which most women prisoners have been jailed. Many incarcerated women were sexually or physically abused as children or adults. The view of the Elizabeth Fry Society is that these women continue to be humiliated and mistreated by the justice and prison systems, which fail to understand the dynamics of abuse.

Soon after arriving in Halifax, Forestell heard about Jane. "I knew her story, but I didn't know she was here until I heard about the work she was doing through contacts in the women's community.

"A woman at the Halifax Correctional Centre who had killed her husband was having a really hard time dealing with what was going on in there. She had been abused by her husband and she wanted to talk to someone. So I called Jane and asked her if she would see her. She went to the correctional centre and helped the woman out and gave her support."

Forestell and Jane talked a lot on the telephone after that, but they didn't meet face to face until 1991, when Forestell asked her to join Elizabeth Fry's board of directors. Jane agreed, and she and Forestell became good friends.

"She was someone I admired and respected and felt a pretty strong connection with," said Forestell. "She was very strong and brave, with a great sense of humour, but certainly there was a lot of pain there."

Forestell considered her appointment of Jane Hurshman to the Elizabeth Fry board one of the shrewdest moves she made as executive director. "She was encouraging and very, very supportive of me," she said. "I used her a lot to check my impressions, and if I was thinking about a program or a strategy, she was my touchstone. She was very bright and she saw through people—she knew the good ones from the bad ones."

Prison facilities and programs for women inmates in Nova Scotia were clearly inadequate, and in October 1991 the provincial government created the Solicitor General's Special Committee on Provincially Incarcerated Women. Its mandate was to study the needs of women inmates and to recommend necessary changes. Solicitor General Joel R. Matheson wanted input from government, prison officials, women's and community groups, and the inmates themselves. He appointed Liz Forestell as co-chair and Jane

Hurshman as a member. Both women relished the assignment. Jane had served her sentence for killing Billy Stafford at the Halifax Correctional Centre in nearby Lower Sackville. It was a men's prison with a women's unit that held as many as twenty-four inmates in maximum-security conditions. Forestell had long advocated that unit be closed.

According to Forestell, most of the women being held at the centre were not a threat to society: in fact, most were serving time for shoplifting or petty fraud. These women, Forestell said, "can be secure in the community in a different kind of setting—one that does not separate them from their families."

(A 1992 study of convictions against women in Halifax showed that most were for crimes of poverty, and that only a fraction involved violence. Poverty was leading women to steal such things as Christmas gifts and clothing for their children. Of the 4,373 charges laid against women in Halifax between 1984 and 1988, 42 per cent were for theft under $1,000. The same study found that violent crimes, such as murder, robbery, and assault, accounted for only 8 per cent of the charges laid against women, while about 67 per cent were for crimes against property, such as theft and petty fraud.)

All Nova Scotia women sentenced to jail terms of less than two years were automatically sent to HCC; those with longer sentences were sent to the archaic Prison for Women, in Kingston, Ontario. In 1993, slightly more than two hundred of the twelve thousand inmates in federal prisons across Canada were women. At the time the Nova Scotia committee was appointed, the federal government had already announced that it would build a network of regional federal prisons—including one in Nova Scotia—to replace the Prison for Women.

Jane Hurshman's contribution to the prison committee was as valuable as her work with the Elizabeth Fry board of directors. "She connected with people and pulled them together in a really interesting way," said Forestell. "Jane would sit through the meetings very quietly—then, when she had something to say, she said it. She was never aggressive, but what she said made sense and it came from the heart and it came from knowledge, and she would fight for it.

"I can remember a woman on the committee from the corrections system saying things had changed at the Correctional Centre and this didn't go on anymore, and that didn't go on, and Jane just had enough. And she said, 'Listen, I was there six years ago, and it's still the same as it was then, so don't say it has improved, because it hasn't.' That was very important coming from Jane.

"She had an incredible power on that committee. Nobody could argue with her because she had been through it. I don't know if she realized how much power she had. Sometimes I think she did and she used it very strategically, very effectively, and for all the right reasons. She didn't use it in a manipulative way at all."

To carry out the mandate of the committee, Forestell, Jane, and others interviewed women incarcerated at HCC. "That was the basis of our research," said Forestell, who coordinated the research and designed the interviews, and who insisted that the inmates not be cut off. "You don't go on to the next question until people are really finished. If it takes six hours, it doesn't matter. Let them tell you what they need to tell you."

In all, the committee interviewed thirty-three women. Twenty-six of them said they had been physically abused, nineteen of them as children or teenagers. Twenty-one had been sexually abused, sixteen as children or teenagers. Spouses or partners were a close second to other family members as the most frequent abusers.

"Typically, the women found little support in surviving the trauma," the committee reported in a summary of its findings. "They often found themselves going from abusive childhood situations into abusive relationships with partners and spouses. Programs, they found, were either not available or did not respond to their needs."

Twelve of the women interviewed had a history of self-mutilation. This was not surprising to the committee, which referred to a 1979 Ontario study that found that 86 per cent of adolescent females in custody in that province had inflicted injuries on themselves. Another study suggested a link between self-injury and early sexual abuse.

"Women talk about self-injury as something that happens when they are in crisis, and say that it actually brings about some release from their pain," the committee stated in its report. "Self-injury includes slashing, burning, and sometimes, breaking bones. Typically, correctional institutions respond to such actions in a punitive, rather than supportive manner, which may in fact exacerbate the crisis."

Most of the women inmates told Jane and the other committee interviewers that they had been treated badly by police during and after arrest. "Complaints included lack of information; rough treatment; not being permitted to change clothing; being shackled and thrown into a police van while pregnant; refusal of treatment for injuries; refusal of phone calls; and verbal abuse."

In an April 9, 1992, letter to the *New York Times*, Ann L. Jacobs, executive director of the Women's Prison Association and Home, wrote that "we're learning that 80 per cent of women in the system have been victims of child abuse, sexual abuse, or domestic violence. They need drug treatment, counselling, education, and job training."

The solicitor general's special committee released its report, *Blueprint For Change*, in April 1992. It recommended that the women's unit at the Halifax Correctional Centre be phased out by 1995 and that "small, community residential facilities be established in the western, central, and eastern regions of Nova Scotia."

It also recommended that prison staff be trained to deal with manifestations of post-traumatic stress, including self-injury, substance abuse, flashbacks, panic attacks, and nightmares, all of these common results of childhood trauma, sexual assault, and spousal battering.

Prison staff, said the report, should be women, but only because the presence of men in positions of control over women who have been victimized "was a real barrier to healing. While it might provide an opportunity for women to see caring males in positions of authority, it perpetuated the inequality of relationships and contributed to women's view of themselves as submissive to male power. Before women survivors of abuse can deal effectively with the men in their world, and enter into healthy relationships based on mutual respect, they must have a safe environment in which to heal from trauma, and then face men on a more equal playing field."

The committee's workload was heavy and demanding. Often Jane attended meetings after long stretches on the night shift at the rehabilitation centre. Whenever she felt the load was too much, she would call Forestell: "Look, I'm just too tired and I can't be there today. I have to look after myself."

"I'm sure it was hard on her," Forestell said. "And I'm sure it wasn't without pain—to go back and look again at the kind of traumatic things that you've been through. But she said that it gave her back a lot and it was very fulfilling."

CHAPTER 21
GHOSTS

When Annette Bushen heard that Jane Hurshman had been acquitted of murdering Billy Stafford in 1982, "I just gave a whoop of joy. I read what she had gone through, and her acquittal couldn't have been more fitting."

Bushen didn't know that within a few months she would be taking a Certified Nursing Assistant course with Jane. And that she and Jane would be in the same group that was sent to Queens General Hospital on Mondays and Tuesdays as part of their training.

Bushen was living in Petite Riviere, and it was a long drive to get to Liverpool for their early-morning hospital assignments. While Bushen was explaining her problem to her instructor, Jane overheard and approached.

"I live a lot closer to the hospital than you," said Jane. "If you don't mind, you can come up to my place on Sunday afternoon and stay overnight Sunday and Monday. It's only fifteen minutes to the hospital. We'll use your car one week and mine the next."

Bushen was impressed with Jane's generosity and agreed immediately. "We got along like sisters right off the bat," she said. "But I still didn't realize who she was." Later that day, Jane took her aside.

"You don't know me, Annette, do you?" asked Jane.

"No I don't. Should I know you?"

"I'm Jane Stafford."

Bushen shrugged.

"Do you remember a trial in Liverpool a while back?" Jane asked.

"Oh my God! You're *that* Jane Stafford."

The following Sunday, Bushen made her first trip to Jane's house in Bangs Falls, where she met Darren, who was then six. When they sat down for dinner in the evening, Bushen noticed that the kitchen table was on an elevated platform.

"We're sitting on his throne," said Jane. "This is where Bill sat when he issued all his orders."

Bushen said it gave her an eerie feeling.

"There's something else I have to tell you," said Jane. "Strange things do happen here."

"What do you mean?"

"The main thing I want to tell you about is the doors."

In the Bangs Falls house, the outside back door to the house opened to a small porch used to store jackets and boots, and the inside door opened to the kitchen. "If at any time you're in the house and I'm not here, don't be alarmed if you hear the doors," said Jane. "The outer door will open. It will close. The inner door to the kitchen will open. It will close too. But nobody will be there and nobody will come in."

Bushen was not overly superstitious, and she was sceptical, but on a later visit it happened just as Jane had described it. "She and I were having coffee one evening. Darren had gone to bed and we were talking when we heard a noise. I looked at Jane and she looked at me, and we looked at the door. And honest to God, I would not lie, both the doors opened and closed and nobody came in. There was no wind, nothing."

Bushen said chills went up and down her spine whenever she recalled the incident. She also remembered Jane sitting deep in thought at the kitchen table and then turning to her. "You know, Annette, Bill Stafford will never be dead."

"I don't know how many times she told me that in the time I knew her," said Bushen. "But I thought, my God, the woman is right."

James Tynes said he too remembered Jane being haunted by Billy Stafford. "When we were living together, she sometimes had bad dreams about Billy, and there was one period when she thought she was possessed by evil spirits. She wouldn't talk much about it. She said she had some little knickknacks Billy had given her over the years when he came in from the ships. She thought they were bad omens and she got rid of them, and after a while the bad feelings went away and she never talked about it anymore." He said her bad dreams ended when she started seeing a psychiatrist.

To those who understand the dynamics of intimate partner violence, Billy's hold on Jane, even after his death, was not surprising. Sleep deprivation and the interminable emotional abuse, strengthened by unpredictable outbursts of physical violence and degrading sexual episodes, were a form of severe brainwashing that left Jane broken and confused. After her release from prison in 1984, she told a friend that she believed her breaking point came after Billy shot at her while she was filling the wood stove, and threatened her that if she ever left him he would kill off her family one by one.

"Never again did I see the slightest ray of hope," Jane said. "That episode left me purposeless. It left me with no choices—nothing to be, nothing to do, nothing to believe in. Nothing but emptiness and death. I didn't know how I was going to cope. Stafford had total control of everything in that house. There was no emotion left in me. I would crawl into bed, tired and worn out, and if I did sleep it was a fitful one. I was just as tired when morning came. Each day was a continuance of the day before. It was never-ending.

"The fear was overwhelming. The pure hate for me and Darren would spew out of his mouth without warning. All activity in the house was tense—hearts pounding, afraid to move, afraid to breathe."

In one of her speeches, Jane said she didn't know if it was love for her children or her "sheer hatred for Stafford" that kept her survival instinct alive. In a letter to her friend Sara, Jane said it was very difficult for those who haven't been abused to understand what it does to a person. "Abuse in any form is so traumatic. And you spend the rest of your life trying to get over it."

In a return letter, Sara asked Jane if she had been able to forgive Billy Stafford.

"I'm not sure if it is forgiveness or understanding," replied Jane. "Probably some of both. For the last couple of years that we were together, I just hated him. I couldn't get beyond that hate, even after his death. When I started my nursing training and we got into psychiatric nursing, I had a fantastic instructor who taught me that Bill was a very sick man, and from there my hate began to change to understanding. And then I was able to put a label on it and put it away.

"It wasn't until 1990 that I went back to our old house where everything happened. It was something I had to do, because I felt part of me was trapped there. I had to go and get it and set it free. It was very difficult and very scary for me, but I went. I got what I went for—forgiveness. I wanted to forgive myself, and that's what I did.

"What Bill did will always have an effect on my life. Sometimes I am very resentful and hateful and unforgiving—

but that is a natural part of healing. To forgive someone does not mean you have to be around them or love them. It just means you have settled something inside yourself and you are at peace with your decision."

It was in the summer of 1990 that Jane returned to Bangs Falls for the first time in six years. Besides wrestling with the ghost of Billy Stafford, she was there to seek answers from her former neighbour, Margaret Joudrey, the woman who once treated her like a daughter but had turned against her on the witness stand.

No one will ever know what Jane was thinking as the single-lane bridge crossing the Medway River came into view, and beyond it Margaret Joudrey's trailer, and then the small weathered barn with its sagging roof. And then, on the gentle slope at the end of a long driveway, flanked by a low, white, board fence, the frame bungalow with its painful memories.

Did she see herself behind the wheel of Billy Stafford's half-ton truck, bouncing over the bridge with the weight of his decapitated body pressing against her and blood and brain tissue splattering on the dash and the windshield?

And when she looked at the house did she see images of Darren being force-fed? Or of Billy's massive fist breaking her nose—as it did at least three times—and loosening her teeth? Did she remember the rifle butt that finished the job, forcing her to have her teeth removed and to lie to her dentist that she'd been in a car accident?

When she stopped at Margaret Joudrey's trailer and stared up to the house, did she remember Billy's voice booming down at her and Darren: "I'm number one, and you look out for number one, and fuck everyone else!"

Or perhaps she was remembering the day she summoned the courage to tell Billy Stafford she was leaving him, and listened as he told her in a cold and measured voice that if she left, she would be back, "because, old woman, I may not know where you are, but I do know where your family is. And I will kill them one at a time until you do come back. I will not be a third-time loser."

Jane never fully understood how Margaret Joudrey could have turned against her on the witness stand. Joudrey's animosity continued after the trial. In a December 1992 interview she said she didn't think it was right for Jane to speak out against spousal violence. "She'd go in front of all them women...and oh my God. I seen her on TV and she'd tell them women about abuse and all this shit, and it's hard to tell what kind of hell she made for them and their husbands by telling them the kind of stuff that she was telling them. It would just cause them more trouble at home."

At Jane's trial, Joudrey said it was her belief that the man should be the head of the household. And in the telephone interview she claimed she told Billy that he was going to have a hard time as long as he lived with Jane. "I told him Jane's got you down as low as she can get you. I said she can't put you down any lower. Everything Jane did, Billy got the blame for."

Jane and her lawyer, Alan Ferrier, theorize that Joudrey turned on her because she thought that her dealings with the police and the courts over Billy's death would somehow result in the loss of the property she was living on. Jane was there to see if she could confirm that theory when she went to the door of Joudrey's trailer in the summer of 1990.

Joudrey's memory of that visit was that they sat at her kitchen table and "just talked ordinary talk. To tell the God's truth, after what she done to Billy, I didn't give a damn if I ever saw her. But I wouldn't turn her away from the door—I wouldn't."

Jane told Liz Forestell that she went to Bangs Falls to talk to Margaret as a kind of closure. "She said Margaret opened the door and they went inside and Jane said all those years just melted away and she felt like she had just gone out to the store for ten minutes. It was like nothing had changed.

"And she ended up saying to Margaret, 'I wanted to come and ask you why you did what you did, but it doesn't matter.' She just had to go back and look. And then she went away. She didn't want to talk to her. It was no longer important."

Forestell said there were occasions when she thought Jane looked very haunted. "I wouldn't describe it as a dark side, but I could certainly see the pain. Sometimes when Jane talked about what happened to her, her eyes got very big and round. It was a very profound kind of thing—very easy to see."

Most of us carry different levels of trauma around with us, Forestell said; the challenge is to turn that into a strength rather than let it cripple you. "And I think Jane did that extraordinarily well."

Jane may have turned past trauma into strength, but the past was always with her. "We would be talking about someone else's situation," said Forestell. "And Jane would say, 'Oh yeah, I remember that happening to me,' and I would say, 'How horrible,' or 'How did you survive that?' And I asked her a few times if she ever thought about it."

"It never leaves you," replied Jane.

Jane told Vern Oickle, a reporter and editor with *The Advance*, a Liverpool weekly newspaper, that she was able to put Billy and the years of abuse "away on a shelf where they can no longer hurt me, although they do come back to haunt me on a regular basis."

She also told Oickle that she was not sorry that Billy was dead. "I've accepted the fact a long time ago that if he wasn't dead, then I would have been."

Oickle said Jane was also concerned about Billy's parents, particularly his father, Lamonte Stafford, who had comforted her after the police picked her up for questioning. While Jane was in jail in the spring of 1984, she was upset when she read a letter from Billy's father that appeared in *The Advance* on March 21. In the letter, Lamonte Stafford accused "the ghouls" at CBC's *fifth estate* of "crucifying" his son and said that Jane's son Allen, and Ronald Wamboldt, who boarded with Jane and Billy, "lived at my son's getting free room and board. They came to my house two or three times a week and I made a number of trips to their home at Bangs Falls. For all the physical abuse they were supposed to have taken from my son, I never saw a mark on either of them.

"My son was on boats for years and he never had any trouble, to my knowledge. It is all very well to give statements in court and to the newspaper when the one person who could deny them is dead... The many people who could have been called to testify on his behalf were never summoned by the Crown."

Jane told Oickle later that she wept after reading Lamonte's letter. "I couldn't get those feelings out of my mind about what I had done to Bill's father," she said. "I kept thinking about how his mother and father must have felt and I could understand how upset all of this must have made them. I didn't wish his family any harm and I regret any pain I may have caused them."

On March 23, 1984, Jane wrote a letter to Oickle from jail, explaining why she didn't want to be interviewed for an *Advance* article. "I read Lamonte's piece that was published this week and I wish no more hurt or bad feelings to him. He is a fine man and I respect him very much, but he has suffered dearly and I choose not to have any more printed, even if only for that reason. He is a man that has been good to me over the years and I just want to let my past rest now."

Jane Hurshman also had a lot of difficulty dealing with the reality that she had been unable to protect Darren against Billy's abuse. The despair she felt over it hit her as hard as any of Billy's punches the day she escorted Donna Smith's two children for a four-hour visit with their father one Christmas. Jane had offered to accompany the children to ease Donna's fears that they might be molested.

Robert knew who Jane was and the atmosphere was tense. She told Donna later that he had purchased a mug inscribed with the words: "World's Greatest Dad." Jane saw a striking similarity in the way Robert and Billy controlled the gift-opening ritual. The children had to wait for their father's permission to open each gift, and had to neatly fold and put away the wrapping paper before they could open another. It triggered memories of Christmas at the Bangs Falls house, where Darren was not even allowed to open his own presents.

When Jane returned to Donna's apartment with Mary and Bobby, she was emotionally drained and said she could never accompany them again. "All the bad feelings from her time with Billy came back," said Donna.

Ann Keith, of SSAV, believed that when a woman is abused, it is akin to a lifelong prison sentence. "People who have not experienced violence don't understand the long-term psychological effects that abuse has on a woman. Flashbacks of the abuse can be triggered by something very minor—a smell, a touch... anything."

Keith believed that every time Jane spoke, it brought back memories of Billy's abuse. "If you heard her speak, you might not get that impression. Especially as she became more polished in her later speeches. But I'm sure that's how she felt, and she did express that.

"If you've been abused, you can put on masks, you can be three or four people. You can be hurting and have the biggest smile on your face. You could be tearing up inside, but you are not going to let anybody know, because you have been conditioned that way all your life."

CHAPTER 22
NIGHT CALLS

Annette Bushen was delighted when, in October 1984, Jane began working at the rehabilitation centre where she had been employed for several months, but she wondered how the others would accept her. "I was scared for her because it was no secret who she was and what she had done." She voiced her concern to Jane.

"Don't worry about it," said Jane. "Those who don't accept me as I am—well, it's their loss."

Bushen needn't have worried. Jane soon gained the respect and affection of both staff and patients. Because of her experience working at a home for the aged when she lived in Bangs Falls, and her brief employment in a similar institution in Ontario, she was assigned to the geriatric section. She was to remain there, working the night shift, for the next six years.

In all that time, Bushen never once heard anything derogatory about Jane, from staff or patients. She was gentle and compassionate with the elderly and a diligent worker. She was always neat and clean and was always in early for her shift, which began at 11:30 p.m.

After receiving patient reports from the outgoing shift, Jane's job was to check every patient on her floor, ensuring they had clean bed linen, pyjamas, and nightshirts. Those who were bedridden were repositioned to prevent bed sores. Most patients were asleep by 1 a.m., but Jane checked on them every hour until about seven, when she would rouse them for breakfast before her shift change at 7:30.

Between 1 a.m. and 7 a.m., Jane had a lot of quiet time to herself. She never wasted it. Between rounds, she wrote letters to friends, family, and abused women, including her pen pal Sara. She also spent a lot of time talking with them on the telephone. Many were abused women who, like Jane, had trouble sleeping at night.

She probably talked most to Donna Smith, who also had trouble sleeping at night. "Jane and I talked every night, and she kept telling me how much strength I had. Our situations were almost identical except that Robert was still alive. She knew nights were always bad for me. That's when everything comes back. Anything—a noise, a smell—and suddenly there's a flashback. It was the same for Jane because Billy never, never died—no matter what, he was still there."

Nights could also be bad for Jane's youngest sister, Mona, who lived near Barrie, Ontario, with her husband, Ed Donnelly. The sisters were close and had kept in touch by letter and telephone. The night calls to Jane's workplace from Mona became more frequent after February 14, 1985, when Ed Donnelly was shot by a disturbed young neighbour who came to the door of their rented cabin late one night. The bullet travelled upward through Ed's neck, exited through his cheek, and penetrated a kitchen cupboard, where police found it in a silverware drawer. Ed eventually recovered from his wound. Mona, a religious person, called it a miracle.

The gunman was initially charged with attempted murder, but a plea bargain reduced it to aggravated assault and he was sentenced to two years less a day, which meant he would serve his time in a provincial prison rather than a federal penitentiary. No motive for the crime was ever established.

After the shooting incident, the Donnellys never entered the cabin without sending their dog in first, and Mona had trouble sleeping. "I have really restless nights and I hear every noise, inside or out," she told Jane. "Eddie was never an edgy person, but now if he hears a noise, he sits and stares."

Every time they entered the rented cabin, they relived the shooting incident, and so several months later, they moved two miles away to a house Ed had built. But the move didn't end the trauma for Mona. "Now I check two or three times to make sure my doors are locked. And I'm a light sleeper and I wake up at the slightest sound."

Mona, an employment counsellor for Simcoe County, in Ontario, said there were many nights when she couldn't sleep and she would call Jane at work to talk.

Carrie Rafuse said that whenever she had a problem, she would also call Jane, usually in the middle of the night. "If the kids were driving me up the wall, boyfriend problems—anything—Jane was always there to cheer me up. If she was your friend, she was your friend—she was loyal to you. I never once in nine years had to say, 'Jane, would you please not tell anybody this.' You didn't have to say this to Jane. You could tell her your deepest secrets and you knew they were safe."

Jo Sheridan, a single mother who lived in a small community near Vancouver, was flipping through the TV channels on the night of March 13, 1984, when on the screen she saw "a woman with huge, agonized eyes."

The eyes were Jane Hurshman's and she was being interviewed by Hana Gartner on CBC's *the fifth estate.* The segment was aired a month after Jane was sentenced for killing Billy Stafford.

"The eyes riveted me," said Sheridan, a financial aid adviser for university students. "I didn't know if it was a soap opera or what it was." The program had just started. "Come and see this face," she called out to her daughter and son, both teenagers. "The three of us sat absolutely thunderstruck on the couch. Her eyes absolutely haunted me—and to this day they haunt me. I wept through most of the show and I stayed up all night, just tormented by this."

She was so struck by Jane that she sat down and wrote to her, care of *the fifth estate.* "If I could have borne just a little of that pain, to alleviate it for you, I would have done it. You are a good woman. You had no choice [in killing Billy] in my opinion. There is something in your eyes and soal that has struck every chord in my heart, and I need you to know that I—a complete stranger—care. I'm thinking positively and projecting lovely thoughts to you and I will never forget what I have seen. You're on the right track—go for it."

All of Jane's mail that came in to the CBC after the TV documentary was screened by her lawyer, and Sheridan was thankful her letter got through. Jane wrote to her immediately, thanking her and saying, "Your approach and your attitude were exactly what I need at this time. You have no idea what you've done for me."

They wrote often after that, and Sheridan sent flowers on the day Jane was released from prison. They learned about each other and their families though letters, photos, voice tapes, and telephone calls.

Sheridan, who was born in Britain, laughed when she recalled Jane's reaction to her English accent whenever she called her from British Columbia. "She preferred to write, but if

I phoned her and we chatted, she used to say to me, 'You sound just like the Queen.' We laughed about that many times."

Sheridan came to consider Jane one of her dearest friends, even though they were never to meet in person. "I knew a lot of her history, and she knew a lot of mine—things that I'd never shared with anyone, very sensitive things," said Sheridan. She believed she and Jane were so compatible because their life experiences, backgrounds, and hopes and dreams were so vastly different. She once asked Jane what she would consider a dream vacation. Jane told her she would like to take a hiking trip, on her own, through a remote and rugged part of Alaska. Sheridan shuddered at the thought.

In 1988 and 1989, Sheridan sensed that the work Jane was doing for abused women, combined with her busy everyday schedule, was exacting too large an emotional toll. In numerous letters, she begged Jane to curtail her speaking engagements. "It's too much for you to handle," she wrote. "It's getting to you badly. I can tell." For a time Jane tried to back off "to find her way," but she continued to be pulled back into speaking, "and there was a lot of agony coming through. I was writing and saying 'Stop it, don't do it anymore. Take a break. You owe it to yourself and your kids. Be selfish, Jane, be selfish.'"

Jane acknowledged that others had been giving her similar advice, but she felt obligated to continue because women continued to be battered and since she had the experience, she had to be their spokesperson. "She believed she had to educate the public, get changes made, and be there for women who were suffering," said Sheridan. "She was on a mission, but she wasn't, in my opinion, a missionary. I realized then that this was, for sure, a most remarkable woman."

CHAPTER 23
TAKING THINGS

Billy Stafford was still alive when Jane was caught shoplifting in Bridgewater in March of 1981. She never told anyone of the stress she was under—stress that she believed led to the incident. Her eldest son, Allen, then a teenager, had a brush with the law while Billy was at sea, and she was terrified Billy might find out about it when he returned. "I knew that if Bill found out he would have killed Allen," she wrote later.

A couple of days before Billy's return, Jane went shopping in Bridgewater with Margaret Joudrey and Roger Manthorne. They went to Zellers shopping plaza in Bridgewater where, said Jane, "an awful feeling came over me, and I walked out of the store with a full shopping cart. Next thing I knew, the man from the store had me by the arm and I was being arrested for shoplifting."

Joudrey said the three of them were taken to the police station, where the car was searched. "And one of them said to me, 'Do you know, Margaret, she had enough money in her purse to buy that stuff three and four times over,' and he said there was stuff she stole that she would never make use of. He wondered what in name of God would she ever do with it."

Billy returned home the day before Jane went to court, and she was terrified that he would find out what she had done. She managed to keep it from him, and Joudrey accompanied her to the court. The judge was lenient, sentencing Jane to fifty hours of community service and one year of probation.

"I never told anyone the real reason I was shoplifting was because I was so worried about what would happen to Allen if Bill found out that he was in trouble," wrote Jane. "And with this happening [shoplifting and court], I had even more to worry about." Jane saw a psychiatrist at that time but could not tell her why she had to keep the shoplifting incident secret from Billy. She couldn't admit to a stranger that she was a battered wife and that Billy would administer a terrible beating if he knew she had been charged.

Being arrested for shoplifting wasn't something new for Jane. She had four convictions against her on the same charge in 1975, and she had stolen from stores many times without being caught.

James Tynes believed he may have inadvertently discouraged Jane from confiding in him about her shoplifting problem when they were living together. "When we first started going together, we used to talk about everything for hours and hours, and one time I told her I didn't like thieves. I said it was wrong to steal and lie. Meantime, I didn't know it but she had already been caught a few times. So she probably thought I would think less of her if I knew about it. But I would have tried to help her—she wasn't a common thief."

It wasn't until the shoplifting charges appeared in the newspapers, and she feared going to jail, that Jane told Tynes about her problem. He wanted to help and offered to go shopping with her. He told her to call him if she felt the urge to shoplift. "She would agree, but I think it was just to get me off her case."

Jane did tell Tynes about one incident after that, but she had already been caught. He went to the manager of the store. "It's in the hands of the police," said the manager.

Tynes went to the police and asked them to drop the charge. "But they said it was already in the computer." He went back to the manager and pleaded with him to drop the charges. The manager refused.

"To them, she was just a common thief," said Tynes.

Donna Smith remembered being in a pet store with Jane when she saw her pick up a dog leash. "It was winter, just before Christmas, and she tucked it under her coat. I thought I was seeing things. She bought something else and paid for it, but she didn't pay for the leash. I was scared. I thought I would get caught too. She didn't say a thing about it. Later the same day, we went into a jewellery store and I was looking at a nice necklace and earrings."

When they returned to the car Jane shifted her body in the seat until her back was to Donna.

"Wait a minute," said Jane. Donna could hear a rustling sound but didn't know what Jane was doing.

"Then she turned and handed me a little red stocking."

"This is for you," said Jane. Inside were the necklace and the earrings, worth about $70. Donna realized that the rustling sound was Jane removing the price tags from the jewellery.

"Jane, no!" protested Donna. "It costs too much, take it back right now."

"It's your Christmas present," said Jane.

"When did you get a chance to buy them? I was in there with you."

"I told the woman to go and do it in the back. It was a surprise for you."

Donna suspected that the jewellery was stolen but she could never bring herself to ask Jane, and Jane never talked about it. There were, however, conversations about shoplifting, and Jane once told Donna it gave her a "high" to get away with shoplifting, although sometimes she wasn't aware she was stealing.

"She said nobody ever listened to her," said Donna. "The shoplifting was a cry for help and she couldn't stop it."

Ann Keith first learned about Jane's problem with shoplifting around 1986, when a friend from the probation office tipped her off. She called Jane and they met for tea at Keith's house. "Jane, you've been shoplifting, haven't you?" said Keith.

"Yeah." Jane nodded.

"Why didn't you come to me?"

Jane grinned and said, "Oh, I knew you'd come to me when you found out."

"Look, I don't want to go and visit you in jail," said Keith. Jane avoided jail on that and another subsequent charge. But when it happened again, she told Keith she had to get help because she had no control over the shoplifting. The psychiatrist she was seeing wasn't helping her.

"I want hypnosis," said Jane. "I have to stop it."

Resources for the type of treatment Jane needed were scarce in Halifax, but Keith knew that if anyone could help her it was John Curtis. Keith called him. "John, I'm begging you," she said. "You've got to take Jane."

Curtis had a string of credentials giving him standing as an expert in psychiatry in Canada and the United States. His specialties were multiple personality disorders, dissociative disorders, and hypnosis.

On February 2, 1989, two months after Jane Hurshman started treatment with Curtis, she was shopping at Towers Department Store in Bedford, just north of Halifax. She was wearing a winter jacket over a red-and-black sweater and pushing a shopping cart with her purse in the upper compartment. Beside the purse were two beige planter trays and a pair of blue jogging pants with matching top. In the lower part of the cart was an audio cassette holder.

In an aisle in the outdoors department, Jane slipped the planter trays into her purse and tucked the jogging suit under her sweater. Gabrielle MacAulay, the store's loss prevention investigator, saw her conceal the items. Jane pushed her shopping cart to cash register No. 1, where she paid for the cassette holder. Then she walked to the front of the store toward the exit. MacAulay approached her as she was leaving.

"Excuse me, ma'am," she said, producing her identification. "I'm loss prevention investigator with Towers Department Store. You have some items concealed that you haven't paid for."

"Yes, I do have items that I didn't pay for," admitted Jane.

MacAulay arrested her, read her her legal rights, and asked if she understood.

"I understand," she said softly.

Jane followed MacAulay to the store's office, where she called a lawyer and waited for the Bedford police to arrive. The total value of the items stolen was $37.96.

At the time of her arrest, Jane had at least seven previous convictions for shoplifting. At her trial for the Towers theft, on July 11, 1989, Jane told defence lawyer Linda Tippett that she remembered taking the jogging suit but not the planter trays. "Who was the track suit for?" asked Tippett.

"It would have fit Darren," she replied.

"Was it something Darren needed?"

"No, he didn't need it."

"Did you have any money in your purse that could have paid for those items?"

"Yes."

"When you took the items did you look around to see who might have been there?"

Jane didn't respond for several seconds. "I don't know. I don't think so. I... didn't think. I just did it."

"What was going through your mind at the time?" asked Tippett.

"That's difficult to say... nothing, really."

Tippett went through Jane's record of convictions and asked her if she remembered when she started shoplifting.

"Not really," she replied. "A long time."

"And other than the times you've been caught, have you taken things on other occasions?"

"Yes."

"When did you start realizing that this was a serious problem?"

There was a lengthy pause, and then Jane gave an inaudible response.

"You'll have to speak up, Mrs. Hurshman," said Provincial Court Judge Patrick Curran. "I can just barely hear you."

"Probably about a year ago or less," said Jane.

"What did you do about it, if anything?" asked Tippett.

"Well, I went to see one doctor and it didn't seem to be doing any good."

She said she was seeing a new psychiatrist, Dr. John Curtis, once a week, and that she wanted to stop shoplifting, but couldn't help herself.

"How much do you want to stop doing it?" asked Tippett.

Jane thought about her response for several seconds.

"In terms of how much... well, if I thought of the thing that I would not want to lose the most, it would probably be my eyesight and I would trade that."

Jane said she would continue to see Dr. Curtis for as long as it took to stop shoplifting.

During cross-examination, Crown counsel Bob McCarroll told Jane she must have realized long ago that she had a serious problem. Jane agreed that she did.

The defence called Dr. Curtis, who told the court that Ann Keith referred Jane to him because "she had no memory of her childhood" and hypnosis might be helpful in recalling childhood trauma.

"It was felt the childhood trauma probably had something to do with her severe depression, her mood swings, even her kleptomania," said the psychiatrist. He defined a kleptomaniac as a person who steals articles they don't really need and are quite capable of paying for. "And often these individuals will describe that it was not something that they had plotted or planned, but more something they found themselves doing or had completed...An awful lot of the people I see with this disorder do not ever remember stealing. Jane's having no recollection at all of stealing the planter bottoms is typical of kleptomania and typical of having a form of dissociative disorder in which you are unaware of certain actions—or amnesic."

Dr. Curtis said Jane did not remember most of her first twelve years of life and had no memory "of other things as well."

"I was aware that kleptomania was a factor," he said, "but it wasn't the focus of what we were doing until February 2, when she arrived late for my appointment because she had been picked up at Towers."

According to Dr. Curtis, Jane led a lifetime of accepting tragedy and problems and had learned to tune them out and ignore them. "It goes back into her childhood and into her family upbringing."

Linda Tippett asked the psychiatrist if he thought Jane was improving—changing.

"Yes, she certainly is," he replied. He added that inducing a trancelike state to bring back Jane's childhood didn't work "because she was literally so totally out of touch with herself and her emotional memories, that when she went into a trance she didn't really recall anything. So we had to institute a kind of therapy in which I've been literally teaching her about families and about herself and what happened to her."

Dr. Curtis described the family system that Jane came out of as a boarding house. "It was a family where there was no discussion of any emotional events whatsoever."

Curtis said that through treatment, Jane was getting very much in touch with herself emotionally. Through hypnosis, they were able to recognize various "ego-states" within her personality. "These are parts of the person," he said. "And there are two ego-states in her which have to do with the shoplifting." One state was associated very much with sadness and had to do with her upbringing "and never having really been nurtured."

The other ego-state was associated with an event that happened in Jane's life when she was twelve and living with her family on a Canadian army base in Germany. Jane was asked to babysit a family of three children for the weekend. The parents didn't tell her where they were going, and when she went to the refrigerator to prepare supper, there was no food.

"And she went to the cupboard and there was nothing in the cupboard," said Dr. Curtis. "There was nothing to eat." Jane went up the street to her parents' house.

"Mother," she said. "I can't believe this, there's no food in the house for the kids for the weekend."

Jane's mother said nothing. "She never commented on it," the psychiatrist said. "She never said this was a terrible thing.

She gave her enough food for one meal and sent her back to the house and made it very plain she didn't want to hear from her for the rest of the weekend. It was very clear to Jane that she should do what her father had done in that household since she was born—as a cook in the army he stole every bit of food they ever ate. And she went out and started shoplifting and that was the origin of this problem.

"What I'm saying here, it was a whole family system—it was something that you just do. And Jane, unfortunately, has within her a belief system that's saying, 'This is something that's all right to do.' She's dealing with that now, but she wasn't even aware of it three months ago."

Tippett asked Dr. Curtis what goes through the mind of a kleptomaniac at the time they are taking things.

"It's something they're quite unconscious of and it's not a predictable thing," he replied. He said he once had a client who stole an item with an RCMP officer standing beside her. He found it interesting that in the two previous months, as Jane became more in touch with her emotions, her urge to shoplift intensified rather than decreased. "Now she can start doing something about it, whereas before she could not. And when she has that urge she's extremely careful when she goes into a store."

The ego-state that told Jane to shoplift was associated with a tremendous amount of anger. "Jane has spent a lifetime of having things done to her—horrible things—and has never really expressed anger. I think a lot of it is encapsulated in that ego-state and in others as well."

He found Jane to be cooperative, bright, and intuitive, and said she was working very hard at her therapy. "Jane herself has no conscious intent or desire to steal. Her everyday self is in fact a very fine, caring, honourable, honest person who would never steal or do anything like that, but she does have ego-states inside her that would do this—for very childlike and immature reasons."

Under cross-examination by McCarroll, Dr. Curtis said the reason Jane had a heightened urge to steal of late "has to do with the fact that she's getting better. Oddly enough, this ego-state inside her cannot tolerate her getting better. That may seem rather odd to you, but Billy, her husband, could not stand her doing well either. Her family—father—could not stand her doing well, and she was continually put down by these people. And this ego-state is modelled after those people. So here you have an ego-state that's going to get you in trouble if you do well."

In her summation to the judge, Tippett said that Jane's was an unusual case and that when she stole items from the store she wasn't thinking like a rational person. "She's appeared before the court with a number of convictions and she's quite well aware that someone with a record like hers could very well be looking at a jail term."

Jane was not a hardened petty thief who needed harsher penalties to rehabilitate her, Tippett said. Rather, she was suffering from an illness that sometimes left her incapable of thinking rationally.

"No one is trying to suggest that she's insane," said Tippett. "However, she does have an illness that at the time of this incident rendered her incapable of forming the type of intent needed to sustain a conviction. A kleptomaniac she is—a thief she is not."

Crown counsel McCarroll agreed that the issue of insanity was not relevant. "What we have here is a competition of egos in this lady," he said. "Every one of us has competition of egos of one type or another. This lady has more of a battle on her hands than most of us, but that doesn't change the fact that she knows what she does. She knows she has a history of it. She's reckless in not taking precautions to prevent herself from losing the battle with her ego."

McCarroll said it was a matter of guilt or innocence, and he suggested that Jane had a guilty mind.

Because of the extraordinary circumstances of the case, Judge Curran reserved his judgment until the following week.

"I'm not aware of any instances of kleptomania being recognized as a defence to a charge such as this," he said. "But I think there's a very important question raised here by the evidence and arguments I heard today."

On July 17, Jane was back in court to hear Judge Curran's decision: "One could conclude from the evidence that Mrs. Hurshman had a reduced degree of responsibility for her actions because of the condition which affected her and that it is something to be taken into account on sentencing rather than when determining guilt or innocence.

"Apart from the evidence of the dissociative state, it's clear that Mrs. Hurshman did steal property of Towers on February 2, 1989, and consequently I find her guilty of that offence."

Jane stood as Judge Curran sentenced her. He said that he accepted her reduced responsibility as outlined by Dr. Curtis, and he commended her for seeking help. He placed her on probation and instructed her to continue with therapy. The judge also recommended that Jane take somebody with her when she went shopping. "Somebody that you're not afraid to tell what the history has been and to be right there with you and make sure it doesn't happen."

Curran tempered his advice with a warning that if the shoplifting continued, Jane would have to face the consequences. "Because, notwithstanding some measure of reduced responsibility, the time is going to come sooner or later when the courts are going to conclude the only way to stop this kind of thing is to put you in jail for some period of time—which would be most unfortunate, especially since it seems in every other way that you live a praiseworthy kind of life."

Victoria Jones recalled shopping at a mall with Jane in the summer of 1990, while she was living with her on Arklow Drive. "I'm not much of a mall person, and I got tired, so I told Jane I would sit on a bench and wait for her."

After an hour, Jane hadn't returned. "I thought, 'What's going on?' so I went in and found her." Jane told her she was looking for strawberries and sent Jones in one direction while she went into the bulk food section. A few minutes later, as they were leaving the store, two security officers stopped them. They accused Jane of theft.

"I don't have anything," protested Jane.

"Either you come with us or we'll send for the police."

Jane handed Jones the keys to the car.

"Wait for me in the car," she said. "I won't be long."

Jane came out a short time later and they drove home.

"She didn't say anything," said Jones, "but I imagine they searched her and didn't find anything. They wouldn't have stopped her unless they were sure. I think she must have got rid of whatever it was she had when she sent me after the strawberries. She used to buy me all these presents and I had kind of an idea where they were coming from, but you can't turn around to the person and say, 'Well, where did this come from?'"

Jane was likely dissociating in the store, and when Jones showed up, it jarred her out of it and she returned the item.

There is no doubt that Jane felt embarrassed and ashamed about her shoplifting. She didn't tell her counsellor, Ann Keith, about it until Keith came to her. And until she began therapy with Dr. Curtis and came to realize that her shoplifting was a disorder, she kept it a secret even from her closest friends. After her arrest at Towers, but before her trial, Jane drove to Bridgewater and revealed her secret to Carrie Rafuse.

"I have problems stealing and I want you to know, because you're going to read about it in the newspaper," said Jane.

To Carrie, her admission was enlightening. "She never wanted to go shopping with me, never—ever. When she told me about her problem, it just clicked."

Carrie remembered one of Jane's laughing refusals to accompany her on a shopping excursion. "Oh, Carrie," she had said, "that's the difference between us. You like the malls and you like shopping, but I don't—I hate it."

Now Carrie understood why, and they hugged and cried. "She told me about her therapy with John Curtis and said she was feeling great—and I could tell it was true. For a long time before that, she was there but she wasn't there. Now it was like my friend Jane was back, and I told her I thought the therapy was doing good for her."

Jane's sister Mona said that Jane was really excited about her therapy. "She felt very good about seeing Dr. Curtis because she was finally doing something for herself. She wouldn't say a lot about the sessions, but she said there was hypnosis involved. She said he gave her books to read and movies to watch and they'd talk about the dominant characters."

What Jane didn't tell Mona was that, through hypnosis, she eventually remembered being sexually assaulted as a child, by someone close to the family—as Ann Keith had long suspected.

Through John Curtis, Jane began to better understand the root cause of her mood swings and her kleptomania, and she began to speak out about it. She was adamant that people aren't born to be victims. "We are born to be what we are taught to be, and what we are conditioned to be. As a child, I grew up in a home with an alcoholic father and a mother who only had time for him. In our home, there was no communication, no positive encouragement, no parental involvement of any kind in my life or in the lives of my older brother or my two younger sisters.

"I watched my mother being verbally and physically abused. Mom withstood this abuse for years and years, always believing that someday things would get better. To this very day, my mom will not discuss her life or the abuse.

"I was very fearful and obedient to my father, always trying to please him, and growing up believing that life should be—please everyone but yourself."

At the time she made that speech, Jane had been seeing Dr. Curtis for just over a year. "I can honestly say that it is the best thing that I have ever done for myself," she said.

She said that being a kleptomaniac was like being an alcoholic. "You can spend the rest of your life clean and sober, but you are always an alcoholic. There is always the chance that you will take that one drink, or for me that I will steal that one item."

On June 9, 1991, less than a year after the conviction for the theft of the planter trays and jogging suit from Towers, Jane Hurshman was arrested for stealing greeting cards and a bottle of cologne from a Dartmouth pharmacy. She pleaded guilty at her court hearing on July 3 and was fined $375. The next day the story was in the news. HURSHMAN FINED FOR THEFT, ran one headline.

The stories always brought up Jane's past and the fact that she killed Billy Stafford. She believed she was being treated unfairly because of who she was.

"She was really upset," said James Tynes.

Jane decided to fight back. She wrote a scathing letter to a Halifax newspaper in which she said her name "still sells your papers after all these years. If everyone that got caught and sentenced for shoplifting got media coverage, there wouldn't be any room in your paper to print anything else.

"Shoplifting—kleptomania—is a disease, the same as alcoholism, compulsive overeating, anorexia, or compulsive gambling." Yet, she pointed out, shoplifting was a crime, "while the others you can do anywhere and there is no repercussion."

Shoplifting, Jane wrote, "brings shame and humiliation to me and my family." She said she was fortunate to have family and friends who supported her, and she urged the media to "put more effort into publishing information about the problem" instead of keeping her in the spotlight. "I am a good, honest, hard-working, caring, and helpful person, and it would be nice to live my life without constant comments from the media."

When people see the word *shoplifting*, wrote Jane, they associate it with "a bad, untrustworthy person. I am neither, nor is anyone else who has the disease of kleptomania. It's because of all the shit and abuse that I have endured during my life that I continually have to fight and struggle every day to live. Just because the abuse is gone, and Stafford is dead, does not mean that everything is okay, or normal.

"Myself and others like me, have no idea what *normal* is. I must spend the rest of my life learning—one day at a time. And when I mess up—as in shoplifting—it is because I cannot believe that I deserve to be happy, or that I am worthy of good things or good people around me."

The Halifax *Chronicle-Herald* assigned reporter Gail Lethbridge to interview Jane about her kleptomania. The story appeared less than a week after the account of her conviction and fine.

"For her, shoplifting is the alcoholic's drinking binge or the over-eater's late night refrigerator raid—the same, except that it's illegal," wrote Lethbridge.

In the article, Jane said kleptomania was "a symptom of the abuse that I suffered, probably from childhood" and to a larger degree from her years with Billy Stafford. She said she was speaking out so that other women with the same problem would know they were not alone.

"I want it brought out in the open so that kleptomania is an issue that is talked about like alcoholism. It's a disease."

Lethbridge wrote that Jane couldn't explain what triggered her to shoplift, but a memory from her past or an act of violence, like the Montreal massacre, "can send her into a swirl of emotional confusion and pain. Most of the time she suppresses the urge, but occasionally she finds herself stealing. Afterwards, the feelings are always the same—sharp disappointment in herself and anger at her inability to shake the urge and forget the past."

The article included a post office box address for Jane, who said she wanted to start a support group for those suffering from kleptomania and other effects of abuse. It was after that appeal that Sara, who had been sexually and physically abused as a child and a young adult, first wrote to her.

"I know you steal and understand that's it's humiliating for you," wrote Sara. "But I do something that's even more humiliating and shameful." She was an obsessive masturbator, which is not uncommon for women who are sexually abused as children. (Donna Smith's daughter Mary, who was discovered masturbating at the age of three at Bryony House, continued the practice indiscriminately and had to undergo therapy.)

Jane responded to Sara by praising her for recognizing her problem and trying to do something about it. They corresponded regularly after that.

Liz Forestell said that Jane's attempt to form a support group for kleptomaniacs illustrated "what I said about her being able to take things that happened to her and turn them into a strength."

Despite the therapy and her efforts to go public with her problem, Jane was frustrated that the urge to steal was greater than ever. "I just can't control it," she said in late 1991. "I am getting help from my doctors, but it isn't easy. It's a constant struggle for me."

She lost the struggle once again when she was arrested for shoplifting from an IGA store in Dartmouth on November 16, 1991. She kept it a secret from her family and pleaded not guilty when she appeared in court on December 17. Her case was put over to March 4, 1992, when she was scheduled to appear in Courtroom No. 2 at 9:30 a.m.

CHAPTER 24
THOUGHTS OF DEATH

Jane Hurshman had often considered suicide during the abusive years with Billy Stafford. Those thoughts receded after his death, but they were never far from the surface. Jane was open about it with some of her friends.

"Jane and I often talked about suicide," said Donna Smith. "If we ever decided to do it, I said I would help her and she said she would help me. Jane kept saying we were so much alike. We laughed about getting older and opening a nursing home together. We pictured ourselves sitting on the porch with our canes and knocking over whoever we wanted to knock over. But suicide was always there. We didn't call it suicide. We called it 'escape.' You know, you can only take so much."

In the summer of 1988, Donna and her children were invited to vacation for a week in Cape Breton with a friend who lived there. The friend arranged to have someone drive Donna to Cape Breton from Halifax. A day or two before they were to leave, Jane called Donna.

"I'm not going to be around when you get back," she said. "I can't take any more. I want to die."

Donna did her best to talk Jane out of it and then called Ann Keith in tears. "Ann, she's going to do it," she cried. "I know she is."

Donna didn't want to leave Jane, but her children were excited about the trip and their ride was already on the way to pick them up. Keith, who was still counselling Jane at the time, called her on a Sunday night under the pretext of changing the time of their session, which was scheduled for the next day.

The session was routine until Jane was preparing to leave. "I'm really glad you called me last night," she said. "I was going to commit suicide, but you jarred me out of it."

Jane told Keith she had put her papers in order and had written letters to her children, the rest of her family, and her friends.

"It was really bizarre," said Keith. "She had a syringe and she said she was going to inject air into her ear. She was a nursing assistant and she had access to needles."

Jane once talked to her sister Mona about using a syringe. "Mona, if I ever wanted to die, I could do it real easy. All I'd have to do is get a needle, inject air into my veins, and I'd be gone just like that."

While Donna Smith was in Cape Breton, her daughter Mary contracted chicken pox, and they ended up staying for two-and-a-half weeks instead of one week. "I kept calling Jane and Ann, but it wasn't until two or three days after I returned home that I thought Jane was over it."

Jane's son Allen didn't realize at the time that his mother's shoplifting was something she had no control over, and he felt badly when he came to understand it was an illness.

"He didn't understand the extent of Jane's hurt inside and how all that stuff could be brought back up and make her feel victimized all over again," said Mona. "He didn't want to see it any more. He didn't want to hear about it. And it seemed like every time he turned around, something was in the paper, and people would ask him about it. It was an embarrassment to

Allen, and I know that would have hurt and upset Jane, but not to the extent that she would want to kill herself."

Ann Keith said the media attention, and the embarrassment it brought to the family, hurt Jane deeply. "Because she loved her family so much, the last thing she wanted to do was to bring disgrace on them. And she felt, personally, that she was letting her family down."

There is no doubt that Jane's inability to stop shoplifting, and the fallout that resulted whenever she was caught, pushed her to contemplate suicide. That was the case in 1988 when twice in three months she was arrested in Dartmouth for shoplifting. It was after the second occasion, on December 3, that James Tynes went to the store manager and the police and sought unsuccessfully to have the charges dropped. (Jane had started seeing Dr. Curtis before the December 3 arrest, but she hadn't told him about her problem or the incident. She told a friend it was too embarrassing for her.)

Jane was scheduled to appear in court in Dartmouth on January 10, and was to report to the police station the day before for mug shots and fingerprints. On Friday, January 6, she was at home sleeping after working the night shift at the rehab centre when the telephone woke her up. The caller said he was a constable with the Dartmouth city police. Jane missed his name and he ignored her when she asked him to repeat it.

"Several times throughout his conversation, I asked him to tell me his name but he just kept talking past me and over me," she said later. The caller told Jane that the newspapers would be present when she appeared in court on the tenth, and that the Children's Aid would be notified "and they would see that the children were dealt with the way they should have been before."

"He said that the newspapers would carry my story," said Jane. "This would be the eighth time I appeared in the

Dartmouth court, and he said that I would be doing jail time and my kids would be taken away and I would be proven to be an unfit mother."

Jane couldn't get back to sleep, and that afternoon, as she lay there agonizing over the telephone call, she decided to kill herself. She booked a room in a Dartmouth motel and went to work that night as usual. At 4 a.m., when her floor at the rehab centre was quiet, she sat down and in a soft voice prepared a suicide audio tape for Tynes:

"James, I want you to know, darling, you are forever in my heart and in my mind. You've been a very special person in my life these last years and you've made up for all the unbearable years I've lived. You've been a lover, a friend, and a companion, and I have been more honest and straightforward to you than I have been with anyone.

"You are a beautiful, special person and I don't want to bring you any more shame and humiliation than I already have. I've brought it to my children too, and I still continue to do so. Allen knows I stole way back when. I don't know what Jamie knows. Darren knows I steal, and he's been quite worried about my going to court."

Jane said it was difficult for her to accept that she wouldn't be seeing him or her children and family again, but her death wouldn't be a surprise to them. She said that only Tynes and her sister Mona were to know that she was killing herself because of the shoplifting. She wanted her sons and the rest of the family to believe that she took her life because she was dying from incurable cancer. That would be "a hundred times more acceptable" than the real reason.

"I don't know if you can agree to a lie—but I do hope you don't tell my kids or parents the truth and I ask the same thing of Mona. What I have is the same as a cancer—it's incurable and it destroys. It eats away just like a cancer—it has been with me all my life, and it has destroyed me a little at a time. And it begins to gnaw and chew anything that I come close to or love...

"I just don't want to be here anymore. I know that's going to cause you to be sad and hurt, and the pain is going to be enormous."

Her voice became stronger and more authoritative when she talked about her remains. "I do not want to be buried in the ground. I want to be cremated and I definitely do not want to be put in any coffin. I want Mom to take my ashes and in the spring when she plants her flowers in her garden, I want her to sprinkle my ashes there. Then I will be at peace at last."

Jane thanked Tynes for trying to get the store manager and the police to drop charges against her. "You'll never know how much that meant to me. Nobody has ever defended me like that."

She asked Tynes to keep the news of her suicide from her children until they were all together at her parents' home in Danesville. "Darren really is a very warm and loving, and extremely sensitive, child, so I'd like his hurt to be buffered by him being with family."

Jane said she hadn't been a good parent "as far as consistency and punishment," and she hoped Darren would go to Ottawa to live with her sister Sandy and that Jamie would go to Mona and Ed in Barrie.

Allen and his girlfriend, Charlene, were planning to marry in September, and Jane hoped "that everything goes well in their life and that they are together forever."

Jane and Tynes had talked about getting married, and she had even bought a dress. Her voice was barely a whisper when she said that two moments she had often visualized were the look in Tynes's eyes as she came down the aisle toward him, and the exchange of rings as they said "I do."

"We have so much love to share with each other, I know we'd have a good life together," she said.

There was a tinge of anger in Jane's voice when she talked about the Dartmouth police and the call she received on Friday. "There is no way, James, that I could ever be an unfit mother. Nobody loves their kids more than I do." Society might consider her to be unfit, she said, but society didn't know the whole story. She said she wouldn't give them the opportunity to declare her unfit or to take her children.

"So I decided Friday afternoon that of my options, suicide was the way to go. That's the solution I came up with, and right or wrong, that's my decision. With that decision, for the first time in my life, I felt an inner peace—knowing that it's soon going to be all over."

Jane asked Tynes to call the court or attend on January 10, "and tell them that I am dead and that I won't be bothering them anymore. Also, I'm supposed to go on the ninth to the Dartmouth police station for mug shots and fingerprints and I don't want these assholes coming to my door. Could you just kindly tell them I'm deceased now and I won't be in for mug shots and fingerprints—which they already got from me less than two weeks ago."

On the tape, Jane read a poem; reminisced about some of their good times together; and played two of their favourite songs, which they had chosen to be played at their wedding. "I do have your memory hard in my mind—you and my children and my family—and I'll die that way," she said. "James, I do know that there is a Heavenly Father and a Lord Jesus Christ, who is our mediator and redeemer. But I also believe that He works for some, and some He can't help, because I think they gave up on Him and vice versa. I think that's the point I'm at in my life now.

"Once again I am hurting so many people, but this will be the last hurt—there'll be no more."

Jane's closing words were barely audible: "You have my endless love and I know I have yours and I have taken yours to my grave—I love you, James."

She told him she took an overdose of sleeping pills because "it just seemed to be the easiest way and the least painful—to lie down and go to sleep and have a sleep that will be forever.

"The inner peace is near, babe, and I ask your forgiveness. Goodnight, my darling. You're very precious, James, very beautiful, and a kind, loving, and caring person. Goodbye, James. May we meet again some day."

She ended the recording with a short prayer: "Dear Heavenly Father, protect him and my children, ease their pain, and fill their hearts with love only..."

The tape was delivered to Tynes by taxi shortly after 7:30 Saturday morning, about the time Jane usually returned home from work. Before leaving, the taxi driver told Tynes where he had picked up the tape. Tynes listened to part of it and immediately called the police. Jane was close to death when they found her. Had they arrived even minutes later, she would probably have died.

She drifted in and out of consciousness for several days, and when she was well enough, she was sent to the Nova Scotia Hospital for psychiatric care. On January 10, Tynes appeared in court in Dartmouth on Jane's behalf and explained the reason for her absence. The case was put over for several months.

Donna Smith called Jane at the hospital during her recovery. "She was really sad, but more embarrassed, at what she had done. She said she could only get so far in her therapy. The hardest part of therapy is that you have to relive everything. Sometimes you feel anger toward the therapist because you go home and keep thinking about it and they just move on to the next patient. You're like a number, and you don't mean anything to them. There are times when you don't want to go because you don't want to talk about it. I know Jane often felt that way."

It wasn't until two weeks after her release from the hospital that Jane told Carrie Rafuse about the suicide attempt.

"I felt so bad," said Carrie, "and I asked her why she didn't call me if she was depressed. What bothered me most is that I didn't detect that she was feeling that way. She must have been depressed for a couple of months, but I didn't notice it."

(About two weeks later, on February 2, 1989, Jane was caught stealing the jogging suit and planter trays at Towers in Bedford. This time Dr. Curtis found out, because her arrest caused her to be late for her appointment with him.)

In a speech a year after her suicide attempt, Jane said she had tried to kill herself because she couldn't deal with her problems and wouldn't discuss them with anyone. "You have the same kind of feelings and thoughts that you have in an abusive situation. The feelings of hopelessness and helplessness and that you are weak and a failure. But mostly, it's a feeling of being incapable of being *normal.*

"Death appeared better to me than having to go to court for shoplifting, and having to be harassed by the media. Worst of all was having everyone know my secret and being told that I was an unfit mother and having my sons taken away."

In the speech, Jane also acknowledged that she had deep-seated problems that she had ignored because she had spent so much time helping others. "Just because I was out of my abusive situation, and just because I had my family together, and just because I allowed everyone to believe all was fine, did not mean that was how it was. I still had not dealt with *me*, personally. I still had a gigantic secret problem [shoplifting]—a problem that was destroying me."

In January 1989, while she was recovering in the Nova Scotia Hospital, Jane told Carrie Rafuse she couldn't think of anything to live for.

"The kids would be better off without me," she said.

Jane began reading in the hospital, searching for answers.

"She thought she might be manic depressive, and she went to her doctor, who put her on lithium," said Carrie. "She was on it for a while, and she said, 'Yes, I can see light at the end of the tunnel and I think I do feel better.' But it didn't work. She was trying to convince herself."

Tynes, who was living on and off with Jane during that period, said she went through dramatic mood swings. "The lithium was supposed to balance things out, and she was doing some exercises and reading, but it wasn't doing any good."

Jane eventually gave up on the lithium. There was improvement when Dr. Curtis began treating her with hypnotherapy.

"The depression wasn't gone away," said Tynes, "but she knew how to control it, and she understood herself a lot more. She seemed better to me."

Victoria Jones noticed the same mood swings when she went to live with Jane a year later, in January 1990. "She wouldn't say much. She was just quiet and she would go into her room and sleep a lot when things were bothering her."

In her job as a counsellor at the Harbour House shelter for battered women, Carrie Rafuse encountered many suicidal women. "Eventually you learn to pick up little warnings, but you couldn't pick up the signs with Jane.

"I was speaking with her every two or three weeks and I never sensed any of this. After her bout at the Nova Scotia

Hospital, I decided I would have to really watch her—to see if there were any clues."

Carrie's vigilance paid off, and she began to notice that Jane became more angry and aggressive than usual when she was despondent. "She would be very preoccupied and a little sarcastic to me. Her fuse was a little shorter. When I noticed her like that, I'd really talk to her. It was a warning signal, but she wouldn't tell you much. You had to either dig it out, or, if she was in the mood, she might just tell you what was bothering her. You might not find out until a month later, but in her own time, she would tell me."

CHAPTER 25
WEDDING BELLS

On Saturday, July 21, 1990, Jane Hurshman decided to drive to Bridgewater to spend the evening with her friend Carrie Rafuse as the kick-off to a two-week vacation at her parents' place in nearby Danesville. Jane had been on her own since she and James Tynes stopped seeing each other several months earlier. The women decided to drive to Mahone Bay and have supper at the Mug and Anchor.

"As usual with Carrie, we were late getting there and the grill was closing," Jane wrote in a letter a year later. "We stayed and sat outside and had a couple of drafts." After their drinks, they returned to Bridgewater to have supper at the Topsail Tavern. A band was playing, and after their meal they decided to have a drink in the bar.

Joel Corkum, a licensed mechanic working locally at Hebb's Cross Esso, was sitting at a table near the band with his friend, Fred. Around 10 p.m., Joel saw Jane and Carrie walk in. He knew Carrie but hadn't seen her in about fifteen years. The place was crowded, and Joel invited Carrie and Jane to join him and his friend. Carrie made the introductions, explaining that she and Jane had met at nursing school.

Joel was soft-spoken and, at thirty-three, eight years younger than Jane. There was an instant mutual attraction. "It was destiny," she wrote later. "I came alive."

Joel and Jane danced until sometime after midnight, when the four of them decided to go for coffee. Carrie noticed that Jane and Joel were holding hands as they left the tavern.

At the coffee shop, "Jane and I did a lot of talking," recalled Joel. Later, the others left and they went to the trailer where Joel was living. They had more coffee and did more talking. The next day was Sunday. It was a day off for Joel, and he asked Jane if he could see her. She agreed.

Joel met Jane's parents when he came by the next day. Then they went to Cherry Hill Beach, where they spent most of the day getting to know each other better. Soon Jane was spending her nights in Joel's trailer.

About a week after they met, Joel went to see Jane at her parents'. "She was sitting at the table with her back to the wall," he recalled. "She had sort of a funny look on her face."

"What did I do now?" He smiled.

"Oh, you didn't do anything," she said. "Have you ever read *Life With Billy*?"

"Yeah, I read that," replied Joel.

"Well, I'm Jane of that book."

"So?" He shrugged.

"Do you want to know about it?"

"That was then, this is now. If you want to talk about it, I'll listen. But if you don't want to talk about it, I'm not going to ask. It doesn't matter to me what happened in your past."

Joel said Jane seemed relieved at his reaction. "I gather some people would have got right nosey—want to know everything about it. Or they would back right away. I didn't do either. I just liked her for who she was."

When Jane left for Cole Harbour at the end of her vacation, she gave Joel a key to her townhouse.

"She invited me up for the weekend a couple of weeks after she went back," he said. "In between, my phone bill was hurtin' bad because I called her every night."

Carrie Rafuse didn't see Jane for a few weeks after their night out. "The next time she came down, I could see she was like a little kid in love. You could see it in her face. She was ecstatic."

Carrie wondered if Jane knew about Joel's past. He seemed harmless enough, but Carrie had heard stories about him.

When Joel was three, his father died. At sixteen, he left home and fell into trouble with the law, serving two six-month sentences on break-and-enter charges as a teenager and three months for dangerous driving in his early twenties. Twice married, he had three children. "I had one kid before I was married—when I was sixteen or seventeen—it was one of those 'oops' things. And I had two more with my first wife, and none with my second."

Joel had no contact with the two children from his marriage. "They were adopted out a long time ago," he said. The son from before his marriage was seventeen when Joel met Jane. She encouraged him to spend time with the boy. "He's being raised by his grandparents [on his mother's side] and they're not really fond of me," Joel told her.

Before becoming a mechanic, Joel had worked on the fishing boats. He had been on his own for about a year before he met Jane.

Jane didn't ask Carrie about Joel's past. "I hinted to her," Carrie said, "but I never, ever, forced my opinion on her or told her what I thought she should do." And Jane appeared so happy that Carrie didn't want to say anything that would break the spell.

Jane soon invited Joel to come to Cole Harbour to live with her, Jamie, and Darren and their two dogs. He found a job with a muffler shop near Halifax, and in early September of 1990 he moved in with them. By late fall of that year, they were engaged.

At the end of September, Jane went into hospital for a hysterectomy. She was told not to return to work until the end of November. On a Sunday afternoon in November, Jane and Joel drove to Bridgewater to visit his seventy-seven-year-old mother. At one point she took Jane aside.

"Joel's finally happy," she said. "I can let go."

"It didn't really make any sense to us at the time," said Joel. But his mother, who suffered from angina, died of a heart attack the following Tuesday.

In April of 1991, Jane and Joel jointly purchased a house just up the street on Arklow Drive. Joel was in debt and had declared personal bankruptcy, so Jane put up most of the down payment. From then on, most of Joel's pay went toward the mortgage. The house was small, but it had a decent yard and "a lot of potential." Joel built a bedroom in the basement for fourteen-year-old Darren, and a wall of shelves for Jane's growing collection of books. He also set up a cubbyhole with a desk, adjoining their bedroom, as an office for Jane.

Jane shared her feelings about Joel with Sara, the abused young woman she was now corresponding with on a regular basis. In September 1991, she wrote: "I have been on my own with my sons for nearly ten years. I have gone out with guys in that time, but none really interested me until Joel—and we spend all of our free time together. He is my best friend, my lover, my companion, and soon to be my husband. We are good for each other."

Jane and Joel set October 10 as their wedding day. She asked her friend, Carrie Rafuse, to be her maid of honour. As the wedding approached, Carrie noticed that Jane was becoming more aggressive and agitated.

"I don't know if I can do this," Jane told her.

"Look," said Carrie, "if you want to change your mind, it's okay, even if you're walking down the aisle. I'll take care of it. I'll explain it to everybody." Her assurances relieved Jane's anxieties.

The ceremony took place at St. John's Evangelical Lutheran Church, a quaint, steepled church facing the water in Mahone Bay. Two ministers jointly conducted the wedding service—Rev. George Wawin, the regular pastor, and Rev. Margie Whynot, whom Jane had befriended in her work with battered women.

Whynot had been sexually abused as a child; pregnant and married as a teenager; and physically and sexually abused by her husband for seventeen years. She finally left, divorcing him in 1978. By 1980 she was at Mount Allison University in New Brunswick; later, she attended the Atlantic School of Theology. In 1985 she was ordained a minister in the United Church of Canada.

Whynot began speaking out on domestic violence, and she met Ann Keith of SSAV and Jane Hurshman, whom she had long admired. "When she shot and killed Billy Stafford, I found a soul mate, even though she didn't know it then," said Whynot. "Twice I had tried to kill my husband, both times in a moment of rage while I was being brutally beaten."

Whynot said her husband was stronger than she was, and that saved him. "I had to live with the knowledge that I, a servant of God, had those feelings—that I wanted to kill. Then, Jane did it." When Jane was acquitted by a jury at her first trial, Whynot said she too felt acquitted—of the guilt over wanting to kill her husband.

"She became my hero," declared Whynot.

Her hero stood before her at 2 p.m. on a sunny autumn afternoon and, before a small gathering of friends and family, was married to Joel Corkum. Ann Keith said that after Jane repeated her vows, "there was a big sigh of relief that could be heard throughout the church. It was as if she was saying, 'I've done it.'"

Joel said he was nervous and hoping he would be third-time lucky. "I didn't have a great batting average, and I was just a little leery, wondering if everything would work out."

Jane described her wedding and five-day honeymoon to her pen pal, Sara: "It was just beautiful how the sun came streaming through the lovely stained glass windows. The ceremony was very spiritual and very uplifting. I wrote out our vows and everything went well. After the ceremony we had a buffet lunch in the church rectory. It was very informal and very relaxed and easy. No booze!

"Both of my sisters came from Ontario—and my best friend since childhood [Valery Cromwell] also came home from Ontario. That was very special. After the ceremony we went down to Mom and Dad's for the evening and later drove home. In the morning, we got ready for our honeymoon. We drove to New Brunswick, took the ferry to Prince Edward Island and went to a gorgeous cottage. It was an old-fashioned place right on the beach. It had a fully equipped kitchen, a dining room, living room with a fireplace, and a bathroom with a huge jacuzzi! WOW! It was a fantasy come true. We had a fantastic time.

"When we left there, we went to Cape Breton and stayed at an old inn that was surrounded by mountains. It was just breathtakingly beautiful with all of its splendid colour! We left there and went to Sydney and the next day we left for home. It was one wonderful experience—a beautiful collection of memories."

What Jane failed to mention was that she and her new husband were not alone. She had invited Carrie and her boyfriend, Bob, to travel with them. A short time before the wedding, Carrie told Jane that she and Bob were planning a trip to Prince Edward Island and Cape Breton.

"Well listen, Carrie," said Jane. "Would you mind if we went with you? We haven't planned a honeymoon or anything, so why don't you just wait till we get married, and then we'll take off together."

Carrie was taken aback. She and Bob had never been away together and she found it somewhat unusual to be invited along on someone else's honeymoon. "I'd want to be alone on my honeymoon, but I thought, oh well—it might be fun."

Although Jane appeared happy after the wedding ceremony, some of her friends noticed that her eyes at times widened and bulged as if she were dissociating.

"Her eyes stuck right out," said Carrie, "but she got through it."

Ann Keith believed that Jane was experiencing flashbacks, a common trait in women who've been battered. Whatever she was going through, everyone close to her agreed that in the days and weeks that followed, they had never seen her so happy.

"Her wrinkles even seemed to have vanished," said Carrie. "It was wonderful to see her like that and know she was truly happy inside."

On the first night at the cottage on Prince Edward Island, Jane and Carrie cooked dinner, turned out the lights, and lit several candles. Carrie began to weep, and her voice cracked as she remembered how happy Jane was that night. "The whole place was full of candles and we all sat around the table and

Jane said, 'Just a minute, I want to say a prayer.' She was so happy. For that week anyway, she was away from all her problems. We all held hands and she just thanked God for her friends and for her new life.

"I wondered about her marrying Joel, but I thought, if it's going to make her feel like this, then fine with me—great."

After the honeymoon, Jane and Joel returned to their daily routine, with Jane working nights at the rehab centre and sleeping during the day while Joel was at work. Jane continued to speak out against domestic violence, and on many afternoons and early evenings she attended meetings or met privately with battered women. Joel knew that her work with women's issues was important to her and did not try to discourage her.

"We managed to get together most evenings and on our days off," he said. "In the good weather we would take the dogs down to the beach and walk away out when the tide was low."

They doted on each other, and Joel often found love notes or cards from Jane. "I'd find them around the house—even in my lunch pail." He had to ask her to stop packing his lunches when his weight ballooned from 175 pounds to 210. "I could hardly close my lunch pail, she put so much into it. Finally I told her to let me make my own lunches."

Ann Keith said that Jane was "just beaming in the weeks after her marriage. I thought, 'This is great.' She had her kids together, she had her work, she had her house—everything."

Jane's feelings toward Joel were summed up in the letter she wrote to him on the anniversary of their first meeting at the tavern in Bridgewater: "Over this past year, we have grown and learned so much about each other. We change every day, yet our love keeps growing stronger and safer! We have no need to fight or argue, although quite often we differ in our opinions—which is great! There is nothing we cannot discuss openly and easily.

"There is no way that I could ever see me without you. I no longer take life for granted, and because of you, I have a very special appreciation of its beauty. Our love is very precious and it certainly will continue to be an amazing, cherished experience.

"I knew in my heart that we would be so good for each other. The emotions you stirred inside were overwhelming and when you kissed me, I knew it was for real—I would lay my life on the line for you anytime."

Carrie Rafuse was relieved. "I thought, my God, finally, I don't have to worry about Jane anymore—because I was worried that someday she was going to kill herself."

CHAPTER 26
'TIS THE SEASON

Despite the contagious excitement her sons were generating as Christmas approached, Jane Hurshman did not welcome the month of December 1991 with much enthusiasm. She had been caught shoplifting at an IGA store in Dartmouth in mid-November, and once again she faced the threat of jail. As usual, she was embarrassed and ashamed, and she kept it from her husband and the rest of her family. Her court hearing was scheduled for December 17.

That pending appearance, before yet another judge, was weighing heavily on her when, on November 26, Jane talked about death in a letter to her pen pal, Sara, who was also suicidal: "There are times when I feel like ending my life also," she wrote. "So I do understand where you are coming from. You do not have to be ashamed of your body—and you do not have to be ashamed of masturbation. Remember my problem? Shoplifting! Well I still do that also and I just hate myself for it. I don't have the control to stop and because of it, there is always the chance of losing my job; losing my family; losing my confidence and self-esteem; and of going to jail.

"The underlying factors are never-ending and I can't stop. When I think negative like that, I wish that I was dead! So you see, Sara, I do understand."

In early December, in the run-up to the second anniversary of the Montreal massacre, the news media were carrying a flood of stories. Toronto writer Donna Laframboise wrote in the *Globe and Mail*: "Having been declared a national memorial day by Parliament, December 6 will become, for many of us, a day to reflect not only on the deaths of those fourteen young women, but on the hundred-odd Canadian females who are murdered by their current or former spouses each year and on the tens of thousands more whose lives are ravaged by sexual and other assaults."

Women's groups in Halifax and Dartmouth planned to mark the event with a press conference and memorial service. Ann Keith was invited to speak, and she called Jane to see if she was interested in joining her on the podium.

"I'm so glad you called," said Jane. "I've been driving around for a week and I can't stop crying, thinking of those women. It brought everything back."

Keith went over to Jane's house.

"I need to do this," said Jane. "When you called, I understood that I had to speak on behalf of those murdered women."

"She told me it was hurting her—eating at her," said Keith. "So I just sat in her house and I didn't say a word and she just wrote and then she went and she spoke."

Carrie Rafuse didn't know that Jane had been arrested for shoplifting again. On a visit with her in November she thought Jane seemed to be on edge and "not quite as patient with Joel. He was going away a lot of weekends. Jane liked her privacy. She wanted to be alone so she would send him down to her mother's. She told me she sent him down to work with her dad on the cars."

Jane had tried the day shift at the rehab centre for a time, but it had not worked out and she went back to nights. "She couldn't sleep at night because she was tormented by memories of Billy," said Carrie. "I noticed that she wasn't as happy as she was. I wondered if the marriage was just like the book—'There, I've accomplished that'—it was over again."

In early December, Jane and Carrie were visiting Jeff, a mutual friend who lived with his wife in Bridgewater. Carrie thought Jane was in an aggressive mood. Darren and Joel and their two dogs were with her, and Carrie was with her boyfriend, Bob. "I remember thinking, why is Jane like this?" said Carrie. "I thought it might be the stress of Christmas."

Jane hugged and kissed Jeff and his wife, and Carrie and Bob, before she left. Victoria Jones, who had continued to live with Jane until shortly before Jane's wedding in October 1991, said she left because she felt uncomfortable around Joel. "I never felt comfortable from the day the man moved in. He came up for the Labour Day holiday in 1990, and the week after that he moved in for good."

Like Carrie, Jones believed that even before the wedding, Jane had become despondent. "She used to go to her bed and sleep for long periods of time when she wasn't working, and that was always an indication that she was depressed. She wanted to get away from everybody."

Jones decided, once again, to return to Montreal to see her son. She left believing Jane felt guilty over Billy Stafford's death. "Two or three times she said, 'Jonesy, I wish Bill hadn't had to die the way he did, but I couldn't see any other way because the police weren't going to do anything about him.'"

Jane was upset the day Jones left. "She wouldn't come home until after I'd gone," said Jones. "I was very fond of Jane and I hated to leave, but I couldn't live where I felt unwanted. I had to sit in my room all the time because I couldn't very well go out where Joel was. He made it obvious he didn't want me there, and I think he realized that I could see things Jane couldn't see."

One night in the first week of December 1991, Donna Smith and Jane met for what had become an annual pre-Christmas Chinese dinner to exchange gifts and enjoy themselves. Ann Keith was usually with them, but Jane hadn't invited her this time. There was a winter storm that night and Donna thought they might have to cancel, but Jane insisted they meet.

"She drove over from Dartmouth and the roads were just wicked," Donna said. "My roommate said she'd watch the kids for me."

The women loved Chinese food and settled on the Princess in Halifax near Donna's place.

"Jane was in a really good mood and she gave me a picture of her wedding in a little frame and I gave her a wind chime with five porcelain doves. My roommate had one, and every time Jane came to the apartment she said how much she loved them. So I got a set for her. Doves are a sign of freedom."

Jane had tea and Donna had coffee. They placed their food order and when the waitress left, Jane leaned in a bit.

"I have to ask you something," she said.

"What is it?" asked Donna.

"What I need is your help," replied Jane. "There's this woman—I won't say who she is, but you know her, and she's very well known."

"Yes?"

"Well, she's dying of cancer and she's really, really ill. She called me and said she would pay $2,000 for someone to shoot her and $1,000 for someone to remove the gun."

Donna could not believe what she was hearing. Her heart was pounding. She thought Jane might have been talking about a mutual friend, but she had already died of cancer. Jane said she would shoot the woman in the head and she wanted Donna to remove the gun.

"Why do you need me?" asked Donna, in a panic. "If you already have the gun, you don't need me."

"I really need you to do this for me, Donna. You know we've always been together and we're so much alike."

"But why do you need me?"

Donna kept asking the question. Jane ignored her and continued outlining details of what was to happen.

"It will happen next Friday night [the 13th]," said Jane. "It's better to do it before Christmas, because at Christmas the woman's whole family would be together. And you have to take the gun because this woman wants to make it look like murder. It would be better for the family if it looked like murder instead of suicide.

"I'll pick you up at Tim Horton's about eight o'clock. Wear old clothes and bring a change of clothes with you." (On the night she shot Billy Stafford, Jane ordered her son Allen to get her a change of clothes, in a garbage bag, before she drove off with Billy's body in the truck.)

Jane told Donna they would drive to the West End Mall on Mumford Road in Halifax and go into Sears, where Donna would be paid $1,000 "right then and there." They would shop a bit, pick up a Sears shopping bag, and then meet the woman in a secluded area of the rear parking lot near the railway tracks.

Donna had a friend, Shelley [pseudonym], living with her at the time and sharing the rent. "What about Shelley?" she asked Jane. "She'll know something's up if I leave wearing old clothes and come back wearing something else."

"You'll think of something," said Jane.

"Why would I need old clothes, anyway?"

"When you shoot someone in the head, blood goes everywhere."

"I could never, ever, do this," said Donna, now frantic. "Doesn't it bring back the memory of Billy for you?"

"I did it once before—I can do it again," said Jane. "I've been having trouble getting a gun. I don't have it yet, but I'll have it in a day or two. It won't have any serial number and they won't be able to trace it. Nothing will ever come back on you. You'll be depressed for a while, but that's normal."

"But why do you need me?" pleaded Donna. "If you're holding the gun, you can get rid of it yourself and leave me out of it."

"No," said Jane sharply. "This woman really needs our help. Somebody has to remove the gun."

Jane told Donna she would be driving Joel's Ford Tempo and not her newer Mustang. "She said she would have a purse and a garbage bag in the back of the car. I was to wear gloves and as soon as the woman was shot I was supposed to take the gun." The gloves, the gun, the purse, and Donna's old clothes, by then presumably bloodied, were to be placed in the garbage bag, which in turn would go into a Sears shopping bag.

"I was supposed to walk out of the mall with the Sears bag, dump the garbage bag over a bridge, or into a bin, and go straight home," said Donna.

"I kept asking her, 'Why do you need me?' but she wouldn't answer my question. She kept repeating, over and over, 'Donna, we're so much alike and I really need your help.' I don't know how many times she said it. And I kept thinking, 'I can't do that, I'm not like that.' I couldn't hurt a flea."

Because of the storm, they were the only two customers in the restaurant. Donna had no appetite when their food came.

"It just sat there. I couldn't eat a thing. Jane ate her meal as if everything was normal—everything was fine."

"I just can't do it," reiterated Donna.

"Don't worry," said Jane. "Don't give me your answer tonight. I want you to think about it for a few days. But I want you to promise me that you will never, ever, say anything about this to anybody—no matter what happens. If you do, it will be your kids that will suffer."

Donna said Jane's eyes were very serious. "I really don't know what she meant by that, but it was scary. That was the first time Jane had ever threatened me. I kept saying to myself, 'Why is she doing this?'"

Donna also had to promise not to talk about it with Jane over the telephone, because she thought her line was tapped.

"We were at the restaurant for over an hour, and when I came home I was really upset," said Donna. "I was in shock. My roommate, Shelley, knew immediately that something was really wrong but I wasn't allowed to talk about it."

Donna was in a fragile emotional state at that stage in her life, and she thought she would have a breakdown if she didn't share her secret. "I kept thinking, 'I can't believe this is real.' I had to tell."

Donna was crying incessantly, but through her tears she told Shelley. "I didn't come right out and tell her," she said. "I got her to ask me questions and eventually she got the story." Beforehand, she had sworn Shelley to secrecy.

Donna didn't hear from Jane for about a week, but they were to see each other at the SSAV Christmas party on December 11, a Wednesday.

"I went through hell for a week," said Donna. "Whenever I fell asleep, I would dream of shooting that woman."

On the morning of the party, she gathered the courage to confront Jane. "I left it to the last minute and then I called her and told her I couldn't do it." Jane was angry with her for discussing the matter over the telephone but even more angry at Donna's refusal to participate.

"You *have* to do it!" declared Jane.

"Jane, I can't. I couldn't live with myself knowing that I helped kill someone."

"And I thought I could count on you."

"Jane, I can't."

"I've got the gun and everything is planned and set up for Friday."

Donna insisted that she couldn't do it, and Jane became more angry and desperate. "Do you know anybody else who can do it?" she asked coldly.

"No, I don't," replied Donna. She said she had never seen Jane so angry. Jane told Donna she would meet her at the Christmas party and drive her home and they could discuss it further then.

"She didn't show up at the party, and I was relieved because I was afraid if we met face to face I wouldn't be able to refuse," said Donna. "I still felt guilty about not going underground after all the work she did, and now I was letting her down again."

On December 16, the day before the court appearance, Jane's dread, anguish, and bitterness surfaced in a letter she wrote to Sara: "I do wish that for people like us there was some type of cure—but I guess we have a cross to bear and it will be with us for a lifetime. Sara, I love Jesus, and I know that both He and Satan are very real. With me, I have a problem believing that I am worthy of Christ. You see, with my shoplifting, I can't see it ever stopping—so if I am continually going to sin, then my coming to Christ and asking, even begging, for His forgiveness, is a mockery when I know I am going to do it again.

"How do you get past that? Is there something that I am missing? I want nothing more than to not sin, yet I constantly do. I am just totally unworthy. I don't know if my torment will ever end—until I die. And there are times that I want to make that happen—one of those times being right now. I have to go to court again tomorrow and I would sooner be dead than go there.

"I know in my heart that JESUS is the only reason why I am not dead—as it is definitely not from my lack of wanting and trying. It is a demon that I can't get rid of. I love Joel and my family very much, but I'd rather be dead than to continually bring them shame and humiliation. I am in a very strong dilemma right now as to living or dying. I am not crazy—yet I know that I cannot continue like this. There is no help available that I haven't already tried—I am so tired. Well, I feel that I have cried on your shoulder long enough and I just had to let it all out to someone. I am glad that you are there to hear me.

"Sara, I don't know how I can help you or others when I can't begin to help myself. Joel knows my problem and is very understanding—in fact, everyone knows my problem because it is public knowledge."

Jane was in a Dartmouth courtroom the next morning, intent on pleading guilty. With her was Kathleen Jennex, executive director of the Coverdale Court Work Services, an organization that gives advice to women facing charges in the courts. Jennex had been with Coverdale for ten years and had worked with women facing charges ranging from disturbing the peace to murder. She had accompanied Jane to court on several occasions.

Jane had also begun therapy with Mary Haylock, an abuse counsellor associated with Coverdale.

"We were very supportive when she was going through the shoplifting charges," said Jennex, who was opposed to Jane pleading guilty on that day. "There was a possibility of her going to jail because of the number of convictions against her. I wanted her to plead not guilty just to get it put over. But she was determined that she was just going to plead guilty, and she kept saying she wasn't going to go to jail. I couldn't convince her to get a lawyer."

While they sat in the courtroom waiting for the case to be called, Jane watched lawyer Pat Duncan defending another woman and was impressed. "I always feel good when Pat represents a woman," said Jennex. "He not only looks after their legal rights—he thinks of them as a whole person."

Finally, Jennex convinced Jane to talk to Duncan. She spoke to him briefly outside the courtroom and agreed to allow him to represent her. The case was put over to March 4, 1992.

The law had recently recognized a state referred to as *automatous* in which a person commits an offence while in a robot-like state, without exercising his or her own will. "That defence is not used very often, but Pat Duncan felt Jane fell within that category," said Jennex. "That was the kind of state she was in when she took things, and he was going to use that as her defence. Jane had more hope, I think, in this case, than she had at any other time that I had seen before."

On the night Jane's case was put over, Carrie Rafuse came over for dinner. After they ate, Joel went out to work on one of the cars, and Jane and Carrie had tea at the kitchen table. Jane was in an unusually talkative mood.

"I shut up because she hardly ever felt like this," said Carrie. "She told me she had been in one of her dark moods again but this time she couldn't seem to shake it."

Jane told her she'd been feeling depressed for about a month. Carrie didn't know it, but it was exactly one month since Jane's latest arrest for shoplifting.

"Jane, did you steal again?" asked Carrie.

Jane lowered her head and nodded.

"Why don't you tell me about it?"

Reluctantly, Jane told her about being caught at the IGA store in Dartmouth. Her voice was very serious but matter-of-fact.

"Look, Carrie," she said. "I'm not going to live like this."

"Oh God, Jane, no! Don't think this way again."

Jane became very stern and stared directly into her eyes.

"I won't kill myself," she said, "but I will not live like this and I will not put my family through this. I won't do this to Joel, or the kids, or my parents, anymore."

She told Carrie that Kathleen Jennex and others from Coverdale had been at the house earlier in the day to work out a strategy to keep her from going to jail on the latest shoplifting charge.

"I steal and I can't do anything about it," said Jane. "I can't stop it, and nobody can help me. I've been to the best. I can't control it, and eventually I'm going to end up in jail."

"Jane, what are you saying?" said Carrie.

"Look, don't worry for now because it's okay. I'm talking to these women and they're working out a defence for me and it looks good. But if that doesn't work out, I won't go to jail and I won't live like this—but I won't kill myself. I have to go back to court in March. I was going to wait until the New Year to tell you this, but I decided to tell you now. I plan to tell Joel and the kids and my family after the New Year.

"Carrie, I want you to know, I don't have a death wish. I'm not crazy. I'm just not going to live like this."

Jane told her she was obsessed with her problem. "Not a day goes by that I don't think about it. If there's something about kleptomania on the TV or radio, I'm right in there watching or listening in case there's anything helpful."

"If you're sent to jail, but you say you're not going to jail, and you're not going to kill yourself—what are you going to do?" asked Carrie.

"You remember when I saw you and Bob at Jeff's a couple of weeks ago?" asked Jane.

"Yes."

"I thought it would be the last time I ever saw the two of you, but it wasn't."

"Jane, what on earth are you talking about?" asked Carrie.

"Last weekend, I sent Joel and the kids down to Mom and Dad's and I hired somebody to shoot me."

Carrie's face paled. "I was in shock for a week," she said. "It was so bizarre—and here was Jane, a normal person telling me this. She was very calm, very calm."

Jane said she had gone to meet the person in her car.

"Where did you go?" asked Carrie.

"We just went down a deserted road and he had a gun and we got out. He put the gun to my head and fired it but it didn't go off." At this point, Carrie felt sick to her stomach.

"There was something wrong with the gun," continued Jane. "A piece was missing or something and it wouldn't go off. I left and went back home and cried all night."

"My God, Jane, who would you get to do this?"

"Carrie, they're a dime a dozen. You can get anybody off the street to do that."

Jane said the person who was to shoot her was going to have the gun repaired and make a second attempt the following day.

"I was ready to go," she said, "but he got picked up by the police on some charges and couldn't meet me."

Carrie was shaken and didn't know what to think. She thought the story might not be true and that Jane was crying out for help. "But knowing Jane, it could have been true. I never knew of her lying to me—ever. I wanted to believe it wasn't true." But she remembered Jane's eyes bulging when she mentioned the person pulling the trigger—as they did when she was having flashbacks of the horrors from her time with Billy Stafford.

Jane told her she was glad she hadn't died.

"Now I'm working on this defence and it looks really good," said Jane. "I'm going to see this through, and see if it will work out."

At that point, Joel came through the door from outside.

"She changed just like that," said Carrie, snapping her fingers. "And there I was, just like a friggin' piece of limp spaghetti. I had no energy whatsoever, and my friend who I loved..." Carrie's voice trailed off and she began weeping as she remembered that night.

She said Jane got up from the table and laughed with Joel as she poured him a cup of tea. "She was another person, and I didn't even know if I could drive. I went home and I was sick to my stomach and I went right to bed."

Carrie's mind raced as she tried to figure out what to do. She thought about calling the police. But what could they do? What *would* they do? And what about Dr. Curtis? Jane was already in therapy with him and he couldn't be with her every minute of her life.

"That night I called Jeff," said Carrie, "because he was the only one I could trust. And he came over the next day and we talked about what we could do—we had to do something." Jane had assured her that she would be okay until the March court hearing. They would have to think of something before that.

Carrie decided to spend as much time as she could with Jane and watch her as closely as she could. "And I decided that when the time was right, I would call John Curtis and her sister Mona. I knew of Ann [Keith], but I didn't know her last name. I would try to get her too. I'd have to be careful because Jane's very smart, but we would have to do something."

The week before Christmas, Joel arrived at Carrie's to pick up gifts for Jane's family, which Carrie was keeping for her in her recreation room. Carrie decided Joel was the closest person to Jane at the time, and without alarming him, she wanted to warn him about her emotional state.

"He didn't have a clue about any of it, and I really felt bad for him," she said. "He's just married two months, he's happy—he thinks everything is fine."

Joel had loaded the gifts into his car and was standing by the door, ready to leave.

"Joel, I've got to talk to you about something," said Carrie. "I've known Jane for a long time and over the years she has times when she feels suicidal. How are you finding her now?"

"She's fine, just great," said Joel.

"Well, you know, Joel, when I was in last week, I sensed she was in one of those moods and I'm really worried. I want you to keep an eye on her."

Joel promised to call Carrie if he noticed anything unusual in Jane's behaviour.

Carrie's anxieties lessened considerably when she saw Jane at Christmas. They made plans to get together for New Year's Eve. "Joel and Jane came down, and Bob and I went with them to dinner at an inn in Mahone Bay. She was in a wonderful mood. We just laughed and talked about our fun times, and it really assured me that she was okay. And I thought, thank God."

On December 18, the day after pleading not guilty at her court appearance, Jane called Donna Smith, who hadn't heard from her for a week. Jane was friendly and they talked for a while. Until the end of their conversation, neither mentioned the plan to kill the woman.

"Oh, by the way," said Jane. "Don't worry about anything. What we talked about before, was taken care of—out of province." Jane never mentioned the plan again.

CHAPTER 27

THREATS AND DISCONTENT

Jane Hurshman learned about Mary Jacquart through a nurse who worked at the Halifax County Regional Rehabilitation Centre. Jane was looking for a tutor for her son Darren, and the nurse gave her Jacquart's name.

"Jane called me and we met and hit it off immediately," said Jacquart, a teacher who tutored after hours. Jane had Darren with her, and when he began acting up, Jacquart, who was used to dealing with rowdy teenagers, told him to sit down and be quiet. The boy eyed her a moment and sat down.

"Oh, you're a schoolteacher," he said.

"Yes, I am, and you're being rude here."

Jane looked at Jacquart with surprise. "I've never really said that to him." She smiled. "But I guess it's time someone did."

Jacquart became Darren's regular tutor after that. "When he first came he was a real hard ticket," she said. "But he's a real likeable kid and we got along just fine. I tutored him in math, science, and other schoolwork and I really enjoyed it."

Jacquart also got along with Jane, and they began confiding in each other.

"We talked quite a bit about my life and her life," said Jacquart. "But she never got into it about Billy. I told her my father was an alcoholic—and he'd come into your bedroom before a major exam for teachers' college and tear up your essays... that sort of thing.

"It was important to Jane that Darren go to university. She didn't want him in a construction job or menial work because she thought he would be frustrated and he would get into trouble."

In a letter to Jo Sheridan in British Columbia, Jane described the importance of Jacquart to Darren. "He just hates school and everything about it," she wrote. "He has a tutor whom he thinks is just wonderful and when he is with her for his two hours a week, he accomplishes more there than he does all week at school."

Arranging a tutor for Darren was another step in the healing process, which Jane knew was so important for her and her son. She had been seeing the Coverdale therapist, Mary Haylock, since August 1991, as her problems with kleptomania continued to distress her.

Jane first heard about Haylock when she was facing one of the shoplifting charges in Dartmouth. A Coverdale court worker told her they had a therapist on staff who might be able to provide support and therapy for her problem. Jane was sceptical but agreed to talk to Haylock.

"I met her at McDonald's for a coffee to see if she wanted to work with this crazy old lady," said Haylock, who had been helping women for more than ten years, including three years at Coverdale. Jane liked her and began weekly therapy sessions.

Haylock, and others close to Jane, believed that she stopped seeing Dr. Curtis because the hypnotherapy was uncovering childhood events that perhaps she did not want to face. In a letter to her friend Sara, Jane once wrote: "There are things that have happened in your past that you may never remember—do not dwell on those. If they ever do come to memory, then you can deal with them—and if they don't, well then I do believe that Jesus has a reason for us not remembering, because in one of His many promises, He says, 'I will never give you more than you can bear.'"

Mary Haylock believed that if Jane had continued with hypnotherapy, she might have come to better understand and control her kleptomania.

"I liked working with Jane," said Haylock. "She was a very intelligent, articulate woman who endured an incredible amount of pain and suffering. She had insight into her total recovery—her move away from violence. But she was not unaware of the fallout from the abuse for herself or her children."

Haylock said that Jane gave too much, and she could sense the pain when Jane spoke out publicly. "It probably did help her at first, but by the time I was seeing her, I think it was taking its toll. She understood that her way out of the pain was to go through it. But what I have to question was this facing it, again, and again, and again."

Haylock believed that Jane was feeling tired by the winter of 1991–92, and that "the time was soon approaching when she would feel that she could let it be." Jane was also telling friends that she was getting more nervous about her high profile. Nova Scotia was not a safe place for women. More than a dozen women had been murdered in the province in the previous two years, and assaults against women were on the rise—there had been 260 in 1990 in Dartmouth alone. Jane began to worry about her safety.

In early December 1991, she asked Joel if he could get a permit for a handgun. She said she would also try to get a gun on her own—perhaps from a motorcycle gang, perhaps Hell's

Angels. She thought they might get her a gun because of her background.

"She had been scared for a while, and it was clear in my mind she wanted it for her own protection," said Joel. "It was going to be small enough so she could carry it in her purse when she was out. At other times it would be locked up and I would have a key and she would have a key."

He asked the police about getting a permit for a handgun and was told he would have to fill out an application and that his chances of getting a gun would improve if he belonged to a pistol club. Rather than a permit, Joel decided to check with people in the Bridgewater area "who I knew were into guns at one time or another, and I really didn't care if it was legal or not. I found one, but the guy wouldn't sell it to me without the certificate you gotta get from the cops."

On Thursday, December 19, eight days after she told Donna Smith that she had acquired a gun, Jane showed Joel an old .38-calibre pistol with no serial number. It was in a clear plastic bag, with six bullets in a smaller plastic bag. "Where'd you get that?" asked Joel.

"You don't want to know," replied Jane. "If you don't know, you can't say."

"Fine." Joel shrugged. He was certain the gun wasn't registered, but never again did he ask about its origin. He promised Jane he wouldn't say anything to anyone about the gun. She wrapped it up and put it in a box. The next day, the Friday before Christmas, Joel and Darren were planning to drive down to Jane's parents' for the weekend. Before they left, Jane handed Joel the box with the pistol and ammunition.

"Take it down home and try it and see if it works right," she said.

Darren didn't know the gun was in the car. Joel dropped the boy at his grandparents' and drove to a friend's place in Bridgewater. "It was all wrapped in a box and I knew my friend wouldn't ask about it."

He had planned to leave the gun there until he had a chance to test it, but Jane called him and told him to bring it back with him when he returned on Sunday. On the drive back to Cole Harbour, Joel, on impulse, pulled the car off the road.

"There's something I want to show you," he said to Darren.

Joel removed the gun from the box and put the shells into it. "Your mom told me to try it out."

Joel lowered his window and was about to fire a shot when he spotted a police car approaching. "The cop car went by and they sort of spooked me, so I put the gun back in the box and brought it home."

Jane was furious with Joel for showing the gun to Darren.

"She was really pissed off at me," he said. "But I can understand her point—she told me not to show it to anybody."

"I got this gun for another lady," Jane told them, "and you're not to say anything about it, because I might get into trouble for giving it to her."

Joel said that although he didn't fire the gun, "I basically checked it over and everything seemed to work properly."

Jane and Joel went into their bedroom, where he removed the shells from the gun. "We cleaned all the fingerprints off," said Joel. "All the shells, the gun—everything was just totally wiped."

The handgun went back into the plastic bag and the bullets into the smaller plastic bag. "I put them up in the attic," said Joel. A few days later, he asked Jane about the gun.

"I got rid of it," she said. "I gave it back."

Joel checked the attic later and it was gone. "I don't know if she was carrying it around with her or not. It wasn't where I put it, so I figured it was gone. I just thought no more about it."

The last public speech Jane Hurshman gave was on behalf of a City of Dartmouth task force on violence against women. It was on November 29, 1991, in a packed, sweltering, second-floor room at the Dartmouth Library. It was the final public event before the task force members sat down to hammer out recommendations, which they hoped would curtail violence against women.

Kathleen Jennex of Coverdale was one of the organizers of the event. She had asked Jane to give the keynote address, and now she introduced her to the crowd of about 150. Ann Keith, who attended the meeting, described Jane's speech as strong and "to the point."

According to Jennex, it was shortly after that speech that a frightening message was recorded on Coverdale's answering machine: "You tell that bitch, Jane Hurshman, that if she doesn't stop speaking out on violence against women, I'll shut her up permanently." Jennex said the voice was definitely male.

Unfortunately, that threat was eventually taped over. But the first week in January, another message threatening to kill Jane came in to Coverdale. This one was preserved, and was turned over later to the RCMP.

"My co-worker Margaret Rodger is from Scotland, and we listened to the tape with the RCMP a couple of times," said Jennex. "Margaret... picks up our dialects much faster than we would. She said the voice was 'South Shore,' and it wasn't until she said that that I listened. And there was no doubt in my mind, it was Bridgewater—down that way. To me, it was definitely a man's voice. We talked about the terminology he used. It's not the type of language a woman would use—the aggression and the tone of voice. No doubt in our minds, it was an older male with a South Shore accent."

Coverdale wasn't the only place receiving threats. On New Year's Day of 1992, Liz Forestell went into her office at the Elizabeth Fry Society and checked her answering machine for messages. On the tape, she heard a muffled male voice make a threat, "and the tone of it was really frightening."

Forestell couldn't make out the name of the person the threat was directed to, but the message was clear: "You better tell [name garbled] to shut her mouth and stop all this talking about battered women. If she doesn't shut up, I'll shut her up."

"I listened to it and listened to it, and it scared me," said Forestell. "People told me that women's groups got these kinds of threats all the time. I had never received one before, but we'd been getting a higher profile in the press with the announcement in December that a prison for women was going to be built in Truro. I'd been on the news, and the committee [on jailed women] had been quite vocal."

On January 2, another telephone threat, similar to the one made against Jane at Coverdale, came in to the rehabilitation centre where she worked in Cole Harbour. Jane was off at the time, but another female staff member heard it.

On the same day, a call was recorded on Jane's answering machine at home. It was from Sergeant Gary Grant, the RCMP's media relations officer for Nova Scotia. He was calling to wish her and Joel a happy New Year. (Years before, it was Grant who had stood toe to toe with Billy Stafford while Billy screamed obscenities at him during an RCMP search at the Bangs Falls house.)

In her daily journal, Jane wrote of Grant's call: "Sort of strange phone call—would not have been unusual if he had called Joel."

Jane and Joel had both known Grant for years before they met each other, and once, before they were married, Grant had visited them at the Arklow Drive townhouse. But Joel too thought Grant's call was out of place: "Before that, Gary never called me unless I called him, and he always called me at work."

Grant, who left the RCMP in August 1992, said there was nothing at all sinister about his call and that the only thing unusual was Jane's reaction.

"It was easy to know it was me," said Grant. "I mean, I left a message on the machine, with my name on it. If it would have been Joel's voice on the machine, I would have left the message for him. I said, 'Look, Jane, it's just Gary calling, sorry I didn't catch you at home but happy New Year and if there's anything I can do, please give me a call, and say hi to Joel'—that was it."

Jane left a return message on Grant's answering machine. "She sounded strange and she asked me if my call was business or personal," he said.

Jane answered when Grant called back again. He remembers that her voice was accusatory, and "it put me on the defensive, and I said, 'Gee, Jane, I was calling merely to say hi and to see how things were going.' She sounded very different, very strange—I thought."

It was during Grant's posting with the RCMP in Liverpool that he had met Joel Corkum. Joel, then in his late teens, had just been released from his second six-month prison stretch, for break and entry, and he provided tips to Grant that led to a couple of successful drug busts.

"There wouldn't have been no busts if I wouldn't have made the calls—I'll put it that way," said Joel. "They were a couple of good ones too." In one instance, he left a Liverpool tavern and was "walking down the street as the SWAT team was ready to go in. That's a lot of years ago."

About the time Grant was transferred from Liverpool to the drug squad in Bridgewater in 1980, Joel was released early from a three-month sentence for dangerous driving. "I did fifty-five days and they booted me out because the jail was full."

Joel was living in Bridgewater with his first wife, and he and Grant got to know each other better. Joel, once a casual drug user, was never a paid police informer, but he continued providing tips to Grant.

"I had seen too many people burn out pretty bad on drugs," said Joel. "I made up my mind, I wanted nothing more to do with drugs."

After heading the drug squad in Bridgewater for several years, Grant was transferred to the RCMP's Cole Harbour detachment; still later, he ran the force's drug awareness program in Nova Scotia. He did that for more than two years before being promoted to sergeant and moving to the Halifax drug squad, and eventually to media relations.

Jane didn't trust Grant or any other police officer, and she told Mary Jacquart she was "a bundle of nerves" when Grant visited for a cup of tea at Joel's invitation in late 1990. Jane told Joel and others she thought Grant or some other police officer was behind the threats against her.

Jane did not consider herself a common criminal, and she resented her treatment by the police when she was arrested for shoplifting.

"Jane was a good example of why I argue with the police all the time," said Kathleen Jennex. "She should not have had to go to the police station for mug shots and fingerprints every time she committed a new offence. They knew who she was and they knew her address. And for a lot of women who have committed more than one offence, to put them through that is just degradation. Jane shouldn't have had to go through that."

It was probable that Jane did not relish Gary Grant's visit or telephone call; almost certainly, they triggered a flood of horrible memories of her time with Billy Stafford. But after thinking about it for two days, she likely decided that facing the pain—as she had when she returned to Bangs Falls to visit Margaret Joudrey—would help her to heal, and she allowed Joel to invite Grant for tea.

In the late 1970s, when Grant was patrolling Liverpool and Queens County, the problem of criminal violence in the home was still in the shadows, and shelters and transition houses were only just being established. If Grant saw bruises on Jane the numerous times he pulled Billy over, he didn't remember them. And even if he had seen evidence of abuse, nothing would have been done unless she filed a complaint—something she wasn't about to do.

"There's no question, the police handled wife battering a hell of a lot differently then," said Grant. "But, in retrospect, I think if I had known Billy was abusing her, I would have probably tried to talk her into doing something—because I wanted that sonofabitch so bad."

Grant had his own theory for Jane's negative feelings toward him. "I had been stopping Billy, and hassling his ass and trying to bust him for every goddamn thing from soup to nuts. Ninety per cent of the time, he would be infuriated when he left me. Then he probably went home and beat the shit out of Jane. Now I'm wondering if there wasn't some transfer of blame, from him to me, on her part—I pissed Billy off, therefore, I caused her pain. I've thought a lot about that, and it really bothers me."

On Friday, January 8, the day after the threat at the rehab centre, Jane called Carrie Rafuse and said that she and Joel wanted to come down to Bridgewater the next day to go to church with her and Bob. Carrie was surprised because Jane hadn't been to church for some time. "She always had a strong faith in God. Then she just stopped going to church. She never talked to me about it, and we didn't discuss religion much after that. But I know she loved God."

It was guilt over shoplifting that prompted Jane to give up church. In a letter to her friend Sara in December, she wrote: "I want to thank you for sharing the sinners prayer with me—but I am having difficulty with prayer lately. I guess that Satan is too powerful, and when I turn to Christ, I feel too guilty and unworthy, so it's easier to just avoid it all."

After the service at the Seventh-day Adventist church on Saturday, January 4, the four of them went to Bob's apartment for lunch. Carrie was relieved that Jane seemed happy. During lunch, Jane told Carrie and Bob about the threats she had been receiving. "She seemed genuinely concerned," said Carrie.

The following day, another death threat against Jane was recorded at her home. She wrote in her daily journal: "Threatening message for me on answering machine. Joel took tape out of machine so he could keep it."

Jane may have appeared happy after attending church with Carrie, but the next day she wrote to Sara: "Until I get rid of the demons inside, I will not be contacting any pastor, nor will I go to church. I have tried that before and I just kept on sinning. I had more guilt to carry around and it made me feel like a hypocrite. I believe in Jesus, I pray, and in general, I do live a good honest life, so I'll have to be judged on that and on what is in my heart."

In the same letter, Jane mentioned that the next day she was planning on having a family photograph taken at Sears, and she promised to send Sara a copy. As Jane drove to the photo session in her 1987 Mustang, with Joel beside her and Darren and Jamie in the rear seat, the car began vibrating.

"It must be that damn muffler," said Jane.

"That's no muffler," said Joel. "Get this thing pulled over. If it ain't the drive shaft loose, it's a wheel." He got out of the car and discovered that the lug nuts on both rear wheels had been loosened. "I put those wheels on the car in November and those nuts were torqued down to one hundred foot pounds—the manufacturer's specification. Somebody loosened those wheels, and if the wheel on the driver's would have fallen off, that car would have swerved into traffic."

Joel tightened the nuts, and they continued on to Sears, where they met Jane's son Allen and his wife Charlene. They all sat for the photo. Later that day, Joel telephoned the RCMP at Cole Harbour and told them about the loosened wheels and the threats Jane had received.

"What do you expect us to do?" said the officer who took the call.

"I know there's probably not a lot you can do right now," said Joel. "But I wanted you guys to know this is going on."

The incident with the loosened wheels scared Joel. "She believed somebody was out to get her. It was after that speech to the mayor's task force that all this started."

Three days later, Jane cancelled a group therapy session at Coverdale with Mary Haylock, stating in her journal: "I need one-on-one therapy and not group."

On January 17, Jane met with Patrick Duncan, the lawyer who was to represent her at her March 4 court appearance on the latest shoplifting charge. The same day, she also met with Liz Forestell and the prison reform committee.

"I had been called by a reporter, from one of the major TV networks, asking if Jane would appear on a national news show," said Forestell. "They wanted to talk about the committee and profile her. There was quite a bit of publicity when the committee was announced—you know, 'husband killer on committee,' that type of thing.

"I had connected Jane with reporters before, and usually she was quite happy to be interviewed. But this time, it was odd because she said no—and there was no hesitation."

The next day, Jane wrote in her journal: "I did nothing except sleep all day—did a bit of housework and took the dogs for a walk."

Around noon on Sunday, January 19, Darren noticed an envelope on the windshield of Jane's car. It was addressed to Jane, but he ripped it open and brought it into the house. Jane had worked nights and was still asleep. Darren handed the envelope to Joel, who read the stencilled message inside.

"Hi bitch!" it said. "I want you to know I haven't forgotten."

Joel waited until Jane woke up at 2:30 before he gave her the note. "You must have really ruffled somebody's feathers with that speech you gave," he said.

Jane's journal entry for the 19th: "Today a letter was found on the windshield of my car. I was at work last night and I drove the car home at 7:30 a.m. So the threatening letter was put there sometime between 7:30 a.m. and noon. Joel called the RCMP at 3 p.m. They returned his call at 4 p.m. They wanted to know what we expected them to do. They are useless!!"

She went on to write: "There is no real way to handle grief. It comes in waves and it will hit you when you least expect it. If anything should happen to me, don't sit and feel sorry for me or for yourselves—just take all of our special memories with you and have a wonderful life, like I would want you to."

Two days later, Jane wrote about the threats in a letter to Sara: "I guess that I just have to be on my guard and take whatever precautions that I feel are necessary. I hate not knowing who wants me to keep my mouth shut or he is going to shut it for me permanently! It is crazies like that who scare you!"

Jane had been cool toward Donna Smith since the December 11 telephone call, when Donna told her she couldn't assist her with the plan to shoot a woman supposedly dying of cancer.

"For quite a while, I kept leaving messages on her answering machine," said Donna. "Or I'd get Jamie or Darren and they kept taking messages but she didn't call me back. It was like she avoided me for a while. I tried calling her at work, but the switchboard had stopped calls going through. You had to leave your name and number and they would call you back. But she didn't call and I kept feeling I had let her down and she was upset."

They resumed their friendship in late January, when Jane talked to Donna and told her about the threats she was receiving. "She said she was really scared and that's why the answering machine was on a lot. And she said the RCMP told her they wouldn't do anything unless something happened."

Jane's forty-third birthday was on January 25, and her childhood friend, Valery Cromwell, called her from Toronto with birthday greetings.

"She told me a few things about the threats," said Valery. "She said she didn't want to be paranoid, but she said somebody was after her and she didn't know who it was."

On January 30, when Jane took Darren for his weekly tutoring session, she asked Mary Jacquart if she and her husband Paul would take Darren if anything happened to her.

"She said she was getting these threats and she wasn't so much worried about herself as she was about Darren," said Jacquart. Jane made the request after earlier overhearing Darren and Jacquart joking about him coming to live with her and her family.

"Would you really let me live here?" asked Darren.

"Sure, if your mother gets fed up with you, you can come here," laughed Jacquart. It was two weeks later that Jane asked her if she was serious.

"Sure," said Jacquart, "I would take him if something happened to you and that's what you wanted."

Until Jane mentioned the threats, Jacquart thought that Jane and Joel might not be getting along. Jane told her she was driving on the highway one night and she thought she heard a rattle in the car. She said it made her think of the loosened lug nuts, and she prayed that the car hadn't been tampered with again.

"I pulled the car over," she told Jacquart, "and I thought, 'My God, if they get me, what will happen to Darren?' And Mary, I said a prayer and it was just like God spoke to me. And I thought of you and Paul, because you said you would take him. I had this great sense of relief, but then I worried that maybe you wouldn't want him."

"No, there's no problem," said Jacquart. "But the main thing for you to do is to get everything in order in case something does happen."

CHAPTER 28
FOREBODING

"I hate this month," Jane Hurshman wrote and underlined in her daily journal on February 1, 1992. It was a month she associated with pain and tragedy, including the death of her pregnant cousin the year before. It was also in the month of February that Jane went to jail for killing Billy Stafford.

On February 4, another stencilled threat against Jane appeared, this time at the rehabilitation centre. It came in a reusable interdepartmental envelope. This time the message read: "I told you to keep your mouth shut, or I would shut it permanently."

In her journal, Jane wrote simply: "It is scary."

On February 9, Jane drove out to the Halifax Correctional Centre with Liz Forestell to conduct interviews with inmates for the prison reform committee. The television reporter who had asked for an interview with Jane had called Forestell again. Once more she passed on the request to Jane, who again refused, explaining that she had received threats and wanted to keep a low profile. "They seem to know everywhere I go and everything I do," said Jane.

"She said she was quite frightened by the threats," said Forestell. "She said she had gone to the police and she was nervous about it because she thought maybe the police were involved, and that's when Gary Grant's name came up. She told me he had called her and she felt very uncomfortable with it. The call came on the same day that a threatening message came in where she worked. She was freaked out and she was scared."

The next day, Forestell listened to the threat Jane had received at the house. It was identical to the one that had come in to the Elizabeth Fry office. In her journal on February 10, Jane wrote: "Liz called—said that message on tape I gave her was exactly like the one she had received on her machine around New Year's."

Jane had been invited to address the Canadian Panel on Violence Against Women during its March 6 swing into Halifax. On February 12, she confirmed that she would speak to the panel. The following day, Jane arrived at Mary Jacquart's home with a will that included a provision for Darren to live there if anything should happen to her. Jacquart signed the will as a witness and gave it back to Jane.

The next day, Valentine's Day, Jane drove down to Danesville to visit her parents. That night, she called Carrie Rafuse, who was at work at the Harbour House women's shelter in nearby Bridgewater.

"She didn't sound good at all," said Carrie. "She said she and Joel had celebrated Valentine's Day the week before."

"I hate Valentine's Day and I hate February," Jane told her.

They agreed to meet the next morning. After she hung up, Jane played Scrabble with her parents. The phone rang while they were playing, and Jane answered it. She listened for a moment and hung up. She told her parents it was nothing important, but in her journal she wrote: "While down at Mom's, I answered the phone while we were playing Scrabble and the man said, 'I just want you to know that I am always aware of where you are at.' It was about 10 p.m. I did not say anything to my family but I plan to tell Liz about it."

On the same day, Valery Cromwell received a short letter from Jane with a colour photo of the family that had been taken at Sears the day the loose lug nuts were discovered. "She told me she was still getting the threats," said Valery, "and if whoever was after her got to her, they would make it look like suicide and her body would probably never be found because it would be out to sea."

On the morning of February 15, Jane drove to Bridgewater from her parents' place to visit Carrie. They talked and laughed and discussed the possibility of another trip to Prince Edward Island at the end of March. But Carrie was still worried, and as Jane prepared to leave for Cole Harbour, Carrie asked if she could come into town for an overnight visit.

"Oh good!" said Jane. "I'd love that."

"I'll call you by seven o'clock tonight," said Carrie, "and let you know if I'm coming for sure." She thought about Jane all day and decided to make the drive in with another woman fricnd.

"Jane and Joel were in the living room having a drink when we got there about 8:30," said Carrie. "Jane looked great. She had her housecoat on and was all fresh and bathed and waiting to get dressed. I never saw her in such a good mood."

As they left the house for a local bar, Carrie asked about the threats. "We gotta do something about this," blurted Joel, "because the police won't do anything. I'm gonna look for a gun."

Carrie was shocked that he would talk about getting a gun after she had warned him, before Christmas, that Jane was in a fragile state.

"No, Jane," said Carrie. "Don't do that. Don't get a gun. What if you had to use it to protect yourself? You know what they would say—'There she goes again.' They wouldn't believe you."

"We've got to do something," said Joel.

Carrie said Jane changed the subject. "We went out to a couple of bars and had a ball. We got feeling really good, except for Joel who was driving and wasn't allowed to drink."

When they returned to the house, Carrie's friend from Bridgewater was tired and went to sleep in the guest room. "The three of us were at the table," recalled Carrie. "It was probably one o'clock and we started eating chocolate bars—Jane's favourite thing."

They had tea and then Joel went to bed at two or three, leaving Carrie and Jane at the table. They were both in a talkative mood because of the drinks.

"Jane," said Carrie, "I've never ever told you what I thought you should do—I've always gone along with what you want."

"I know that, Carrie, and I love you for it," said Jane.

"You're my friend and I've got to tell you how I feel," said Carrie. "I think you're making up those threats."

"No, I'm not," Jane replied evenly.

"Okay, I believe you. I thought maybe you were still going to kill yourself and you were setting it up."

"No, I told you, I'm not going to do anything until after my court appearance on March 4," said Jane.

As they continued talking, the conversation drifted back to Billy Stafford. "It always came back to Billy when we talked late at night," said Carrie.

"When am I going to get over this?" asked Jane. "When is it going to go away?"

Later, they talked about abuse, and Jane told her she was going to stop speaking about it in public. Later still, they talked about Jane dying.

"I'm not going to do it," she reiterated. "And now that we're talking about this again, I've been meaning to tell you how sorry I am for telling what I told you that day. I just want you to know I would never hurt you and I know it upset you and put a lot on you. I'm sorry."

"Jane, you can tell me anything. *You've* always been here for me."

Jane assured her once again that she wasn't going to do anything drastic. "I didn't know," said Carrie. "I was praying it was the truth. Then we talked about the possibility of the trip to P.E.I. and she seemed fine."

Carrie became more inquisitive than she had ever dared in the past.

"Jane, do you know if you have a split personality?" she asked.

"No, I don't think so," replied Jane.

"I'm not saying you have. I'm just curious, because I know about three or four different Janes. Sometimes you get in a dark mood. And then you have a very aggressive, sarcastic mood. And sometimes, you're just Jane."

"John Curtis said what I've got is a dissociative disorder," said Jane. "I do have times that I forget things."

"Is everything okay with you and Joel?" asked Carrie. "Are you happy?"

"Yes, everything is fine. I'm glad now that I had Christmas and it didn't happen, and I don't plan for it to happen. I'm going to wait until March when I have my court appearance—and it's looking very good."

"I was very worried about you, Jane."

"You don't have to worry."

Carrie said Jane was very convincing. "I told her I had thought of going to John Curtis, and Mona, and Ann. I thought she might react—but nothing. She wasn't threatened by that a bit."

"No, I'm really fine now," said Jane.

"Jane, I love you and I don't want anything to happen to you. I wish you would go back to John Curtis."

"He did all he can do," said Jane. "We reached a point, and I can't get beyond that point—there's nothing else he can do."

"Jane, I think there's a lot here that I don't know about, and other people don't know about, and I think it's probably from a long time ago—maybe even before Billy. And with Billy, are there things I don't know about?"

"Yes," said Jane.

"Look," said Carrie, "have you been completely honest with John Curtis?"

"Well... I haven't said everything."

"Why don't you go back to him? Just give it one more try, but be completely honest. Get it out, and you can break through and get help for the stealing."

"Nope," said Jane. "I'm not going back to him. He did what he could."

"But, Jane, people have therapy for years." But Jane was adamant.

"I know she had very little memory of her first twelve years and I know that's what she didn't want to face," said Carrie. "That's why she stopped seeing John Curtis. It was very hard for her. Jane was in control of everything in her life—except the stealing."

The conversation returned to Billy Stafford.

"The only way for you to beat him is to live and be happy," said Carrie.

Jane looked at her friend sharply.

"She didn't like it when I said that," said Carrie. "She didn't want to hear it. And then she said she was tired and she got up and went to bed. And I thought, 'Oh God, everything is *not* all right.'"

Jane gave her a hearty hug before she left the next morning, but Carrie was uneasy and decided she would have to do something soon. "But I thought everything would be okay up to the March 4th court date."

Jane spent Monday, February 17, at an all-day meeting of the committee studying incarcerated women. Recommendations were formulated and readied for inclusion in a draft report.

Over lunch, Jane told Liz Forestell about the threat she received at her mother's house on Friday night. "She was really freaked out by that call. She thought maybe her phone was tapped because she had gone down there at the last minute, and nobody other than her family would have known that she was going."

Forestell said there had been problems with the telephones at the Elizabeth Fry offices since late January, and she also wondered if their phones might not be tapped. "The phones were malfunctioning and we were hearing strange sounds," she said. "It was weird. The lines weren't connecting properly and we'd get cut off on calls."

"This is too crazy, Jane," said Forestell. "You can't go on like this."

Forestell suggested mentioning the threats to a contact in the solicitor general's department. Jane agreed it was a good idea. Forestell's contact thought the situation was serious, and together they arranged a meeting with Deputy Solicitor General Nadine Cooper-Mont.

In the second week of February, Jane's sister Mona received a troubling letter from Jane in which she said there were some strange things happening and that she was concerned.

Over the weekend of February 15, Mona called her sister Sandy, in Ottawa, to see if she had heard anything from Jane. "Sandy didn't know anything about it," said Mona. "Jane had contacted her to see if Darren could come up to Ottawa for the

March break, but that was it. Sandy had said, 'Sure, let him come up,' and she was going to confirm it with Jane."

Mona was concerned over Jane's letter, and telephoned her on Tuesday, February 18. Jane told her about the threats, and that she thought they might be from Gary Grant. She planned to write them down in detail while she was at work in the early hours of the coming Saturday (February 22), and she planned to include them in a letter to a friend [the author] in Toronto.

On Wednesday, February 19, Jane and Liz Forestell met with Nadine Cooper-Mont, the Nova Scotia deputy solicitor general.

"Jane brought the threatening letters and tapes," said Forestell. "And she had written down everything that happened."

Cooper-Mont took the threats seriously and told Jane and Forestell that she knew a police officer "she would trust with her life." The officer was the RCMP's chief superintendent, Allen Burchill, who would later be appointed the force's assistant commissioner for Nova Scotia.

"I'll arrange for him to meet with you," Cooper-Mont told Jane. "He'll appoint an internal investigator. I know they've done this before, and I trust this guy."

After the meeting, Jane and Forestell went to a restaurant for breakfast. Jane said she was satisfied that something was being done. "We talked for a couple of hours about all sorts of things," said Forestell. "Nadine [Cooper-Mont] called me later to say that Burchill would meet with us on Monday morning. I called Jane and she said that was fine."

After leaving Forestell, Jane went home and taped a lengthy audio message for Joel and her family. She began by saying she had just come from meeting Cooper-Mont: "And I was speaking to her in regards to what has been happening with me this last while, and the threats being made by phone and by note.

Just in case anything does happen, I want you to know it's been reported to the top."

The taped message was to serve as an addendum to her will, and hinted strongly that she expected to die very soon. She talked about financial matters that would need immediate attention, including the receipt of a paycheque that was expected "at any time."

On the same tape, Jane talked about her cousin who, along with her husband, was killed in a fiery highway crash: "This is the day, one year ago, that Patricia and Philip and their unborn baby had their lives snatched away so quickly. Since that day, I've thought of a lot of things that had to be done. It doesn't make the pain any easier, to lose a loved one, especially one so young and vibrant and full of life. And I guess there's not been one day since their deaths that I haven't thought about that or them, and just how easily life can be taken away and how precious it is."

Jane went to work on Wednesday night. Sometime in the quiet morning hours, she wrote at least two letters—one to Sara and the other to Jo Sheridan in British Columbia. The letter to Sheridan was upbeat when she talked about her family and job and her appointment to the special committee studying the plight of incarcerated women.

But the tone changed when she talked about the threats. Jane said it was "creepy" to think an unknown person wanted to hurt her. But, she wrote, "life continues on anyway."

In the letter to Sara, Jane said of Billy Stafford: "He was a miserable S.O.B. who deserved what he got—but, Sara—it is extremely hard for me to deal with. And I figure that is why I still shoplift—because I cannot forgive myself! No matter what, Bill was a human being. I am not sorry that he is dead, but I am sorry his life had to end the way it did—so violently!

"There are times I am angry over what he did—and all of its after-effects (I mean my shoplifting). By continuously doing that, I shame and humiliate my kids and family and hurt myself. It is my way of punishing myself for what I did—because of what he did to me."

Jane also mentioned her visit with Nadine Cooper-Mont, and added: "Even though I do not have much faith in the system, I got enough courage to go beyond the RCMP, who aren't doing anything."

She said she still had doubts that people believed her when she told them something. "That all comes from my time with Bill. So much damage gets done to persons from our backgrounds. I am not a liar—never have been. Nor do I exaggerate the truth—yet Bill always made me feel like a babbling idiot, and at times I still feel that way. But I was believed [by Cooper-Mont], although I don't know what is going to be done yet."

About her pending shoplifting charge, Jane wrote: "My case goes to court on March 4, but I don't have to go. My lawyer will go and he will get a new date, which will be as long away as possible so he can establish the defence he wants. When I know more about it, I will explain it to you."

Finally, Jane confirmed in the letter that she had agreed to the terms of a "suicide contract" contained in the book *The Courage to Heal*, which Jane had sent to Sara. Sara said that under the terms of the "contract," they would give each other at least three weeks' notice, by letter or telephone, if they planned to commit suicide.

"That would give her three weeks to tell me why I shouldn't commit suicide," said Sara. "And it would be the same for me if she wanted to kill herself."

Jane wrote of the "contract": "I take your word on what you wrote, and I shall pledge the same to you, okay?"

On Thursday evening, Jane took Darren to Mary Jacquart, his tutor. She had with her a copy of her will, but Jacquart said it wasn't the one she had signed the week before. "My signature wasn't there, but Joel's was," she said.

While she was there, Jane told Jacquart about her meeting with Nadine Cooper-Mont, and she talked about the threats. "If they get me, it will be one of two things, Mary," said Jane.

"What?" asked Jacquart.

"They'll either never find my body, or they'll make it look like suicide."

Jacquart said that as they talked about the threats, Jane was sitting in a rocking chair and Darren was across from her in another chair.

"Mom," he said, "if anybody ever hurt you, I'd kill them."

"Darren!" said Jacquart.

"If they did get me, Darren, fight it and find out who did it, but be on the right side of the law," said Jane. "By you living here with Mary, I *know* she'll make you mind, I *know* she'll make you go to school, and I *know* she'll make you go to university. Darren, you be a lawyer, and you be a good one, and an honest one. Because if anything ever happens to me, I don't need a guilt trip of you killing someone."

Darren didn't mention killing again. Jane left about 10 or 10:30. Mary never saw her again.

At work that night, Jane wrote to her mother, telling her she had picked out material for living room drapes, which she would make up and install for her parents when she came down for the March break. "They will look real nice with sheers… Give Dad my love and I will see you on Tuesday the 25th for your doctor's appointment. I love you both. Janie."

CHAPTER 29

MISSING

Shortly after Jane arrived home from the night shift on the morning of February 21, her son Allen drove up in his new half-ton truck. He was there to pick up his brother Jamie and drive him to visit their father, Jane's first husband, who lived in Milton, near Liverpool.

Usually, Jamie had the use of Joel's 1985 Ford Tempo, because Joel had his own half-ton and Jane had her Mustang. But Jane had warned him a week or two earlier that she would need the Tempo on this night, because Joel was taking the Mustang to her parents' for the weekend to tune it up and change the oil. She told Jamie that before going to work, she would need the Tempo to drive to Halifax to see a battered woman who had called her for help.

"Why don't you use Joel's truck?" asked Jamie.

"Because I already told the lady what the car looks like," said Jane, "and if I go there with the truck, she won't recognize it."

"Why don't you call her and describe the truck to her?"

"I can't phone her, because I don't have her number," said Jane.

Allen agreed to drive Jamie to Milton so that he wouldn't have to take a bus. "Until I got there, Mom was going to take him over to the bus station," said Allen. "She had her housecoat on and I knew she was getting ready to sleep after working all night."

"Don't speed," Jane told him. "You don't want no tickets with that new truck."

Jamie gave his mother a hug and kiss while Allen stood by the door. "I was waiting for her to come over to me and hug me, but she didn't," said Allen. "She went into the living room by the table and she didn't say goodbye to me. I should have told her I loved her but I didn't. It was something I always did, even on the telephone."

Jane was up by early afternoon, and Ann Keith telephoned about 4 p.m. Other than the November 29 speech on behalf of the Dartmouth task force, and the December 6 news conference marking the anniversary of the Montreal massacre, Keith had seen little of Jane since the October wedding. "She had Joel in her life and she seemed happy," recalled Keith.

Keith decided to call Jane after reading about plans to begin shooting a television movie based on *Life With Billy*. Jane was happy to hear from Keith but told her she couldn't say much.

"I've been getting threats and I think my phone might be tapped," Jane told her.

"Oh-oh," said Keith. "Well I won't say too much."

"I'd really like to see you," said Jane. "How about Monday?"

"Sure," said Keith. "Noon time and we'll go for lunch."

That was the first and only time Jane mentioned the threats to Keith.

Carrie Rafuse also called Jane at home on Thursday. "I had talked to her the day before and she didn't sound too bad—maybe a little flat, like the blahs," said Carrie. "I thought she was tired and busy, but nothing unusual. I told her I was thinking of coming in Friday, and she told me to come ahead. But my plans changed and I called her on Friday to say I couldn't make it. She understood and there was no problem."

Joel left work a bit early that Friday because a storm was on the way and it was already starting to snow. He wanted to get an early start on the drive to Jane's parents'. Traffic would be heavy on Friday night, and the storm would add to the congestion.

Jane had partially loaded the Mustang by the time Joel got home. He placed a couple more bags in the back seat along with Jane's dogs, Sasha and Oreo, and he was ready to go. He and Jane hugged and kissed, and he told her he loved her.

"I'll call you when I get down there," he said.

"You don't have to, I'll call you tomorrow night," Jane replied.

"No," said Joel, "you know I'll call you when I get there—I always do." Jane smiled and shrugged.

Shortly after 6 p.m., Joel left for Danesville, about eighty miles away. He was to return on Sunday. Allen, meanwhile, had dropped Jamie off at their father's place in Milton and was home by four in the afternoon.

Jane had asked Darren if he wanted to go down with Joel and spend the weekend with his grandparents, but the boy declined. With Joel and Jamie away, Anita Bruce, Jamie's girlfriend, agreed to stay overnight at Jane's so that Darren wouldn't be alone. She was there most of the day. About 7 p.m. she saw Jane dial a number and speak briefly on the telephone, describing the Tempo to the woman she was apparently supposed to meet in Halifax.

Anita also heard Jane say: "There's things I can't get into over the phone, because my line is tapped."

Jane had purchased and wrapped a birthday gift for Larry, one of the clients at the rehab centre. When she got off the phone, she told Anita and Darren she planned to take the gift with her to work that night.

She put on a pair of Joel's jogging pants. Then, about 7:30 p.m., she said she was going to the nearby Mic Mac Shopping Mall to pick up a cake to go with Larry's gift. "Then I'm going to meet a lady in Halifax," she continued. "I'll phone you from work at twelve o'clock. Leave the side door unlocked so I can get in when I come home in the morning."

Jane turned to them as she slipped on her jacket.

"You know what I did," she said. "I forgot my purse in my car [the Mustang]."

"Well, do you have any money?" asked Anita.

"Yeah, I have money, but I don't have anything else."

Jane telephoned her father in Danesville and told him about the purse.

"When Joel gets there, tell him to bring it into the house," she said. "There's nothing important that I really need."

"She kissed Darren and hugged him like she usually did," said Anita. "All she had was her jacket when she walked out."

The drive to Danesville usually took about an hour and fifteen minutes, but tonight it took Joel about two hours because of the snow storm and heavy traffic. He arrived shortly after 8 p.m.

"Jane just called a little while ago," said Maurice Hurshman. "She left her purse in the car."

Joel went back out to the car, found the purse in the back seat, brought it into the house, and called home.

"She left a little while ago," Anita told him. "She's gone over to Mic Mac to buy a cake for Larry and she's going to meet a lady in Halifax."

"Well okay," said Joel. "If she wants her purse, I can drive right back and get it to her. Tell her to call me when she gets in."

About 9 p.m., Anita and Darren were startled by a loud banging noise in the basement. They ran to the kitchen, thinking someone had broken into the house. Darren grabbed a knife from a drawer and they went to the basement.

"There was nothing there," said Anita. "We don't know what it was."

Later as they sat at the kitchen table, the light in the hall went on and off. "We were nowhere near the switch and there was nobody else in the house," said Anita. "It was very weird. After that, we were scared and we took off."

She and Darren returned to the house just before midnight, the time Jane said she would call them. But Jane didn't call.

Joel said he tried calling a couple of times to get Jane before she went to work, but there was no answer, and he gave up about 11 p.m.

"She's probably at work," said Jane's mother.

Joel was not overly concerned because Jane had met battered women in the past and didn't always make it back to the house before she went to work. Also, she had told him not to bother calling that night and that she would call on Saturday. He decided to go to bed.

When Jane didn't show up for work on Friday night and she couldn't be reached at home, the Cole Harbour RCMP were notified by the hospital.

Maurice and Gladys Hurshman were asleep when the telephone rang about 1:15 a.m. Maurice answered it.

"Hello, Gramp, it's Darren. Is Joel there?"

"Yes, he's in bed."

"Can you get him?"

"Well, he's asleep."

"This is very important, Gramp."

Hurshman hollered to Joel, who jumped to his feet and went to the phone.

"Mom never showed up for work, and the police are here," said Darren.

"I'm on my way," said Joel.

The roads were bad from the winter storm, but traffic was light at that hour, and Joel made much better time on the return trip. The police were gone by the time he arrived home. He called the rehab centre and they told him to call the police, "but they couldn't tell me nothing. I didn't know if I should go and look for her or if I should stay at home and wait in case she called." He decided to drive Jane's normal route to work, in case the car had slipped off the road, but there was no sign of her.

The RCMP detachment at Cole Harbour was just blocks from Jane's Arklow Drive home. When officers there were alerted that she was missing, they treated it seriously because of the reported threats against her.

Sergeant Keith Crosland, a twenty-five-year veteran, was assigned to the investigation. A bulletin with her description, and that of the Ford Tempo, was sent across the province through the police computer network, CPIC (Canadian Police Information Centre).

"In her case, she was receiving threats," said Crosland. "That's a little different twist as opposed to other missing persons, but in every case we put out reports as a matter of course. A lot of times it's for naught, because within twenty-four hours many missing persons are discovered or come back on their own. But you can't sit back and wait for that."

Allen and Charlene had planned to go out Friday night, but Charlene felt a cold or flu coming on and they decided, instead, to go to bed early. Allen, a sound sleeper, said he was awakened by several phone calls, including one from a neighbour and two from callers who dialed the wrong number. He was sound asleep when the last call came shortly after 1 a.m. It was Darren, but Allen was groggy and didn't recognize his voice. He thought it was a crank call.

"Were the police over there yet?" asked Darren.

"No," replied Allen.

"Well, come over right away."

"Okay, bye," said Allen, replacing the receiver.

"Who was that?" asked Charlene.

"I don't know—something about the police and wondering if they were here."

Allen rolled over and went back to sleep. He and Charlene were awakened about 7 a.m. when Joel called.

"Your mother didn't go to work last night, and she's nowhere to be found," he said.

Allen went immediately to the house. While he was there, several calls came in that were "hang-ups—call and hang up, call and hang up. I answered four myself. The police said it was probably people who knew Mom was missing and they were concerned." But Allen was suspicious because the number was unlisted.

Joel asked the police if the line was tapped, as Jane had suspected. The police checked it and said it wasn't. Allen said the police then put a device on the phone that would record a caller's number so it could be traced. "As soon as the police did that, the calls stopped," he said.

Joel called Ann Keith at 8:30 a.m. "I thought, who the hell is calling me at this hour on a Saturday morning," she said.

"Have you seen Jane?" asked Joel.

"No," replied Keith. "I was talking to her at four o'clock yesterday and we were planning to meet for lunch on Monday."

"Well, she didn't go to work last night and she hasn't come home."

Keith was at Jane's house by 9 a.m. Then she went over to the Cole Harbour RCMP detachment and gave her statement about her telephone conversation with Jane.

"I came back to Jane's and Carrie was there," said Keith. "I'd never met her before. She came in with Jeff and his wife, who were also friends of Jane."

Joel told Keith that Jane had been going to see a battered woman in Halifax. The police were now trying to determine the woman's identity. Keith decided to look around the house, and she came across Jane's desk off the bedroom. Joel showed Keith Jane's diary and the black organizer in which she kept her accounts. On top were instructions to Joel to immediately close her accounts and put them into his name if anything should happen to her.

"Until Jane went missing, I never, ever looked in that book," said Joel. "She had it all written what I was supposed to do." She instructed him not to turn any of her personal papers or writings over to the police. But Keith told Joel the police should see the diaries and organizer.

"I can't do that," said Joel. "I have to obey Jane's wishes. She said not to give the police anything in her handwriting."

"I'm sorry, Joel, but you have to give them to the RCMP."

Eventually Joel did turn them over to the police.

The RCMP at Cole Harbour were heading the investigation, but police in Halifax and Dartmouth were also looking for Jane, although no extra patrols or officers were assigned to the case. Through CPIC, regular patrols had her description and the licence number, model, and colour of the car.

Allen saw the card and gift Jane had wrapped, and Joel explained it was for Larry, the client at the rehab centre. "Joel wanted me to take it over there because it was this guy's birthday that day," said Allen. "So I run it up on my way home because I wanted to take my time and drive the road Mom takes to work. It's a pretty dark road at night and it had been snowing so I thought maybe she went off into the woods or something." But he saw nothing to indicate that a car had left the road.

After dropping off the gift, Allen and Charlene drove around every parking lot and hotel in Dartmouth searching for the Ford Tempo. They thought she had to be close by because the tires on the Tempo were bald and "she couldn't have gone far." As the day wore on, Allen's anxiety grew.

Liz Forestell was at work in her office at the Elizabeth Fry Society when an officer from the Cole Harbour RCMP telephoned around noon on Saturday to tell her Jane was missing.

Forestell said her heart stopped, "and I had a sick feeling in my stomach that something really bad had happened to her."

"Do you have any idea where she might be?" asked the officer.

"No."

"Has she been depressed lately? Is she suicidal?"

"What are you talking about? Why would you say that? No! She's not suicidal."

"Well, she's missing, and we always ask that."

"Don't you know that she's been getting threats for the last month?" asked Forestell.

"Yes, we know that but we have to look at everything."

Ann Keith made call after call from Jane's house to women who might know where Jane was or who might know the identity of the mystery woman she said she was to meet in Halifax. It was a dead end, and eventually Keith went home. She decided to call Donna Smith so that she wouldn't hear about Jane from the media first.

"Donna, I hate to tell you this, but Jane's missing," said Keith, who briefly explained what she knew.

"What was she wearing?" asked Donna.

"She had on Joel's dark-coloured jogging suit," said Keith, who thought it an odd question. "She was supposed to have gone to meet a woman in Halifax."

Keith promised to keep Donna informed. After she hung up, she returned to Jane's to see if there was anything more she could do.

As soon as Keith told her that Jane was wearing the jogging suit, Donna knew that Jane was dead. "Jane and I often went to meet other women who had been battered, and she always dressed nicely. She would never wear a jogging suit to go and meet a stranger."

Donna remembered the scenario that Jane had laid out in December for killing the woman dying of cancer, and realized for the first time that there *was* no other woman: Jane was talking about killing *herself*. That was why she insisted that Donna be there—to remove the gun.

After the call from Keith, Donna was shattered. Her daughter, Mary, and her roommate, Shelley, could see her concern.

"Jane's missing," said Donna. Shelley, too, thought back to the scenario Donna had outlined the night she returned from her dinner with Jane. Donna arranged for a babysitter, and she and Shelley went out about 7 p.m. to look for Jane.

"We drove and drove," said Donna. "We went to all the malls and checked the lot behind Sears that she had talked about in December."

Donna also checked the parking lot of a particular hotel because Jane once told her that a simple way to overdose was to rent a room there under a fictitious name, and "go in and do it and they wouldn't find your body until the next day."

Donna and Shelley returned home at 11 p.m. A few minutes later the RCMP called and asked Donna if she knew Jane's whereabouts. "I told them I didn't know where she was."

Donna began pacing while Shelley drove the babysitter home. "I kept thinking, I've got to tell Ann what I know—I've got to tell somebody—even if I get arrested."

Shelley returned, and minutes later Ann Keith called. "It was like she had ESP," said Donna. Donna told Keith the full story, and expressed her belief that Jane would never have dressed in a jogging suit to meet a woman she didn't know.

"We've got to go to the police right now," said Keith. "I'll call you right back."

Keith met an RCMP officer at a doughnut shop and told him the story. Then she telephoned Donna to tell her she would be over with the officer, who would take her statement.

"They came over around midnight, and I told him everything," said Donna. "Then the RCMP called me back around three o'clock in the morning to get my full name. I wasn't asleep—I couldn't."

On Sunday morning, February 23, Joel discovered the audiotape Jane had recorded four days earlier as an addendum to her will. The tape was in the strongbox Jane kept under their bed. "We kept money in there," he said. "She and I were the only ones who had a key for it. I saw the tape, and it said 'Last Will and Testament' on it."

He played the tape and showed it to Darren.

"You don't have to listen to it if you don't want to," said Joel.

He played it partway through for the boy. "He heard the part about him and he cried a bit," said Joel. "Then he said, 'I got to leave,' and he went out."

Joel decided he would not tell the police about the tape.

CHAPTER 30
ANOTHER BODY

On Saturday, February 22, 1992, between 9 and 10 a.m., a worker with East Coast Towing, a tugboat company on the Halifax waterfront, noticed a lone blue Ford Tempo in an adjacent parking lot. The car was parked near the water a considerable distance from several other cars bunched at the top of the lot across the street from Brewery Market, a collection of upscale shops, restaurants, and offices.

The Tempo was still there at three the next afternoon when Roy and Yvonne Kline drove about two-thirds of the way into the lot and parked their car. Roy, recently retired after forty-five years with a local dairy, and Yvonne, who worked for the provincial transportation department, drove down to the waterfront two or three times a week to watch the ships in the busy harbour. There was snow on the ground and a biting wind was blowing from the north as they stepped from their car. Yvonne decided it was too cold to stray very far, and stood near the car as her husband walked toward the water.

"I was just pokin' along, heading south towards the entrance to the harbour, when I noticed the car there," recalled Roy. "When I was four or five feet from it, on the driver's side, I noticed a lady slumped over in the front seat. The first thing that came to my mind was, my gosh, that could be somebody's mother in there and she probably has children waiting for her to come home. I thought maybe she had a drink or something and she was just resting, or else she tried to start the car and it wouldn't go.

"The snow had fallen through the night, and I observed there was no marks or footprints around the car. And I took a closer look and I didn't like the colour of her face. I thought, 'There's something wrong here.' I thought she might have had the car going and she was asphyxiated."

The cold, meanwhile, had got to Yvonne Kline, and she was back in the car watching her husband. "He just stood there and looked into that car," she said. "He wasn't moving—wasn't saying a word." She called out, and Roy Kline returned to the car. He sat silent behind the steering wheel for a few moments.

"You won't believe this," he said finally, turning to his wife. "There's a woman in that car."

"What does she look like?"

"She doesn't have very good colour."

"Well, maybe she's dead. We better go call the police."

They drove two or three blocks to a pay telephone, but vandals had damaged it. They found another phone booth, and Roy told police about the woman and gave them the licence number of the car.

"We decided to come back and watch," he said.

They chose an adjacent lot, where snow collected from city streets was being dumped at the water's edge and pushed into the harbour. A police cruiser arrived within minutes, sliding to a stop near the Tempo. A bulldozer operator and a truck driver stopped to watch along with the Klines.

"There were two officers, a man and a woman," recalled Yvonne Kline. "They walked over to the car and looked into it."

The officers then moved away and pulled on white surgical gloves before approaching the car again. As they watched, the Klines overheard the bulldozer operator say to the dump truck driver, "They're putting on their white gloves. That means there must be something wrong."

Another police car arrived a short time later. The Klines decided it was too cold to wait around until the body was removed.

"We may as well go home and see it on the TV," said Yvonne. Roy nodded in agreement.

"I figure they must know who she is by now," he said. "I gave them the licence number. They can tell from that."

Kline was right. The Tempo was registered to Jane Hurshman, and the police had been looking for her since late Friday.

Constables Bryan Naas and Colleen Kelly were in the marked cruiser that slid to a stop in the parking lot several yards from the 1985 Ford Tempo. From a distance, no one was visible in the car. Naas was a veteran officer who once worked for the Metropolitan Toronto Police Department. As he and Kelly approached the car, they noticed only one set of footprints—Roy Kline's—visible in the snow near the vehicle.

As they drew closer, the officers saw a woman slumped over. She was wearing an open, multicoloured jacket over a black jogging suit. It was obvious that she was dead.

Peter Astephen, one of two corporals on the Halifax Police Department's fifteen-member major crime unit, was at his in-laws' in Dartmouth for Sunday dinner when he was informed on his cellular phone that a woman had been found dead in a car.

The plainclothes members of the major crime unit worked from 8:30 a.m. to 4:30 p.m., Monday to Friday. There was also a rotation system under which someone was always on call for nights and weekends. On this weekend it was Astephen's turn, which meant that the dead woman would be his investigation. He went immediately to the waterfront.

Astephen was of average height and weight and his stiff black hair was beginning to turn grey. He was into his twenty-fifth year with the Halifax department but was just forty-five, with a daughter in college and a son on the police force. He had been a plainclothes investigator for eighteen years, the first six on the drug squad. In the field, he seemed always serious and more often than not a plastic-tipped Old Port Colt cigar was clenched between his teeth.

By the time Astephen arrived on the waterfront, Naas and Kelly had strung yellow police tape to cordon off a wide perimeter around the Ford Tempo. Several other Halifax officers, some in uniform and some not, were already at the scene, along with Dr. Kim McBride from the medical examiner's office and Sergeant Keith Crosland from the RCMP Cole Harbour detachment.

Crosland was in his Cole Harbour office, working on Jane's disappearance, when Halifax police notified him that they had found the missing woman and the car. He arrived at the waterfront with Constable Angus Emberly.

"I remember it was very cold, with the wind coming off the water," said Crosland. "I talked to Peter [Astephen] for a few minutes at the scene and then stood back as he did his thing."

Corporal James Griffin, head of the Halifax department's identification [Ident] section, pulled up at the same time as Astephen. Griffin was also a twenty-five-year veteran. The on-duty member of the Ident unit, Wayne Fraser, had already taken still photographs and video shots, and Dr. McBride had confirmed that the woman was dead.

According to Astephen, Naas, Kelly, and Dr. McBride used the same path to and from the vehicle, on the driver's side, to protect the scene as best they could.

Although there were officers on the scene who outranked Astephen, including Staff Sergeant Mike Mahar, there was an unwritten rule that as soon as the investigator arrived, he was in charge.

Astephen and Griffin surveyed the area around the car and noticed that icicles had formed from the car to the ground behind the rear wheels. "That indicated that the car was there for some time," said Astephen. "It had snowed, melted some, and frozen again." He concluded later that the car had probably been there since Friday night.

Jane's body, he said, was "slumped toward the passenger's side from the driver's side, and that was the reason nobody spotted her earlier... Where the car was situated, with the sun and the glare, you'd almost have to walk right up to it and look in to see anything."

Vehicle tracks and footprints indicated that through the night, other vehicles had parked as close as four or five feet on either side of the Tempo. That area of the parking lot was notorious for attracting prostitutes and their clients. On Sunday mornings, discarded condoms and empty liquor and beer bottles could be found strewn on the ground. That fact that it had snowed on Friday and Saturday night and that Jane's body was slumped over reduced the possibility of anyone spotting her, "especially," said Astephen, "when you consider the reason some of these people were down there. The hookers are around in the early evening and after the clubs close. There's a lot of room in that lot and they would be down away from the street and the traffic. It's common knowledge that they either meet their clients there or go down there with them."

Joel's car was a four-door, and only the front door on the passenger's side was locked when Naas and Kelly arrived. No purse or identification of any kind was found on Jane or in the car, but police knew who she was through the licence plate and because her face was familiar from her media profile as a spokesperson for battered women.

In the left pocket of her jacket, police found a sealed envelope. Inside was another of the stencilled threats, this one stating, "No more talk from you—Gotcha!"

Crosland had informed Astephen about the reported threats against Jane, and as Astephen approached the car, suicide was the last thing on his mind. "We were treating it as a homicide investigation at that point, which is the way we treat any type of sudden death."

The body had not been moved in any way when Astephen approached from the driver's side and Griffin from the passenger's side.

"We did a visual check of the body first," said Astephen. "She was in the same position as when they found her—slouched over toward the passenger side." The keys were in the ignition, and the officers noticed a folded flannel sheet, draped partially over Jane's lap, her right hand, and the seat.

On the floor was a paper cup partially filled with coffee. The cup was standing upright on the passenger's side beside three plastic grocery bags, one inside the other. Inside the bags were a large, empty plastic bag and a plastic sandwich bag containing three .38-calibre bullets. In the back seat was a loaf of bread and the boxed birthday cake that Jane had purchased at the Mic Mac Shopping Mall for Larry, the rehab centre client.

Astephen decided to move the body. "Jim Griffin was taking pictures and I began to carefully move her into a more upright position—back to where she would have been sitting," he said.

As they moved the body out of its slouched position, the officers noticed the barrel of a handgun. "It was on her lap, and the sheet was sort of around and under it," said Astephen.

While holding Jane's body upright, Astephen looked for a gunshot wound and noticed a small hole through the black, hooded jogging top. "It wasn't much more than a pin-hole in the front," said Astephen. "I didn't notice it at first because it was so small."

The bullet had entered the centre of Jane's chest and travelled on a slight angle, upward and to the right, exiting just below her right shoulder blade. A small hole was visible in the back of the seat. A single, deformed, .38-calibre slug was later found lodged in the seat. The location of the hole in the seat matched that of the exit wound in Jane's back when she was in the upright position behind the steering wheel. No blood was visible on Jane's jacket or on the back of the seat where the bullet entered.

"Once we verified there was a shot and we could see the hole in the seat, we took a closer look—with the doctor—as the body was placed on the stretcher," said Astephen. "Because it was so cold, the blood had coagulated quickly, but there was some blood visible on the inside of the jogging top."

Under police guard, a nondescript white van from Eastern Removal Service, a private company that transports bodies for the medical examiner, funeral homes, and others, delivered Jane's body to the morgue at Victoria General Hospital at South Street and Tower Road in downtown Halifax.

Once the body was removed, the Ident men, Griffin and Fraser, carefully catalogued and removed the handgun, bullets, and other items found in the car. The car was then impounded and towed to the police garage to be screened—inside and out—for fingerprints, hair, and fibres. The gun, coffee cup, and other items would also be checked for prints, and then sent for forensic examination to the RCMP's Crime Detection Laboratory in Halifax. Ballistics tests would be conducted to determine whether the bullet found in the seat came from the handgun in the car.

After the car was towed, all of the police officers involved met at Astephen's office in the Halifax police building to review the evidence and information gathered so far and to coordinate strategy for the investigation.

"We put our heads together to determine exactly what we were dealing with," said Astephen. "Keith Crosland had a better background on who she was. We basically decided to work on the investigation with the RCMP because they reported her missing and they were investigating the threats."

Crosland went into details about the threats and other information the RCMP had gathered. "We were assisting Halifax police because the body was found in their jurisdiction. My investigation initially pertained only to the threats. Then it became a missing person. Then it became a missing person found dead, but I was still dealing with the threats."

About 4:30 Sunday afternoon, Joel Corkum was sitting at home "watching every car that went by" when an RCMP cruiser with two officers pulled into the yard.

"Mr. Corkum, we've found your wife and she is deceased," said one of the officers. Darren was standing in the kitchen, and Joel went to him.

"Darren, they found Mom and she's dead," he said, putting his arms around the teenager's shoulders. Darren pulled away, kicked a hole in the basement door, and went down to his room.

"Are there any guns in the house?" asked one officer.

"Yes," replied Joel.

"Can we take them as a safety precaution?"

"Yeah, sure, take them."

The police removed three shotguns and two rifles from the house.

Ann Keith was at the house Sunday night and noticed a remarkable change in Darren. The hurt and anger had left him and he had become animated and almost euphoric—perhaps a form of delayed shock.

"It was so peculiar," she said. "He was at one end of the table and Joel was sitting there and I was sitting there. And Darren seemed up and elated and he was just talking and babbling away. He mentioned how Billy used to swat him or something. It was the first time I ever heard him talk about Billy."

When Joel interrupted Darren at one point, the boy said, "Shut up there, Joel, I'm talking."

"It was as if Darren was taking over the role of father and Joel was becoming the little kid," said Keith. "It was hard to explain. Joel was playing right into it."

Just before Darren went to bed, he approached Keith and told her he wouldn't be having any more nightmares.

"He told me about a dream he had in which he got out of bed and went into the kitchen where he saw a man standing outside the window. He said the man had blond hair and he had a shotgun, which he cocked and fired at him. The time on the clock in his dream was 2:30 a.m."

Darren told Keith that with the blast of the shotgun, he woke up and went into the kitchen and looked at the clock. It was the same time as in his dream—2:30 a.m.

Keith had never seen Darren show physical affection, but after he told her about the nightmare, "he came over and gave me a hug and said, 'I hope we see more of you,' and he went to bed. I couldn't believe it."

Keith described what she saw that evening as "bizarre," and added, "I made sure I had my back to the wall."

Wendy Annand, Jane's former parole officer, was distraught when she learned that Jane was missing. "I talked to her just two nights before. She was going to be our special guest for International Women's Day, and she was also planning a presentation to the Canadian Panel on Violence Against Women.

"I was beside myself, so I went to a friend of mine who is a psychic to see if she could track it. She felt Jane had been kidnapped and was being held on the waterfront, but had dissociated. It turned out she was very close with the geography."

Annand was about to drive to Halifax to search for Jane when Joel called and told her Jane was dead. "I was a wreck. She was one of my best friends, and to have her die that way just seemed so unbelievable and so unjust, after what she'd been through. You wanted her to be ninety years old and die surrounded by family."

Annand's psychic wasn't the only one thinking about the waterfront. Liz Forestell spent most of Sunday morning driving around Halifax harbour. "I'm not sure what drew me there," she said. "I had the licence plate number and I was looking for her car."

Early in the afternoon, she drove to the Dartmouth side of the harbour, picked up a hamburger, and sat facing Halifax from the Dartmouth Ferry Terminal parking lot. "I sat there looking over to the other side of the water and I kept thinking she was there somewhere."

Later in the afternoon she returned to the Elizabeth Fry offices in Halifax. "When I arrived there, I found footsteps in the snow going up to my window at the rear of the building and, from there, around to each of the windows in front. I wondered if Jane had been there or if someone was looking for me.

"It could have been anything, but I didn't feel very comfortable at the office, so I went home." About 5 p.m., Joel telephoned her and told her Jane was dead.

"I guess I knew it all along," said Forestell, "but I just couldn't believe it. I was sort of calm, but it just didn't seem possible. The whole time we were waiting, it seemed like weeks and weeks instead of a day. And I kept imagining what they would find and what had happened to her. I had some pretty awful images."

The news reports on radio and television in the Halifax area late Sunday afternoon said that a woman had been found dead in a blue car at the waterfront. When Donna Smith heard the news, she had a strong feeling it was Jane.

"They showed pictures of the car and I ran in and taped it so we could see the car again," said Donna. "Then the RCMP called and said it was Jane's body."

As Donna hung up, a song that she and Jane liked was playing on the radio. "I broke down," said Donna. Shelley, her roommate, saw Donna crying and tried to distract Mary, who was playing in the bedroom, but the child came into the living room.

"Jane's dead, isn't she, Mommy?" she asked.

"Yes," sobbed Donna.

Bobby, then six years old, was the strongest. "I was crying so much," Donna remembered, "and Mary was bawling while Shelley tried to calm her, but Bobby didn't cry at all."

"It's okay to cry, Mommy," said the boy, "because if you cry it means you care."

It was dark by then, and Bobby went to the window and looked out. A single star was visible in the sky. "Mommy, look at that star," he said, motioning Donna to the window. "That's Jane looking over us."

As word spread that the dead woman was Jane, Donna was inundated with telephone calls. "We had so many calls because when anybody at Bryony House wanted to get in touch with Jane, they called me. It reached the point I was so upset I couldn't handle any more calls.

"It took the kids a while to get over it, especially Mary. They were so close to Jane, and she always brought them something. I think she bought them every kids' movie going. Eventually Mary came to realize Jane was at peace."

Carrie Rafuse called Jane at work at three on Saturday morning. "They said she didn't come in to work tonight, and I thought, 'Oh God, I wonder if I should call her house.' It sort of shocked me because Jane never missed work. I thought she was probably not feeling well and had stayed home and gone to bed."

At 6 a.m., Joel called her to tell her Jane was missing.

"And I knew," said Carrie. "I just knew."

It was obvious to her that Jane planned her death. It wasn't only that she knew Jane was suicidal. "I knew Jane," she said, "and she would never, ever, leave her purse behind. And if she did, she'd go right after it—it's as simple as that. She wanted to leave her purse in the car. She wanted it to go somewhere else. And it didn't surprise me that she had the old car, because she probably wanted Jamie to have her new car."

The morgue at Victoria General Hospital is on the first floor of the D.J. MacKenzie Building. It includes a refrigerated body storage room; two modern autopsy suites; a lab for storage and examination of tissues; a small photo lab; two offices; and a change room and showers.

In the body storage room, a dozen or so pull-out drawers are built into the wall. Each has a door of stainless steel. Jane's body was placed in one of the drawers, which was rolled into its compartment. The door was closed behind her, and a police officer secured it with a padlock.

Ten years earlier, almost to the day, an autopsy on the body of Billy Stafford had been conducted in the sub-basement of the same building.

Dr. Malcolm MacAulay, the province's acting chief medical examiner, was called at his home Sunday night and notified that the police required an autopsy on Jane's body the next day. He informed the hospital and arranged for X-rays of the body to be taken in the morning before the autopsy. Dr. MacAulay taught pathology at Dalhousie University and at Victoria General Hospital, and was one of three doctors who performed forensic autopsies at Victoria General for the medical examiner's office.

On Monday morning, February 24, the drawer containing Jane's body was unlocked and the X-rays MacAulay had requested were taken. The body was then removed to a stainless steel table in one of the two autopsy rooms across the hall from the body storage room.

When he entered the room at 11:20 a.m. to begin the autopsy, Dr. MacAulay was dressed in full operating-room garb, including surgical mask, gown, and gloves, eye protection, and shoe covers.

Photographers from the hospital and from the Halifax police department's Ident section took photographs while he worked. In addition, the police used a standard kit to check for gunpowder residue on Jane's hands. The samples collected would be sent to the RCMP laboratory in Ottawa for analysis.

Dr. MacAulay reported that the entrance wound in Jane's body was seven millimetres in diameter and that the bullet passed through the breastbone, the sac surrounding the heart (pericardium), the right lung, and the ninth rib. The bullet barely grazed the heart but came close enough to tear a large hole in the wall of the right ventricle.

The exit wound in the right upper back was six millimetres in diameter, and MacAulay said that the absence of blood on the seat or Jane's outer clothing was consistent with her "immediately falling over to one side." Most of the blood drained into the right chest cavity.

The bullet had pierced the back of Jane's jacket and the front and back of her black jogging top, but had not gone through the pink camisole she was wearing underneath. That there was no hole in the back was easy enough to explain: it was cut low, and the bullet came out on an upward angle. And in front, MacAulay explained, the camisole had three buttons and the barrel had been placed in the gap between the first two.

"The camisole itself was not damaged by the bullet," said Dr. MacAulay. "But all the blow-back [soot] from the explosion was on the inside of the camisole."

Entrance wounds are designated as *distant*, *close*, or *contact*. With a *distant* wound there is no powder residue on the target or victim but there will be considerable residue if it is a *contact* wound. Contact wounds are further described as *loose contact* or *tight contact*. Jane's wound was described as *loose contact* because the jogging top was between the muzzle of the handgun and her chest. Police believe that Jane loaded two bullets into the gun in case she was still conscious after firing the first shot.

When Jane's youngest sister, Mona Donnelly, arrived in Cole Harbour on Monday from Barrie, Ontario, she was upset that no one from the family had been to identify or look at Jane's body.

"Why didn't you go over and look at the body?" she asked Allen. "How do you even know it's your mom? You're allowed to see her."

"I don't want to," said Allen. "They know it's her."

He said he didn't want to go into a cold morgue. Mona telephoned Peter Astephen and insisted on seeing her sister's body.

"Her body is under the control of the medical examiner," explained Astephen.

"I don't care, I want to see her," said Mona.

"Well, I don't think you can see her at this point, but if you really insist, I'll make inquiries."

Mona also asked Astephen why no one from the family was asked to identify the body. "He said that one of the officers identified her and they wanted to spare the family the pain. And I told him the family should have had the option of making that decision."

She waited and waited for Astephen to call back, "and finally I called him."

"The autopsy has been completed," said Astephen. "They won't let you see her but they will give you a photograph if you want."

"I don't want a photograph," said Mona. "I want to see Jane and I want to see her now, and so does her mother, and so does her husband. I'm a pretty strong person and I want to see her."

Astephen said the autopsy had just been completed, but he agreed to call the medical examiner's office once again. This time he was given the go-ahead to allow the family to view Jane's body at the pathology lab.

According to Dr. MacAulay, in cases of suspicious death the family members are not allowed to see the body before the autopsy, because in their grief they might do something that would interfere with or alter evidence. "We usually hold the body until the next day, in case we want to go back to check something. It's kind of a safety precaution."

Mona, Joel, and Jane's mother, Gladys, met Astephen at the police station and went with him to the morgue. Jane's body was on an elevated stretcher that had been wheeled into an alcove off a hallway in the Mackenzie Building.

"She was lying there with a white sheet over her and plastic bags on her feet," said Mona. "All I could really see was her face. And when I first saw her, I thought, 'I've got to get her out of here.' She looked so lost and alone and innocent, and I just didn't want to leave her there. Her face was so white and she looked like she was sleeping but her eyes were half open. I remember looking down and just thinking about her blue eyes."

Dr. MacAulay now felt certain that Jane's death was a suicide, but he needed more information to make a definitive ruling.

"The attitude of the weapon and the attitude of the victim were compatible with her doing it herself," he said. "But somebody else could have rigged it. It's possible to stage a suicide. I mean, there's no magic to that."

The fact that the bullet did not go through the front of the camisole was one of the factors that pointed to suicide. If Jane had felt one of the camisole buttons digging into her chest from the pressure of the revolver, her automatic response would have been to shift the button aside with the muzzle before squeezing the trigger, "especially if you're sitting there deciding whether you're actually going to do this or not."

If someone else shot Jane, it's extremely unlikely they would have been aware of the button beneath the jogging top, or would have bothered to push it aside.

There were no visible injuries on Jane's body other than a slight discoloration on her lower lip. But Dr. MacAulay said that in gunshot suicides it is not uncommon for a person to bite his or her lower lip when squeezing the trigger. He felt that it would have been improper for him to label Jane's death as a definite suicide while forensic results and investigation of the threats against her were still outstanding. "I had no doubt that it was suicide," he said, "but you need to know information about the person's state of mind. And so, before I became convinced, I needed to hear the information that the police gathered. Eventually, they had some fifty or sixty statements, most of which I went through."

On Monday night, most of Jane's family gathered in the living room of her home, and Joel played the audiotape she recorded two days before her disappearance. Present were her parents; her sister Mona; her sons Darren, Jamie, and Allen; and Allen's wife, Charlene.

Jane talked about her meeting with Liz Forestell and Nadine Cooper-Mont, the deputy solicitor general. "Just in case anything does happen, I want you to know it's been reported to the top," she said.

She then went into a detailed review of the financial aspects of her will and of how her assets, including insurance policies, RRSPs, and pension benefits, were to be divided.

The family listened to her talk calmly and clearly about her feelings and list the things she wanted done in the event of her death. She urged Jamie and Darren to stay in school. Her voice broke only when she talked about the possibility of her dogs being put to sleep.

Jane wanted only her immediate family to view her body, and asked to be cremated in an inexpensive casket. She also said that Darren was to maintain close ties to his brothers, the rest of her family, and Joel, if he went to live with Mary and Paul Jacquart.

On the tape she also read a letter she had written to Joel and her family three months earlier, on November 20, 1991: "My precious loved ones, Joel, my sons, my parents, my sisters and brother, and their families: Life has been good to me this past couple of years. I fell in love with a fantastic man and got married. A miracle. We bought a home and turned it into our castle, and all of this is more than I ever believed to be possible. Happiness has been overwhelming. There is a future. Life is good. I am safe and loved.

"I am writing this letter because I am positive that was exactly how Patricia Parnell and Phillip Nickerson [Jane's pregnant cousin and her husband, who were killed in a car accident] felt just before life was so abruptly taken away. I have not been able to get them out of my mind, so I decided to write this letter to accompany my will. I want everything to be as clear as possible in the event of the inevitable—my death."

Listening to Jane's voice was very difficult for Mona and for Jane's sons. "I was crying," Mona said. "And at one point I even felt a little angry at Jane for not telling me what she was really feeling. You know, 'Why didn't you let me in on everything? You could have been here today if you would have reached out.' It was very emotional."

It was particularly emotional when Jane said she was at peace and addressed each of them individually: "Joel . . . I love you dearly and deeply. When the time is right, and you and the kids are settled, consider getting yourself a new partner. Get yourself a lady that is good, and caring, and loving, to you and to my kids.

"To Al and Char [Allen and Charlene], I want only the best for both of you and I ask your understanding and forgiveness for the shame and humiliation I have caused you. Remember the good times and live your lives to the fullest and carry my love in your hearts.

"Jamie, I love you dearly. I am so very happy and proud that we have had the time and the opportunity to get to know how much alike we really are—so sensitive, caring, and loving.

"Darren, my precious pride and joy, I love you. You and Jamie and Joel be good to each other, take care of each other, love and talk, and understand each other. Try to keep out of trouble and get your education. I will always know that I am alive in your heart and in your mind.

"Mom and Dad, I am glad that we had these days and years to really get to know each other and I am thankful we are such a good family. I love you both so very much. Please take care of yourselves and of Joel and my sons.

"Mona, Sandy, and Skipper [Jane's brother], I love you all very much and I am so proud to call you sisters and brother. I thank you all for all your support and love, and your caring and kindness. Now just show it to Joel and my sons as much as ever."

Jane also emphasized that she didn't want law enforcement officers to have access to her private papers: "And remember, should anything happen to me, and the police come here, don't you allow them to take anything that's mine that I have written in, or written on, or any documents or papers."

CHAPTER 31

QUESTIONS

On Tuesday, February 25, the day after the autopsy, Dr. MacAulay made public his initial findings. In his view, Jane's death was consistent with suicide, but he had not ruled out homicide. The Halifax police also said that Jane's death was probably suicide, but added that their investigation was continuing.

The news media reported both statements the next day and carried stories about the threats that had been made against Jane. Allen Burchill, the RCMP's chief superintendent, said that Jane hadn't thought the police would take the threats seriously, because she had served time in prison.

"It wasn't a case of faith in their [the RCMP's] competence," Burchill was quoted as saying, but rather a fear that she wouldn't be taken seriously.

Burchill told the media about the Monday meeting he had set up to discuss the threats with Jane and to tell her they *would* be taken seriously. "Unfortunately, I never got the chance to give her my assurances," he said.

The police investigation, meanwhile, was proceeding on several fronts. After interviewing Donna Smith and Carrie Rafuse, the investigators began to feel strongly that Jane had intended to kill herself and make it look like a murder. They believed she had paid someone to put the gun, the bullets, and the blanket into the plastic bags and remove them from the car. But the person had failed to follow through with the plan.

Peter Astephen and other investigators determined that Jane was last seen shortly before 8 p.m. on Friday, February 21, at the Mic Mac Shopping Mall, where she purchased the birthday cake. The coffee cup found in the car was from Perks Coffee on the harbour side of Lower Water Street near the Dartmouth Ferry docks, about three blocks from the parking lot where her body was found.

Given the times and locations, it was assumed that the coffee had been purchased sometime after Jane left the Mic Mac Mall. She seldom drank coffee, and police were unable to determine whether she or someone else picked it up from Perks.

No drugs or alcohol were found in Jane's system, and no clear fingerprints were found on the coffee cup or on the handgun—a military issue .38-calibre Smith and Wesson that had been manufactured without a serial number in the late 1930s or early 1940s. The letters R.A.F. (Royal Air Force) were inscribed on the gun, which according to the police had been widely issued within the Canadian military during World War II.

Jane did not have a permit to own or carry a handgun, and in initial discussions with the Cole Harbour RCMP, Joel did not mention that she had obtained a revolver. Eventually, a man from the Bridgewater area came forward and informed police that Joel had been looking for a handgun. Ten days after Jane was reported missing, Joel and Darren were brought in for intensive questioning. It was then that police learned that Jane had obtained a gun.

Astephen said that although police never showed Joel the gun found in the car with Jane, he gave police an exact description of it, including the R.A.F. inscription. He also described the bags used to contain the bullets and the gun. "He knew it was a .38 because he saw it on the back side of the bullets," said Astephen. "He said it was an old gun and demonstrated how it broke down—the chamber goes out to the side. It's not your typical gun of today."

Astephen's boss, Staff Sergeant Don Thomander, said that the flannel sheet around the gun would have protected Jane's hands from gunpowder residue, muffled the sound of the shot, and masked the resulting flash. By chance, the sheet also kept the gun from falling to the floor as Jane slumped to one side.

Astephen said that forensic evidence later revealed powder residue on the flannel sheet and on "the webs of both hands between the thumb and forefinger. In a close area like that, it wouldn't be uncommon for residue to be in lots of places, but the chances of it getting on both hands, in areas consistent with the hands being around the gun, I think would be almost impossible. Griffin [from Ident] and I feel that her thumbs were hooked through the trigger."

Dr. MacAulay said that because the handgun was held so close to Jane's chest, some of the residue from the blow-back would have come from the muzzle when the shot was fired but most of it would have come from "the break between the cylinder and the barrel. With a revolver, the hands of the shooter—whether it's the victim or not—receive residue that comes from the break between the cylinder and the barrel."

Dr. MacAulay also believed it was suicide because "a killer shooting for the body, logically, would shoot twice—at least."

As part of their investigation, the police attempted to find the man that Jane claimed to have hired to shoot her in the head. In her story to Carrie Rafuse, she said that after the gun misfired on the first attempt, the man was to try a second time.

However, before he was able to do so, the police picked him up on an unrelated charge.

"There was one way of finding out whether or not that was true, and that would be to find the guy," said Sergeant Keith Crosland of the Cole Harbour RCMP. "And there's no ifs, ands, or buts—we have not found the guy." He said that police checked arrest records around the dates that Jane had indicated to Carrie. "Nothing came of it," said Crosland. "It was a nice lead that dead-ended. The other side of the coin is, even if you did come up with the guy, virtually all you're getting is a little more information that's going to corroborate the suicide theory. I felt from the start that we would find her and we would find that she committed suicide."

Some of Jane's friends and associates believed that she spent so much time helping other women that she had not allowed herself enough time to heal. She was also worried about how her sons would turn out. But overshadowing all of that was Jane's continuing battle with kleptomania—an affliction she found humiliating, as well as hurtful to her family. It had brought on her 1989 suicide attempt, and the problem had worsened since then.

She was facing a court hearing on March 4, and she hadn't told her family about it. Her lawyer would have had the case put over, probably for several weeks, even months, but she was afraid the media would see her name on the court docket and play up the story, as they had in the past.

Jane had been scheduled to address the Canadian Panel on Violence Against Women on March 4, two days after her next court appearance. The thought of public humiliation and embarrassment one day, and a public appearance the next, was probably more than she could bear.

The story of Jane's death—of the threats against her, of her likely suicide, of the possibility of homicide—unleashed a tide of fear, anger, and confusion among many women in Nova Scotia and Atlantic Canada, where she had such a high profile.

Darlene Darrington, one of the victims of the motorcycle rapist, said she believed it was suicide, but "if that's what she needed to do to end her pain and suffering, I can understand it. My suicidal feelings still come and go today. After what happened to me, I wanted to commit suicide, and a lot of the women in the group that we have felt the same way. You do begin to get on with your life, but there's always something that brings it back—some times worse than others."

Jane's childhood friend, Valery Cromwell, didn't believe it was suicide. "I feel somebody out there had something to do with it, and whoever it is they are not going to the grave with their secret. They must confess before they die."

Valery's cousin, and Jane's former boyfriend, James Tynes, said he wasn't really surprised to learn Jane was dead: "I felt real bad about it." He could not understand Joel going along with Jane's attempt to get a gun when he knew how distressed she was about her shoplifting. "I think I know Jane as well as anybody and probably better than most," he said. "If she wanted a gun, I would know she wouldn't want it for protection. She would want it to kill herself."

Margaret Joudrey, alone in her trailer below the house where Jane lived with Billy Stafford in Bangs Falls, heard on the five o'clock news that a woman had been found dead in a car on the Halifax waterfront.

"They didn't give no name," she said. "And I said, 'For godsakes that makes it bad. Why don't they tell us the name?' Then I think it was nine o'clock that they told the name and I said, 'Hallelujah!' I said there's one damn piece of trash gone. That's the way I felt. I'm happy that she's dead. I said if she goes to heaven, none of us has got to worry. I guess we'll all go there. Yes sir, if that woman lands in heaven, we ain't got nothin' to worry about. We can do mostly anything and get away with it."

The police asked Joudrey if she had a copy of *Life With Billy* in her house. "I told them I wouldn't put that book in no outside toilet. They said, 'You didn't think much of her?' and I said I did at first because we was together all the time, but after she killed Billy I didn't want a thing to do with her." (Joudrey died in her late seventies on March 25, 1993, two weeks after the tenth anniversary of Billy Stafford's death, and thirteen months after Jane's death.)

Donna Smith believed that Jane killed herself and that she had planned it for some time. "Once she married Joel, she felt she could die knowing somebody would look after Darren. I think she had it in her mind to kill herself before she was married. Jane and I were always open about suicide. She just couldn't take it anymore. She had court coming up again—and that panel (on violence against women). There's no way she could handle that. I don't condemn what she did. Some people think I should be angry with her for what she put me through, but I'm not mad at her. They don't know what she went through."

Donna didn't believe the story that Jane told Carrie Rafuse. "We figured out the dates, and when she told Carrie about hiring somebody, it would have been me she was talking about."

After the initial shock over Jane's death, Maurice Hurshman thought back to the night she went missing, and he was convinced she died about 3:30 a.m. on Saturday morning, February 22. Joel had left the Hurshman house about 1:30 a.m. after the call from Darren informing him Jane was missing. About two hours later, Hurshman heard footsteps at the front door. "It was just the same as if someone walked right across the steps. I said, 'That's Joel coming back,' and I got up and came out and opened the door." No one was there, and the only footprints in the snow were those left by Joel when he went to his car two hours earlier.

"I heard it clear as that," said Hurshman. "It was like someone coming right to the door. Even the dogs started barking. But there was no one there. I think that's when she died. That's what's on my mind all the time."

Gladys and Maurice Hurshman didn't believe Jane killed herself. They pointed to the letter she wrote to them indicating she would be down to visit them during the March break and to take her mother to the doctor. "She never talked about suicide to us," said Hurshman. "I can't see her doing this."

Victoria "Jonesy" Jones, the retired nursing assistant, who once lived with Jane, was at a friend's house "and it came on the news they'd found a woman's body in a car in Halifax. They didn't give any name, and I thought, the poor soul. And the next day Charlene called me and she said you know that woman that they found in a car was Jane."

Jones, bored with retirement, had been working for a private nursing agency when, on the weekend before her death, Jane called and invited her for dinner and an overnight. "I'd been working two or three twelve-hour shifts and I was really, really tired," said Jones.

"Could I take a rain check on it?" she asked Jane. "I don't feel ill exactly, but I don't feel great."

"That's all right," Jane said. "We'll do it another day."

Jones believed that the dinner and overnight stay was Jane's way of saying goodbye to her. "I had no inkling that she was going to die that week. When Charlene told me Jane was dead, I felt dreadful—I felt guilty too. I hadn't a clue she was going to do it. I cried for a week. I was just sick. How do you know you'll never, ever, see a person again? I often think about Jane and what I might have done to prevent this."

Jane's pen pal, Sara, wanted to die when she learned of her friend's death. "I thought, 'Oh—she left me stranded,' you know. If there was no hope for her, then there was no hope for me. I wanted to kill myself."

Jane's other long-time pen pal, Jo Sheridan in British Columbia, was unequivocal in her belief that Jane did not kill herself. "I am absolutely convinced she was murdered," she said. "There's not one shadow of doubt in my mind. I feel that she was snatched away and I didn't get to say goodbye and I never touched her hand because I never saw her—she was my pen friend. She was clearly afraid and she said someone out there wanted to hurt her. If she was planning suicide, there's no way she would have done that just to put people off track. She was not an unkind or cruel person—in any way."

Alan Ferrier, the legal aid lawyer who defended Jane when she killed Billy Stafford, believed she committed suicide, and it did not surprise him. "I saw her as an ongoing victim," he said. "She never got off the treadmill." He said her kleptomania was out of control and was a symptom of deeper problems. "It was overwhelming. Some people asked why she didn't come back to me when she was caught shoplifting. It was because she was so embarrassed and felt she had let me down. That's why she changed lawyers so often."

Before all the details of Jane's death were made public, a Bridgewater police officer asked Ferrier if he thought it was suicide or murder.

"I think she concocted the whole thing to make it look like murder," replied Ferrier.

"What makes you think that?" asked the officer.

"Well, I just knew Jane."

During their conversation, the police officer said that in addition to Jane's many convictions for shoplifting, there were many occasions when charges against her were withdrawn. He said that as part of one investigation, police went to her Cole Harbour home with a warrant and discovered numerous items "with the tags still on them."

"Here I'm telling him how this [suicide] is all concocted and he's telling me how serious the kleptomania was," said Ferrier. In his view, Jane would have wanted her death to look like murder because if it was suicide "she would have felt she was letting people down—more recently, the feminist groups she was involved with."

But Liz Forestell was convinced that Jane couldn't have faked the fear she felt over the threats. Forestell's voice was to become one of the loudest in the chorus of Jane's friends and associates demanding a public inquiry. She was concerned that the police were discounting the threats against Jane.

Gary Grant was on vacation in Florida when he learned of Jane's death, and said he was shocked and was unaware she had been receiving threats. When he returned to Halifax from Florida, he heard rumblings in police circles and "through jiggin' the reels, I got word that maybe someone was thinking I was making these phone calls and I said, 'Wait a minute! What is going on?' As soon as I heard, I went over to the Cole Harbour detachment and said to the investigator [Keith Crosland], 'Listen, let's have a chat here.' I told him exactly what had gone on with the phone calls between us and that was it. I said anything else you need—come and see me. They were doing their job and I was helping them. And I heard no more about it after that."

Grant had great sympathy and respect for Jane, and believed she must have been out of control to accuse him of threatening her after an innocent phone call in which he identified himself.

"The whole thing is a bit bizarre," he said. "I think at the time her mind was probably not working as it should."

During their questioning of Joel Corkum after Jane's body was found, the police discovered more evidence to bolster their belief that Jane had planned her suicide to look like murder. He told them that most of Jane's financial dealings were done through Ora Harkins, a financial planner for Investors Group.

A week or so before Jane disappeared, Joel saw her with $1,000 to $1,200 in cash, which was never accounted for later. "I had my cheque, and two cheques that she hadn't got around to cashing. She sent me out to cash them and I brought her home the money. She said she had to take it to Ora to dump in her RRSP to reduce her taxes or something. It was cash money, which I thought was a little odd, because she usually just wrote him a cheque. It made me think a bit—why cash this time?

"Ora did not receive any money. The bank accounts did not go up, and the money was nowhere to be found in the house. It's gone without a trace."

Police believed that Jane had earmarked that money to pay for someone to remove the gun, blanket, and bullets from the car after she shot herself. The amount fit the scenario Jane had outlined to Donna Smith, who was to be paid $1,000 in cash for removing the gun after Jane shot the woman in the parking lot.

"For a thousand dollars, all that person had to do was to open that door, pick up the gun, and dispose of it," said Staff Sergeant Thomander. "Disposing of the gun would be very, very simple. You could take it down to one of the piers, you could bury it... I mean, as long as nobody sees you, there's no problem—the only one that's going to know about it is you. There are people who will kill for a thousand dollars."

Police speculated that the person hired to remove the gun didn't do it because their tracks would have been visible in the new snow, or because the person had no intention of following through with the plan once Jane was dead.

The RCMP's Keith Crosland envisioned a similar scenario. "If you got paid $1,000 or $1,200 and you went out and removed the gun to make the scene look like a murder, as opposed to a suicide, you're altering the evidence, and that's obstruction," he said. "But if they get the money but they don't remove the gun, they haven't committed any offence. That person definitely isn't going to jump up and walk into the office and say, 'Guess what I did?' They're just sitting down there, drinking it up and having a good laugh."

Crosland doubted that Jane obtained the handgun from a member of Hell's Angels or some other gang. "With these guys there's definitely a possibility, but if you wanted to go and get a gun, you could get a gun anywhere. We all know that."

Police were further convinced that Jane wanted her death to look like murder when they looked into the life insurance policies in her name. If she was murdered, the ten-month-old mortgage on her Arklow Drive house would have been automatically paid off, and various insurance policies would have paid out in excess of $300,000.

In the life insurance industry, there are standard clauses that state that if a policy has been in effect less than two years, claims can be rejected if there were misrepresentations on the original application, or in the event of suicide.

The suicide clause states: "If the insured commits suicide while sane or insane, within two years from the date of issue, the company will pay an amount equal only to the premiums paid since such date."

The two-year stipulation did not affect the life insurance policy at the Halifax County Regional Rehabilitation Centre, because Jane had worked there for more than six years. That policy paid out $54,000.

Other claims, totalling $246,000, were rejected. This could have been because of the suicide clause, but in fact the insurance company, Great West Life, rejected them on the grounds that there were substantial misrepresentations in Jane's application for insurance.

The "misrepresentations" likely involved Jane's failure to disclose that she suffered from depression. Possibly, if Jane had died two-and-a-half weeks later, after March 21, Great West might have paid out the full amount, because the two-year deadline would have passed.

CHAPTER 32
REMEMBERING

Following Jane's wishes, her family held a private viewing of her body before she was cremated. "It was very quiet and it was close to home," said Jane's sister Mona. "I picked Jane's clothes out and I went in to make sure she looked nice before the family came in. She looked mean, and they had sort of a frown on her face. She was pale, so I put a little bit of colour on her cheeks. I moved her collar up a bit but she still didn't look like herself."

The viewing was tough on the family. "I didn't think my dad was going to make it through," said Mona. "He broke right down and I don't think my mom could really let her feelings out because she was worried about my dad and afraid she would fall apart. When Darren was looking at Jane, he thought he could almost see her heart beating."

Allen could see how difficult it was for his grandfather. "If she had died from a heart attack, or old age, or even a car accident, he could deal with that—but this was hard to accept."

When Allen approached his mother, "she was just lying there, and I told her I was sorry for everything that happened and I told her I loved her a lot. I wish she could have come to me and said, 'Look, I got a real problem,' or whatever. But it didn't happen like that."

Jane's remains were cremated, and on Friday, Joel picked up the urn with her ashes from the funeral home.

On the afternoon of Friday, February 28, the weather was crisp as more than one hundred of Jane's friends and relatives attended her funeral service at St. John's Evangelical Lutheran Church at Mahone Bay. On a small table at the front of the church were a framed picture of Jane and the urn containing her ashes. Four months earlier, she and Joel Corkum were married in the same church. Rev. George Wawin and Rev. Margie Whynot, the same ministers who officiated at her wedding, conducted the service.

Rev. Whynot said that Jane's spirit would live on through all the lives she had touched. "Ten years ago, we cheered her strong spirit when she took action to free herself and her children from a madman who was destroying them," she said. "And when she began to speak out in public about her experiences, she opened the door for many other victims to do the same—to break the conspiracy of silence that surrounded their lives.

"I will never forget the first time I shared a certain part of my own story [of abuse] in public. It was the most tense and draining experience you could ever imagine. Some amount of telling is healing. Some sharing is healthy, but her public audience kept calling on Jane... to talk, to share, to give—for the past eight or nine years. We kept her immersed in the past, with all its pain and ugliness, and she tried not to let us down. We *liked* that brave mask she wore in public.

"There are those who don't like the idea of her being depressed in the midst of her new-found happiness, when everything seemed to be falling into place for her. By making Jane our larger-than-life hero, we didn't give her the time or the space to stop and forget the past for a while. You see, by asking so much of her, we were able to avoid our own responsibility for speaking out to help make our society a better, safer place."

Rev. Whynot said that Jane was a "strong feminist but . . . she was different from many of the feminists I have encountered. Jane did not show any prejudice against other victims who would not, or could not, follow in her large footsteps. She allowed us to go on at our own pace and in our own way—as long as we did something.

"She knew real pain and fear . . . and depression was part of her life. She also had her faults and weaknesses . . . nevertheless, she was my hero."

Rev. Whynot omitted part of her written address because she wanted her words to be positive and comforting to her family, friends, and admirers. The section omitted stated that regardless of how Jane died, Billy Stafford "has reached out of his grave and finally claimed his victim. You see, if Jane died because someone wanted to silence her feminist voice, remember that she started speaking out in the first place because of his abuse.

"And if she died at her own hand because she was tired of living with the constant pain and had nothing left for herself because she gave so much for so long to others—then remember who was the cause of that pain. I can't presume to know the cause of her death, but I know she was tortured by a lot of things in her past and no one should stand in judgment of her, nor let it detract from the good she has done."

Mona Donnelly, speaking on behalf of the family, said that Jane was a "woman with a mission" and that her struggle to put an end to violence in society must be continued.

Valery Cromwell, Jane's childhood friend, came from Toronto for the service; James Tynes was also there. Donna Smith's emotional state was fragile, and she found it difficult to accept that all that was left of her friend was the ashes in the urn at the front of the church.

Smith had always had trouble sleeping at night because of the abuse she had endured, but with Jane gone from her life her insomnia worsened. "We used to talk at night all the time and I miss her so much. I found myself calling her at work without realizing what I was doing. Then I would remember and hang up before anyone answered."

Jane's friend and co-worker, Annette Bushen, and her daughter, Charlene, also attended the Mahone Bay funeral service. "It was a last goodbye," said Bushen. "If her death was suicide, it was because of deep despair, but it takes great courage to take what cannot be bought, borrowed, or stolen. Whether it was murder or suicide, we all lost. I know many tears were shed by people who loved and respected her. To many she was a hero."

On Monday, March 2, three days after the funeral service in Mahone Bay, a candlelight vigil was held at St. John's United Church in Halifax. The church was filled to near capacity for the half-hour of poetry, song, and testimonials. It was billed as a celebration of Jane's life, not a mourning of her death, but there were many tears among the family, friends, and strangers who gathered to honour her.

Several framed photographs of Jane and her family, surrounded by candles and flowers, were set up on a table near the lectern at the front of the church. Once again Mona Donnelly spoke on behalf of the family, which she said had "drawn close" since Jane's death. "We've committed ourselves to care for each other. I know it would please Jane. Jane was truly a symbol of hope to the abused people in our society. We want you to know that her death was not a defeat for them, but a rallying point. And we vow to continue this work to create the society which Jane so desperately wanted—where love, caring, and respect for one another surpasses the evils of anger, hatred, and violence. We have to continue on…and carry her banner until all the pain stops."

One battered woman told the gathering that like Jane, she had suffered her own nightmare. "On Sunday, I decided to follow in Jane's footsteps by speaking out against violence." Others tearfully vowed to keep alive Jane's memory and spirit by fighting the "evil force"—domestic violence.

Three days after Jane's body was found, a simple memorial appeared in the snow in the parking lot near the spot where her car had been parked. It was a bouquet of flowers in a soft drink bottle with an attached note that read, "In remembrance of Jane—the pain has to stop. We can be silent no longer." It was signed, "A man who never knew you (unfortunately)." From that poignant tribute, to items and editorials in the local and national media, the public outpouring of grief was unabated.

Judy Hughes, Nova Scotia's representative on the Canadian Panel on Violence Against Women, which Jane had been scheduled to address when it came to Halifax on March 6, spoke about Jane in an interview with the Halifax *Daily News*: "Her death makes the reality of violence against women so crystal clear to me. I just feel sick about it. She was so symbolic of the women coming to the panel. The fact that she's dead is very disheartening."

One editorial said that Jane "broke the silence and focused public attention on an issue once buried under private shame. Through women like her, we've learned the shame must not be borne by the victim, but by the men who commit the abuse and by a society that has done too little to face this problem."

Daily News columnist Joyce Deveau Kennedy wrote that "grace under pressure" and "courage under fire" are stock phrases applied to athletes and soldiers. "Yet this grace and this courage may mark [an abused woman] even more."

She cited Jane Hurshman as an example. "Used as a punching bag for years, unable to protect herself or her children against the assaults of her husband, driven to mutiny and murder, tried twice for her treason—i.e., attacking her superior—jailed and finally set free, she was never able to escape her servitude.

"Jane wanted to help other women like herself who had been victims of abuse. She wanted to be the true athlete, whose competition is really with self. She wanted to be the soldier who pulls others from the trenches and leads them back to safety."

Instead, said Kennedy, Jane found a bullet through the heart. "When will we learn the grace of women like Jane Hurshman, to dance the dance of life even in the face of death? I don't know, but such women give me hope."

In a letter written after Jane's death, her pen pal in British Columbia, Jo Sheridan, wrote, "This remarkable, compassionate woman has been so cruelly and suddenly taken from us, but she made her mark—oh, how she made her mark. And it's indelible."

Vernon Oickle, reporter and editor with the Liverpool *Advance*, spoke with Jane on the telephone two days before she was reported missing. He had interviewed her at his home in mid-September of 1991 for a lengthy article he planned to run on the tenth anniversary of Billy Stafford's death. Jane told Oickle that she did not like being considered a celebrity.

"That's a hard thing to live up to," she said. "It doesn't give you a chance to fall down once in a while. It's really not fair that people put you on a pedestal. Sometimes I feel like I am under a microscope…but you learn to cope with the attention and live with it."

Jane's death was devastating for Maurice and Gladys Hurshman because they'd grown so close to Jane, after the years of emotional separation. She loved visiting them because it provided the peace and quiet she so desperately craved.

Her parents weren't aware of the extent of Jane's problem with shoplifting, nor did they realize the depth of her involvement in the fight to end violence against women and children. "I couldn't believe how many women she touched," said Maurice Hurshman. "I didn't realize this until after her death. I don't know where she found the time. When Jane came here, she never talked about that stuff. She came here to relax."

Hurshman suffered from diabetes and did a lot of walking "to keep the sugar out of me." Jane often walked along with him. "We'd drive over to Mill Village, about five minutes out the old No. 3 highway, and walk from there. There was a big rock up there and sometimes we would sit there and talk and she would say what she was going to do when she retired."

It was Jane's favourite spot, and she talked about building a small home where she could look after the elderly. It was the same dream she and Donna Smith often talked about. "She was going to try to get that piece of land up there, and she showed me how she was going to have it all landscaped and have flowers growing," said Hurshman. "She planned to do that when she retired. She told me that many a time."

"She seemed so happy," said Gladys Hurshman. "I can't understand."

CHAPTER 33
CONTROVERSY

On June 8, 1992, three-and-a-half months after Jane's death, the Halifax Police Department closed its file on the case, concluding that she had killed herself. The announcement was made after the department received forensic results from RCMP laboratories in Ottawa. Chief medical examiner Dr. Roland Perry agreed with the finding. Staff Sergeant Don Thomander said that Jane died between 9 p.m., February 21, and 9 a.m., February 22. The bullet that killed her came from the gun found on her lap in the car. Forensic tests confirmed that residue from the shot was on her hands and on the flannel sheet that had been used to muffle the sound.

Seven months after the Halifax police closed the case, the RCMP announced that forensic tests on the written and telephone threats against Jane had been unable to establish whether Jane herself had orchestrated them. "There is no firm evidence to prove where the threats came from," said RCMP Constable Dave Pike. He added that whoever sent the threats obviously went to great lengths to remain anonymous.

The lack of DNA on the envelopes indicated that a liquid dispenser had been used to seal them. Also, no fingerprints were found on the stencilled threats or on the envelopes they came in. RCMP lab technicians weren't able to definitely prove that the telephone threats had been made by a man or a woman, but did determine that they were pre-recorded and then played over the phone.

"It is possible the pre-recorded message was made by a female," said Pike. "As the lab results have not offered us any new information, there is nothing further police can do at this time."

The Halifax police and RCMP investigators believed the threats were made by a woman disguising her voice to sound like a man. But Liz Forestell, Kathleen Jennex, and Margaret Rodger (who worked with Jennex at Coverdale) also heard the tapes, and were certain the threats were made by a male.

Forestell told the Halifax *Chronicle-Herald*: "I'm still of the opinion she was murdered. I'm not satisfied they investigated with an open mind. But it's tragic no matter how she died. Whether she committed suicide or was murdered, she died from the violence that she suffered and survived for a while. I think there are answers we'll never have. I think there are things we'll never know about it."

Maurice Hurshman said his daughter had too much to live for and would never have killed herself. And Mona Donnelly told the Liverpool *Advance* that she was "very disappointed and saddened by the outcome of this investigation. You may be thinking that our family does not want to admit that Jane took her own life. Jane is dead—nothing will bring her back, I know that. I wish that this was a clean-cut case, but it is not."

Staff Sergeant Thomander was convinced that Jane's death was a long-planned suicide that she had arranged to look like murder. He said the threats, the coffee cup found in the car, and all the business she left unfinished—such as delivering the cake and gift to the rehab centre, sewing drapes for her mother, taking her parents to the doctor, and scheduling meetings with

Ann Keith and other associates—were all part of her plan. The plan fell apart, he said, because the person she depended on to remove the evidence—the gun, the extra bullets, and the blanket—didn't show up.

Thomander said Jane was sitting straight back behind the steering wheel, and given the angle of the bullet, "for someone to shoot her they would have to be almost sitting in her lap. And there was no sign of a scuffle. Obviously, if someone tried to do it this way, they would have tipped that coffee over. And if there had been someone in that car, there would have been a footprint."

The policeman disputed claims that footprints made Friday night on the weekend Jane went missing would have been obliterated by Saturday's snowfall. "The snow melted to a certain degree on Saturday, but it would have been quite obvious if someone had been in that car. There was no indication of any exit whatsoever from that vehicle—from the driver's side or from the other side."

The two officers first on the scene reported that only the front door on the passenger's side was locked. Jane's son Jamie, who drove the Ford Tempo most of the time, said the handle on that door was broken and could not be opened from the inside. So if there was a killer in the front seat with Jane, he would have had to climb over the back seat or over her to get out of the car after shooting her. And if a killer opened her door and shot her, he would have had to shoot with his left hand and crouch or bend down, since the bullet went slightly upward and slightly to the right through her chest. And if he did come at Jane from that side, why would she remain seated square in the normal driving position? Finally, how did blow-back residue get on the web of skin between the thumbs and forefingers of both her hands?

Police also pointed to the scenario laid out by Jane to Donna Smith in early December. The details closely paralleled those of her death, including the old clothes, the older car, the handgun, the parking lot, and the plastic bags.

Under the byline "Some Angry Women," several of Jane's friends, including Liz Forestell and Wendy Annand, wrote a seven-page cover story for the July/August 1992 edition of *New Maritimes*. The title of the article was "Why Did Jane Hurshman Have to Die?"

The media coverage of Jane's death "upset me so much for months and months," said Annand. "That's why we finally wrote the article." The women suspected that the police investigation was not thorough, and that "there is a real possibility that there is a cold-blooded murderer on the loose who stalks women who speak out against violence against women."

They also wrote of the closeness of Jane's death to the tenth anniversary of Billy Stafford's death. "Both were shot. Both died in vehicles. It is too coincidental. It doesn't have the feel of a 'guilty suicide.' It has the feel of a 'hit.' Jane had survived too much in life to give it up when she was the happiest she had ever been."

Allen Whynot and his wife Charlene concede that Jane may have committed suicide, but added that a lot of unanswered questions remained. "I didn't want it to be suicide," said Allen. "It's an awful thing to think about—that your mother shot herself—took her own life. I honestly believe that somebody was there with her. I don't know whether she pulled the trigger or they pulled the trigger."

Allen wished that he had understood that kleptomania was an illness. "I figured if I stayed right away from her she might stop stealing, but I guess, in all honesty, it hurt her—did more harm than good."

Charlene was pregnant within three months of Jane's death, and Allen wished it had happened before she died. "I could have told her, "you're going to be a grandmother" and she might have had a different outlook."

Jane's sister, Sandy Thomson, who lived in Ottawa, said that after listening to the tape Jane made two days before she disappeared, "I honestly believe that Jane played a part in this. I listened to the tape a couple of times and I put it on pause and just really pondered some things. I'm really convinced that Jane knew this was going to happen—that this was planned. There are a lot of things that don't make sense and I don't know if she pulled the trigger, but when I listen to that tape, I'm convinced."

Jane's other sister, Mona Donnelly, didn't believe that Jane pulled the trigger. "To me, it's a very violent way to die and violence is what Jane fought against." Mona, like Jane, was a Seventh-day Adventist. "The church doesn't have any stand on suicide," she said. "To me, only the Lord can judge something like that. Only He knows the motives behind your actions and only He knows what's in your heart at the time. We don't believe in hell.

"I feel that when I die, I'm going to meet my Maker and I look forward to the day that the Lord does come again and the righteous will be in heaven. And I'm looking forward to seeing Jane there."

CHAPTER 34
WHISPERS

Much of the abuse and sexual degradation Jane Hurshman was subjected to, including bestiality, was related in *Life With Billy*, but she told the author and others that there were incidents and practices she did not divulge, and that she had suppressed other memories. After her death, it was whispered among some of Jane's friends that she may have been a victim of ritual abuse by others, in concert with Billy, and that she may have been "triggered" to kill herself.

Liz Forestell considered that a possibility. "Laying out the whole scenario to someone [Donna Smith] leads me to believe she could have been triggered," she said. "We know that it happens. We know that people are programmed and that there are ways of triggering them."

Jane had trouble sleeping at night because she associated darkness with the terror and abuse she went through. This is common among victims of ritual assault. She had been sexually abused as a child by someone close to the family and apparently had quit seeing Dr. John Curtis because she did not want to learn the extent of that abuse, or because recalling it was so painful.

It seems unlikely that Jane was the victim of satanic or ritual abuse as a child, but in her five years with Billy

Stafford she suffered experiences similar to those of ritual abuse victims.

In his own crude way, Billy Stafford was a one-man cult—and the abuse he inflicted on Jane was certainly as severe and structured as that reported by ritual abuse victims. He didn't wear the black robes of a satanist, but he would not allow a Bible in the house, he banned church-going, and he often said he was sent by the Devil or that he was the Devil incarnate.

Wendy Annand did some research into ritual abuse survivors, and "Boy, so many things just fall into place. Just the way Jane's eyes were sometimes, I would say she was dissociating. Although it could be caused by other kinds of trauma, it's so typical of ritual abuse survivors."

Kathleen Jennex of Coverdale said that people who experience the kind of severe abuse Jane did "have to compartmentalize to survive, and that's how split personalities develop. They're finding that multiple personality is related to sexual abuse and it makes so much sense. If you're a little kid and someone's doing those things to your body, well, your mind can't handle it, so it goes someplace else."

Some of Jane's friends wondered if Jane was afflicted with a mild form of multiple personality disorder. All of them had seen her eyes bulging abnormally when she was dissociating, and Carrie Rafuse and Donna Smith occasionally saw her in a rigid, near-robotic state. Alan Ferrier, Jane's former lawyer, had also witnessed this.

"There were definitely different Janes," said Carrie. "I'm not saying she had different personalities. We don't know that. But after Jane's death I talked to Donna Smith, and the person Donna told me about and the person I knew were different." A week before her death, Jane was quick to deny to Carrie that she had a split personality, saying that Dr. Curtis had diagnosed her as having a dissociative disorder. But multiple personality disorder is a dissociative disorder—albeit the most extreme form.

Dr. Marlene Hunter, a Vancouver hypnotherapist, told *Maclean's* in November 1989 that multiple personality disorder is "a very creative, sophisticated way of coping with an intolerable situation."

The coping method may work for a time, but Dr. Colin Ross, director of the dissociative disorders clinic at Winnipeg's St. Boniface General Hospital, said in the same article that more than 70 per cent of multiple personality disorder patients attempt suicide.

Dr. Curtis told *Maclean's* that although multiple personality disorder appears to be the worst of the psychological conditions, "it's the one you seem to be able to do the most for." The drawback is that treatment can take up to six years. Curtis said that the personalities within a person with the disorder can display marked differences in the way they speak, dress, and act, and even in their handwriting.

When Carrie Rafuse and Ann Keith went through Jane's diary on the weekend Jane went missing, they noticed extreme changes in her handwriting.

"There were at least three different types of handwriting," said Keith.

"It was crazy, but it was almost like she was different people. I was wondering about dissociation and multiple personalities."

Jane's normal handwriting slanted to the right and was free-flowing and open. But in late January and early February, before her death, the handwriting in her diary was often tight and straight up and down. "It started to change around February and then became erratic," Keith said.

Those who believed Jane Hurshman was murdered said that she wouldn't have killed herself without leaving a note. In fact, Jane left many messages, including a will, a tape, and letters.

And in her daily journal on January 19, she wrote a brief goodbye to her family, which she expanded on in the audiotape she recorded two days before she disappeared. She also left detailed instructions, in which she allocated chores to be shared by Darren, Jamie, and Joel in the event of her death.

Jane believed that her affairs were in perfect order and that upon her death all of the family bills would be paid (including the mortgage on the house); Darren would go to live with Mary and Paul Jacquart; the Arklow Drive house would be jointly owned by Joel, Jamie, and Darren; Joel and each of her three sons would receive $25,000; and Joel's life insurance would list Jamie and Darren as beneficiaries.

Jane was confident that Joel would look after her sons as if she were around. "Take time to get to know each other and to love each other," she had told them in her audio message. But the family was upset with Joel for not immediately telling them or the police about Jane having a gun and long-simmering resentments between Joel and her children, held in check while she was alive, now quickly surfaced.

None of Jane's plans for Joel and her sons turned out as she hoped. Within weeks of her death they were estranged from him; her last will was ruled invalid; most of her insurance claims were rejected; her sons received virtually nothing; Darren went to live with his grandparents; and Joel moved in with another woman.

CHAPTER 35
LEGACY

Besides raising public awareness about widespread violence against women, Jane Hurshman, in a very real way, helped change the law as it applies to battered women who kill their spouses.

The Nova Scotia Supreme Court ordered a new trial when the Crown appealed the jury's not guilty verdict in Jane's 1982 murder trial, ruling that the evidence of Billy Stafford's brutality against Jane, her children, and others "served only to create sympathy for the Respondent [Jane], and for this reason should have been excluded."

The appeal court also ruled that the defence of self-defence was improper in Jane's case because Billy was asleep in the truck at the time she shot him, and the jury "should not have been permitted to consider a possible assault as a justification of her deed, and section 37 (self-defence) of the Code should not have been left with them."

But in May 1990 the Supreme Court of Canada unanimously ruled that a battered woman should be allowed to use a plea of self-defence as a reason for killing her abuser, even if an attack against her was not in progress or imminent. It also ruled that evidence of the battered wife syndrome and evidence of the deceased's character were admissible to support the self-defence plea.

The court made the ruling in the case of Angelique Lavallee, a Winnipeg woman who in 1986 shot her common-law husband in the back of the head as he was walking away from her. Like Jane, she had been severely abused over many years and believed if she didn't kill her tormenter, he would kill her. On September 22, 1987, after deliberating more than nine hours, a jury found her not guilty of second-degree murder.

Lavallee's defence was based on the battered wife syndrome. At her trial, Dr. Peter Markesteyn, Manitoba's chief medical officer, testified that a woman trapped by the syndrome "finds herself in a situation of either physical, emotional, sexual—or a combination of—abuse. This occurs in all levels of society. It does not only occur in lower socio-economic classes. It can occur in the professional strata of society."

Dr. Markesteyn characterized the condition medically as one that got worse without intervention, and that very seldom got better. He added that women in this situation usually attempt to hide their bruises and injuries from their friends.

Lavallee's lawyer, G. Greg Brodsky, introduced evidence that proved the battered wife syndrome was recognized as a psychiatric diagnosis.

The Supreme Court also ruled that battered women themselves are in the best position to assess whether a lethal attack against them is likely to take place. It also rejected arguments that evidence from experts on battering is improper.

The Court said that experts were necessary to explain the dynamics of the battered wife syndrome so that jurors would understand why abused women are unable to leave their situation.

"We would expect the woman to pack her bags and go," said the judges. "Where is her self-respect? Why does she not cut loose and make a new life for herself? Such is the reaction of the average person confronted with the so-called battered wife syndrome. We need help to understand it, and help is available from professionals."

Jane's lawyer, Alan Ferrier, said that in retrospect, "we were essentially trying to argue the battered wife syndrome, although we didn't know it and we didn't call it that. I guess the significance from a legal perspective was the law was out of sync with the feelings of the people. We all know what the jury felt and what the public felt. It took a lot of those types of cases, in which cumulative provocation couldn't be used, that forced the Supreme Court to say, 'Well, we've got to have an out here.'"

EPILOGUE

The preponderance of evidence confirms Jane Hurshman fired the bullet that killed her, but there can be no doubt that society loaded the gun and helped pull the trigger.

Jane was a fighter, and her instinct to survive brought her through a loveless childhood, a depressing, numbing marriage to an alcoholic, and five years of severe physical, emotional, and sexual abuse with Billy Stafford.

In describing what can happen to severely battered women like Jane, Winnipeg psychiatrist Dr. Fred Shane said that there comes a point "that an act or a series of acts crosses that line of total unacceptability. It may be precipitated by a violent act of a sexual nature, or of an aggressive nature... or some behaviour toward their children which becomes totally revolting.

"Once they feel that this line has been crossed, and also that their sense of hope has been obliterated, the need to do something to escape and to mitigate the threats becomes overwhelming. Suddenly, there is energy that was not available before and the primal need to survive asserts itself."

It was that energy and need that led Jane to kill Billy Stafford.

"Paradoxically," said Dr. Shane, "after the death of the spouses of those women involved in homicide, is often a deep, profound remorse, a difficulty in accepting that they have been part of this act."

There can be no argument that Jane was a tireless fighter against criminal violence in the home and that she touched the lives of hundreds, perhaps thousands, of women across Canada. She had the toughness to survive and eventually work out her inner turmoil. What she couldn't survive was the kleptomania. She couldn't understand it, and she couldn't control it. It was like a train bearing down on her. There was no escape, so she killed herself.

Jane was convinced that if her body was found with a bullet wound and no gun present, her death would unquestionably be treated as murder. Wasn't that the case when RCMP Staff Sergeant Peter Williamson peered into the cab of Billy Stafford's half-ton truck and saw his bloodied corpse? "Okay, boys, there's no gun. We've got a homicide here. No gun—no suicide."

Jane paid to have the gun, blanket, and extra bullets removed from the car after she shot herself. Suicide would be letting others down. Better if they thought it was murder. But as often happened in her life, someone let her down.

Regardless of how Jane died, the reality is that if she had not been a battered woman raised in a society that has readily accepted abuse and treated women as inferior, she would not have died as she did.

There is an image of Jane in 1963, when she was fourteen, a strong and determined cross-country runner, facing a hundred competitors from three Canadian military bases in a seven-mile race through the German countryside. She came second and won a medal. At the same meet, her basketball team won a first-place ribbon and her volleyball team a second-place ribbon. Jane also won other athletic awards, all the while continuing to excel at school. It was this grit and intelligence that helped her survive the emotional and physical brutalities for as long as she did.

Wendy Annand said that no matter how Jane died, "she's still a hero and we all need to remember that, because women have so few heroes of whom we can say, 'Look at what this woman did.' And it's not because she had money behind her, and it's not because she had powerful friends. It's because of what she lived through and her own grit and determination."

Considering the cards she was dealt in her abbreviated life, Jane's accomplishments are remarkable. The tragedy of her death is that the promise of this spirited, intelligent, and brave woman must remain unfulfilled. Imagine what she might have become if she had grown up loved and self-confident in a society where women and men are equal—where women and children are not forced to live in fear.

TRANSITION HOUSES AND EMERGENCY SHELTERS

Abused women seeking information on transition houses and emergency shelters anywhere in Canada can call toll-free to the National Clearinghouse on Family Violence in Ottawa at:

1-800-267-1291
Website: www.phac-aspc.gc.ca/nc-cn
Email: ncfv-cnivf@phac-aspc.gc.ca

OR

Telephone transition house and shelter associations in your home province or territory:

ALBERTA
Alberta Council of Women's Shelters
Toll-free: 1-866-331-3933
Edmonton: (780) 456-7000

BRITISH COLUMBIA & YUKON
British Columbia/Yukon Society of Transition Houses
Vancouver: (604) 669-6948

MANITOBA
Manitoba Association of Women's Shelters
Toll-free: 1-877-977-0007
Selkirk: (204) 623-7427

NEW BRUNSWICK
New Brunswick Coalition of Transition Houses
St. Stephen: (506) 466-5879
Email: syn456@nb.sympatico.ca

NEWFOUNDLAND
Transition House Association of Newfoundland and Labrador
St. John's: (709) 739-6759

NORTHWEST TERRITORIES
N.W.T. Association of Family Violence Prevention
Iqaluit: (867) 979-4566

NOVA SCOTIA
Transition House Association of Nova Scotia
Halifax: (902) 429-7287

ONTARIO
Ontario Association of Interval and Transition Houses
Toronto: (416) 977-6619

PRINCE EDWARD ISLAND
Prince Edward Island Transition House Association
Charlottetown: (902) 894-3354

QUÉBEC

Fédération des ressources d'hébergement pour femmes violentées et en difficulté du Québec
Montréal: (514) 878-9757
Website: www.fede.qc.ca/federation.html

SASKATCHEWAN

Provincial Association of Transition Houses and Services of Saskatchewan
Regina: (306) 522-3515
Email: paths@sasktel.net

INDEX OF NAMES